THE TARIFF HISTORY
OF THE
UNITED STATES

The Tariff History
of the
United States

THE EIGHTH REVISED EDITION

F. W. Taussig

L 42

with an Introduction by
DAVID M. CHALMERS
UNIVERSITY OF FLORIDA

Capricorn Books, New York

TARIFFS, TAUSSIG, AND THE CHANGING WORLD OF TRADE

David M. Chalmers

UNIVERSITY OF FLORIDA

With the reemergence of Western Europe as a viable trading area, the protective tariff has regained the spotlight as an important factor in world trade. A tariff is, very simply, a list or schedule of the taxes levied against goods carried in trade across political boundaries. The word "duties" is often used interchangeably with tariffs and describes such taxes placed upon both incoming and outgoing goods.

At the drafting of the American Constitution, many Southerners were fearful that a strong central government might levy taxes on exports, which at that time were primarily composed of Southern agricultural staples. A prohibition against export taxes was written into the Constitution and Americans became accustomed to thinking of tariffs as import duties only. For most nations this is the principal form of tariff, for it has long been considered good policy to stimulate rather than hinder exports. A favorable balance of trade, or an excess of exports over imports, meant building up credit abroad and often an influx of gold into the creditor nation.

In those countries where the central government handles all economic life, obviously tariffs would not be of much point, for imports, exports, and revenues are already controlled. However, even authoritarian and collectivist societies such as Nazi Germany and the Soviet Union have been unable to maintain autarchic isolation and have been faced with tariff barriers around those markets in which they sought to sell their goods. Primarily, however, tariffs have been a meaningful instrument of policy only when commerce moves through private hands and governments use their taxing power either to share in the profits or to channel the direction of economic activity at home.

The two major purposes of the tariff have been to provide revenue and protection. Between the two, when each is carried to its logical conclusion, there is conflict. A revenue tariff should be sufficiently low to encourage the entrance of goods, so that the government may gain as much income as possible from the tax. A protective tariff, on the other hand, is intended to discourage trade, and in some cases to cut it off entirely. In the latter case, a tariff would yield little revenue. Usually governments have sought a balance, although a high degree of protection may be used to shield particular products against competition. This may be done either to channel resources into productive areas that are felt to be nationally desirable or merely to aid particular domestic producers who have sufficient political power to use the tariff for their own gain. Whatever the initial reason for the protection, it is almost always easier to institute than remove tariffs, which, once passed, build up special interests and political power behind them.

Tariff duties were collected at least as far back as ancient Greece and Rome. With the decline of the Roman Empire, its vast trading area was broken into countless fragments, and the myriad duties levied by numerous princes, potentates, lords and barons, contributed to a stifling of trade. In feudal Europe, the practice of every lord being his own tariff collector, in a world in which revenue and plunder were often indistinguishable, operated to keep the economy of Western Europe at the subsistence level. The rise of the national monarchies aided the restoration of a market economy by removing most of these local, internal restrictions on trade. At the same time the new national states pursued the bullionist path. This meant encouraging domestic manufactures and production, and the use of tariffs and other devices to maintain a favorable balance of trade that would bring an influx of gold and silver in settlement. As England expanded her production and began to industrialize, her statesmen, led by William Pitt in 1787, codified, simplified and, in less than a century, practically removed her tariff walls. By 1860 Great Britain was unparalleledly close to free trade; France was influenced to reduce her restrictions, and the United States also moderated her young tariff barriers.

With the advent of the Civil War, the United States began to move her tariffs upward again; and in the 1880's the nationalistic and imperialistic upsurge in Europe led to a movement of neo-mercantilist tariff construction. The United States played her part. In 1888 President Grover Cleveland became convinced that a presumably revenue tariff was not justified when the nation was actually accumulating a surplus in its treasury. This led to the emergence of the tariff as a major political issue, the result of which was a series of higher, overtly protective tariffs (McKinley, 1890; Dingley, 1897; Payne-Aldrich, 1909; Fordney-McCumber, 1922; and Hawley-Smoot, 1930). Efforts in the other direction, under Cleveland and Woodrow Wilson (Wilson-Gorman, 1894; and Underwood-Simmons, 1913) were either aborted by politics or by the outbreak of World War I. With a frankly protectionist tariff and with the federal income tax made constitutional by the Sixteenth Amendment, the tariff yielded up its accustomed revenue role. For one hundred and twenty-four years, dating from the introduction of the tariff as the first bill presented to the new House of Representatives, it had been the primary source of governmental income. With the Hawley-Smoot Tariff Act of 1930, the United States moved to her highest, overtly protective position, even though she had enjoyed a favorable balance of trade since 1874 and had become the foremost creditor nation after World War I.

It was during this period of American tariff nationalism that Frank William Taussig emerged as America's great tariff historian, a world-famous expert on international trade, and perhaps the most influential teacher of economists in America. As editor, author, teacher, theorist, text-book writer, and government official, Taussig was a major figure in the world of economics.

F. W. Taussig was born in St. Louis, Missouri, in 1859. His parents had come to America in the 1840's, each seeking greater freedom and opportunity than were to be found in their former homes in the Austrian Empire and Germany. Taussig's father prospered in the new world in a succession of careers in business and public life. His most lasting achievement came in the successful fight for a single central terminal for all railroads entering St. Louis. After a year at Washington University of St. Louis, young Frank Taussig went on to Harvard, which was to be his pulpit and his love for the remainder of his life. As a student he combined academic success with fraternity life and intramural athletics. Graduating in 1879, with highest honors, he went off on the grand tour of Europe, lingering to study a touch of political economy and Roman law in Berlin.

On his return he became secretary to Charles W. Eliot, the chemist-president who was revolutionizing Harvard. Taussig worked on his doctorate in economics, taught for a year, and then earned an advanced degree in law. But his choice of profession was teaching, and his field was economics. For almost half a century, until he retired at the age of seventy-five in 1935, he reached successive generations of Harvard students in his introductory and advanced theory courses, which were basic requirements for freshmen and graduate students. In addition he taught classes in banking, taxation, transportation, and his most famous area, international trade.

Although teaching was the center of his life, it was only one of Taussig's many roles. For forty-one years he was editor and chief manuscript reader for the influential *Quarterly Journal of Economics.* He wrote thirteen books and over two hundred articles.* His *Principles of Economics,* first published in 1911 and last revised in 1939, became a standard introductory text and probably reached tens of thousands of students. His primary interest was the field of international trade, to which he devoted many books and articles. Among them were his most original work, *International Trade* (1927), and his classic study, *The Tariff History of the United States.*

When the Tariff Commission was first set up, Woodrow Wilson selected the Harvard don to head it. From 1917 to 1919, Taussig shaped the Commission, particularly developing its fact-finding function, sending out his bright young men to make scholarly studies of comparative costs in foreign industries. A trusted adviser to President Wilson, Taussig served on the price-fixing War Industries Board and participated in the President's postwar Industrial Conference. Taussig helped shape the third of Wilson's famous Fourteen Points, calling for the removal of economic barriers and the "equality of trade conditions among all nations," and he went to the Peace Conference as the President's adviser on trade matters.

* For a Taussig bibliography, see *Explorations in Economics: Notes and Essays Contributed in Honor of F. W. Taussig* (New York, 1936), pp. 535-539.

There was in Taussig's outlook a concern for the policy application of his economic knowledge, and it was probably this concern that helped lead him into government service. His philosophy was based upon the writings and intuitions of the classical economists, which tended to place him in the conservative camp. He looked suspiciously at governmental intervention in the economy and the growth of organized labor, believing that the incentives of inequality, efficiency, and the market were the best regulators of economic activity. His analysis of market behavior was based upon marginal utility, which he called "vendibility" analysis. However, patrician security, humanism, intelligence, and a concern for information and its practical application served to prevent shrillness or doctrinaire rigidity in his thinking and writing.*

Frank W. Taussig's ideological convictions, temperament and experience blended together best in his famous *Tariff History of the United States.* After three quarters of a century, it is still the standard work on the subject. The first edition of the *Tariff History* appeared in 1888, but its printed origins went back further. Taussig had written a prize-winning essay on tariff origins and then expanded it into his doctoral dissertation, published in

* For further information on the life and thought of F. W. Taussig, see Joseph Dorfman, *The Economic Mind in American Civilization* (New York, 1959), Vol. III, Ch. XII; Vol. IV, Ch. IX; Howard S. Ellis, "Frank William Taussig, 1859-1940," *American Economic Review,* 31 (1941), 209-211; J. A. Schumpeter, A. H. Cole, & E. S. Mason, "Frank William Taussig," *Quarterly Journal of Economics,* 55 (1941), 337-363; Ben B. Seligman, *Main Currents in Modern Economics* (New York, 1962), pp. 623-628.

1883 as *Protection to Young Industries as Applied to the United States*. This and another book bringing his account of the tariff up to the 1880's were combined to form his *Tariff History*. Over the next forty-three years, the book went through eight editions, as Taussig kept the story up to date. With his chapter on the Hawley-Smoot bill of 1930, the last of the great old-style tariff acts, Taussig concluded his final revision in 1931.

In his *Tariff History,* Taussig most clearly showed the influence of his intellectual mentors, Adam Smith, David Ricardo, and John Stuart Mill. Taussig was a free trader, believing in the benefits of specialization and increased trade. In the book he delighted in adding fragments of Congressional debates that Smith himself might well have used as illustrations. However, it was with Ricardo's development of Smith's theory that he felt most in tune, and in his own *International Trade* he made his greatest contribution by a definitive working-out of the theory of comparative advantage. John Stuart Mill's influence was the acknowledged underpinning of Taussig's theoretical outlook and of his *Principles of Economics*. Mill contributed to Taussig's understanding of the nature of trade and tariffs by lending justification for the limited and temporary protectionist encouragement of the growth of new industries in young nations.

Although Smith, Ricardo, and Mill shaped his thinking, perhaps no one has known quite as much about the theory and practice of tariffs as Frank W. Taussig. His *Tariff History of the United States* is not a history of international economics and trade, nor is it a definitive treatment of either the politics of tariff-making or the international impact of American tariff policy. The *History* approaches the tariff in the way that Americans looked at it up to 1930. Tariffs were concerned with revenue or the protection of home industries, and that was a matter of unilateral, domestic concern. The series of informative and graceful essays that compose the *History* unfold the results of tariff protection in the United States. In doing this, Taussig wrote an important industrial history, perhaps the first and still one of the best, and he offered many insights into the politics of tariff-making. For the study of the three most important "protected" industries in American development, iron, wool and cotton textiles, Taussig's *Tariff History* remains the essential primer.

Taussig began his book by accepting "the argument for protection," not for all infant industries, but rather for those which necessitated new departures in technique and skills in a country that had hitherto devoted its energies to agriculture. He not only limited his approval to the protectionist aid to those industries which would have not developed without it, but set standards for performance. Echoing John Stuart Mill, he explained that it was "an essential condition for the usefulness of assistance given to a young industry, that the industry shall ultimately supply its products at least as cheaply as they can be obtained by importation." Protection thus had to prove its value.

This, unfortunately, had not been the case in the United

States. The cotton and woolen industries gained their major tariff protection after they were already established and strong enough to sustain themselves, while it was the discovery of anthracite in the 1830's, not tariff protection, that enabled the iron industry to develop production at a competitive price. In short, Taussig maintained, it was not the tariff but resources, technical ingenuity and inventiveness that carried American manufacturing forward prior to the Civil War.

The postwar appearance of the argument that the tariff was needed to protect high American wages was a sign that the "infant industries" argument had been unsuccessful. Taussig found this new line of reasoning to be no more sound, for he continued to demonstrate that the position of American industry, and wages, rested on natural resources and mechanical skill. Productivity, not protection, was the source of national strength. With the policy-oriented practicality that marked his approach, Professor Taussig did, however, defend the protection offered to those industries with a large investment in a fixed physical plant, such as the Louisiana sugar producers, which could not be easily changed to other uses. On the other hand, although he maintained that combination and concentrated economic power were the products of large-scale production rather than protection, he recognized the political pressures that resulted from the popular tendency to see a connection between trust and tariff.

And so, as tariff walls rose, and sometimes fell a little, Frank W. Taussig described the diversity of pressures and politics that directed them. As he surveyed the history of the American tariff, he tended to find that the forces that led to greater protectionism seldom stemmed directly from the popular will. In his final chapter, as he analyzed the farmers' stake in the Hawley-Smoot Tariff of 1930, he decried the futility of tariffs as a basic solution to economic problems.

The Hawley-Smoot Act, with which Taussig concluded his eighth and final revision of *The Tariff History of the United States,* was the last of the old-style tariffs. It was probably one of the most disastrous tariffs in world history. Because the United States was a major exporter of manufactured goods and the world's prime creditor nation, it would have been hard for the Hawley-Smoot tariff to have been more badly conceived and timed. Its effect was to worsen the depression that was expanding through the world's trading nations. It helped bring retaliatory barriers against American products, including Great Britain's creation of an imperial preference system, and a general drop in the nation's share of world trade.

The bitter depression days of the 1930's initiated a revolution in American tariff history. This revolution was marked by three characteristics: 1) the abandonment of general tariff-making by the Congress, 2) the growing realization that tariffs had to be made with the world market as well as domestic industry in mind, and 3) an international shift from tariffs to other means to control national trade policy.

With widespread unemployment and sluggish demand at home and decreased trade and higher tariff barriers abroad, many nations chose additional means for controlling entry into their domestic markets. Led by France, they initiated quota systems to control the course and size of trade. Arrangements were made more and more on bilateral bases as pairs of nations entered into agreements that discriminated against all outsiders. Nazi Germany sought barter deals, and international trading accounts were balanced on bilateral bases. As war approached in the late 1930's, countries either stockpiled or sought to make themselves as self-sufficient and as little dependent on trade as possible.

When Franklin Roosevelt became President of the United States in 1933, he came pledged to seek freer trade, and in 1934 an amendment was added to the Hawley-Smoot Tariff of 1930. Better known as the Reciprocal Trade Act, it was adopted as an "emergency" depression measure, an explanation that was carried in the text of subsequent renewals until 1949. In this Act, Congress delegated tariff-making power to the President, for the legislators had come to feel that they were not capable of producing a lower tariff. The details were too intricate and the political pressures were too great. Inasmuch as the purpose was not protection but, rather, the encouragement of trade and the expansion of markets for American goods, successful tariff-making could be achieved only by international negotiation. That brought it in the purview of the President and Secretary of State Cordell Hull, a strong-willed free-trading Wilsonian from Tennessee. The chosen path was selective tariff reduction through bilateral agreements. Cuts were authorized up to fifty per cent of the Hawley-Smoot rates, and since the treaties incorporated the unconditional "most favored nation" principle, the reductions were automatically extended to all other treaty partners.

Growing international conflict and the outbreak of World War II disrupted the increasing flow of trade, and governments took over direct control. They issued quotas and licenses, rationed exchange, and made decisions about purchases, prices, and distribution. Beginning with Lend-Lease, America's shipment of goods to the Allies was not placed on normal repayment basis, and often not upon repayment at all.

Nor did the advent of peace return international trade to normal conditions. Drastically changed societies and reorganized governments faced the problems of rebuilding their devastated economies through planning and controls. In most countries, the government used exchange controls and quantitative restrictions to husband scarce foreign, and particularly American, currencies. Until production could approach pre-war levels, the tariff would not be a major factor in world trade. Altogether, it took the efforts of UNRRA, a three and three-quarter billion dollar loan to Britain, the Marshall Plan (European Recovery Program), inter-European cooperation, widespread currency devaluation, and the Korean War boom to revitalize production and trade and narrow the dollar gap.

Nevertheless, throughout the difficult postwar years, the non-Communist countries continued to look toward the day when controls would yield to a more normal, freer, multi-lateral trading world. Attention was once again focused on the tariff. It was hoped that other forms of depression, war, and reconstruction restrictions would go, and that tariff walls could be further breached.

In 1945 the Reciprocal Trade Agreements Act was extended again, with the President given power to negotiate tariff reductions to a limit one-half of the then existing rates, or, in effect, one quarter of what American tariffs had been in 1930. This Act was to be the high point of American tariff liberality until the radical Extension Act of 1962. Under the impetus of the 1945 law, most of the world's trading nations met in Geneva in 1947 to form the General Agreement on Tariffs and Trade.

The purposes of the General Agreement, or GATT, were to lay down rules for national commercial behavior and to end special quota-type restrictions as soon as possible. The member countries sat down to round-table negotiations of bilateral agreements, whose benefits were thereby extended, under the "most favored nation" policy, to all members. Altogether, one hundred and twenty-three such agreements, covering close to fifty thousand commodities, were made at Geneva, and more were added at subsequent conferences. Although the principles of GATT were derived from American trade agreement policies, many nations were skeptical over the extent of American commitment to trade liberalization, and the progress of the Geneva

Conference was closely watched. At a critical juncture, President Truman vetoed a congressional bill raising the American duties on wool, despite the pleas of his political aides that to do so would cost him the vote of six states in the next election.

There was some basis for foreign apprehensions, because protectionist sentiment was rising in the United States. If the Trade Agreement Act of 1945 represented a high point of anti-restrictionism, the tide was soon changed. As a part of the postwar reaction against government, reform, the Democrats, and President Truman, a number of qualifications were placed upon the President's tariff-negotiating powers. The "Mexican escape clause," which provided for modification or withdrawal of concessions that seriously injured domestic producers, was now added to all trade treaties. In 1951 the "peril point" amendment, which was inserted in 1948 and withdrawn the next year, again became part of the law. By its provisions the Tariff Commission was to survey all those commodities that were to be up for negotiation and indicate the minimum tariff level necessary to preserve American producers. The President was thereupon expected, though not required, to observe these minimums.

With the election of Dwight D. Eisenhower in 1952, the nation faced the paradox of a trade-oriented President heading a traditionally protectionist Republican Party, now back in full control of the government for the first time since 1930. President Eisenhower's appointees to the Tariff Commission were protectionist-minded, and in a wave of escape clause cases the Commission tended to recommend support for distressed American industries, whether or not foreign competition lay at the heart of the trouble. Backed up by the State and Commerce Departments, the latter headed by Sinclair Weeks, a protectionist businessman who fashioned his "team" role to the President's freer-trade convictions, Eisenhower resisted the pressures. Between 1947 and 1962 the Tariff Commission recommended use of the escape clause in only a third of some 106 cases, and in only fifteen of these did the three postwar Presidents raise the duties. By 1964, American tariff rates averaged only eleven per cent.

By the 1960's, protectionism had few national champions. Although the traditionally anti-tariff South was becoming more protectionist as it industrialized, and Washington often besought other countries to impose voluntary limitations on the quantity of particular commodities, such as textiles, shipped into the American market, the general sentiment was for freer trade. Interested in investment opportunities and foreign markets, American business was not protectionist. This attitude was part of a general awareness that trade was but a part of a national involvement in the well-being of the greater world society.

This realization, plus shrewd political wooing, enabled President Kennedy to win acceptance of a potentially radical Trade Extension Act in 1962. The Act was directed toward negotiations with the European Economic Community (Common Market), which had emerged as a

major productive and trading area, and one whose po-
tential tariff walls threatened to exclude American commerce. For the first time the President's authority was
granted him for five rather than three years. He could
negotiate cuts up to fifty per cent in the 1962 tariff levels
and even eliminate duties on those products that were
supplied eighty per cent or more by the U.S. and the EEC.
The Act itself was based upon the premise that Great
Britain would become a member of the EEC. With President Charles De Gaulle's rising anti-Anglo-Saxon nationalism, the French veto of British admission to the
Common Market, and strong European sentiment for agricultural protectionism, hope for immediate revolutionary
changes appeared slight in the mid-sixties. However, one
thing seemed clear, and that was the increased importance
of tariff policy in a world in which Europe and America
were growing in economic health and reshaping their
international commercial outlooks.*

* Henry Chalmers, *World Trade Policies* (Berkeley, 1953); Gott-
fried Haberler, "Integration and Growth of the World Economy in
Historical Perspective," *American Economic Review*, LIV (1964),
1-22; William B. Kelley, ed., *Studies in United States Commercial
Policy* (Chapel Hill, 1963); Frank W. Taussig and Henry Chalmers,
"Tariffs," *Encyclopedia Britannica* (1962); United States Council of
the International Chamber of Commerce, *United States Trade Policy
in a Changing World Economy* (New York, 1959).

NOTE TO THE FIRST EDITION.

OF the papers printed in this volume none is now presented to the public for the first time. The essay on "Protection to Young Industries as Applied in the United States" was first published in Cambridge in 1882, and was republished in a revised edition in New York in 1883. The paper on "The Tariff of 1828" appeared in the *Political Science Quarterly* for March, 1888. That on "The History of the Tariff between 1830 and 1860" was printed in the *Quarterly Journal of Economics* for April, 1888. "The History of the Present Tariff" was published in New York in 1885. All, however, have been revised for the present volume, and considerable additions have been made. I have avoided repetitions, so far as this was possible, and have attempted to connect the narrative of the separate parts. Although not originally written with the design of presenting a complete history of our tariff legislation, these papers cover in some sort the entire period from 1789 to 1887.

F. W. T.

CAMBRIDGE, MASS.

NOTE TO THE EIGHTH EDITION.

IN the present edition the narrative, which in the previous editions had been brought to date by chapters on the successive tariff acts of 1890, 1894, 1897, 1909, 1913, and 1922, is again brought to date by a chapter on the tariff of 1930. In the appendix, certain tables which have now largely lost their interest have been omitted, while the others have been brought to date.

As a companion volume I venture to ask the reader's attention to *Some Aspects of the Tariff Question* (new edition, 1931). In that I have considered much more fully than is here possible the economic principles involved in tariff legislation, and the substantive effect of the duties, particularly as regards sugar, iron and steel, silks, cottons, wool and woollens.

CONTENTS.

PART I.

CONTENTS.

CONTENTS

CONTENTS.

CONTENTS.

CONTENTS

to Agricultural Commodities.—Sugar, Wheat, Long-staple Cotton, Other Articles.—Some Higher Duties on Manufactured Products, Usually Petty in Scope.—General Comparison of the Rates of 1930 with Those of 1922.—The Act in General Futile.—The Tariff Commission and the Flexible Provisions.—Unsatisfactory Situation During 1922–30.—The Tariff Commission Retained, with Changed Membership, but no Essential Changes in Duties or Powers.

THE TARIFF HISTORY OF THE
UNITED STATES.

PART I
CHAPTER I

PROTECTION TO YOUNG INDUSTRIES AS APPLIED IN THE UNITED STATES.

I.

THE ARGUMENT FOR PROTECTION TO YOUNG INDUSTRIES.

OF the arguments in favor of protection, none has been more frequently or more sincerely urged than that which is expressed in the phrase "protection to young industries." None has received so generally the approval of economists, even of those little disposed to acknowledge the validity of any reasoning not in accordance with the theory of free exchange. Mill gave it the weight of his approval in a passage which has been frequently cited. Later English writers have followed him in granting its intrinsic soundness. The reasoning of List, the most prominent protectionist writer among the Germans, is based, so far as it is purely economic, on this argument, and since List's time the argument has taken an established place in German treatises on political economy, even though it be admitted that the conditions to which it fairly applies belong to the past.

The argument is, in brief, that it may be advantageous to encourage by legislation a branch of industry which might be profitably carried on, which is therefore sure to be carried on eventually, but whose rise is prevented for the time being by artificial or accidental causes. The essential point of the argument lies in the assumption that the causes which prevent the rise of the industry, and render protection necessary, are not natural and permanent causes,—not such as would permanently prevent, under a state of freedom, the growth of the industry. Let it be supposed, for instance, that the industry to be encouraged is the cotton manufacture. The natural advantages of a given country for making cotton cloths are good, we may suppose, in comparison with the advantages for producing other things. The raw material is cheap, power for machinery is abundant, the general intelligence and industry of the people—which, since they admit of but very slow change, must be considered natural advantages—are such as to fit them for complex industrial operations. There is no permanent cause why cotton goods should not be obtained at as low cost by making them at home as by importing them ; perhaps they can even be produced at lower cost at home. But the cotton manufacture, let it be further supposed, is new ; the machinery used is unknown and complicated, and requires skill and experience of a kind not attainable in other branches of production. The industry of the country runs by custom in other grooves, from which it is not easily diverted. If, at the same time, the com-munication of knowledge be slow, and enterprise be hesitating, we have a set of conditions under which the establishment of the cotton manufacture may be pre-vented, long after it might have been carried on with advantage. Under such circumstances it may be wise to encourage the manufacture by duties on imported goods, or by other analogous measures. Sooner or later the cotton manufacture will be introduced and carried on, even without assistance; and the government's aid will only cause it to be established with less friction, and at an earlier date, than would otherwise have been the case.

It may illustrate more clearly the conditions under which such assistance may be useful, to point out those under which it is superfluous. The mere fact that an industry is young in years—has been undertaken only within a short period of time—does not supply the con-ditions under which protection is justified by this argu-ment. An industry recently established, but similar in kind to other branches of production already carried on in the country, would hardly come within its scope. But where the industry is not only new, but forms a departure from the usual track of production; where, perhaps, ma-chinery of an entirely strange character, or processes hitherto unknown, are necessary; where the skill and ex-perience required are such as could not be attained in the occupations already in vogue; under these circumstances protection may be applied with good results, if no natural disadvantages, in addition to the artificial obstacles, stand in the way. The manufacture of linen goods in the United States, at the present time, probably supplies an example of an industry which, though comparatively new, can hardly be said to deserve protection as a young industry. The methods and machinery in use are not essentially different from those of other branches of textile manufactures. No great departure from the usual track of production is necessary in order to make linens. Manufactures of the same general character are established on all sides. Work-people and managers with experience in similar work can be easily found. Moreover, the means of obtaining and communicating knowledge at the present time are such that information in regard to the methods and machinery of other countries can be easily obtained, while workmen can be brought from abroad without difficulty. Those artificial obstacles which might temporarily prevent the rise of the industry do not exist, and it may be inferred that, if there are no permanent causes which prevent linens from being made as cheaply in the United States as in other countries, the manufacture will be undertaken and carried on without needing any stimulus from protecting duties.

There are two sets of conditions under which it is supposable that advantages not natural or inherent may be found in one country as compared with another, under which causes merely temporary and accidental may prevent the rise of certain branches of industry in the second country, and under which, therefore, there may be room for the application of protection. These are, first, the state of things in a new country which is rapidly growing in population, and in which, as population becomes more dense, there is a natural change from exclusive devotion to the extractive industries toward greater attention to those branches of production classed as manufactures. The transition from a purely agricultural state to a more diversified system of industry may be retarded, in the complete absence of other occupations than agriculture, beyond the time when it might advantageously take place. Secondly, when great improvements take place in some of the arts of production, it is possible that the new process may be retained in the country in which they originate, and may fail to be applied in another country, through ignorance, the inertia of habit, and perhaps in consequence of restrictive legislation at the seat of the new methods. Here, again, the obstacles to the introduction of the new industry may be of that artificial kind which can be overcome most easily by artificial means. Now, both these sets of conditions seem to have been fulfilled in the United States in the beginning of the 19th century. The country was normally emerging, to a considerable extent, from that state of almost exclusive devotion to agriculture which had characterized the colonies. At the same time great changes were taking place in the mechanical arts, and new processes, hardly known outside of England, and held under a practical monopoly there, were revolutionizing the methods of manufacturing production. Under these circumstances there would seem to have existed room for the legitimate application of protection for young industries.

The more detailed examination in the following pages of the industrial condition of the country during the earlier part of the 19th century will bring out more clearly the reasons why protection may then have been useful. It may be well, however, to notice at this point one difference between those days and the present which must seriously affect the application of the argument we are considering. Even if we were to suppose the conditions of 1810 to exist now; if the country were now first beginning to attempt manufactures, and if a great revolution in manufacturing industry happened to make the attempt peculiarly difficult; even then the obstacles arising from the force of custom, and from the want of familiarity with new processes, would be much more easy to overcome now than sixty years ago. The ties of custom in industry have become much loosened in the last half century; capital and labor turn more easily to new employments. The railroad, the telegraph, the printing-press, the immense increase in the facility of communication, the constant change in methods of production in all industries, have tended to make new discoveries and inventions common property, and to do away with advantages in production based on other than permanent causes. It is true that there are still appreciable differences in the arts of production in different countries, and that some may have a superiority over others based on the merely accidental or temporary possession of better processes or more effective machinery. But the United States hardly lag behind in the industrial advance of the present day, and where they do labor under artificial or factitious disadvantages, these cannot endure long or be of great consequence under a system of freedom.

Eighty years ago, however, the state of things was very different. The conditions were then in force under which protection might be needed to enable useful industries to be carried on. The argument for protection to young industries was accordingly the most effective of those urged in favor of the protective policy. During the twenty years which followed the war of 1812 the protective controversy was one of the most important features in the political life of the nation; and the young industries argument was the great rallying-cry of the protectionists. It is of interest to examine how far protection of the kind advocated was actually applied, and how far it was the cause, or an essential condition, of that rise of manufactures which took place. The object of this paper is to make such an investigation.

THE INDUSTRIAL HISTORY OF THE UNITED STATES, AND
THE COURSE OF PROTECTIVE LEGISLA-
TION, FROM 1789 TO 1838.

THE early economic history of the United States may
be divided into two periods. The first, which is in the
main a continuation of the colonial period, lasted till about
the year 1808 ; the embargo marks the beginning of the
series of events which closed it. The second began in
1808, and lasted through the generation following. It
was during the second period that the most decided attempt was made to apply protection to young industries
in the United States, and with this period we are chiefly
concerned.

During the first period the country was, on the whole,
in the same industrial condition in which the colonies had
been. The colonies had been necessarily engaged almost
exclusively in agriculture, and in the occupations closely
connected with it. The agricultural community could
not get on without blacksmiths, carpenters, masons, shoemakers, and other artisans, and these existed side by side
with the farmers. In those days, it must be remembered,

handicraft workmen of this kind occupied a more important place in industrial organizations than they do at the
present time.   They made many articles and performed
many services which are now the objects of manufacturing
production and of extensive trade, and come within the
range of international dealings.   Many tools were then
made by individual blacksmiths, many wares by the car-
penter, many homespun cloths fulled and finished at the
small fulling-mill.   Production of this kind necessarily
takes place at the locality where consumption goes on.
In those days the division of labor between distant bodies
of men had been carried out to a comparatively slight
extent, and the scope of international trade was therefore
much more limited.   The existence of these handicraft
workmen accounts for the numerous notices of "manufactures" which Mr. Bishop industriously collected in his
"History of Manufactures," and is not inconsistent with
the mainly extractive character of the industry of the
colonies.   What could be imported at that time was im
ported, and was paid for by the exportation of agricultural produce.   The exportation took place, so far as the
northern colonies were concerned, largely to the West
Indies.   From the West India trade the means for paying indirectly for the imported goods were mainly obtained.   There were some important exceptions to this
general state of things.   Ship-building was carried on to a
considerable extent in New England, where abundance of
material and the necessity of transportation by water

made such an industry natural.   The production of unmanufactured iron was carried on to a considerable extent;
for at that time the production of pig and bar iron tended
to fix itself in those countries where wood, the fuel then
used, was abundant, and was therefore an industry much
more analogous to agriculture than it has been since the
employment of coal as fuel.   In the main, however, the
colonies made only such manufactures as could not be imported.   All manufactured goods that could be imported
were not made at home, but obtained in exchange for
agricultural exports.

   This state of things was little changed after the end of
the Revolutionary war and the adoption of the Constitution.   The year 1789 marks no such epoch in economic as it
does in political history. Agriculture, commerce, and the
necessary mechanic arts, continued to form the main occupations of the people.   Such goods as could be imported
continued to be obtained from abroad in exchange for
exports, mainly of agricultural produce.   The range of
importable articles was, it is true, gradually extending.
Cloths, linens, and textile fabrics were still chiefly homespun, and fine goods of this kind were still in the main
the only textile fabrics imported.   But with the great
growth of manufacturing industry in England during this
time, the range of articles that could be imported was
growing wider and wider. During the Napoleonic wars the
American market was much the most important for the
newly established English manufactures.   Large quanti-

ties of cotton and woollen goods were imported, and the importations of manufactures of iron, in regard to which a similar change in production was then taking place, also increased steadily. Sooner or later the change in the course of production which was going on in England must have had, and did have, a strong influence on the economic condition of the United States; but for the time being this influence was little felt, and the country continued in the main to run in the grooves of the colonial period.

This absence of development was strongly promoted by the peculiar condition of the foreign trade of the country up to 1808. The wars of the French Revolution opened to this country profitable markets for its agricultural products in the West Indies and in Europe, and profitable employment for its shipping, both in carrying the increased exports and in a more or less authorized trade between the belligerent countries and their colonies. For many years the gains arising from these sources, though not regular or undisturbed, were great, and afforded every inducement to remain in the occupations that yielded them. The demand for agricultural products for exportation to the belligerent countries and their colonies was large, and the prices of wheat, corn, and meat were correspondingly high. The heavy exports and the profits on freights furnished abundant means for paying for imported goods. Importations were therefore large, and imported goods were so cheap as to afford little inducement for engaging in the production of similar goods at home.[1]

The tariff legislation of this period was naturally much influenced by the direction taken by the industries of the

---

[1] The following tables of imports and exports show the influence of these circumstances on the foreign trade of the country. The exports of foreign produce show the swelling of the carrying-trade. The price of flour shows the effect on the prices of agricultural produce. The influence of the temporary stoppage of the war in Europe during the time of the Peace of Amiens is clearly seen.

Year.	Gross Imports. 000 Omitted.	Gross Exports. 000 Omitted.	Exports of Foreign Produce. 000 Omitted.	Price of Flour per Bbl.
1791	29,200	19,000	500	. . .
92	31,500	20,700	1,750	$ 5.07
93	31.100	26,100	2,100	6.21
94	34,600	33,000	6,500	7.22
95	69,750	48,000	8,500	12.05
96	81,400	67,000	26,300	12.43
97	75,400	56,800	27,000	9.00
98	68,500	61,500	33,000	8.78
99	79,000	78,600	45,500	9.62
1800	91,200	71,000	39,100	9.85
01	111,300	94,000	46,600	10.45
Peace of ⎰ 02	76,300	72,000	35,700	6.75 ⎱
Amiens. ⎱ 03	64,700	55,800	13,600	6.73 ⎰
04	85,000	77,700	36,200	8.22
05	120,600	95,500	53,200	10.28
06	129,400	101,500	60,300	7.30
07	138,500	108,300	59,600	7.00
08	57,000	22,400	13,000	5.60
09	59,400	52,200	20,800	6.90
10	85,400	66,700	24,400	9.66
11	53,400	61,300	16,000	10.00
12	77,000	38,500	8,500	8.75
13	22,000	27,900	2,800	8.50
14	13,000	6,900	150	7.70

The tables of imports and exports are from the Treasury Reports. The last table, giving the price of flour, is in " American State Papers, Finance." III., 536.

country. The peculiarly favorable conditions under which agriculture and commerce were carried on prevented the growth of any strong feeling in favor of assisting manufactures. Much has been said in the course of the protective controversy about the views of the fathers of the republic. But for nearly twenty years after the formation of the Union other subjects so absorbed the attention of public men that no distinct opinion appears in their utterances for or against protective duties. Considering the state of economic knowledge in those days, the example set by European countries, and the application of the colonial system before the days of independence, we cannot be surprised that some disposition was shown to impose protective duties. It is curious that in the first session of Congress these were advocated most earnestly by the representatives from Pennsylvania, who took their stand from the first as unflinching advocates of a protective policy. On the other hand, the current toward more liberal views, which had set in so strongly after the writings of the French economists and the publication of the "Wealth of Nations," had made its way to the United States. One might expect to find its influence most strong among the followers of Jefferson, whose political philosophy led them in general to oppose government interference. But both Federalists and Republicans were influenced in their attitude to the question of protection most of all by its bearing on the other more prominent questions on which parties began to be divided.

Madison had maintained the principle of free intercourse in 1789,[1] and Jefferson in 1787 had extolled the virtues of a simple agricultural State.[2]   But in 1793, when the Federalists and Republicans began to differ on questions of foreign policy, and especially on the attitude the country should take in the wars of the French Revolution, Jefferson advocated vigorous measures of protection directed against England, and Madison brought forward a set of resolutions based on his recommendations.[3] On the other hand, Fisher Ames had said, in 1789, that the general government should nurture those industries in which the individual States had an interest ; but in 1794, when his political views led him to oppose Madison's resolutions, he called the whole theory of protection an exploded dogma.[4]

The first tariff act, that of 1789, was protective in intention and spirit.   The Congress of the Confederation had framed a plan for a general five per cent. duty, with a few specific duties on articles like tea, coffee, and sugar, —a plan whose failure was one of the most important events leading to the adoption of the Constitution.   When Congress met in 1789, this scheme, which had aimed solely at procuring the needed revenues, was presented

---

[1] "Annals of Congress," 1789, pp. 112–114.

[2] "Notes on Virginia, Works," VIII., 404.

[3] See Jefferson's "Report on Commerce, Works," VII., 637 ; and Madison's resolutions of 1794, based on Jefferson's Report, "Annals of Congress," 1794, pp. 155, 209.

[4] "Annals of Congress," 1789, p. 221 ; 1794, p. 342.

anew by Madison, who advocated it not only on financial grounds but on the general principles of free trade. But several of the States, especially Massachusetts and Pennsylvania, had imposed protective duties before 1789; and they were desirous of maintaining the aid then given to some of their industries. Moreover, the feeling of resentment against Great Britain was strong. Consequently, Madison's simple proposal was replaced by a more complicated scheme. The general duty of five per cent. was retained on all goods not otherwise enumerated. On certain articles of luxury, higher ad valorem rates were fixed, the highest, on carriages, being fifteen per cent. Specific duties were imposed on some selected articles, such as hemp, cordage, nails, manufactures of iron, and glass. These articles were selected, and made subject to the specific duties, with the clear intent of stimulating domestic production. The general range of duties was by no means such as would have been thought protective in later days; but the intention to protect was there.[1]

The legislation of the next twenty years, however, brought no further appreciable development of the protective policy. For a short time after 1789, it may be possible to detect a drift in favor of protective duties,

---

[1] On the act of 1789, see the monograph by William Hill, "The First Stages of the Tariff Policy of the United States," in Publications of the American Economic Association, vol. VII., No. 6. This valuable paper has led to a modification of the account of the act of 1789 given in previous editions of the present book

which doubtless was strengthened by the powerful advocacy of protection in Hamilton's "Report on Manufactures" (1792). But that famous document had little, if any, effect on legislation. The moderate policy of 1789 was maintained. The duties were increased from time to time as more revenue was needed, but they were in all cases moderate. Those which were most distinctly protective had no appreciable influence in diverting the industry of the country into new channels. No action at all was taken for the encouragement of the production of textiles, of crude iron, and of the other articles which later became the great subjects of dispute in the protective controversy.

The industrial situation changed abruptly in 1808. The complications with England and France led to a series of measures which mark a turning-point in the industrial history of the country. The Berlin and Milan decrees of Napoleon, and the English orders in Council, led, in December, 1807, to the Embargo. The Non-Intercourse Act followed in 1809. War with England was declared in 1812. During the war, intercourse with England was prohibited, and all import duties were doubled. The last-mentioned measure was adopted in the hope of increasing the revenue, but had little effect, for foreign trade practically ceased to exist. This series of restrictive measures blocked the accustomed channels of exchange and production, and gave an enormous stimulus to those branches of industry whose products had before been imported. Establishments for the manufacture of cotton goods, woollen cloths, iron, glass, pottery, and other articles, sprang up with a mushroom growth. We shall have occasion to refer more in detail to this growth when the history of some of these manufactures comes to be considered separately. It is sufficient here to note that the restrictive legislation of 1808-15 was, for the time being, equivalent to extreme protection. The consequent rise of a considerable class of manufacturers, whose success depended largely on the continuance of protection, formed the basis of a strong movement for more decided limitation of foreign competition.

Some signs of the gradual growth of a protective feeling appear before the close of the war.[1] It was natural that the patriotic fervor which the events of the period of restriction and war called out for the first time in our history, should bring with it a disposition to encourage the production at home of a number of manufactured articles, of which the sudden interruption in the foreign supply caused great inconvenience. Madison, whose views on this subject, as on others, shifted as time went on and circumstances changed, recommended the encouragement of manufactures ; and in some of Clay's earlier speeches we can see the first signs of the American system of the

---

[1] It is curious to note that in 1802–1804, during the temporary lull that followed the Peace of Amiens, the committee reports seem to show a drift toward protection. See " American State Papers, Finance," II., pp. 29, 80, and the report on the Barbary Powers Act of 1804, " Annals of Congress," 1804, pp. 946–950.

future.[1] The feeling in favor of the manufactures that had sprung up during the time of restriction obtained some clear concessions in the tariff act of 1816. The control of the policy of Congress at that time was in the hands of a knot of young men of the rising generation, who had brought about the war and felt in a measure responsible for its results. There was a strong feeling among these that the manufacturing establishments which had grown up during the war should be assisted. There was little feeling, however, either in Congress or among the people, such as appeared in later years, in favor of a permanent strong protective policy. Higher duties were therefore granted on those goods in whose production most interest was felt, textile fabrics; but only for a limited period. Cotton and woollen goods were to pay 25 per cent. till 1819; after that date they were to pay 20 per cent. A proviso, intended to make more secure this measure of protection, was adopted in regard to a minimum duty on cotton goods, to which reference will be made in another connection. These and some other distinctly protective provisions were defended by Calhoun, mainly on the ground of the need of making provision for the exigencies of another war; and on that ground they were adopted, and at the same time limited. The general increase of

---

[1] See Madison's message of 1809, "Statesman's Manual," I., 289; and Clay's speech of 1810, "Works," I., 195. Madison never gave up his general acceptance of the principle of free trade, but admitted it to be inapplicable to articles needed in time of war, and in circumstances to which the young-industries' argument applied. See his "Works." III., 42.

duties under the act of 1816, to an average of about twenty per cent., was due to the necessity of providing for the payment of the interest on the heavy debt contracted during the war.

For some time after the close of the war and the enactment of the tariff of 1816, there was no pressure for a more vigorous application of protective principles. The general expectation was, that the country would fall back into much the same state of things as that which had existed before 1808 ; that agriculture and commerce would again be as profitable as during the previous period, and would be as exclusively the occupations of the people. Such an expectation could not in the nature of things be entirely fulfilled, but for a time it was encouraged by several accidental circumstances. The harvests in Europe for several seasons were bad, and caused a stronger demand and higher price for the staple food products. The demand for cotton was large, and the price high. Most important of all, the currency was in a state of complete disarrangement, and concealed and supported an unsound economic condition. Under cover of the excessive issues of practically irredeemable bank-notes, the prices of all commodities were high, as were the general rates of wages and rents. The prices of bread-stuffs and provisions, the staples of the North, and of cotton and tobacco, the staples of the South, were high, not only absolutely, but relatively, and encouraged continued large production of these articles. The prices of most manufactured

goods were comparatively low.   After the war the imports of these from England were very heavy.   The long
pent-up stream of English merchandise may be said to
have flooded the world at the close of the Napoleonic wars.
In this country, as in others, imports were carried beyond
the capacity for consumption, and prices fell much below
the normal rates.   The strain of this over-supply and
fall of prices bore hard on the domestic manufacturers,
especially on those who had begun and carried on operations during the restrictive period ; and many of them were
compelled to cease production and to abandon their works.

This abnormal period, which had its counterpart of
feverish excitement and speculation in Europe, came to
an end in 1818–19.   The civilized world then settled
down to recover slowly from the effects of a generation
of war and destruction.   In the United States the currency bubble was pricked in the latter part of 1818.
Prices began to fall rapidly and heavily, and continued to
fall through 1819.   The prices of the agricultural staples
of the North and South underwent the greatest change,
for the harvests in Europe were again good in 1818, the
English corn-laws of 1816 went into operation, and the
demand for cotton fell off.   A new scale of monetary exchange gradually went into operation.   During the period
of transition there was, as there always is in such periods,
much suffering and uneasiness ; but gradually the difficulties of adjusting old contracts and engagements were
overcome, and the habits of the people accommodated

themselves to the new régime. Within three or four
years after 1819 the effects of the crash were no longer
felt in most parts of the country.

Two results which it is important to note in this connection followed from the crisis of 1819: first, a great
alteration in the position and prospects of manufacturing
industries; and second, the rise of a strong public feeling
in favor of protecting these industries, and the final enactment of legislation for that purpose. The first of
these results was due primarily to the fact that the fall in
prices after 1819 did not so greatly affect most manufactured goods as it did other articles. The prices of manufactured goods had already declined, in consequence of
the heavy importations in the years immediately following the war. When, therefore, the heavy fall took place
in 1819 in the prices of food and of raw materials, in the
gains of agriculture, in money wages and money rents,
the general result was advantageous for the manufacturers.
They were put into a position to produce with profit at
the lower prices which had before been unprofitable, and
to meet more easily foreign competition. After the first
shock was over, and the system of exchange became
cleared of the confusion and temporary stoppage which
must attend all great fluctuations in prices, this result
was plainly felt.[1] It is easy to see that the whole process

---

[1] "The abundance of capital, indicated by the avidity with which loans
are taken at the reduced rate of five per cent., the reduction in the wages of
labor, and the decline in the price of property of all kinds, all concur favorably for domestic manufactures."—Clay Speech of 1820. "Works," I., 419.

was nothing more than the evolution of the new state of
things which was to take the place of that of the period
before 1808.   In that earlier period manufactured goods,
so far as they could be obtained by importation at all,
were imported cheaply and easily by means of large exports and freight earnings.   These resources were now
largely cut off.   Exports declined, and imports in the end
had to follow them.   The tightening of the English
corn-law, and the general restriction of trade and navigation by England and other countries, contributed to
strengthen this tendency, and necessarily served to stimulate the growth of manufactures in the United States.
That growth was indeed complicated and made more
striking by the revolution which was then taking place in
many departments of manufacturing industry.   Especially
in the production of textile fabrics, machinery was rapidly
displacing—in England had already largely displaced—
production by hand on a small scale.   Home-spun textiles
were gradually making room for the products of the spinning-jenny and the power-loom.   The state of things that
followed the crisis of 1818–19 was favorable to the rise of
manufactures; but the change took place not so much by
an increase in the relative number of persons engaged in
such occupations, as in the substitution of manufactures
in the modern sense for the more simple methods of the
previous period.[1]

---

[1] According to the census returns of 1820 and 1840, the only two of the
earlier returns in which occupations are enumerated, there were engaged

The second effect of the change that followed the financial crisis of 1819, was the strong protective movement which exercised so important an influence on the political history of the next generation. The diminution of the foreign demand, and the fall in the prices of staple products, naturally gave rise to a cry for a home market. The absence of reciprocity and the restrictive regulations of England, especially in face of the comparatively liberal import duties of this country, furnished an effective argument to the advocates of protection. Most effective, however, was the argument for protection to young industries, which was urged with persistency during the next ten or

in manufactures and the mechanic arts in 1820, 13.7 per cent. of the working population ; in 1840, 17 1 per cent. In New England 21 per cent. were so engaged in 1820, 30.2 per cent. in 1840 ; in the Middle States 22.6 per cent. in 1820, 28 per cent. in 1840. Mac Gregor, " Progress of America," II., 101. There are no census figures before 1820. In 1807 it was loosely estimated that out of 2,358,000 persons actively employed, 230,000 were engaged in mechanics and manufactures—less than 10 per cent. Blodgett, " Thoughts on a Plan of Economy," etc. [1807] p. 6.

The fluctuations in the exports of wheat flour, which was the most important article of export among agricultural products during the early part of the century, tell plainly the story of the country's foreign trade. They were as follows, the figures indicating millions of dollars :

Yearly average,	1803–7 (expanded trade)	.	.	.	.	8.2
"	"	1808–10 (restriction)	.	.	.	4.0
"	"	1810–12 (restrictions removed)	.	.	13.5
"	"	1813–15 (war)	.	.	.	5.5
"	"	1816–17 (temporary revival)	.	.	14.5
	Year 1818	.	.	.	.	6.0
	" 1819	.	.	.	.	5.0
	" 1820	.	.	.	.	4.3

During the decade 1820–1830, when matters settled down to a normal state, the yearly export was between four and five millions of dollars. See "Quarterly Reports of the Bureau of Statistics," 1883–84, No. 4, pp. 523, 24.

fifteen years. The character and history of this early protective movement will be discussed elsewhere.[1] Here it is
sufficient to note that its effect on legislation was not
merely to maintain the protective provisions of the tariff
of 1816, but much to extend the protective element in
tariff legislation. Already in 1818 it had been enacted
that the duty of 25 per cent. on cottons and woollens
should remain in force till 1826, instead of being reduced
to 20 per cent. in 1819, as had been provided by the act of
1816. At the same time the duty on all forms of unmanufactured iron was considerably raised ; a measure to
which we shall have occasion to refer in another connection. In 1820, while the first pressure of the economic
revulsion bore hard on the people, a vigorous attempt
was made to pass a high protective tariff, and it barely
failed of success, by a single vote in the Senate. In 1824
the protectionists succeeded in passing the tariff of that
year, which increased all duties considerably. Four years
later, in the tariff of 1828, the protective movement
reached its highest point. The measures which followed
in 1832 and 1833 moderated the peculiarly offensive provisions of the act of 1828, but retained the essential parts
of protection for some years longer. On the whole, from
1816 on, there was applied for some twenty years a continuous policy of protection ; for the first eight years with
much moderation, but after 1824 with high duties, and
stringent measures for enforcing them.

---

[1] In the next essay, pp. 68–75.

III.

THE COTTON MANUFACTURE.

WE turn now to the history of some of the industries to which protection was applied during this long period, in order to determine, so far as this is possible, how far their introduction and early growth were promoted or rendered possible by protection. We shall try to see how far and with what success protection to young industries was applied. The most important of them, on account both of its magnitude and of the peculiarly direct application of protection to it, is the cotton manufacture; and we are fortunate in having, at the same time, the fullest and most trustworthy accounts of the early history of this industry.[1]

During the first of the two periods into which we have divided the early economic history of the United States, several attempts were made to introduce the manufacture of cotton by the machinery invented by Hargreaves and Arkwright in the latter part of the 18th century. One or

---

[1] In S. Batchelder's "Introduction and Early Progress of the Cotton Manufacture in the U. S." (1863); G. S. White's "Memoir of Samuel Slater" (1836); and N. Appleton's "Introduction of the Power-loom and Origin of Lowell" (1858).

two of these attempts succeeded, but most of them failed, and the manufacture, which then was growing with marvellous rapidity in England, failed to attain any considerable development in this country. In 1787 a factory using the new machinery was established at Beverly, Mass., and obtained aid from the State treasury; but it was soon abandoned. Similar unsuccessful ventures were made at Bridgewater, Mass., Norwich, Conn., and Pawtucket, R. I., Paterson and Philadelphia. The spinning-jenny was introduced in all these, but never successfully operated.[1] The first successful attempt to manufacture with the new machinery was made by Samuel Slater, at Pawtucket. Slater was a workman who had been employed in Arkwright's factories in England. He joined to mechanical skill strong business capacity, and had become familiar with the system of carding, drawing, roving, and mule-spinning. Induced to come to the United States in 1789 by prizes offered by the Pennsylvania Society for the Encouragement of Manufactures, he took charge in the following year of a cotton-factory which had been begun and carried on with little success by some Quakers of Pawtucket. He was successful in setting up the Arkwright machinery, and became the founder of the cotton manufacture in this country. Through him machinery, and instruction in using it, were obtainable; and a few other factories were begun under

---

[1] Batchelder, p. 26 *seq.;* White, ch. III. The cotton-mill at Norwich, built in 1790, was operated for ten years, and then abandoned as unprofitable.—Caulkins, " Hist. of Norwich," p. 696.

his superintendence. Nevertheless, the manufacture hardly maintained its hold. In 1803 there were only four factories in the country.[1] The cotton manufacture was at that time extending in England at a rapid rate, and the imports of cotton goods from England were large. The Treasury reports of those days give no separate statements of the imports of cotton goods; but in 1807 it was estimated that the imports of cotton goods from England amounted to eleven million dollars' worth—a very large sum for those days.[2] The consumption of cotton goods was large; but only an insignificant part of it was supplied by home production, although later developments showed that this branch of industry could be carried on with distinct success. The ease with which these imports were paid for, and the stimulus which this period, as described in the preceding pages, gave to agriculture and commerce, account in part for the slowness with which the domestic manufacture developed. The fact that raw cotton was not yet grown to any considerable extent in the country, together, doubtless, with the better machinery and larger experience and skill of the English, account for the rest.

When, however, the period of restriction began, in 1808, the importation of foreign goods was first impeded, and soon entirely prevented. The domestic manufacture accordingly extended with prodigious rapidity. Already

---

[1] Bishop, " Hist. of Manufactures," II., 102.

[2] See the pamphlet by Blodgett " On a Plan of Economy," etc., already cited, p. 26.

during the years 1804–8 greater activity must have prevailed ; for in the latter year fifteen mills had been built, running 8,000 spindles. In 1809 the number of mills built shot up to 62, with 31,000 spindles, while 25 more mills were in course of erection.[1] In 1812 there were 50 factories within thirty miles of Providence, operating nearly 60,000 spindles, and capable of operating 100,-000.[2] During the war the same rapid growth continued, rendered possible as it was by the increasing supply of raw cotton from the South. The number of spindles was said to be 80,000 in 1811, and 500,000 in 1815. In 1800, 500 bales of cotton had been used ; in 1805, 1,000 bales. In 1810 the number consumed rose to 10,000; in 1815, it was 90,000.[3] These figures cannot be supposed to be

---

[1] Gallatin's Report on Manufactures in 1810 ; " Amer. State Papers Finance," II., 427.

[2] White: " Memoir of Slater," p. 188.

[3] See the Report of a Committee of Congress on the Cotton Manufacture in 1816 ; " Amer. State Papers, Finance," III, 82, 84. This estimate refers only to the cotton consumed in factories, and does not include that used in household manufacture. The number of spindles for 1815, as given in this report, is probably much too large. In Woodbury's Report of 1836 on cotton, the number of spindles in use in factories is given as follows :

In 1805	.	.	4,500 spindles.
" 1807	.	.	8,000 "
" 1809	.	.	31,000 "
" 1810	.	.	87,000 "
" 1815	.	.	130,000 "
" 1820	.	.	220,000 "
" 1821	.	.	230,000 "
" 1825	.	.	800,000 "

" Exec. Doc.," 1 Sess., 24 Congr., No. 146, p. 51. It need not be said that these figures are hopelessly loose ; but they are sufficient to support the general assertions of the text

at all accurate; but they indicate clearly an enormously rapid development of the manufacture of cotton.

The machinery in almost all these new factories was for spinning yarn only. Weaving was still carried on by the hand-loom, usually by weavers working in considerable numbers on account for manufacturers. Toward the end of the war, however, a change began to be made almost as important in the history of textile manufactures as the use of the spinning-jenny and mule: namely, the substitution of the power-loom for the hand-loom. The introduction of the power-loom took place in England at about the same time, and some intimation of its use seems to have reached the inventor in this country, Francis C. Lowell. He perfected the machine, however, without any use of English models, in the course of the year 1814. In the same year it was put in operation at a factory at Waltham, Mass. There for the first time the entire process of converting cotton into cloth took place under one roof. The last important step in giving textile manufactures their present form was thus taken.[1]

When peace was made in 1815, and imports began again, the newly established factories, most of which were badly equipped and loosely managed, met with serious embarrassment. Many were entirely abandoned. The manufacturers petitioned Congress for assistance; and they received, in 1816, that measure of help which the public was then disposed to grant. The tariff of 1816

---

[1] Appleton, pp. 7–11; Batchelder, pp. 60–70.

levied a duty of 25 per cent. on cotton goods for three years, a duty considered sufficiently protective in those days of inexperience in protective legislation. At the same time it was provided that all cotton cloths, costing less than 25 cents a yard, should be considered to have cost 25 cents and be charged with duty accordingly; that is, should be charged 25 per cent. of 25 cents, or 6¼ cents a yard, whatever their real value or cost. This was the first of the minimum valuation provisos which played so considerable a part in later tariff legislation, and which have been maintained in large part to the present time. A similar minimum duty was imposed on cotton-yarns.[1] At the time when these measures were passed, the minimum provisos hardly served to increase appreciably the weight of the duty of 25 per cent. Coarse cotton cloths were then worth from 25 to 30 cents, and, even without the provisos, would have paid little, if any thing, less than the minimum duty. But, after 1818, the use of the power-loom, and the fall in the price of raw cotton, combined greatly to reduce the prices of cotton goods. The price of coarse cottons fell to 19 cents in 1819, 13 cents in 1826, and 8½ cents in 1829.[2] The minimum duty became proportionately heavier as the price decreased, and, in a few years after its enactment, had become prohibitive of the importation of the coarser kinds of cotton cloths.

---

[1] The minimum system seems to have been suggested by Lowell. Appleton, p. 13. Compare Appleton's speech in Congress in 1833.—"Congressional Debates," IX., 1213.

[2] Appleton, p. 16.

During the years immediately after the war, the aid given in the tariff of 1816 was not sufficient to prevent severe depression in the cotton manufacture. Reference has already been made to the disadvantages which, under the circumstances of the years 1815–18, existed for all manufacturers who had to meet competition from abroad. But when the crisis of 1818–19 had brought about a re-arrangement of prices more advantageous for manufacturers, matters began to mend. The minimum duty became more effective in handicapping foreign competitors. At the same time the power-loom was generally introduced. Looms made after an English model were introduced in the factories of Rhode Island, the first going into operation in 1817 ; while in Massachusetts and New Hampshire the loom invented by Lowell was generally adopted after 1816.[1] From these various causes the manufacture soon became profitable. There is abundant evidence to show that shortly after the crisis the cotton manufacture had fully recovered from the depression that followed the war.[2] The profits made were such as to cause a rapid

---

[1] Appleton, p. 13 ; Batchelder, pp. 70–73.

[2] The following passage, referring to the general revival of manufactures, may be quoted : " The manufacture of cotton now yields a moderate profit to those who conduct the business with the requisite skill and economy. The extensive factories at Pawtucket are still in operation. . . . In Philadelphia it is said that about 4,000 looms have been put in operation within the last six months, which are chiefly engaged in making cotton goods, and that in all probability they will, within six months more, be increased to four times that number. In Paterson, N. J., where, two years ago, only three out of sixteen of its extensive factories were in operation . . . all are now in vigorous employment."—" Niles's Register," XXI., 39 (1821). Com-

extension of the industry.   The beginning of those manufacturing villages which now form the characteristic
economic feature of New England falls in this period.
Nashua was founded in 1823.   Fall River, which had
grown into some importance during the war of 1814, grew
rapidly from 1820 to 1830.[1]   By far the most important
and the best known of the new ventures in cotton manufacturing was the foundation of the town of Lowell, which
was undertaken by the same persons who had been engaged in the establishment of the first power-loom factory
at Waltham.   The new town was named after the inventor
of the power-loom.   The scheme of utilizing the falls of
the Merrimac, at the point where Lowell now stands, had
been suggested as early as 1821, and in the following year
the Merrimac Manufacturing Company was incorporated.
In 1823 manufacturing began, and was profitable from the
beginning ; and in 1824 the future growth of Lowell was
clearly foreseen.[2]

---

pare *Ibid.*, XXII., 225, 250 (1822) ; XXIII., 35, 88 (1823) ; and *passim.*
In Woodbury's cotton report, cited above, it is said (p. 57) that " there was
a great increase [in cotton manufacturing] in 1806 and 1807 ; again during
the war of 1812 ; again from 1820 to 1825 ; and in 1831–32."

[1] Fox's " History of Dunstable " ; Earl's " History of Fall River," p. 20
seq.

[2] See the account in Appleton, pp. 17–25.   One of the originators of the
enterprise said in 1824 : " If our business succeeds, as we have reason to
expect, we shall have here [at Lowell] as large a population in twenty
years from this time as there was in Boston twenty years ago."—Batchelder, p. 69.

In Bishop, II., 309, is a list of the manufacturing villages of 1826, in
which some twenty places are enumerated.

From this sketch of the early history of the cotton manufacture we may draw some conclusions. Before 1808 the difficulties in the way of the introduction of this branch of industry were such that it made little progress. These difficulties were largely artificial; and though the obstacles arising from ignorance of the new processes and from the absence of experienced workmen, were partly removed by the appearance of Slater, they were sufficient, when combined with the stimulus which the condition of foreign trade gave to agriculture and the carrying trade, to prevent any 'appreciable development. Had this period come to an end without any accompanying political change—had there been no embargo, no non-intercourse act, and no war with England—the growth of the cotton manufacture, however certain to have taken place in the end, might have been subject to much friction and loss. Conjecture as to what might have been is dangerous, especially in economic history, but it seems reasonable to suppose that if the period before 1808 had come to an end without a jar, the eager competition of well-established English manufacturers, the lack of familiarity with the processes, and the long-continued habit, especially in New England, of almost exclusive attention to agriculture, commerce, and the carrying trade, might have rendered slow and difficult the change, however inevitable it may have been, to greater attention to manufactures. Under such circumstances there might have been room for the legitimate application of protection to the cotton manufacture as a young industry.   But this period, in fact, came to an end with a violent shock, which threw industry out of its accustomed grooves, and caused the striking growth of the cotton manufacture from 1808 to 1815. The transition caused much suffering, but it took place sharply and quickly.   The interruption of trade was equivalent to a rude but vigorous application of protection, which did its work thoroughly.   When peace came, in 1815, it found a large number of persons and a great amount of capital engaged in the cotton manufacture, and the new processes of manufacture introduced on an extensive scale.   Under such circumstances the industry was certain to be maintained if it was for the economic interest of the country that it should be carried on.

The duties of the tariff of 1816, therefore, can hardly be said to have been necessary.   Nevertheless, they may have been of service.   The assistance they gave was, it is true, insignificant in comparison with the shelter from all foreign competition during the war.   Indeed, most manufacturers desired much higher duties than were granted.[1] It is true, also, that the minimum duty on cottons was least effective during the years immediately after the war, when the price of cottons was higher, and the duty was therefore proportionately less high.   But these years be-

---

[1] " In 1816 a new tariff was to be made.   The Rhode Island manufacturers were clamorous for a very high specific duty.   Mr. Lowell's views on the tariff were much more moderate, and he finally brought Mr. Lowndes and Mr. Calhoun to support the minimum of 6¼ cents a yard, which was carried."—Appleton, p. 13.

tween the close of the war and the general fall of prices in 1819 were trying for the manufacturers. The normal economic state, more favorable for them, was not reached till the crisis of 1818–19 was well over. During the intervening years the minimum duty may have assisted the manufacturers without causing any permanent charge on the people. The fact that careful and self-reliant men, like the founders of the Waltham and Lowell enterprises, were most urgent in advising the adoption of the rates of 1816—at a time, too, when the practice of appealing to Congress for assistance when in distress had not yet become common among manufacturers—may indicate that those rates were of service in encouraging the continuance of the manufacture. How seriously its progress would have been impeded or retarded by the absence of duties, cannot be said. On the whole, although the great impulse to the industry was given during the war, the duties on cottons in the tariff of 1816 may be considered a judicious application of the principle of protection to young industries.

Before 1824, the manufacture, as we have seen, was securely established. The further application of protection in that and in the following years was needless, and, so far as it had any effect, was harmful. The minimum valuation was raised in 1824 to 30 cents, and in 1828 to 35 cents. The minimum duties were thereby raised to $7\frac{1}{2}$ and $8\frac{3}{4}$ cents respectively. By 1824 the manufacture had so firm a hold that its further extension should have been left to individual enterprise, which by that time might have been relied on to carry the industry as far as it was for the economic interest of the country that it should be carried. The increased duties of 1824 and 1828 do not come within the scope of the present discussion.

IV.

THE WOOLLEN MANUFACTURE.

THE sudden and striking growth of the cotton manufacture in the last hundred years has caused its history, in
this country as in others, to be written with comparative
fulness. Of the early history of the manufacture of
woollen goods in the United States we have but scanty
accounts ; but these are sufficient to show that the general
course of events was similar to that in cotton manufacturing. During the colonial period and the years immediately after the Revolution, such woollen cloths as were
not spun and woven in households for personal use were
imported from England. The goods of household manufacture, however, formed, and for many years after the introduction of machinery continued to form, by far the
greater part of those in use. The first attempt at making
woollens in large quantities is said to have been made at
Ipswich, Mass., in 1792 ; but no machinery seems to have
been used in this undertaking. In 1794 the new machinery was for the first time applied to the manufacture of
wool, and it is noteworthy that, as in the case of the cotton manufacture, the machinery was introduced by En-

lish workmen. These were the brothers Arthur and John Scholfield, who came to the United States in 1793, and in the next year established a factory at Byfield, Mass. Their machinery, however, was exclusively for carding wool, and for dressing (fulling) woollen goods; and for the latter purpose it was probably in no way different from that of the numerous fulling-mills which were scattered over the country during colonial times. Spinning and weaving were done, as before, on the spinning-wheel and the hand-loom. The Scholfields introduced carding-machinery in place of the hand-cards, and seem to have carried on their business in several places with success. A Scotchman, James Saunderson, who emigrated in 1794, also introduced carding-machines at New Ipswich, N. H., in 1801. Their example, however, was followed by few. Carding-machines were introduced in a few other places between 1800 and 1808; but no development of the business of systematically making cloth, or preparing wool for sale, took place. The application of machinery for spinning does not seem to have been made at all.[1] One great difficulty in the way of the woollen manufacture was the deficient supply and poor quality of wool. The means of overcoming this were supplied when in 1802 a large flock of fine merino sheep was imported from Spain,

---

[1] See a sketch of the early history of the woollen manufacture in Taft's "Notes on the Introduction of the Woollen Manufacture." Compare the same writer's account in "Bulletin National Ass. of Wool Manufacturers," II., 478-488 and the scattered notices in Bishop, "Hist. of Manufactures," I., 421, and II., 106, 109, 118, etc.

followed in 1809 and 1810 by several thousand pure me-
rinos from the same country.[1] But imports from England
continued to be large, and those woollen cloths that were
not homespun were obtained almost exclusively from the
mother country.[2]

When the period of restriction began in 1808, the woollen manufacture received, like all other industries in the
same position, a powerful stimulus. The prices of broad-
cloth, then the chief cloth worn besides homespun, rose
enormously, as did those of flannels, blankets, and other
goods, which had previously been obtained almost exclusively by importation. We have no such detailed statements as are given of the rise of the cotton manufacture.
It is clear, however, that the manufacture of woollen
goods, which had had no real existence before, began,
and was considerably extended. The spinning of wool by

---

[1] Bishop, II., 94, 134.

[2] The United States were important customers of woollens for England,
as appears from the following figures, which give in millions of pounds
sterling the total exports of woollens from England, and those of exports to
the United States.

	Total	To the U. S.
1790	5.2	1.5
1791	5.5	1.6
1792	5.5	1.4
1793	3.8	1.0
1794	4.4	1·4
1795	5.2	2.0
1796	6.0	2.3
1797	4.9	1.9
1798	6.5	2.4
1799	6.9	2.8

Brothers, "Wool and Wool Manufactures of Great Britain," 143, 144

machinery was introduced, and goods were made for sale on a large scale. As early as 1810 the carding and spinning of wool by machinery was begun in some of the cotton mills in Rhode Island.[1] In Northampton, Mass., Oriskany, N. Y., and other places, large establishments for the manufacture of woollen goods and of satinets (mixed cotton and woollen goods) sprang up. The value of woollen goods made in factories is said to have risen from $4,000,000 in 1810 to $19,000,000 in 1815.[2]

After 1815 the makers of woollens naturally encountered great difficulties in face of the renewed and heavy importations of English goods. The tariff of 1816 gave them the same duty that was levied on cottons, 25 per cent., to be reduced in three years to 20 per cent. The reduction of the duty to 20 per cent., which was to have taken place in 1819, was then postponed, and in the end never took place. No minimum valuation was fixed for woollen goods ; hence there was not, as for cotton goods, a minimum duty. Wool was admitted at a duty of 15 per cent. The scheme of duties, under the tariff of 1816, thus afforded no very vigorous protection. Nor did the provisions of the act of 1824 materially improve the position of the woollen manufacturers. The duty on woollen goods was in that act raised to 30 per cent. in the first instance, and to 33⅓ per cent. after 1825. At the same time the

---

[1] Gallatin's report of 1810, "Am. State Papers, Finance," II. 427 ; Taft, 44.

[2] "Bulletin Wool Manufacturers," II., 486. This is hardly more than a loose, though significant, guess.

duty on wool (except that costing ten cents a pound or less) was raised to 20 per cent. in the first place, to 25 per cent. after 1825, and to 30 per cent. after 1826. If foreign wool had to be imported to supplement the domestic supply,—and such a necessity has constantly existed in this country since 1816,—the increased price of wool in this country, as compared with other countries which admitted wool free or at a lower duty, would tend to make the effectual protection to woollen manufacturers far from excessive.

Notwithstanding the very moderate encouragement given from 1816 to 1828, the woollen manufacture steadily progressed after the crisis of 1819, and in 1828 was securely established. During the years from the close of the war till 1819 much embarrassment was felt, and many establishments were given up; but others tided over this trying time.[1] After 1819 the industry gradually responded to the more favorable influences which then set in for manufactures, and made good progress. During 1821 and 1822 large investments were made in factories for making woollen cloths, especially in New England.[2] In 1823 the manufacturers of woollens in Boston were sufficiently numerous to form an independent

---

[1] Thus a large factory in Northampton, built in 1809 (Bishop, II., 136), was still in operation in 1828 ("Am. State Papers, Finance," V., 815). In Taft's " Notes " there is mention (pp. 39–40) of the Peacedale Manufacturing Company, which began in 1804, and has lasted to the present time. It is said that the spinning-jenny was first applied to wool in this factory.

[2] Bishop, II., 270, 294 ; Niles, XXII., 225.

organization for the promotion of their interests, which
were, in that case, to secure higher protective duties.[1]
The best evidence which we have of the condition of the
industry during these years is to be found in the testimony given in 1828 by various woollen manufacturers before the Committee of the House of Representatives on
Manufactures. This testimony shows clearly that the
industry was established in 1828 on such a scale that the
difficulties arising from lack of skill and experience, unfa-
miliarity with machinery and methods, and other such
temporary obstacles, no longer had influence in preventing its growth.[2] The capital invested by the thirteen
manufacturers who testified before this committee varied
from $20,000 to $200,000, the average being $85,000.
The quantity of wool used by each averaged about 62,000
pounds per year. These figures indicate a scale of operation very considerable for those days. Six of the factories referred to had been established between 1809 and
1815. With the possible exception of one, in regard to
which the date of foundation was not stated, none had been
established in the years between 1815 and 1820; the remaining six had been built after 1820. Spinning-machinery was
in use in all. Some used power-looms, others hand-looms.
The application of the power-loom to weaving woollens, said
one manufacturer, had been made in the United States

---

[1] Niles, XXV., 148, 189,

[2] The testimony is printed in full in "American State Papers, Finance,"
V., 792–832.

earlier than in England.[1] An indication, similar to this, of the point reached by the American producers in the use of machinery, was afforded by the difference of opinion in regard to the comparative merits of the jenny, and of the " Brewster," a spinning-machine of recent invention. Goods of various kinds were made—broadcloths, cassimeres, flannels, satinets, and kerseys. The opinion was expressed by several that the mere cost of manufacturing was not greater in the United States than in England ; that the American manufacturer could produce, at as low prices as the English, if he could obtain his wool at as low prices as his foreign competitor.[2] This testi-

---

[1] Testimony, p. 824. The same statement is made by Bishop, II., 317. In Taft's " Notes," p. 39, there is an account of the application of the power-loom to weaving saddle-girths as early as 1814. In 1822 the power-loom for weaving broadcloths seems to have been in common use.— Taft, p. 43.

[2] " Broadcloths are now (1828) made at much less expense of labor and capital than in 1825, by the introduction of a variety of improved and labor-saving machinery, amongst which may be named the dressing-machine and the broad power-loom of American invention " (p. 824). The power-loom was very generally used. " Since the power-looms have been put in operation, the weaving costs ten cents per yard, instead of from eighteen to twenty-eight cents " (p. 814). Shepherd, of Northampton, to whose factory reference has already been made (*ante* p. 44, note 1), said : " The difference in price of cloths (in the United States and in England) would be the difference in the price of the wool, as, in my opinion, we can manufacture as cheap as they (the English) can " (p. 816). In the same connection another manufacturer said : " The woollen manufacture is not yet fairly established in this country, but I know no reason why we cannot manufacture as well and as cheap as they can in England, except the difference in the price of labor, for which, in my opinion, we are fully compensated by other advantages. Our difficulties are not the cost of manufacturing, but the great fluctuations in the home market, caused by the excessive and irreg-

mony seems to show conclusively that at the time when it was given the woollen manufacture had reached that point at which it might be left to sustain itself; at which accidental or artificial obstacles no longer stood in the way of its growth. That many of the manufacturers themselves wanted higher duties, is, for obvious reasons, not inconsistent with this conclusion. Progress had been less certain and rapid than in the case of the kindred cotton manufacture, for the conditions of production were less distinctly favorable. The displacement of the household products by those of the factory was necessarily a gradual process, and made the advance of the woollen manufacture normally more slow than that of the kindred industry. But the growth of the cotton manufacture, so similar to that of wool, of itself removed many of the obstacles arising from the recent origin of the latter. The use of machinery became common, and, when the first great steps had been taken, was transferred with comparative ease from one branch of textile production to another. In 1828, when for the first time heavy protection was given by a complicated system of minimum duties, and when the actual rates rose, in some cases, to over 100 per cent., this aid was no longer needed to sus-

---

ular foreign importations. The high prices we pay for labor are, in my opinion, beneficial to the American manufacturer, as for those wages we get a much better selection of hands, and those capable and willing to perform a much greater amount of labor in a given time. The American manufacturer also uses a larger share of labor-saving machinery than the English" (p. 829).

tain the woollen manufacture. The period of youth had then been past.

It appears that direct protective legislation had even less influence in promoting the introduction and early growth of the woollen than of the cotton manufacture. The events of the period of restriction, from 1808 to 1815, led to the first introduction of the industry, and gave it the first strong impulse. Those events may indeed be considered to have been equivalent to effective, though crude and wasteful, protective legislation, and it may be that their effect, as compared with the absence of growth before 1808, shows that protection in some form was needed to stimulate the early growth of the woollen manufacture. But, by 1815, the work of establishing the manufacture had been done. The moderate duties of the period from 1816 to 1828, partly neutralized by the duties on wool, may have something to sustain it; but the position gained in 1815 would hardly have been lost in the absence of these duties. By 1828, when strong protection was first given, a secure position had certainly been reached.

V.

THE IRON MANUFACTURE.

WE turn now to the early history of the iron manufacture,—the production of crude iron, pig and bar. We shall examine here the production, not of the finished article, but of the raw material. It is true that the production of crude iron takes place under somewhat different conditions from those which affect cotton and woollen goods. The production of pig-iron is more in the nature of an extractive industry, and, under ordinary circumstances, is subject in some degree to the law of diminishing returns. To commodities produced under the conditions of that law, the argument for protection to young industries has not been supposed, at least by its more moderate advocates, to apply, since the sites where production will be carried on to best advantage are apt to be determined by unalterable physical causes.[1] It happens, however, that changes in the processes of production, analogous to those which took place in the textile industries, were made at about the same time in the manufacture of crude

[1] See, for instance, List, "System of National Economy," Phila., 1856, pp. 296-300.

iron. These changes rendered more possible the successful application of the principle of protection to young
industries, and make the discussion of its application
more pertinent. There is another reason why we should
consider, in this connection, the raw material rather than
the finished article. The production of the latter, of the
tools and implements made of iron, has not, in general,
needed protection in this country, nor has protection often
been asked for it. The various industries by which crude
iron is worked into tools and consumable articles were
firmly established already in the colonial period, and since
then have maintained themselves with little difficulty.
The controversy on the protection of the iron manufacture has been confined mainly to the production of pig-
and bar-iron. It is to this, therefore, that we shall direct
our attention. The production of pig- and bar-iron will
be meant when, in the following pages, the " iron manufacture " is spoken of.

During the eighteenth century England was a country
importing, and not, as she is now, one exporting, crude
iron. The production of pig- and bar-iron was accordingly
encouraged in her colonies, and production was carried on
in them to an extent considerable for those days. Large
quantities of bar-iron were exported from the American
colonies to England.[1] The manufacture of iron was

---

[1] See the tables in Bishop, I., 629, and Scrivenor, " History of the Iron
Trade," p. 81. In 1740 the total quantity of iron produced in England
was about 17,000 tons ; at that time from 2,000 to 3,000 tons annually were
regularly imported from the American colonies.

firmly established in the colonies according to the methods common at the time.   During the second half of the
eighteenth century, however, the great change took place
in England in the production of iron which has placed
that country in its present position among iron-making
countries, and has exercised so important an influence on
the material progress of our time.   Up to that time charcoal had been used exclusively for smelting iron, and the
iron manufacture had tended to fix itself in countries
where wood was abundant, like Norway, Sweden, Russia,
and the American colonies.   About 1750 the use of coke
in the blast furnace began.   The means were thus given
for producing iron in practically unlimited quantities,
without dependence for fuel on forests easily exhaustible ;
and in the latter part of the century, when the steam-
engine supplied the motive power for the necessary strong
blast, production by means of coke increased with great
rapidity.[1]   At the same time, in 1783 and 1784, came the
inventions of Cort for puddling and rolling iron.   By these
the transformation of pig-iron into bar-iron of convenient
sizes was effected in large quantities.   Before the inventions of Cort, pig-iron had been first converted into bar
under the hammer, and the bar, at a second distinct operation in a slitting mill, converted into bars and rods of convenient size.   The rolled bar made by the processes of
puddling and rolling—which are still in common use—is

---

[1] See the good account of the importance of the use of coke (coal) in Je-
vons, " The Coal Question," ch. XV., pp. 309-316.

inferior in quality, at least after the first rolling, to the hammered and slit iron, known as hammered bar, produced by the old method. Cort's processes, however made the iron much more easily and cheaply, and the lower price of the rolled iron more than compensated, for most purposes, for its inferior quality. At the same time these processes made easy and fostered the change from production on a small scale to production on a large scale. This tended to bring about still greater cheapness, and made the revolution in the production of iron as great as that in the textile industries, and similar to it in many important respects.

During the period 1789–1808 these changes in the iron manufacture were too recent to have had any appreciable effect on the conditions of production and supply in the United States. The manufacture of iron, and its transformation into implements of various kinds, went on without change from the methods of the colonial period. Pig-iron continued to be made and converted into hammered bar in small and scattered works and forges.[1] No pig-iron seems to have been imported. Bar-iron was imported, in quantities not inconsiderable, from Russia[2]; but no crude iron was imported from England. The importations of certain iron articles, not much advanced beyond the crude state, such as nails, spikes, anchors, cables, showed a perceptible increase during this period.[3]

---

[1] French, "Hist. of Iron Manufacture," p. 16.   [2] *Ibid.*, p. 13.

[3] The imports of iron, so far as separately stated in the Treasury reports, may be found in Young's Report on Tariff Legislation, pp. XXV., XXXVI. Cp. Grosvenor, "Does Protection Protect?" pp. 174, 175.

Whether this increase was the result of the general conditions which tended to swell imports during this period, or was the first effect of the new position which England was taking as an iron-making country, cannot be determined.   Information on the state of the industry during this period is meagre ; but it seems to have been little affected by the protective duties which Congress enacted on nails, steel, and some other articles.   No protection was attempted to be given to the production of pig or bar-iron, for it was thought that the domestic producers would be able to compete successfully with their foreign competitors in this branch of the iron-trade.

During the period of restriction from 1808 to 1815, the iron and manufactures of iron previously imported, had to be obtained, as far as possible, at home.   A large increase in the quantity of iron made in the country accordingly took place.   The course of events was so similar to that already described in regard to textile manufactures that it need not be referred to at length.   When peace came, there were unusually heavy importations of iron, prices fell rapidly, and the producers had to go through a period of severe depression.

In 1816 Congress was asked to extend protection to the manufacture of iron, as well as to other industries. The tariff of 1816 imposed a duty of 45 cents a hundred-weight on hammered-bar iron, and one of $1.50 a hundred-weight on rolled bar, with corresponding duties on sheet, hoop, and rod iron.   Pig-iron was admitted under an *ad valorem* duty of 20 per cent. At the prices of bar-iron in 1816, the specific duty on hammered bar was equivalent to about 20 per cent.,[1] and was, therefore, but little higher than the rates of 15 and 17½ per cent. levied in 1804 and 1807. The duty on rolled bar was much higher, relatively to price, as well as absolutely, than that on hammered bar, and was the only one of the iron duties of 1816 which gave distinct and vigorous protection. These duties were not found sufficient to prevent the manufacturers from suffering heavy losses, and more effective protection was demanded. In 1818, Congress, by a special act, raised the duties on iron considerably, at the same time, as was noted above,[2] that it postponed the reduction from 25 to 20 per cent. on the duty on cottons and woollens. Both of these measures were concessions to protective feeling, and they may have been the result of an uneasy consciousness of the disturbed state of the country and of the demand for protection which was to follow the financial crisis of the next year.[3] The act of 1818 fixed the duty on pig-iron at 50 cents per hundred-weight—the first specific duty imposed on pig-iron; hammered bar was charged with 75 cents a hundred-weight, instead of 45 cents, as in 1816; and higher duties were put on castings, anchors, nails, and spikes.[4] These duties

[1] See the tables of prices in French, pp. 35, 36.

[2] *Ante*, p. 27.

[3] There is nothing in the Congressional debates on the acts of 1818 to show what motives caused them to be passed.

[4] "Statutes at Large," III., 460.

were comparatively heavy ; and with a steady fall in the price of iron, especially after the crisis of 1818–19, they became proportionately heavier and heavier. Nevertheless, in the tariff of 1824 they were further increased. The rate on hammered bar went up to 90 cents a hundred-weight ; that on rolled bar still remained at $1.50, as it had been fixed in 1816. In 1828 a still further increase was made in the specific duties on all kinds of iron, although the continual fall in prices was of itself steadily increasing the weight of the specific duties. The duty on pig-iron went up to 62½ cents a hundred-weight ; that on hammered bar to a cent a pound (that is, $1.12 a hundred-weight) ; that on rolled bar to $37 a ton. In 1832 duties were reduced in the main to the level of those of 1824, and in 1833 the Compromise Act, after maintaining the duties of 1832 for two years, gradually reduced them still further, till in 1842 they reached a uniform level of 20 per cent. On the whole, it is clear that after 1818 a system of increasingly heavy protection was applied to the iron manufacture, and that for twenty years this protection was maintained without a break. From 1818 till 1837 or 1838, when the reduction of duty under the Compromise Act began to take effect to an appreciable extent, the duties on iron in its various forms ranged from 40 to 100 per cent. on the value.

It is worth while to dwell for a moment on the heavy duty on rolled iron—much higher than that on hammered iron—which was adopted in 1816, and maintained throughout this period. Congress attempted to ward off the competition of the cheaper rolled iron by this heavy discriminating duty, which in 1828 was equivalent to one hundred per cent. on the value. When first established in 1816, the discrimination was defended on the ground that the rolled iron was of inferior quality, and that the importation of the unserviceable article should be impeded for the benefit of the consumer. The scope of the change in the iron manufacture, of which the appearance of rolled iron was one sign, was hardly understood in 1816 and 1818, and this argument against its use may have represented truthfully the animus of the discriminating duty. But in later years the wish to protect the consumer from impositions hardly continued to be the motive for retaining the duty. Rolled bar-iron soon became a well-known article, of considerable importance in commerce. The discriminating duty was retained throughout, and in 1828 even increased; it was still levied in the tariff of 1832; it reappeared when the Whigs carried the tariff of 1842; and it did not finally disappear till 1846. The real motive for maintaining the heavy tax through these years undoubtedly was the unwillingness of the domestic producers to face the competition of the cheaper article. The tax is a clear illustration of that tendency to fetter and impede the progress of improvement which is inherent in protective legislation. It laid a considerable burden on the community, and, as we shall see, it was of no service in encouraging the early growth of the iron industry. It is curious to note that the same contest against improved processes was carried on in France, by a discriminating duty on English rolled iron, levied first in 1816, and not taken off till 1860.[1]

After 1815 the iron-makers of the United States met with strong foreign competition from two directions. In the first place, English pig and rolled iron was being produced with steadily decreasing cost. The use of coke became universal in England, and improvements in methods of production were constantly made. Charcoal continued to be used exclusively in the furnaces of this country; for the possibility of using anthracite had not yet been discovered, and the bituminous coal fields lay too far from what was then the region of dense population to be available. While coke-iron was thus driving out charcoal-iron for all purposes for which the former could be used, the production of charcoal-iron itself encountered the competition of Sweden and Russia. As the United States advanced in population, the more accessible forests became exhausted, and the greater quantity of charcoal-iron needed with the increase of population and of production, could be obtained at home only at higher cost. The Scandinavian countries and Russia, with large forests and a population content with low returns for labor, in large part supplied the increased quantity at lower rates than the iron-makers of this country. Hence the imports of iron show a steady increase, both those of pig-iron and

---

[1] Amé, " Études sur les Tarifs de Douanes," I., 145.

and those of rolled and hammered bar; the rolled bar coming from England, and the hammered bar from Sweden and Russia. The demand for iron was increasing at a rapid rate, and there was room for an increase both of the domestic production and of imports; but the rise in imports was marked. Notwithstanding the heavy duties, the proportion of imported to domestic iron from 1818 to 1840 remained about the same.[1]

Since importations continued regularly and on a considerable scale, the price of the iron made at home was clearly raised, at the seaboard, over the price of the foreign iron by the amount of the duty. The country, therefore, paid the iron tax probably on the greater part used, whether of foreign or domestic origin, in the shape of prices from forty to one hundred per cent. higher than those at which the iron could have been bought abroad.

---

[1] On the production and imports of iron in the years after 1830 the reader is referred to the remarks on p. 124, and to the " Quarterly Journal of Economics," vol. II., p. 377. Until the middle of the decade 1820–30 the annual product of pig-iron is supposed to have been about 50,000 tons. while in the second half of the decade it is put at 100,000 tons and more. The imports of crude iron averaged about 20,000 tons per year in 1818–21, about 30,000 tons in 1822–27, and rose to an average of about 40,000 tons in 1828–30. These figures as to imports refer mainly to bar-iron ; and as it required in those days about $1\frac{2}{8}$ tons of pig to make a ton of bar (French, p. 54), some additions must be made to the imports of bar before a proper comparison can be made between the domestic and the imported supply. An addition must also be made for the considerable imports of steel, sheet-iron, anvils, anchors, and other forms of manufactured iron. Figures of imports are given in Grosvenor, pp. 198, 199 ; of domestic production, by R. W. Raymond, in A. S. Hewitt's pamphlet on " A Century of Mining and Metallurgy," page 31.

The fact that the manufacture, notwithstanding the heavy and long-continued protection which it enjoyed, was unable to supply the country with the iron which it needed, is of itself sufficient evidence that its protection as a young industry was not successful.   It is an essential condition for the usefulness of assistance given to a young industry, that the industry shall ultimately supply its products at least as cheaply as they can be obtained by importation; and this the iron manufacture failed to do. There is, however, more direct evidence than this, that the manufacture was slow to make improvements in production, which might have enabled it eventually to furnish the whole supply needed by the country, and in this way might have justified the heavy taxes laid for its benefit.   Pig-iron continued to be made only with charcoal.   The process of puddling did not begin to be introduced before 1830, and then inefficiently and on a small scale.[1]   Not until the decade between 1830 and 1840, at a time when the Compromise Act of 1833 was steadily decreasing duties, was puddling generally introduced.[2]   The iron rails needed for the railroads built at this time—the first parts of the present railroad system—were supplied exclusively by importation.   In 1832 an act of Congress had provided that duties should be refunded on all imported rails laid down within three years from the date

---

[1] See an excellent article, by an advocate of protection, in the *American Quarterly Review*, Vol. IX. (1831), pp. 376, 379, which gives very full information in regard to the state of the iron manufacture at that date.

[2] French, p. 56.

of importation. Under this act all the first railroads imported their rails without payment of duty. Finally, the great change which put the iron manufacture on a firm and durable basis did not come till the end of the decade 1830–40, when all industry was much depressed, and duties had nearly reached their lowest point. That change consisted in the use of anthracite coal in the blast-furnace. A patent for smelting iron with anthracite was taken out in 1833; the process was first used successfully in 1836. In 1838 and 1839 anthracite began to be widely used. The importance of the discovery was promptly recognized; it was largely adopted in the next decade, and led, among other causes, to the rapid increase of the production of iron, which has been so often ascribed exclusively to the protection of the tariff of 1842. With this change the growth of the iron manufacture on a great scale properly begins.[1]

It seems clear that no connection can be traced between the introduction and early progress of the iron manufacture, and protective legislation. During the colonial period, as we have seen, under the old system of production of iron, the country had exported and not imported iron. The production of charcoal-iron and of hammered bar was carried on before the adoption of the Constitution. During the first twenty years after 1789, the iron-makers

---

[1] Swank's Report on "Iron and Steel Production," in the Census of 1880, p. 114. A fuller discussion of the introduction of the use of anthracite, and of the effect of protective duties after this had been done, will be found at pages 122–134.

still held their own, although the progress of invention
elsewhere, and the general tendency in favor of heavy imports, caused a growing importation from abroad. The
production of iron by the old methods and with the use
of charcoal was therefore in no sense a new industry. If
the business of making charcoal-iron could not be carried
on or increased during this and the subsequent period,
the cause must have lain in natural obstacles and disadvantages which no protection could remove. After 1815,
the new régime in the iron trade had begun ; the use of
coke in the blast-furnace, and the production of wrought-
iron by puddling and rolling, had changed completely the
conditions of production. The protective legislation
which began in 1818, and continued in force for nearly
twenty years, was intended, it is true, to ward off rather
than to encourage the adoption of the new methods ; but
it is conceivable that, contrary to the intentions of its authors, it might have had the latter effect. No such effect,
however, is to be seen. During the first ten or fifteen
years after the application of protection, no changes of
any kind took place. Late in the protective period, and
at a time when duties were becoming smaller, the puddling process was introduced. The great change which
marks the turning-point in the history of the iron manufacture in the United States—the use of anthracite—began when protection ceased. It is probably not true, as
is asserted by advocates of free trade,[1] that protection had

---

[1] *E. g.*, Grosvenor, p. 197.

any appreciable influence in retarding the use of coal in making iron. Other causes, mainly the refractory nature of the fuel, sufficiently account for the failure to use anthracite at an earlier date. The successful attempts to use anthracite were made almost simultaneously in England and in the United States.[1] The failure to use coke from bituminous coal, which had been employed in England for over half-a-century, was the result of the distance of the bituminous coal-fields from the centre of population, and of the absence of the facility of transportation which has since been given by railroads. It is hardly probable, therefore, that protection exercised any considerable harmful influence in retarding the progress of improvement. But it is clear, on the other hand, that no advantages were obtained from protection in stimulating progress. No change was made during the period of protection which enabled the country to obtain the metal more cheaply than by importation, or even as cheaply. The duties simply taxed the community; they did not serve to stimulate the industry, though they probably did not appreciably retard its growth. We may therefore conclude that the duties on iron during the generation after 1815 formed a heavy tax on consumers; that they impeded, so far as they went, the industrial development of the country; and that no compensatory benefits were obtained to offset these disadvantages.

---

[1] Swank, pp. 114, 115.

VI.

CONCLUDING REMARKS.

THE three most important branches of industry to which protection has been applied, have now been examined. It has appeared that the introduction of the cotton manufacture took place before the era of protection, and that—looking aside from the anomalous conditions of the period of restriction from 1808 to 1815—its early progress, though perhaps somewhat promoted by the minimum duty of 1816, would hardly have been much retarded in the absence of protective duties. The manufacture of woollens received little direct assistance before it reached that stage at which it could maintain itself without help, if it were for the advantage of the country that it should be maintained. In the iron manufacture twenty years of heavy protection did not materially alter the proportion of home and foreign supply, and brought about no change in methods of production. It is not possible, and hardly necessary, to carry the inquiry much further. Detailed accounts cannot be obtained of other industries to which protection was applied; but so far as can be seen, the same course of events took place in them as in the three whose history we have followed. The same general conditions affected the manufactures of glass, earthenware, paper, cotton-bagging, sail-duck, cordage, and other articles to which protection was applied during this time with more or less vigor. We may assume that the same general effect, or absence of effect, followed in these as in the other cases. It is not intended to speak of the production of agricultural commodities like sugar, wool, hemp, and flax, to which also protection was applied. In the production of these the natural advantages of one country over another tell more decidedly and surely than in the case of most manufactures, and it has not often been supposed that they come within the scope of the argument we are considering.

Although, therefore, the conditions existed under which it is most likely that protection to young industries may be advantageously applied—a young and undeveloped country in a stage of transition from a purely agricultural to a more diversified industrial condition; this transition, moreover, coinciding in time with great changes in the arts, which made the establishment of new industries peculiarly difficult—notwithstanding the presence of these conditions, little, if any thing, was gained by the protection which the United States maintained in the first part of this century. Two causes account for this. On the one hand, the character of the people rendered the transition of productive forces to manufactures comparatively easy; on the other hand, the shock to economic habits during the restrictive period from 1808 to 1815 effectually prepared the way for such a transition. The genius of the people for mechanical arts showed itself early. Naturally it appeared with most striking results in those fields in which the circumstances of the country gave the richest opportunities; as in the application of steam-power to navigation, in the invention and improvement of tools, and especially of agricultural implements, and in the cotton manufacture. The ingenuity and inventiveness of American mechanics have become traditional, and the names of Whitney and Fulton need only be mentioned to show that these qualities were not lacking at the time we are considering. The presence of such men rendered it more easy to remove the obstacles arising from want of skill and experience in manufactures. The political institutions, the high average of intelligence, the habitual freedom of movement from place to place and from occupation to occupation, also made the rise of the existing system of manufacturing production at once more easy and less dangerous than the same change in other countries. At the same time it so happened that the embargo, the non-intercourse acts, and the war of 1812 rudely shook the country out of the grooves in which it was running, and brought about a state of confusion from which the new industrial system could emerge more easily than from a well-settled organization of industry. The restrictive period may indeed be considered t have been one of extreme protection. The stimulus which it gave to some manufactures perhaps shows that the first steps in these were not taken without some artificial help. The intrinsic soundness of the argument for protection to young industries therefore may not be touched by the conclusions drawn from the history of its trial in the United States, which shows only that the intentional protection of the tariffs of 1816, 1824, and 1828 had little effect. The period from 1808 till the financial crisis of 1818–19 was a disturbed and chaotic one, from which the country settled down, with little assistance from protective legislation, into a new arrangement of its productive forces.

The system of protective legislation began in 1816, and was maintained till toward the end of the decade 1830–40. The Compromise Act of 1833 gradually undermined it. By 1842 duties reached a lower point than that from which they had started in 1816. During this whole period the argument for protection to young industries had been essentially the mainstay of the advocates of protection, and the eventual cheapness of the goods was the chief advantage which they proposed to obtain. It goes without saying that this was not the only argument used, and that it was often expressed loosely in connection with other arguments. One does not find in the popular discussions of fifty years ago, more than in those of the present, precision of thought or expression. The "home market" argument, which, though essentially distinct from that for young industries, naturally suggests itself in connection with the latter, was much urged during the period we are considering. The events of the War of 1812 had vividly impressed on the minds of the people the possible inconvenience, in case of war, of depending on foreign trade for the supply of articles of common use; this point also was much urged by the protectionists. Similarly the want of reciprocity, and the possibility of securing, by retaliation, a relaxation of the restrictive legislation of foreign countries, were often mentioned. But any one who is familiar with the protective literature of that day,—as illustrated, for instance, in the columns of "Niles's Register,"—cannot fail to note the prominent place held by the young-industries argument. The form in which it most commonly appears is in the assertion that protection normally causes the prices of the protected articles to fall,[1] an assertion which was supposed, then as now, to be sufficiently supported by the general tendency toward a fall in the price of manufactured articles, consequent on the great improvement in the methods of producing such articles.

Shortly after 1832, the movement in favor of protection, which had had full sway in the Northern States since 1820, began to lose strength. The young-industries

---

[1] See, for instance, the temperate report of J. Q. Adams, in 1832, in which this is discussed as the chief argument of the protectionists. Adams, though himself a protectionist, refutes it, and bases his faith in protection chiefly on the loss and inconvenience suffered through the interruption of foreign trade in time of war. The report is in "Reports of Committees, 22d Congress, 1st Session, vol. V., No. 481.

argument at the same time began to be less steadily pressed. About 1840 the protective controversy took a new turn. It seems to have been felt by this time that manufactures had ceased to be young industries, and that the argument for their protection as such, was no longer conclusive. Another position was taken. The argument was advanced that American labor should be protected from the competition of less highly paid foreign labor. The labor argument had hardly been heard in the period which has been treated in the preceding pages. Indeed, the difference between the rate of wages in the United States and in Europe, had furnished, during the early period, an argument for the free-traders, and not for the protectionists. The free-traders were then accustomed to point to the higher wages of labor in the United States as an insuperable obstacle to the successful establishment of manufactures. They used the wages argument as a foil to the young-industries argument, asserting that as long as wages were so much lower in Europe, manufacturers would not be able to maintain themselves without aid from the government. The protectionists, on the other hand, felt called on to explain away the difference of wages; they endeavored to show that this difference was not so great as was commonly supposed, and that, so far as it existed, it afforded no good reason against adopting protection.[1] About 1840, the positions of the con-

---

[1] See, among others, Clay's Tariff Speech of 1824, "Works," I., 465 466.

tending parties began to change.[1] The protectionists began to take the offensive on the labor question: the free-traders were forced to the defensive on this point. The protectionists asserted that high duties were necessary to shut out the competition of the ill-paid laborers of Europe, and to maintain the high wages of the laborers of the United States. Their opponents had to explain and defend on the wages question. Obviously this change in the line of argument indicates a change in the industrial situation Such an argument in favor of protection could not have arisen at a time when protective duties existed but in small degree, and when wages nevertheless were high. Its use implies the existence of industries which are supposed to be dependent on high duties. When the protective system had been in force for some time, and a body of industries had sprung up which were thought to be able to

---

[1] Same signs of the appeal for the benefit of labor appear as early as 1831 in a passage in Gallatin's '' Memorial,'' p. 31, and again in a speech of Webster's in 1833, '' Works,'' I., 283. In the campaign of 1840, little was heard of it, doubtless because other issues than protection were in the foreground. Yet Calhoun was led to make a keen answer to it in a speech of 1840, '' Works,'' III., 434. In the debates on the tariff act of 1842, we hear more of it ; see the speeches of Choate and Buchanan, *Congr. Globe,* 1841-42, pp. 950, 953, and Calhoun's allusion to Choate, in Calhoun's '' Works,'' IV., 207. In 1846 the argument appeared full-fledged, in the speeches of Winthrop, Davis, and others, *Congr. Globe,* 1846, Appendix, pp , 967, 973, 1114. See also a characteristic letter in Niles, vol. 62, p. 262. Webster's speech in 1846, '' Works,'' V., 231, had much about protection and labor, but in a form somewhat different from that of the argument we are nowadays familiar with. See also the monograph by G. B. Mangold, '' The Labor Argument in the American Protective Tariff Discussion,'' *Bulletin of the University of Wisconsin,* No. 246 (1908).

pay current wages only if aided by high duties, the wages argument naturally suggested itself. The fact that the iron manufacture, which had hitherto played no great part in the protective controversy, became, after 1840, the most prominent applicant for aid, accounts in large part for the new aspect of the controversy. The use of the wages argument, and the rise of the economic school of Henry C. Carey, show that the argument for young industries was felt to be no longer sufficient to be the mainstay of the protective system. The economic situation had changed, and the discussion of the tariff underwent a corresponding change.

CHAPTER II.

THE EARLY PROTECTIVE MOVEMENT AND THE TARIFF OF 1828.

IN the present essay we shall consider, not so much the economic effect of the tariff, as the character of the early protective movement and its effect on political events and on legislation.

The protective movement in this country has been said to date from the year 1789, even from before 1789; and more frequently it has been said to begin with the tariff act of 1816. But whatever may have been, in earlier years, the utterances of individual public men, or the occasional drift of an uncertain public opinion, no strong popular movement for protection can be traced before the crisis of 1818–19. The act of 1816, which is generally said to mark the beginning of a distinctly protective policy in this country, belongs rather to the earlier series of acts, beginning with that of 1789, than to the group of acts of 1824, 1828, and 1832. Its highest permanent rate of duty was twenty per cent., an increase over the previous rates which is chiefly accounted for by the heavy interest charge on the debt incurred during the war. But after the crash of 1819, a movement in favor of protection set in, which was backed by a strong popular feeling such as had been absent in the earlier years. The causes of the new movement are not far to seek. On the one hand there was a great collapse in the prices of land and of agricultural products, which had been much inflated during the years from 1815 to 1818. At the same time the foreign market for grain and provisions, which had been highly profitable during the time of the Napoleonic wars, and which there had been a spasmodic attempt to regain for two or three years after the close of our war in 1815, was almost entirely lost. On the other hand, a large number of manufacturing industries had grown up, still in the early stages of growth, and still beset with difficulties, yet likely in the end to hold their own and to prosper. That disposition to seek a remedy from legislation, which always shows itself after an industrial crisis, now led the farmers to ask for a home market, while the manufacturers wanted protection for young industries. The distress that followed the crisis brought out a plentiful crop of pamphlets in favor of protection, of societies and conventions for the promotion of domestic industry, of petitions and memorials to Congress for higher duties. The movement undoubtedly had deep root in the feelings and convictions of the people, and the powerful hold which protective ideas then obtained influenced the policy of the nation long after the immediate effects of the crisis had ceased to be felt.[1]

---

[1] The character of the protective movement after 1819 is best illustrated by the numerous pamphlets of Matthew Carey. See especially the " Appeal

The first effect of this movement was seen in a series of measures which were proposed and earnestly pushed in Congress in the session of 1819–20. They included a bill for a general increase of duties, one for shortening credits on duties, and one for taxing sales by auction of imported goods. The first of these very nearly took an important place in our history, for it was passed by the House, and failed to pass the Senate by but a single vote. Although it did not become law, the protective movement which was expressed in the votes and speeches on it remained unchanged for several years, and brought about the act of 1824, while making possible the act of 1828. Some understanding of the state of feeling in the different sections of the country is necessary before the peculiar events of 1828 can be made clear, and it may be conveniently reached at this point.

The stronghold of the protective movement was in the Middle and Western states of those days—in New York, New Jersey, Pennsylvania, Ohio, and Kentucky. They were the great agricultural States ; they felt most keenly the loss of the foreign market of the early years of the century, and were appealed to most directly by the cry for a home market. At the same time they had been most deeply involved in the inflation of the years 1816–19, and were in that condition of general distress and confusion which

to Common Sense and Common Justice " (1822) and " The Crisis : A Solemn Appeal," etc. (1823). " Niles's Register," which had said little about tariff before 1819. thereafter became a tireless and effective advocate of protection.

leads people to look for some panacea. The idea of protection as a cure for their troubles had obtained a strong hold on their minds. It is not surprising, when we consider the impetuous character of the element in American democracy at that time represented by them, that the idea was applied in a sweeping and indiscriminate manner. They wanted protection not only for the manufactures that were to bring them a home market, but for many of their own products, such as wool, hemp, flax, even for wheat and corn. For the two last mentioned they asked aid more particularly in the form of higher duties on rum and brandy, which were supposed to compete with spirits distilled from home-grown grain. A duty on molasses was a natural supplement to that on rum. Iron was already produced to a considerable extent in Pennsylvania and New Jersey, and for that also protection was asked.

In New England there was a strong opposition to many of these demands. The business community of New England was still made up mainly of importers, dealers in foreign goods, shipping merchants, and vessel-owners, who naturally looked with aversion at measures that tended to lessen the volume of foreign trade. Moreover, they had special objections to many of the duties asked for by the agricultural states. Hemp in the form of cordage, flax in the form of sail duck, and iron, were important items in the cost of building and equipping ships. The duties on molasses and rum were aimed at an industry carried on almost exclusively in New England:

the importation of molasses from the West Indies in exchange for fish, provisions, and lumber, and its subsequent
manufacture into rum.   Wool was the raw material of a
rapidly growing manufacture.   So far the circumstances
led to opposition to the protective movement.   On the
other hand, the manufacture of cotton and woollen goods
was increasing rapidly and steadily, and was the moving
force of a current in favor of protection that became
stronger year by year.   We have seen that the beginning
of New England's manufacturing career dates back to the
War of 1812.   Before 1820 she was fairly launched on it,
and between 1820 and 1830 she made enormous advances.
The manufacturers carried on a conflict, unequal at first,
but rapidly becoming less unequal, with the merchants
and ship-owners.   As early as 1820 Connecticut and
Rhode Island were pretty firmly protective; but Massachusetts hesitated.   Under the first weight of the crisis of
1819, the protective feeling was strong enough to cause a
majority of her congressmen to vote for the bill of 1820.
But there was great opposition to that bill, and after 1820
the protective feeling died down.[1]   In 1824 Massachusetts
was still disinclined to adopt the protective system, and it
was not until the end of the decade that she came

---

[1] The vote on the bill of 1820, by States, is given in Niles, XVIII.,
169. Of the Massachusetts members 10 voted yes, 6 no, and 4 were absent. Of the New England members 19 voted yes, 9 no, and 9 were absent. The opposition to the bill in Massachusetts was the occasion of a
meeting at which Webster made his first speech on tariff, which is not reprinted in his works, but may be found in the newspapers of the day.

squarely in line with the agricultural states on that subject.

The South took its stand against the protective system with a promptness and decision characteristic of the political history of the slave states. The opposition of the Southern members to the tariff bill of 1820 is significant of the change in the nature of the protective movement between 1816 and 1820. The Southern leaders had advocated the passage of the act of 1816, but they bitterly opposed the bill of 1820. It is possible that the Missouri Compromise struggle had opened their eyes to the connection between slavery and free trade.[1] At all events, they had grasped the fact that slavery made the growth of manufactures in the South impossible, that manufactured goods must be bought in Europe or in the North, and that, wherever bought, a protective tariff would tend to make them dearer. Moreover, Cotton was not yet King, and the South was not sure that its staple was indispensable for all the world. While the export of cotton on a large scale had begun, it was feared that England, in retaliation for high duties on English goods, might tax or exclude American cotton.

Such was in 1820 the feeling in regard to the protective system in the different parts of the country. After the failure of the bill of that year, the movement for higher duties seems for a while to have lost headway. The low-

---

[1] But no reference was made to the Missouri struggle in the debates on the tariff bill of 1820.

est point of industrial and commercial depression, so far as indicated by the revenue, was reached at the close of 1820, and, as affairs began to mend, protective measures received less vigorous support. Bills to increase duties, similar to the bill of 1820, were introduced in Congress in 1821 and 1822, but they were not pressed and led to no legislation.[1]

Public opinion in most of the Northern States, however, continued to favor protection; the more so because, after the first shock of the crisis of 1819 was over, recovery, though steady, was slow. As a Presidential election approached and caused public men to respond more readily to popular feeling, the protectionists gained a decided victory. The tariff of 1824 was passed, the first and the most direct fruit of the early protective movement. The Presidential election of that year undoubtedly had an effect in causing its passage; but the influence of politics and political ambition was in this case hardly a harmful one. Not only Clay, the sponsor of the American System, but Adams, Crawford, and Jackson were declared advocates of protection. Party lines, so far as they existed at all, were not regarded in the vote on the tariff. It was carried mainly by the votes of the Western and Middle

---

[1] See the interesting account of a Cabinet meeting in November, 1821. in "J. Q. Adams's Memoirs," vol. V., pp. 408–411. "The lowest point of the depression was reached at the close of last year" [1820]. Calhoun thought "the prosperity of the manufacturers was now so clearly established that it might be mentioned in the message as a subject for congratulation." Crawford said "there would not be much trouble in the ensuing session with the manufacturing interest," and Adams himself "had no apprehension that there would be much debate on manufacturing interests."

states. The South was in opposition, New England was divided ; Rhode Island and Connecticut voted for the bill, Massachusetts and the other New England states were decidedly opposed.[1]

The opposition of Massachusetts was the natural result of the character of the new tariff. The most important changes made by it were in the increased duties on iron, lead, wool, hemp, cotton-bagging, and other articles whose protection was desired chiefly by the Middle and Western States. The duties on textile fabrics, it is true, were also raised. Those on cotton and woollen goods went up from 25 to 33⅓ per cent. This increase, however, was offset, so far as woollens were concerned, by the imposition of a duty of 30 per cent. on wool, which had before been admitted at 15 per cent. The manufacturers of woollen goods were, therefore, as far as the tariff was concerned, in about the same position as before.[2] The heavier duties

---

[1] John Randolph said, in his vigorous fashion, of the tariff bill of 1824 : " The merchants and manufacturers of Massachusetts and New Hampshire repel this bill, while men in hunting shirts, with deerskin leggings and moccasins on their feet, want protection for home manufactures."—" Debates of Congress, 1824, p. 2370.

[2] This can be shown very easily. The cost of the wool is about one half the cost of making woollen goods. Then we have in 1816 :

Duty on woollens	25	per cent.
Deduct duty on wool, ½ of 15 cent. .	7½	"
Net protection in 1816	17½	"

And in 1824 we have:

Duty on woollens	33⅓	per cent.
Deduct duty on wool, ½ of 30 per cent. .	15	"
Net protection in 1824 . . .	18⅓	"

The rise in duties both on wool and on woollens took place gradually by the terms of the act of 1824. The calculation is based on the final rates. which were reached in 1826.

on iron and hemp, on the other hand, were injurious to the ship-builders.

The manufacture of textiles was rapidly extending in all the New England States. At first that of cottons received most attention, and played the most important part in the protective controversy. But by 1824 the cotton industry was firmly established and almost independent of support by duties. The woollen manufacture was in a less firm position, and in 1824 became the prominent candidate for protection. Between 1824 and 1828 a strong movement set in for higher duties on woollens, which led eventually to some of the most striking features of the tariff act of 1828.

The duties proposed and finally established on woollens were modelled on the minimum duty of 1816 on cottons. By the tariff act of that year, it will be remembered, cotton goods were made subject to a general *ad valorem* duty of 25 per cent.; but it was further provided that "all cotton cloths, whose value shall be less than 25 cents per square yard, shall be taken and deemed to have cost 25 cents per square yard, and shall be charged with duty accordingly." That is, a specific duty of six and a quarter cents a square yard was imposed on all cotton cloths costing twenty-five cents a square yard or less. The minimum duties, originally intended to affect chiefly East Indian goods and goods made from East Indian cotton, had an effect in practice mainly on goods from England, whether made of American or of Indian cotton. In a few years, as the use of the power loom and other improvements in manufacture brought the price of coarse cottons much below twenty-five cents, the minimum duties became prohibitory. How far they were needed in order to promote the success and prosperity of the cotton manufacture in years following their imposition, we have already discussed.[1] At all events, whether or not in consequence of the duties, large profits were made by those who entered on it, and in a few years the cheaper grades of cotton cloth were produced so cheaply, and of such good quality, that the manufacturers freely asserted that the duty had become nominal, and that foreign competition no longer was feared.

This example had its effect on the manufacturers of woollen goods, and on the advocates of protection in general. In the tariff bill of 1820, minimum duties on linen and on other goods had been proposed. In 1824 an earnest effort was made to extend the minimum system to woollens. The committee which reported the tariff bill of that year recommended the adoption in regard to woollens of a proviso framed after that of the tariff of 1816 in regard to cottons, the minimum valuation being eighty cents a yard. The House first lowered the valuation to forty cents and finally struck out the whole proviso by a scant majority of three votes.[2] There was one great obstacle in the way of a high duty on cheap woollen

---

[1] See above, pp. 25–36.
[2] The vote was 104 to 101. " Annals of Congress," 1823–24, p. 2310.

goods: they were imported largely for the use of slaves on Southern plantations. Tender treatment of the peculiar institution had already begun, and there was strong opposition to a duty which had the appearance of being aimed against the slave-holders. The application of the minimum principle to other than cheap woollen goods apparently had not yet been thought of; but the idea was obvious, and soon was brought forward.

After 1824 there was another lull in the agitation for protection. Trade was buoyant in 1825, and production profitable. For the first time since 1818 there was a swing in business operations. This seems to have been particularly the case with the woollen manufacturers. During the years from 1815 to 1818–19, they, like other manufacturers, had met with great difficulties; and when the first shock of the crisis of the latter year was over, matters began to mend but slowly. About 1824, however, according to the accounts both of their friends and of their opponents on the tariff question, they extended their operations largely.[1] It is clear that this expansion, such as it was, was not the effect of any stimulus given by the tariff of 1824, for, as we have seen, the encouragement given the woollen manufacturers by that act was no greater than had been given under the act of 1816. At all events, the upward movement lasted but a short time.

---

[1] See the Report of the Harrisburg Convention of 1827 in Niles, XXXIII., 109; Tibbits, "Essay on Home Market" (1827), pp. 26, 27; Henry Lee, "Boston Report of 1827," pp. 64 *seq.*

In England a similar movement had been carried to the extreme of speculation and had resulted in the crisis of 1825–26. From England the panic was communicated to the United States; but, as the speculative movement had not been carried so far in this country, the revulsion was less severely felt. It seems, however, to have fallen on the woollen manufacturers with peculiar weight. Parliament, it so happened, in 1824 had abolished almost entirely the duty on wool imported into England. It went down from twelve pence to one penny a pound.[1] The imports of woollen goods into the United States had in 1825 been unusually large; the markets were well stocked; the English manufacturers were at once enabled to sell cheaply by the lower price of their raw material, and pushed to do so by the depression of trade.

A vigorous effort was now made to secure legislative aid to the woollen makers, similar to that given the cotton manufacturers. Massachusetts was the chief seat of the woollen industry. The woollen manufacturers held meetings in Boston and united for common action, and it was determined to ask Congress to extend the minimum sys-

---

[1] It is sometimes said that this reduction of the wool duty in England was undertaken with the express purpose of counteracting the protective duties imposed on woollens in the United States. But there is little ground for supposing that our duties were watched so vigilantly in England, or were the chief occasion for English legislation. The agitation for getting rid of the restriction on the import and export of wool began as early as 1819, and during its course very little reference, if any, was made to the American duties. See the sketch in Bischoff's "History of the Woollen and Worsted Manufactures," vol. II., chapters 1 and 2.

tem to woollen goods.[1] The legislature of the **State** passed resolutions asking for further protection for woollens, and these resolutions were presented in the federal House of Representatives by Webster.[2] A deputation of manufacturers was sent to Washington to present the case to the committee on manufactures. Their efforts promised to be successful. When Congress met for the session of 1826–27, the committee (which in those days had charge of tariff legislation) reported a bill which gave the manufacturers all they asked for.

This measure contained the provisions which, when finally put in force in the tariff of 1828, became the object of the most violent attack by the opponents of protection. It made no change in the nominal rate of duty, which was to remain at 33⅓ per cent. But minimum valuations were added, on the plan of the minima on cottons, in such a way as to carry the actual duty far beyond the point indicated by the nominal rate. The bill provided that all goods costing less than 40 cents a square yard were to pay duty as if they had cost 40 cents; all costing more than 40 cents and less than $2.50 were to be charged as if they had cost $2.50; all costing between $2.50 and $4.00 to be charged as if they had cost $4.00. A similar

---

[1] The memorial of the manufacturers to Congress is in Niles, XXXI., 185. It asks for minimum duties, on the ground that *ad valorem* duties are fraudulently evaded. For the circular sent out by this committee, see *ibid.*, p. 200.

[2] "American State Papers, Finance," V., 599; "Annals of Congress," 1826–27, p. 1010.

course was proposed in regard to raw wool. The *ad valorem* rate on raw wool was to be 30 per cent. in the first place, and to rise by steps to 40 per cent.; and it was to be charged on all wool costing between 16 cents and 40 cents a pound as if the wool had cost 40 cents. The effect of this somewhat complicated machinery was evidently to levy specific duties both on wool and on woollens. On wool the duty was to be, eventually, 16 cents a pound. On woollens it was to be $13\frac{1}{3}$ cents a yard on woollens of the first class, $83\frac{1}{3}$ cents on those of the second class, and $\$1.33\frac{1}{3}$ on those of the third class.

The minimum system, applied in this way, imposed *ad valorem* duties in form, specific duties in fact. It had some of the disadvantages of both systems. It offered temptations to fraudulent undervaluation stronger than those offered by *ad valorem* duties. For example, under the bill of 1827, the duty on goods worth in the neighborhood of 40 cents a yard would be $13\frac{1}{3}$ cents if the value was less than 40 cents; but if the value was more than 40 cents, the duty would be $83\frac{1}{3}$ cents. If the value could be made to appear less than forty cents, the importer saved 70 cents a yard in duties. Similarly, at the next step in the minimum points, the duty was $83\frac{1}{3}$ cents if the goods were worth less than $\$2.50$, and $\$1.33\frac{1}{3}$ cents if the goods were worth more than $\$2.50$. The temptation to undervalue was obviously very strong under such a system, in the case of all goods which could be brought with any plausibility near one of the minimum points.

On the other hand, the system had the want of elasticity which goes with specific duties. All goods costing between 40 cents and $2.50 were charged with the same duty, so that cheap goods were taxed at a higher rate than dear goods. The great gap between the first and second minimum points (40 cents and $2.50) made this objection the stronger. But that gap was not the result of accident. It was intended to bring about a very heavy duty on goods of the grade chiefly manufactured in this country. The most important domestic goods were worth about a dollar a yard, and their makers, under this bill, would get a protective duty of 83⅓ cents a yard. The object was to secure a very high duty, while retaining nominally the existing rate of 33⅓ per cent.

The woollens bill of 1827 had a fate similar to that of the general tariff bill of 1820. It was passed in the House, but lost in the Senate by the casting vote of the Vice-President. In the House the Massachusetts members, with one exception, voted for it, and both Senators from Massachusetts supported it.[1]

This bill having failed, the advocates of protection determined to continue their agitation, and to give it wider scope. A national convention of protectionists was determined on.[2] Meetings were held in the different States

---

[1] "Congressional Debates," III., 1099, 496.

[2] It is not very clear in what quarter the scheme of holding such a convention had its origin. The first public suggestion came from the Philadelphia Society for the Promotion of Domestic Industry, an association founded by Hamilton, of which Matthew Carey and C. J. Ingersoll were at this time the leading spirits.

in which the protective policy was popular, and delegates were appointed to a general convention. In midsummer of 1827 about a hundred persons assembled at Harrisburg, and held the Harrisburg convention, well known in its day. Most of the delegates were manufacturers, some were newspaper editors and pamphleteers, a few were politicians.[1] The convention did not confine its attention to wool and woollens. It considered all the industries which were supposed to need protection. It recommended higher duties for the aid of agriculture; others on manufactures of cotton, hemp, flax, iron, and glass; and finally, new duties on wool and woollens. The movement was primarily for the aid of the woollen industry; other interests were included in it as a means of gaining strength. The duties which were demanded on woollens were on the same plan as those proposed in the bill of 1827, differing only in that they were higher. The *ad valorem* rate on woollen goods was to be 40 per cent. in the first place, and was to be raised gradually until it reached 50 per cent. It was to be assessed on minimum valuations of fifty cents, two dollars and a half, four dollars, and six dollars a yard. The duty on wool was to be twenty cents a pound in the first instance, and was to be raised each year by $2\frac{1}{2}$ cents until it should reach fifty cents a pound. Needless to say, the duty would be pro-

---

[1] Among the politicians was Mallary of Vermont, who had been chairman of the committee on manufactures in the preceding Congress, and became the spokesman of the protectionists in the ensuing session, when the tariff of 1828 was passed.

hibitory long before this limit was reached. Wool costing less than eight cents was to be admitted free.[1]

At this point a new factor, which we may call " politics,"
began to make itself felt in the protective movement.
The natural pressure of public opinion on public men had
exercised its effect in previous years, and had had its
share in bringing about the tariff act of 1824 and the
woollens bill of 1827. But the gradual crystallization of
two parties, the Adams and Jackson parties,—Whigs and
Democrats, as they soon came to be called—put a new
face on the political situation, and had an unexpected
effect on tariff legislation. The contest between them
had begun in earnest before the Harrisburg convention
met, and some of the Jackson men alleged that the convention was no more than a demonstration got up by the
Adams men as a means of bringing the protective movement to bear in their aid ; but this was denied, and such
evidence as we have seems to support the denial.[2]   Yet

---

[1] The proceedings of the convention, the address of the people, the memorial to Congress, etc., are in Niles, XXXII. and XXXIII.

[2] I have been able to find little direct evidence as to the political bearing
of the Harrisburg convention. Matthew Carey, in a letter of July, 1827,
while admitting he is an Adams man, protests against " amalgamating the
question of the presidency with that for the protection of manufactures."
Niles, XXXII., 389. The (New York) *Evening Post*, a Jackson paper,
said the convention was a manœuvre of the Adams men ; see its issues of
August 1 and August 9, 1827. This was denied in the *National Intelligencer* (Adams) of July 9th, and also in the (New York) *American* (Adams) of
July 9th. The *Evening Post* admitted (August 11th) that " doubtless many
members of the convention were innocent of political views," and that " the
rest were induced to postpone or abandon their political views." Van
Buren apparently suspected that the convention might have a political

the Adams men were undoubtedly helped by the protective movement. Although there was not then, nor for a number of years after, a clear-cut division on party lines between protectionists and so-called free traders, the Adams men were more firmly and unitedly in favor of protection than their opponents. Adams was a protectionist, though not an extreme one; Clay, the leader and spokesman of the party, was more than any other public man identified with the American system. They were at least willing that the protective question should be brought into the foreground of the political contest.[1]

The position of the Jackson men, on the other hand,

---

meaning, and warned its members against forming "a political cabal"; *cf.* the *National Intelligencer* of July 26th. But among the delegates from New York were both Jackson and Adams men. See Hammond, "Political History of New York," II., 256-258; Niles, XXXII., 349. Niles, who was an active member of the convention, denied strenuously that politics had any thing to do with it. Niles, XXXIV., 187.—Since the above was put in type, however, a letter of Clay's has been found which seems to indicate that the movement for holding such a convention was at least started by the anti-Jackson leaders. The letter is printed in the "Quarterly Journal of Economics," vol. II., July, 1888.

[1] There is ground for suspecting that the Adams party would have been willing to make the tariff question the decisive issue of the presidential campaign. Clay made it the burden of his speeches during his journey to the West in the early summer of 1827. Very soon after this, however, the correspondence between Jackson and Carter Beverly was published, and fixed attention on the "bargain and corruption" cry. That was the point which the Jackson managers succeeded in making most prominent in the campaign. Clay dropped the question of protection; he found enough to do in answering the charge that in 1825 a corrupt bargain had made Adams President and himself Secretary of State. See Clay's speech at Pittsburg. June 20, 1827, in Niles, XXXII., 299. On June 29th, Clay published his first denial of the "bargain and corruption" charges. *Ibid.*, p. 350 *Cf.* Parton, "Life of Jackson," III., 111.

was a very difficult one.   Their party had at this time no settled policy in regard to the questions which were to be the subjects of the political struggles of the next twenty years.   They were united on only one point, a determination to oust the other side.   On the tariff, as well as on the bank and internal improvements, the various elements of the party held very different opinions.   The Southern members, who were almost to a man supporters of Jackson, were opposed unconditionally not only to an increase of duties, but to the high range which the tariff had already reached.   They were convinced, and in the main justly convinced, that the taxes levied by the tariff fell with peculiar weight on the slave States, and their opposition was already tinged with the bitterness which made possible, a few years later, the attempt at nullification of the tariff of 1832.   On the other hand, the protective policy was popular throughout the North, more especially in the very States whose votes were essential to Jackson, in New York, Pennsylvania, and Ohio.   The Jackson men needed the votes of these States, and were not so confident of getting them as they might reasonably have been. They failed, as completely as their opponents, to gauge the strength of the enthusiasm of the masses for their candidate, and they did not venture to give the Adams men a chance of posing as the only true friends of domestic industry.

The twentieth Congress met for its first session in December, 1827.   The elections of 1826, at which its members were chosen, had not been fortunate for the administration. When Congress met there was some doubt as to the political complexion of the House; but this was set at rest by the election to the speakership of the Democratic candidate, Stephenson of Virginia.[1] The new Speaker, in the formation of the committees, assumed for his party the direction of the measures of the House. On the committee on manufactures, from which the tariff report and the tariff bill were to come, he appointed five supporters of Jackson and two supporters of Adams. The chairmanship, however, was given to one of the latter, Mallary, of Vermont, who, it will be remembered, had been a member of the Harrisburg convention.

Much doubt was entertained as to the line of action the committee would follow. The Adams men feared at first that it would adopt a policy of simple delay and inaction. This fear was confirmed when, a few weeks after the beginning of the session, the committee asked for power to send for persons and papers in order to obtain more information on the tariff,—a request which was opposed by Mallary, their chairman, on the ground that it was made only as a pretext for delay. The Adams men, who formed the bulk of the ardent protectionists, voted with him against granting the desired power. But the Southern members united with the Jackson men from the

---

[1] Stephenson's election is said to have been brought about by Van Buren's influence; Parton, "Life of Jackson," III., 135. It is worth while to bear this in mind, in view of the part played by Van Buren later in the session.

North, and between them they secured the passage of
the resolution asked by the committee.[1] The debate and
vote on the resolution sounded the key-note of the events
of the session.   They showed that the Jackson men from
the South and the North, though opposed to each other
on the tariff question, were yet united as against the
Adams men.[2]

But the policy of delay, if such in fact had been entertained by the opposition, was abandoned. On January
31st, the committee presented a report and a draft of a
tariff bill, which showed that they had determined on a
new plan, and an ingenious one. What that plan was,
Calhoun explained very frankly nine years later, in a
speech reviewing the events of 1828 and defending the
course taken by himself and his Southern fellow-members.[3]
A high-tariff bill was to be laid before the House. It was
to contain not only a high general range of duties, but
duties especially high on those raw materials on which
New England wanted the duties to be low. It was to
satisfy the protective demands of the Western and Middle
States, and at the same time to be obnoxious to the New
England members. The Jackson men of all shades, the
protectionists from the North and the free-traders from

---

[1] The power granted to the committee by this resolution, to examine
witnesses, was used to a moderate extent. A dozen wool manufacturers
were examined, and their testimony throws some light on the state of the
woollen manufacture at that time. See the preceding essay, pp. 42–44.

[2] In "Congressional Debates," IV., 862, 870.

[3] Speech of 1837 ; "Works," III., 46–51.

the South, were to unite in preventing any amendments:
that bill, and no other, was to be voted on. When the
final vote came, the Southern men were to turn around
and vote against their own measure. The New England
men, and the Adams men in general, would be unable to
swallow it, and would also vote against it. Combined,
they would prevent its passage, even though the Jackson
men from the North voted for it. The result expected was
that no tariff bill at all would be passed during the session,
which was the object of the Southern wing of the opposition. On the other hand, the obloquy of defeating it
would be cast on the Adams party, which was the object
of the Jacksonians of the North. The tariff bill would be
defeated, and yet the Jackson men would be able to
parade as the true " friends of domestic industry."

The bill by which this ingenious solution of the difficulties of the opposition was to be reached, was reported to
the House on January 31st by the committee on manufactures.[1] To the surprise of its authors, it was eventually
passed both by House and Senate, and became, with a
few unessential changes, the tariff act of 1828.

The committee's bill in the first place proposed a large
increase of duties on almost all raw materials. The duty
on pig-iron was to go up from 56 to 62½ cents per hundredweight, that on hammered bar-iron from 90 to 112
cents per hundredweight, and that on rolled bar from $30

---

[1] The bill as reported by the committee is printed in " Congressional
Debates," IV., 1727 ·

to $37 per ton. The increase on hammered bar had been asked by the Harrisburg convention. But on pig and on rolled bar no one had asked for an increase, not even the manufacturers of iron who had testified before the committee.[1]

The most important of the proposed duties on raw materials, however, were on hemp, flax, and wool. The existing duty on hemp was $35 per ton. It was proposed to increase it immediately to $45, and further to increase it by an annual increment of $5, till it should finally reach $60. Hemp of coarse quality was largely raised in the country at that time, especially in Kentucky. It was suitable for the making of common ropes and of cotton bagging, and for those purposes met with no competition from imported hemp. Better hemp, suitable for making cordage and cables, was not raised in the country at all, the supply coming exclusively from importation. The preparation of this better quality (" water-rotted " hemp) required so much manual labor, and labor of so disagreeable a character, that it would not have been undertaken in any event by the hemp growers of this country.[2]

---

[1] See the testimony of the three iron manufacturers who were examined, " American State Papers, Finance," V., 784–792. Mallary, in introducing the bill, said : " The committee gave the manufacturer of iron all he asked, even more." " Congressional Debates," IV., 1748.

[2] Gallatin, " Memorial of the Free-Trade Convention " (1831), p. 51. This admirable paper, perhaps the best investigation on tariff subjects ever made in the United States, is unfortunately not reprinted in the edition of Gallatin's collected works. The original pamphlet is very scarce. The memorial is printed in U. S. Documents, 1st session, 22d Congress, Senate Documents, vol. I., No. 55.

Under such conditions an increase of duty on hemp could be of no benefit to the American grower. Its effect would be simply to burden the rope makers and the users of cordage, and ultimately the ship-builders and ship-owners. Essentially the same state of things has continued to our own day. The high duties on hemp have never succeeded in checking a large and continuous importation. The facts were then, and are now, very similar with flax; yet the same duty of $60 per ton was to be put on flax.

On wool a proposal of a similar kind was made. The duty under the tariff of 1824 had been 30 per cent. This was to be changed to a mixed specific and *ad valorem* duty, the first mixed duty of importance in the United States.[1] Wool was to pay seven cents a pound (this was reduced to four cents in the act as finally passed), and in addition 40 per cent. in 1828, 45 per cent. in 1829, and thereafter 50 per cent. The object of the mixed duty was to make sure that a heavy tax should be put on coarse wool. The coarse wool, used in the manufacture of carpets and of some cheap flannels and cloths, was not then grown in the United States to any extent, and, indeed, has been grown at no time in this country, but has always been imported, mainly from Asia Minor and from South America. Its cost at the place of exportation was in 1828 from four to ten cents a pound.[2] The

---

[1] In the earlier editions of this volume it was stated that this was *the* first mixed duty ever imposed. Professor D. R. Dewey has called my attention to the fact that in 1824 mixed duties were imposed on certain kinds of glassware.

[2] Gallatin. "Memorial," p. 67.

price being so low, a·simple *ad valorem* duty would not have affected it much. But the additional specific duty of seven (four) cents weighted it heavily. The *ad valorem* part of the duty reached the higher grades of wool, which were raised in this country ; it was calculated to please the farmer. The specific part reached the lower grades, which were not raised in this country, and was calculated to annoy and embarrass the manufacturers. This double object, and especially the second half of it, the Jackson men wanted to attain, and for that reason the policy of admitting the cheap wool at low rates was set aside,—a policy which has been followed in all our protective tariffs, with the sole exception of that of 1828.[1]

Another characteristic part of the scheme was the handling of those duties on woollens that corresponded to the duties on cheap wool. It had been customary to fix low duties on the coarse woollen goods made from cheap wool, partly because of the low duty on the wool

[1] It was followed in 1824, 1832, 1842, and again in the wool and woollens act of 1867, on which the existing duties [1887] are based. The rates on wool have been :

	1828	1832	1842	1867
General duty on wool	30 per cent.	4c. plus 40 per cent.	3c. plus 30 per cent.	10c.–12c. plus 11 per cent.
Duty on cheap wool	15 per cent. on wool under 10c.	free, wool under 8c.	5 per cent. on wool under 7c.	3c. on wool under 12c.

itself, and partly because coarse woollens were used largely for slaves on Southern plantations. Thus in 1824 woollen goods costing less than 33⅓ cents a yard had been admitted at a duty of 25 per cent., while woollens in general paid 33⅓ per cent. In 1828 this low duty on coarse woollens was continued, although the wool of which they were made was subject for the first time to a heavy duty. The object again was to embarrass the manufacturers, and make the bill unpalatable to the protectionists and the Adams men.

The same object appeared in the duty on molasses, which was to be doubled, going from five to ten cents a gallon. A spiteful proviso was added in regard to the drawback which it had been customary to allow on the exportation of rum distilled from imported molasses. The bill of 1828, and the act as finally passed, expressly refused all drawbacks on rum; the intention obviously being to irritate the New Englanders. The animus appeared again in the heavy duty on sail-duck, and the refusal of drawback on sail-duck exported by vessels in small quantities for their own use.[1]

In the duties on woollen goods the changes from the schedule proposed by the Harrisburg convention were on the surface not very great; but in reality they were important. The committee gave up all pretence of *ad*

---

[1] Sail-duck was charged 9 cents a yard, with an increase of ½ cent yearly, until the duty should finally be 12½ cents. This was equivalent to 40 or 50 per cent. In 1824 the duty had been 15 per cent. Drawback was refused on any quantity less than 50 bolts exported in one vessel at one time.

valorem duties. This was not an insignificant circumstance; for the *ad valorem* rate of the minimum system
was said by its opponents to be no more than a device
for disguising the heavy duties actually levied under it.
The committee brushed aside this device, and made the
duties on woollens specific and unambiguous. On goods
costing 50 cents a square yard or less, the duty was 16
cents; on goods costing between 50 cents and $1.00, 40
cents; on those costing between $1.00 and $2.50, $1.00;
and on those costing between $2.50 and $4.00, $1.60.
Goods costing more than $4.00 were to pay 45 per cent.
These specific duties, it will be seen, were the same as if an
ad valorem duty of 40 per cent. had been assessed, on the
minimum principle, on valuations of 50 cents, $1.00,
$2.50, and $4.00. The changes from the Harrisburg convention scheme were, therefore, the arrangement of
specific duties in such a way that they were equivalent to
an *ad valorem* rate of but 40 per cent. (the convention had
asked 50 per cent.); and, next, the insertion of a minimum
point of $1.00, the Harrisburg scheme having allowed no
break between 40 cents and $2.50. The first change
might have been submitted to by the protectionists; but
the second was like putting a knife between the crevices
of their armor. We have already noted the importance
of the gap between the minimum points of 40 cents and
$2.50. A very large part of the imported goods were
worth, abroad, in the neighborhood of $1.00; and the
largest branch of the domestic manufacture made goods

of the same character and value. The original scheme had given a very heavy duty, practically a prohibitory duty, on these goods, while the new scheme gave a comparatively insignificant duty of 40 cents. As one of the protectionists said : "The dollar minimum was planted in the very midst of the woollen trade." [1]

The bill, in fact, was ingeniously framed with the intention of circumventing the Adams men, especially those from New England. The heavy duties on iron, hemp, flax and wool were bitter pills for them. The new dollar minimum took the life out of their scheme of duties on woollen goods. The molasses and sail-duck duties, and the refusal of drawbacks on rum and duck, were undisguised blows at New England. At the same time, some of these very features, especially the hemp, wool, and iron duties, served to make the bill popular in the Western and Middle States, and made opposition to it awkward for the Adams men. The whole scheme was a characteristic product of the politicians who were then becoming prominent as the leaders of the Democracy, men of a type very different from the statesmen of the preceding generation. Clay informs us that it was one of the many devices that had their origin in the fertile brain of Van

---

[1] "Congressional Debates," IV., 2274. See the statement of the effect of the minimum system in "State Papers," 1827–28, No. 143. Davis (of Massachusetts) said that the minimum of $1.00 "falls at a point the most favorable that could be fixed for the British manufacturer. * * * It falls into the centre of the great body of American business." "Congressional Debates," IV., 1894, 1895. See to the same effect the speech of Silas Wright, *Ibid.*, p. 1867.

Buren.[1]   Calhoun said in 1837 that the compact between the Southern members and the Jackson leaders had come about mainly through Silas Wright ; and Wright made no denial.[2]

The result of this curious complication of wishes and motives was seen when the tariff bill was finally taken up in the House in March.   Mallary, as chairman of the committee on manufactures, introduced and explained the bill.   Being an Adams man, he was of course opposed to it, and moved to amend by inserting the scheme of the Harrisburg convention.   The amendment was rejected by decisive votes, 102 to 75 in committee of the whole [3] and 114 to 80 in the House. The majority which defeated

---

[1] " I have heard, without vouching for the fact, that it [the tariff of 1828] was so framed on the advice of a prominent citizen, now abroad [Van Buren had been made minister to England in 1831], with the view of ultimately defeating the bill, and with assurances that, being altogether unacceptable to the friends of the American system, the bill would be lost." Clay's speech of February, 1832.   " Works " II., 13.

[2] See Calhoun's speech of 1837, as cited above, p. 88.   In the debate of 1837, Wright admitted the compact with the Southern members, but said that he had warned them that the New England men in the end might swallow the obnoxious bill.   " Congressional Debates," XIII., 922, 926–927. Wright was a member of the committee on manufactures, was the spokesman of the Jackson men who formed the majority of its members, and had charge of the measure before the House.   Jenkins, " Life of Wright," pp. 53–60.

The Adams men saw through the scheme at the time.   Clay wrote to J. J. Crittenden, in February, even before the House began the discussion of the bill : " The Jackson party are playing a game of brag on the subject of the tariff.   They do not really desire the success of their own measure ; and it may happen in the sequel that what is desired by neither party will command the votes of both."   " Life of Crittenden," I., 67.

[3] " Congressional Debates," IV.. 2038.

the amendment was composed of all the Southern members, and of the Jackson members from the North, chiefly
from New York, Pennsylvania, Ohio, and Kentucky. The
minority consisted almost exclusively of friends of the
administration.[1] Mallary then moved to substitute that
part only of the Harrisburg convention scheme which
fixed the duties on wool and woollens ; that is, the original
minimum scheme, with a uniform duty of forty per cent.
on wool. This too was rejected, but by a narrow vote,
98 to 97.[2] The Jackson men permitted only one change
of any moment : they reduced the specific duty on raw
wool from seven cents, the point fixed by the committee,
to four cents, the *ad valorem* rate remaining at 40 per
cent.[3] The duty on molasses was retained, by the same
combination that refused to accept the Harrisburg
scheme.[4] The Southern members openly said that they
meant to make the tariff so bitter a pill that no New England member would be able to swallow it.[5]

---

[1] See Niles, XXXV., 57, where the various votes on the bill are analyzed. The vote on Mallary's amendment was :

Yeas . . .	78 Adams men,	2 Jackson men	. . .	80
Nays . . .	14 "	" 100 " "	. . .	114

[2] "Congressional Debates," IV., 2050.

[3] The Adams men seem to have opposed this reduction. The vote was :

Yeas . . .	10 Adams men,	90 Jackson men	. . .	100
Nays . . .	79 "	" 20 " "	. . .	99

[4] On reducing the molasses duty, the vote was :

Yeas . . .	72 Adams men,	10 Jackson men	. . .	82
Nays . . .	19 "	" 95 " "	. . .	114

[5] Most of the Southern members kept silence during the debates on the
details of the bill. After its third reading, McDuffie and others made long
speeches against it. One of the South Carolina Congressmen, however

When the final vote on the bill came, the groups of members split up in the way expected by the Democrats. The Southern members, practically without exception, voted against it. Those from the Middle and Western States voted almost unanimously for it. The Jackson men voted for their own measure for consistency's sake; the Adams men from these States joined them, partly for political reasons, mainly because the bill, even with the obnoxious provisions, was acceptable to their constituents. Of the New England members, a majority, 23 out of 39, voted in the negative. The affirmative votes from New England, however, were sufficient, when added to those from the West and the Middle States, to ensure its passage. The bill accordingly passed the House.[1]

This result had not been entirely unexpected. The real struggle, it was felt, would come in the Senate, where the South and New England had a proportionately large representation. In previous years the Senate had maintained, in its action on the tariff bills of 1820 and 1824, a

---

said frankly: " He should vote for retaining the duty on molasses, because he believed that keeping it in the bill would get votes against its final passage" "Congressional Debates," IV., 2349. The Jackson free-traders from the North (there were a few such) followed the same policy. See Cambreleng's remarks, *ibid.*, 3326. See also the passage quoted in Niles, XXXV., 52.

[1] The vote was:

Yeas	. . . .	61 Adams men,	44 Jackson men	. . .	**105**
Nays	. . . .	35 " "	59 " "	. . .	**94**

If six of those New England members who voted yea, had voted nay, the bill would have failed. Niles, *loc. cit.*

much more conservative position than the House.[1] But in 1828 the course of events in the Senate was in the main similar to that in the House. The bill was referred to the committee on manufactures, and was returned with amendments, of which the most important referred to the duty on molasses and to the duties on woollen goods. The duty on molasses was to be reduced from 10 cents, the rate fixed by the House, to 7½ cents. The duties on woollen goods, in the bill as passed by the House, had been made specific, equivalent to 40 per cent. on minimum valuations of 50 cents, $1.00, $2.50, and $4.00. The Senate committee's amendment made the duties *ad valorem* in form, to be assessed on the minimum valuation just mentioned. The rate was to be 40 per cent. for the first year; thereafter, 45 per cent.[2]

---

[1] The tariff of 1824 was much changed in the Senate from the shape in which it had been passed by the House. " Annals of Congress," 1823–24, pp. 723–735.

[2] It was expected that this change to *ad valorem* duties would have still another effect. According to the method then in use for assessing *ad valorem* duties, the dutiable value of goods imported from Europe was ascertained by adding 10 per cent. to the cost or invoice value. See the act of 1828, " Statutes at Large," IV., 274, substantially re-enacting the provisions of the revenue-collection act of 1789, " Statutes at Large," I., 141. It was expected that by the force of this provision the effect of the *ad valorem* rate, under the Senate amendment, would be to increase the duty not merely to 45 per cent., but to 49½ per cent. Hence Webster, in his speech on the bill, spoke of the amendment as carrying the duty " up to 45 or perhaps 50 per cent. *ad valorem.*" " Works." III., 231. But the Secretary of the Treasury, Rush, finally decided, very properly, that the provision did not apply to duties assessed on minimum valuations, thereby causing much dissatisfaction among the protectionists. See " Congressional Debates." VI., 800.

Other amendments were proposed, all tending to make the bill less objectionable to the New England Senators. Most of them were rejected. The proposed reduction on molasses was rejected by the same combination that had prevented the reduction from being made in the House. The Southern Senators, and those from the North who supported Jackson, united to retain the duty of 10 cents. When Webster moved to reduce the duty on hemp, only the New England Senators voted with him. Again, an attempt was made to increase the duty on coarse woollens, on which, it will be remembered, the House had put a low rate, notwithstanding the heavy duty on coarse wool. The Senate, by a strict party vote, retained the duty as the House had fixed it. One of the amendments, however, was carried—that which changed the duties on woollens to an *ad valorem* rate of 45 per cent. Two Democratic Senators, Van Buren and Woodbury, who had voted with the South against other amendments, voted in favor of this one. It was carried by a vote of 24 to 22, while all others had been rejected by a vote of 22 to 24.[1]

With this amendment, the bill was finally passed by the Senate, the vote being 26 to 21. The Southern Senators (except two from Kentucky, and one each from Tennessee and Louisiana) voted against it. Those from the Middle and Western States all voted for it. Those from New England split; six voted yea, five nay. The result

---

[1] The votes in the Senate are given in Niles, XXXIV., 178, 179, 196.

seems to have depended largely on Webster. His colleague Silsbee voted nay, and Webster himself had been in doubt a week before the final vote.[1] Finally he swallowed the bill; and he carried with him enough of the New England Senators to ensure its passage.

Webster defended his course to his constituents on the ground that the woollens amendment (fixing the 45 per cent. *ad valorem* rate) had made the bill much more favorable to the manufacturers. He said he should not have voted for it in the shape in which the House passed it.[2] Calhoun made the same statement in 1837, in the speech to which reference has already been made.[3] No doubt the slight change on woollens mollified in some degree the New England men; but after all, political motives, or, as Webster put it, "other paramount considerations," caused them to swallow the bill. They were afraid to reject it, for fear of the effect in the approaching campaign and election.[4]

---

[1] "Memoirs of J. Q. Adams," VII., 530, 534.

[2] In a speech made a month later; printed in his "Works," I., 165. In the House, the representative from Boston had voted against the bill, and Webster commended his action. In his Senate speech Webster had said that, even at the 45 per cent. rate, the duty on woollens was barely sufficient to compensate for the duty on wool. "Works," III., 241.

[3] "Works," III., 50, 51. Calhoun even accused Van Buren of being the "real author" of the tariff of 1828. He said that, but for Van Buren's vote in favor of the woollens amendment, there would have been a tie on the amendment; his own casting vote as Vice-President would have defeated it; the bill, without the amendment, would have been rejected by Webster and the other New England Senators. Therefore, Van Buren was responsible for its having been passed.

[4] After the final vote in the House, John Randolph said: " The bill re-

The act of 1828 had thus been passed in a form approved by no one. It was hardly to be expected that a measure of this kind should long remain on the statute-book, and it was superseded by the act of 1832. During the intervening four years several causes combined to lead to more moderate application of the protective principle. The protective feeling diminished. Public opinion in the North had been wellnigh unanimous in favor of protection between 1824 and 1828; but after 1828, although there was still a large preponderance for protection,[1] there was a strong and active minority against it. The tariff question ceased to be an important factor in politics, so that this obstacle to its straightforward treatment was removed. And, finally, there was a strong desire to make

---

ferred to manufactures of no sort or kind, except the manufacture of a President of the United States." In 1833, Root, a representative from New York, said: "The act of 1828 he had heard called the bill of Abominations. . . . It certainly grew out of causes connected with President-making. It was fastened on the country in the scuffle to continue the then incumbent in office, on one side, and on the other to oust him and put another in his stead. . . . The public weal was disregarded, and the only question was: Shall we put A or B in the presidential chair? When it was thought necessary to secure a certain State in favor of the then incumbent, a convention was called at Harrisburg to buy them over. [See, however, the note to p. 84, above.] On the other side another convention was called, who mounted the same hobby. The price offered was the same on both sides: a high tariff. One candidate was thought to be a favorite, because he was supposed to be a warm friend of the protective system, and would support a high tariff; but they were told, on the other side, that their candidate would go for as high a tariff." "Congressional Debates," IX., 1104, 1105.

[1] As Gallatin admits: "It is certain that at this time (1832) the tariff system is supported by a majority of the people and of both Houses of Congress." "Works," II., 455.

some concession to the growing opposition of the South. It is true that in 1832 Clay and the more extreme protectionists wished to retain the act of 1828 intact, and to effect reductions in the revenue by lowering the non-protective duties only.[1] But most of the protectionists, led by Adams, took a more moderate course, and consented to the removal of the abominations of 1828.

Even before 1832 some changes were made. In 1830 the molasses abomination was got rid of. The duty on molasses was reduced from ten cents a gallon to five cents, the rate imposed before 1828, and the drawback on exportation of rum was restored.[2] At the same time the duties on tea, coffee, and cocoa were lowered, as one means of reducing the revenue.[3]

The most important step taken in 1832 was the entire abolition of the minimum system. Woollen goods were subjected to a simple *ad valorem* duty of 50 per cent. The minimum system, as arranged in the act of 1828, had been found to work badly. The manufacturers said it had been positively injurious to them.[4] As might have been expected, it led to attempts at evasion of duties, to undervaluation, and to constant disputes at the cus-

---

[1] "Works," I., 586–595.

[2] "Statutes at Large," IV., 419. The act seems to have passed without debate or opposition.

[3] *Ibid.*, p. 403.

[4] Browne, of Boston, a manufacturer who had actively supported the minimum system, declared: "I could manufacture to better advantage under the tariff of 1816 than under that of 1828; for the duty on wool was then lower, and that on cloths a better protection." Niles. XLI., 204.

tom-houses. The troubles arose mainly under the dollar minimum. Goods worth $1.25 or $1.50 were invoiced so as to bring their values below $1.00, in order to escape the duty under the next minimum point, $2.50. The difficulties were ascribed to the depravity of foreign ex- porting houses and to the laxity of the revenue laws, and in 1830 a special act in regard to goods made of cot- ton or wool was passed, making more stringent the pro- visions for collecting duties. But the troubles continued nevertheless,[1] and, in truth, they were inevitable under a system which imposed specific duties graded accord- ing to the value of the goods. Similar duties were much in use during the period of high protection after the Civil War, and led to the same unceasing complaints of dishonesty and fraud, and the same efforts to make the law effective by close inspection and severer penalties. In 1832, the protectionists themselves swept away the minimum system. The *ad valorem* duty of 50 per cent. which was put in its place was felt to be not without its

---

[1] "Statutes at Large," IV., 400. See the speeches of Mallary, "Congres- sional Debates," VI., 795–803, and of Davis, *ibid.*, p. 874, for instances and proofs of the frauds. The act provided for forfeiture of goods fraudulently undervalued ; but no verdicts under it could be obtained. At the protec- tionist convention held in New York in 1831, one of the speakers said : "The same mistaken current of opinion which prevailed on 'change, en- tered and influenced the jury-box. Men thought the law rigorous and severe. They considered it hard that a man should forfeit a large amount of property for a mere attempt to evade an enormous duty. In two years there was but a single case pursued into a court of justice." Niles, XLI., 203. See also the Report on Revenue Frauds, made by a committee of this same convention, in Niles, XLI., Appendix, p. 33.

dangers in the matter of fraud and under-valuation, but it was harmless as compared with the minimum system of 1828.[1]

The other " abominations " of the act of 1828 were also done away with in 1832. The duty on hemp, which had been $60 a ton in 1828, was reduced to a duty of $40. Flax, which had also been subjected to a duty of $60 a ton in 1828, was put on the free list. The duties on pig- and bar-iron were put back to the rates of 1824. The duty on wool alone remained substantially as it had been in 1828, being left as a compound duty of 4 cents a pound and 40 per cent. But even here the special abomination of 1828 was removed; cheap wool, costing less than 8 cents a pound, was admitted free of duty. In fact, the protective system was put back, in the main, to where it had been in 1824. The result was to clear the tariff of the excrescences which had grown on it in 1828, and to put it in a form in which the protectionists could advocate its permanent retention.

Even in this modified form, however, the system could not stand against the attacks of the South. In the following year, 1833, the compromise tariff was passed. It provided for a gradual and steady reduction of duties. That reduction took place; and in July, 1842, a general

---

[1] J. Q. Adams, who was most active in framing the act of 1832, tried to embody the " home valuation " principle into it ; but in vain. " Congressional Debates," VIII., 3658, 3671. He also tried to give the government an option to take goods on its own account at a slight advance over the declared value ; but this plan also was rejected. *Ibid.*, p. 3779.

level of 20 per cent. was reached.   Two months later, in
September, 1842, a new tariff act, again of distinctly pro
tective character, went into effect.   But this act belongs
to a different period, and has a different character from
the acts of 1824, 1828, and 1832.   The early protective
movement, which began in 1819, and was the cause of
the legislation of the following decade, lost its vigor after
1832.   Strong popular sentiment in favor of protection
wellnigh disappeared, and the revival of protection in
1842 was due to causes different from those that brought
about the earlier acts.   The change in popular feeling is
readily explained.   The primary object of the protective
legislation of the earlier period had been attained in
1842.   The movement was, after all, only an effort, half
conscious of its aim, to make more easy the transition from
the state of simple agriculture and commerce which prevailed before the war of 1812, to the more diversified condition which the operation of economic forces was reasonably certain to bring about after 1815.   The period of transition was passed, certainly by 1830, probably earlier.   At
all events, very soon after 1820 it was felt that there was
not the same occasion as in previous years for measures
to tide it over, and a decline in the protective feeling
was the natural consequence.

Not the least curious part of the history of the act of
1828 is the treatment it has received from the protectionist writers.   At the time, the protectionists were far
from enthusiastic about it.   Niles could not admit it to

be a fair application of the protective policy,[1] while Matthew Carey called it a "crude mass of imperfection," and admitted it to be a disappointment to the protectionists.[2] In later years, however, when the details of history had been forgotten, it came to be regarded with more favor. The duties being on their face higher than those of previous years, it was considered a better application of protective principles. Henry C. Carey, on whose authority rest many of the accounts of our economic history, called it "an admirable tariff."[3] He represented it as having had great effect on the prosperity of the country, and his statements have often been repeated by protectionist writers.

It is almost impossible to trace the economic effect of any legislative measure that remains in force no more than four years; and certainly we have not the materials for ascertaining the economic effects of the act of 1828. Taken by itself, that act is but a stray episode in our political history. It illustrates the change in the character of our public men and our public life which took place during the Jacksonian time. As an economic measure, it must be considered, not by itself, but as one of a series of

---

[1] Niles, XXXVII., 81; XXXVI., 113, and elsewhere. Niles objected especially to the $1.00 minimum on woollens.

[2] See his "Common-Sense Address" (1829), p. XI.; "The Olive Branch," No. III., p. 54; No. IV., p. 3 (1832).

[3] See his "Review of the Report of D. A. Wells" (1869), p. 4; and to the same effect, "Harmony of Interests," p. 5, and "Social Science," II., 225.

measures, begun tentatively in 1816, and carried out more vigorously in 1824, 1828, and 1832, by which a protective policy was maintained for some twenty years. It is very doubtful whether, with the defective information at our disposal, we can learn much as to the effect on the prosperity of the country even of the whole series of tariff acts. Probably we can reach conclusions of any value only on certain limited topics, such as the effects of protection to young industries during this time ; as to the general effect of the protective measures we must rely on deduction from general principles. At all events, no one can trace the economic effects of the act of 1828. To ascribe to it the supposed prosperity of the years in which it was in in force, as Henry C. Carey and his followers have done, is only a part of that exaggeration of the effect of protective duties which is as common among their opponents as among their advocates.

CHAPTER III.

THE TARIFF, 1830–1860.

————

In the years between 1832 and 1860 there was great
vacillation in the tariff policy of the United States; there
were also great fluctuations in the course of trade and industry. A low tariff was succeeded by a high tariff, which
was in turn succeeded by another low tariff. Periods of
undue inflation and of great demoralization, of prosperity
and of depression, followed each other. The changes in
the rates of duty and the fluctuations in industrial history
have often been thought to be closely connected. Protectionists have ascribed prosperity to high tariffs, depression
to low tariffs; free traders have reversed the inference.
It is the object of the present essay to trace, so far as
this can be done, the economic effect of tariff legislation
during the thirty years of varying fortune that preceded
the civil war.

First, by way of introduction, a sketch must be given
of the history of the tariff. We begin with the tariff act
of 1832, a distinctly protectionist measure, passed by the
Whigs, or National Republicans, which put the protective
system in a shape such as the advocates of protection
hoped it might retain permanently. It levied high duties

on cotton and woollen goods, iron, and other articles to which protection was meant to be applied. On articles not produced in the United States, either low duties were imposed, as on silks, or no duties at all, as on tea and coffee. The average rate on dutiable articles was about 33 per cent.

In 1833, the Compromise Tariff Act was passed, and remained in force until 1842. That act, there can be little doubt, was the result of an agreement between Clay and Calhoun, the leaders of the protectionists and free traders, while it secured also the support of the Jackson administration. Clay had been hitherto the most uncompromising of the protectionists; Calhoun had represented the extreme Southern demand that duties should be reduced to a horizontal level of 15 or 20 per cent.[1] The compromise provided for the retention of a considerable degree of protection for nearly nine years, and thereafter for a rapid reduction to a uniform 20 per cent. rate. The tariff of 1832 was the starting-point. All duties which in that tariff exceeded 20 per cent. were to have one tenth of the excess over 20 per cent. taken off on January 1, 1834; one tenth more on January 1, 1836; again one tenth in 1838; and another in 1840. That is, by 1840, four tenths of the excess over 20 per cent. would be gone.

---

[1] The Nullifiers had said that such a horizontal rate was the least they were willing to accept. See the Address to the People of the United States by the South Carolina Convention, in the volume of " State Papers on Nullification," published by the State of Massachusetts, p. 69.

Then, on January 1, 1842, one half the remaining excess was to be taken off; and on July 1, 1842, the other half of the remaining excess was to go. After July 1, 1842, therefore, there would be a uniform rate of 20 per cent. on all articles. Obviously, the reduction was very gradual from 1833 till 1842, while in the first six months of 1842 a sharp and sudden reduction was to take place.

Considered as a political measure, the act of 1833 may deserve commendation. As an economic or financial measure, there is little to be said for it. It was badly drafted. No provision was made in it as to specific duties; yet it was obviously meant to apply to such duties, and the Secretary of the Treasury had to take it on himself to frame rules as to the manner of ascertaining the *ad valorem* equivalents of specific duties and making the reductions called for by the act.[1] Again, the reductions of duty were irregular. Thus on one important article, rolled bar-iron, the duty of 1832 had been specific, —$1.50 per hundredweight. This was equivalent, at the prices of 1832, to about 95 per cent. The progress of the reductions is shown in the note.[2] Up to 1842, they were

---

[1] The instructions issued from the Treasury Department may be found in " Exec. Doc." 1833–34, vol. I., No. 43. It has been thought that the act did not apply to specific duties; but this is a mistake.

[2]

Year.	Duty, per cent.
1834	87
1836	80
1838	72.5
1840	65
Jan. 1, 1842	42.5
July 5, 1842	20

This calculation is on the basis of the prices of 1833. If prices changed

comparatively moderate; but in the six months from January 1 to July 1, 1842, the duty dropped from 65 to 20 per cent. Producers and dealers necessarily found it hard to deal with such changes. It is true that a long warning was given them; but, on the other hand, Congress might at any moment interfere to modify the act. Finally, and not least among the objections, there was the ultimate horizontal rate of 20 per cent.—a crude and indiscriminating method of dealing with the tariff problem, which can be defended on no ground of principle or expediency. The 20 per cent. rate, according to the terms of the act, was to remain in force indefinitely, that being the concession which in the end was made to the extremists of the South.[1]

As it happened, however, the 20 per cent. duty remained in force for but two months, from July 1 till September 1, 1842.[2] At the latter date the tariff act of 1842 went

---

(and they did change greatly), the rates under the Compromise Act would vary materially from those given in the text ; since the *ad valorem* equivalent of the specific duty, and its excess over 20 per cent., were ascertained for each year according to the prices of that year.

[1] Clay, who drafted the act, probably had no expectation that the 20 per cent. rate ever would go into effect. He thought Congress would amend before 1842, and intended to meet by his compromise the immediate emergency only. See his " Works," vol. II., pp. 131, 132. He tried to show Appleton and Davis, two leading representatives of the protectionists, that " no future Congress would be bound by the act." See Appleton's speech on the Tariff Act of 1842, " Appendix to Cong. Globe," 1841–42, p. 575.

[2] The Compromise Act was so loosely constructed that doubt was entertained whether under its terms any duties at all could be collected after June 30, 1842. The point was carried before the Supreme Court, which decided, however, that the rate of 20 per cent. was in effect during the two

into force. That act was passed by the Whigs as a party measure, and its history is closely connected with the political complications of the time. The Whigs had broken with President Tyler, and had a special quarrel with him as to the distribution among the States of the proceeds of the public lands. Tyler vetoed two successive tariff bills because of clauses in them in regard to distribution. The bill which he finally signed, and which became law, was passed hurriedly, without the distribution clause. Attention was turned mainly to the political quarrel and to the political effect of the bill in general.[1] The act, naturally enough, was a hasty and imperfect measure, of which the details had received little consideration. The duties which it levied were high,—probably higher than they would have been had the tariff discussion been less affected by the breach between Tyler and the Whigs. Though distinctively protective, and proclaimed to be such by the Whigs, it had not such a strong popular feeling behind it as had existed in favor of the protective measures of 1824, 1828, and 1832. In the farming States the enthusiasm for the home-market idea had cooled perceptibly ; and in the manufacturing States the agitation came rather from the producers directly interested than

---

months before the act of 1842 went in force. (Aldridge *vs.* Williams, 3 Howard, 9.) Justice McLean dissented ; and there is much force to his dissenting opinion and to the argument of Reverdy Johnson, the counsel against the government.

[1] A full account of this struggle is in Von Holst's " Constitutional History," vol. III., pp. 451–463.

from the public at large. There is much truth in Calhoun's remark that the act of 1842 was passed, not so
much in compliance with the wishes of the manufacturers,
as because the politicians wanted an issue.[1]

The act of 1842 remained in force for but four years.
It was in turn superseded by the act of 1846, again a
political measure, passed this time by the Democrats.
The act of 1846 carried out the suggestions made by
Secretary Walker in his much debated Treasury Report
of 1845. Indeed, it may be regarded as practically framed
by Walker, who professed to adhere to the principle of
free trade ; and the act of 1846 is often spoken of as an
instance of the application of free-trade principles. In
fact, however, it effected no more than a moderation in
the application of protection. The act established several
schedules, indicated by the letters A, B, C, D, and so on.
All the articles classed in schedule A paid 100 per cent.,
all in schedule B paid 40 per cent., all in schedule C paid
30 per cent., and so on for the rest. Schedule C, with the
30 per cent. duty, included most articles with which the
protective controversy is concerned, — iron and metals in
general, manufactures of metals, wool and woollens, manufactures of leather, paper, glass, and wood. Cottons
were in schedule D, and paid 25 per cent. Tea and coffee,
on the other hand, were exempt from duty.

---

[1] " Works," vol. IV., pp. 199, 200. Calhoun thought that a good deal
was due also to the influence of the " moneyed men " who wanted the
Treasury to be filled.

The act of 1846 remained in force till 1857, when a still further reduction of duties was made. The revenue was redundant in 1857, and this was the chief cause of the reduction of duties. The measure of that year was passed with little opposition, and was the first tariff act since 1816 that was not affected by politics.[1] It was agreed on all hands that a reduction of the revenue was imperatively called for, and, except from Pennsylvania, there was no opposition to the reduction of duties made in it. The framework of the act of 1846 was retained,—the schedules and the *ad valorem* duties. The duty on the important protective articles, in schedule C, was lowered to 24 per cent., cottons being transferred, moreover, to that schedule. Certain raw materials were at the same time admitted free of duty.

The act of 1857 remained in force till the close of the period we now have under examination. We begin with a high protective tariff in 1832 ; then follows a gradual reduction of duties, ending in 1842 with a brief period of very low duties. In the four years 1842–46 we have a strong application of protection. In 1846 begins what is often called a period of free trade, but is in reality one of moderated protection. In 1857 the protection is still further moderated, and for a few years there is as near an approach to free trade as the country has had since 1816.

---

[1] Seward said, in 1857, that "the vote of not a single Senator will be governed by any partisan consideration whatever." Appendix to "Congressional Globe," 1856–57, p. 344 ; and see Hunter's speech. *ibid.,* p. 331.

Turning now to the economic effect of this legislation, we have to note, first, its connection with the general prosperity of the country. That there was a distinct connection is asserted by both protectionists and free traders. The protectionists tell us that the compromise tariff caused the disastrous crises of 1837 and 1839; that the high tariff of 1842 brought back prosperity; that depression again followed the passage of the act of 1846, and that the panic of 1857 was precipitated by the tariff act of 1857. On the other hand, free traders not infrequently describe the period between 1846 and 1860 as one of exceptional prosperity, due to the low duties then in force.

It would not be worth while to allude to some of these assertions, if they were not so firmly imbedded in current literature and so constantly repeated in many accounts of our economic history. This is especially the case with the curious assertion that the crises of 1837 and 1839 were caused by the compromise tariff of 1833, or connected with it. This assertion had its origin in the writings of Henry C. Carey, who has been guilty of many curious versions of economic history, but of none more remarkable than this. It may be found in various passages in his works; and from them it has been transferred to the writings of his disciples and to the arguments of protectionist authors and speakers in general.[1] Yet no fair-

---

[1] References to the supposed effects of the act of 1833 abound in Carey's works. As good a specimen as any is this: "Agitation succeeded in producing a total change of system in the tariff of 1833. * * * Thencefor-

minded person, having even a superficial knowledge of the economic history of these years, can entertain such notions.   The crises of 1837 and 1839 were obviously due to quite a different set of causes—to the bank troubles, the financial mistakes of Jackson's administration, the inflation of the currency, and to those general conditions of speculation and unduly expanded credit which give rise to crises.   The tariff act had nothing whatever to do with them.   Indeed, the reductions in duty under it, as we have

---

ward the building of furnaces and mills almost wholly ceased, the wealthy English capitalists having thus succeeded in regaining the desired control of the great American market for cloth and iron.   As a consequence of their triumph there occurred a succession of crises of barbaric tendency, the whole terminating, in 1842, in a scene of ruin such as had never before been known, bankruptcy among the people being almost universal," etc.   "Letters on the Iron Question" (1865), p. 4, printed in his "Miscellaneous Works" (1872).   To the same effect, see his "Financial Crises," p. 18; "Review of Wells' Report," p. 5; "Social Science," II., p. 225.   Professor Thompson makes the same statement in his "Political Economy," p. 353. See also Elder, "Questions of the Day" (1871), pp. 200, 201.   Senator Evarts, in a speech made in 1883, ascribed to the act of 1833 "a bankruptcy which covered the whole land, without distinction of sections, with ruin."   The pedigree of statements of this kind, which are frequent in campaign literature, can be traced back to Carey.   Doubtless Carey wrote in good faith; but his prejudices were so strong as to prevent him from taking a just view of economic history.

Oddly enough, Calhoun ascribed the crisis of 1837 to the fact that duties under the act of 1833 remained *too high*.   The high duties brought in a large revenue and caused a surplus in the Treasury; the deposit and distribution of this brought inflation and speculation, and eventually a crisis ("Works," IV., p. 174).   No doubt the high duties were one cause of the government surplus, and thereby aided in bringing about the crisis, so that this view, incomplete as it is, has more foundation than Carey's explanation.   On the other hand, Clay, as might be expected, took pains to deny that the act of 1833 had any thing to do with the troubles of the years following its passage ("Works," II., pp. 530, 531; edition of 1844).

seen, were slight until 1840, and could hardly have influenced in any degree the breaking out of the panics. Even if the reductions of duty had been greater, and had been made earlier, they would probably have had no effect, favorable or unfavorable, on the inflation of the earlier years or on the depression which followed.

We may dispose at this point of a similar assertion occasionally made in regard to the crisis of 1857,—that the tariff act of 1857 caused or intensified it. This view also is traceable, probably, to Carey. It appears in his writings and in those of his disciples.[1] In fact, the crisis of 1857 was an unusually simple case of activity, speculation, over-banking, panic, and depression; and it requires the exercise of great ingenuity to connect it in any way with the tariff act. As it happened indeed. the tariff was passed with some hope that it would serve to prevent the crisis. Money was accumulating in the Treasury; and it was hoped that by reducing duties the revenue would be diminished, money would be got out of the Treasury, and the stringency, which was already threatening, prevented.[2]

---

[1] Carey speaks in one place of "the terrific free-trade crisis of 1857." "Letters to Colfax," p. 15 : "Financial Crises," p. 8 ; "Review of Wells," p. 5 (all in his "Miscellaneous Works"). Thompson ("Political Economy," p. 357) says : "In 1857, Congress reduced the duties twenty-five per cent. * * * It at once intensified all the unwholesome tendencies in our commercial and industrial life. * * * Another great panic followed through the collapse of unsound enterprises."

[2] See a letter from a Boston merchant to Senator Wilson, "Congr. Globe, 1856–57, Appendix," p. 344 ; and the statement by Senator Hunter *ibid.*, 329.

The reduction failed to prevent the panic; but, at the time, it would have been considered very odd to ascribe the disaster to the tariff act.

On the other hand, it has been very often said that the activity of trade in 1843–44 was due to the enactment of the protective tariff act of 1842. There may be a degree of truth in this. The unsettled state of legislation on the tariff before the act of 1842 was passed must have been an obstacle to the revival of confidence. After July 1, 1842, there was the uniform duty of 20 per cent.; nay, it was doubtful whether there was by law even that duty in force. It was certain that Congress would wish not to retain the horizontal rate, but would try to enact a new tariff law; yet the quarrel between the Whigs and Tyler made the issue quite doubtful. Such uncertainty necessarily operated as a damper on trade; and the passage of any act whatever, settling the tariff question for the time being, would have removed one great obstacle to the return of activity and prosperity. It is even possible that the passage of the act of 1842 may have had a more direct effect than this. No doubt, in the regular recurrence of waves of activity and depression, the depression of 1840–42 would soon have been followed, in any event, by a period of activity. The point at which activity will begin to show itself under such circumstances is largely a matter of chance. It begins, for some perhaps accidental reason, with one industry or set of industries, and, the materials for general revival being ready, then spreads

quickly to the others. In the same way, when the materials for a crisis are at hand, a single accidental failure
may precipitate a general panic. In 1842–43 the high
duties of the tariff act probably helped to make profits
large for the time being in certain manufactures, notably
those of cotton and iron. Prosperity in these set in, and
may have been the signal for a general revival of confidence and for a general extension of business operations.
To that extent, it is not impossible that the protective
tariff of 1842 was the occasion of the reviving business
of the ensuing years. But it is a very different thing
from this to say that the tariff was the cause of
prosperity, and that depression would have continued
indefinitely but for the re-establishment of high protective duties.

In truth, there has been a great deal of loose talk about
tariffs and crises. Whenever there has been a crisis, the
free traders or protectionists, as the case may be, have
been tempted to use it as a means for overthrowing the
system they opposed. Cobden found in the depression of
1839–40 a powerful argument in his crusade against the
corn laws, and knew that a return of prosperity would
work against him.[1] Within a few years, the opponents
of protection in this country have found in general depression a convenient and effective argument against the
tariff. In the same way, the protectionists have been
tempted to use the crises of 1837 and 1857, and conversely

---

[1] See passages in Morley's " Life of Cobden," pp. 162, 163, 210.

the revival of 1843–44, to help their case. But the effect of tariffs cannot be traced by any such rough-and-ready method. The tariff system of a country is but one of many factors entering into its general prosperity. Its influence, good or bad, may be strengthened or may be counteracted by other causes ; while it is exceedingly difficult, generally impossible, to trace its separate effect. Least of all can its influence be traced in those variations of outward prosperity and depression which are marked by "good times" and crises. A protective tariff may sometimes strengthen other causes which are bringing on a commercial crisis. Some such effect is very likely traceable to the tariff in the years before the crisis of 1873. It may sometimes be the occasion of a revival of activity, when the other conditions are already favorable to such a revival. That may have been the case in 1843. But these are only incidental effects, and lie quite outside the real problem as to the results of protection. As a rule, the tariff system of a country operates neither to cause nor to prevent crises. They are the results of conditions of exchange and production on which it can exercise no great or permanent influence.

Remarks of the same kind may be made on the frequent assertion that the prosperity of the country from 1846 to 1860 can be traced to the low duties then in force. He who is convinced, on grounds of general reasoning and of general experience, that the principles of

free trade are sound and that protective duties are harmful, can fairly deduce the conclusion that the low tariffs
of 1846 and 1857 contributed, so far as they went, to general prosperity. But a direct connection cannot be traced.
A number of favorable causes were at work, such as the
general advance in the arts, the rapid growth of the railway system and of ocean communication, the Californian
gold discoveries. There is no way of eliminating the
other factors, and determining how much can be ascribed
to the tariff alone. Even in the growth of international
trade, where some direct point of connection might be
found, we cannot measure the effect of low duties; for
international trade was growing between all countries
under the influence of cheapened transportation and the
stimulus of the great gold discoveries.[1] The inductive,
or historical, method absolutely fails us here.

---

[1] The growth of foreign trade under the tariffs of 1846 and 1857 was certainly very striking. In Grosvenor's "Does Protection Protect?" there is
a table showing the imports and exports per head of population from 1821
to 1869, in which it is stated that the annual average per head of population was:

	Imports.	Exports.
In 1843–46,	$4.66	$5.22
" 1847–50,	6.35	6.32
" 1851–55,	9.10	7.35
" 1856–60,	10.41	9.45

The imports and exports were, in millions of dollars:

	Imports.	Exports.
Annual average of the four years 1843–46,	92.7	100
" " " " " " 1847–50,	138.3	136.8
" " " " five " 1851–55,	231.	186.2
" " " " " " 1856–60,	305.	278.2

But how are we to measure the share which low duties had in promoting
this growth?

We turn now to another inquiry, as to the effect of the fluctuating duties of this period on the protected industries. That inquiry, it is hardly necessary to say, leads us to no certain conclusion as to the effect of the duties on the welfare of the country at large. It is quite conceivable, and indeed on grounds of general reasoning at least probable, that any stimulus given to the protected industries indicated a loss in the productive powers of the community as a whole. But it has often been asserted, and again often denied, that the duties caused a growth of certain industries; and it is worth while to trace, if we can, the tangible effect in this direction, even though it be but a part of the total effect.

It is the production of iron in the unmanufactured form that has been most hotly discussed in the protective controversy. And in regard to this, fortunately, we have good, if not complete, information.

The duty on pig-iron had been 62½ cents a hundredweight under the tariff act of 1828. In 1832 it was reduced to 50 cents, or $10 per ton. This rate was equivalent to about 40 per cent. on the foreign price at that time; and, under the Compromise Act of 1833, it was gradually reduced, until it reached 20 per cent. in 1842. Under the act of 1842, the duty was again raised to $10 a ton. In 1846 it was made 30 per cent. on the value, and in 1857 24 per cent. As the value varied, the duty under the last two acts varied also. In 1847, a time of high prices, the duty of 30 per cent. was equal to $5.75 per

ton; in 1852 it was only \$3.05; in 1855 it was as high as
\$6; in 1860 it again fell to \$3.40.[1]

The duty on bar-iron was of two kinds until 1846,—a
duty on hammered bar-iron, and another heavier duty on
rolled bar-iron. The duty on hammered bar was, in 1832,
fixed at 90 cents per hundredweight, or \$18 per ton.
That on rolled bar was nearly twice as heavy, being \$30
per ton, or nearly 100 per cent. on the value. These duties
were reduced under the Compromise Act; and, as we
have seen, the reduction on rolled bar was very great,
and, in 1842, very sudden. Under the act of 1842, the
duty on hammered bar was made \$17 per ton, that on
rolled bar \$25 per ton. The act of 1846 gave up finally
the discrimination between the two kinds, and admitted

---

[1] The duty from year to year, on the average, for the fiscal years ending
June 30th, is given in the following table. The foreign value, on which the
duty was computed, is also given. The figures are compiled from the tables
given in French, " History of Iron Manufacture," p. 70, and in the " Report of the Iron and Steel Association for 1876," p. 182.

Year ending June 30th.	Average value.	Duty (30 per cent. till 1857, 24 per cent. after 1857.)
1847	\$19.90	\$5.95
1848	15.80	4.75
1849	13.30	4.00
1850	12.70	3.80
1851	12.60	3.75
1852	10.20	3.05
1853	13.40	4.00
1854	18.00	5.40
1855	20.00	6.00
1856	19.80	5.95
1857	19.50	5.85
1858	17.60	4.20
1859	15.20	3.65
1860	14.10	3.40

both alike at a duty of 30 per cent.; and the act of 1857 admitted them at 24 per cent.[1]

Before proceeding to examine the economic effect of these duties, it should be said that our information as to the production of iron is in many ways defective, and that the statements relating to it in the following paragraphs cannot be taken to be more than roughly accurate. The government figures give us trustworthy information as to the imports; but for the domestic production we must rely, at least for the earlier years, on estimates which are often no more than guesses. Nevertheless, the general trend of events can be made out pretty clearly, and we are able to draw some important conclusions.[2]

It seems to be clear that the importation of iron was somewhat affected by the duties. The years before 1842, when the compromise tariff was in force, were years of such disturbance that it is not easy to trace any effects clearly to the operation of the tariff; but imports during these years were a smaller proportion of the total consumption of iron than they were during the period after

---

[1] Between 1832 and 1842, an exception had been made for one class of rolled iron,—iron rails actually laid down on railroads. These were admitted free of duty; or, rather, a drawback was granted of the full amount of duty due or paid on them. Between 1828 and 1832, a drawback had been granted such as to make the duty on railroad iron only 25 per cent. After 1842, however, it was charged with duty like any other iron.

[2] The reader who wishes to examine further the data as to the production of iron before 1860, is referred to the Appendix to the *Quarterly Journal of Economics* for April, 1888, vol. II., pp. 377–382, where I have considered the figures in detail.

1846. It must be remembered that from 1830 till 1842 all railroad iron was admitted free of duty, and that a large part of the imported iron consisted of rails. If this quantity be deducted from the total import, the remaining quantity, which alone was affected by the duties, becomes still smaller as compared with the domestic product. In 1841 and 1842, when duties began to be low under the operation of the Compromise Act, imports were larger in proportion to the home product. On the other hand, in the four years, 1843–46, under the act of 1842, they show a distinct decrease. After 1847, they show as distinct an increase, and continue to be large throughout the period until 1860. In the speculative and railroad-building years, from 1852 to 1857, the importation was especially heavy; and in 1853 and 1854 the total quantity of iron imported was almost as great as the home product.

The most effective part of the iron duties until 1846 was the heavy discriminating duty on rolled bar-iron. That duty amounted (from 1818 till 1846, except during a few months in 1842) to about 100 per cent. Rolled iron, made by the puddling process and by rolling, is the form of bar-iron now in common use. The process was first applied successfully by Cort in England about 1785, and in that country was immediately put into extensive use. It made bar-iron much more cheaply and plentifully than the old process of refining in a forge and under a hammer; and, at the present time, hammered bar of the old-fashioned kind has ceased to be made, except in comparatively small quantities for special purposes. Cort's processes of puddling and rolling were practicable only through the use of bituminous coal and coke. The abundant and excellent coal of Great Britain gave that country an enormous advantage in producing rolled iron, as it had already done in smelting pig-iron, and put her in that commanding position as an iron producer which she continues to occupy to the present day. When rolled iron first began to be exported from England to foreign countries, it aroused strong feelings of jealousy, being so much cheaper than other iron. Several countries fought against the improvement by imposing discriminating duties on it.[1] That course was adopted in the United States. In 1818, a discriminating duty was put on rolled iron, partly because it was said to be inferior in quality to hammered iron, and partly from a feeling in favor of protecting the domestic producers of hammered iron. The duty was retained, as we have seen, till 1846. Its effect was neutralized in part by the free admission of railroad iron, which was one form of rolled iron; but, so far as it was applied to rolled iron in general, it simply prevented the United States from sharing the benefit of a great improvement in the arts. It had no effect in hastening the use of the puddling and rolling processes in the country. Though introduced into the United States as early as

---

[1] In France a discriminating duty equivalent to 12⟩ per cent. was imposed in 1833 on iron imported by sea, *i. e.,* on English iron. Amé, "Tarifs de Douanes," I., 144, 145. The discrimination was maintained until 1855. *Ibid.,* 271.

1817, these processes got no firm hold until after anthracite coal began to be used, about 1840, as an iron-making
fuel.[1]

We turn now to the history of the domestic production.
By far the most important event in that history is the use
of anthracite coal as a fuel, which began about 1840.
The substitution of anthracite for wood (charcoal) revolutionized the iron trade in the United States in the same
way as the use of bituminous coal (coke) had revolution-

---

[1] The first puddling and rolling mill in the United States was put up in
Pennsylvania in 1817.   The first puddling in New England was done as
late as 1835.   Wood was used as fuel at the outset.   Swank, "Iron in All
Ages," 166, 330.   The effect of the duty on rolled iron cannot be better
described than in the clear and forcible language used by Gallatin in 1831 :
" It seems impracticable that iron made with charcoal can ever compete
with iron made from bituminous coal. * * * A happy application of
anthracite coal to the manufacture of iron, the discovery of new beds of
bituminous coal, the erection of iron-works in the vicinity of the most East-
erly beds now existing, and the improved means of transportation, which
may bring this at a reasonable rate to the sea-border, may hereafter enable
the American iron-master to compete in cheapness with foreign rolled iron
in the Atlantic districts.   On those contingencies the tariff can have no
effect.   To persist, in the present state of the manufacture, in that particular competition, and for that purpose to proscribe the foreign rolled iron, is
to compel the people for an indefinite time to substitute a dear for a cheap
article.   It is said that the British iron is generally of inferior quality ; this
is equally true of a portion of that made in America.   In both cases the
consumer is the best judge,—has an undoubted right to judge for himself.
Domestic charcoal iron should confine itself to a competition with the foreign iron made from the same fuel."   Gallatin added, prophetically :
" Your memorialists believe that the ultimate reduction of the price of
American iron to that of British rolled iron can only, and ultimately will,
be accomplished in that Western region which abounds with ore, and in
which are found the most extensive formations of bituminous coal."—
" Memorial of the Free-Trade Convention," pp. 60, 61.

ized the English iron trade nearly a century before. Up to 1840, pig-iron had been smelted in this country with charcoal, a fuel which was expensive, and tended to become more and more expensive as the nearer forests were cut down and wood became less easily attainable. Charcoal pig-iron could not have competed on even terms with the coal-made English iron. But between 1830 and 1840 it was protected by the heavy duties on English iron; and, under their shelter, the production in those years steadily increased. There seems to be no doubt that, with lower duties or no duties at all, the domestic production would have been less, and the import greater. In other words, the duty operated as a true protective duty, hampering international trade and increasing the price of the home product as well as of the imported iron.

In 1840, however, anthracite coal began to be applied to the making of pig-iron. The use of anthracite was made possible by the hot blast,—a process which was put in successful operation in England at nearly the same time.[1] The importance of the new method was immediately appreciated, and predictions were made that henceforth there would be no longer occasion for importing iron, even under the 20 per cent. duty of the Compromise Act. Many furnaces were changed from the charcoal to the

---

[1] The hot blast was successfully applied in a furnace in Pennsylvania in 1835, but the experiment was not prosecuted. In 1837, Crane applied it in Wales, and about the same time the process was successfully used in this country. Swank, "Iron in All Ages," 268–273, French. "History of the Iron Trade," 58–60.

anthracite method.[1] At very nearly the same time, as it
happened, the tariff act of 1842 was passed, imposing
heavy duties on all kinds of iron, among others on the
railroad iron which had hitherto been admitted free.
Very shortly afterwards a general revival of trade set in.
Under the influence of these combined causes, the production of iron was suddenly increased.   The exact
amount of the increase is disputed; but the production
seems to have risen from somewhere near 300,000 tons in
1840-41, to 650,000 or more in 1846-47.   Some part of
this great growth was certainly due to the high protection
of 1842 ; but, under any circumstances, the use of anthracite would have given a great stimulus to the iron trade.
This is shown by the course of events under the tariff
acts of 1846 and 1857.   The production remained, on the
whole, fairly steady throughout the years when these acts
were in force.   There was, on the whole, an increase from
between 500,000 and 600,000 tons in the earlier years of
the period to between 800,000 and 900,000 tons in the
later years.   For a few years after the passage of the act
of 1846, the reduction of the duty to 30 per cent. had
little, if any, effect.   Prices were high both in England
and in the United States ; for it was a time of active
railroad building in England, and consequently of great
demand for iron.   The *ad valorem* duty was correspond-

---

[1] See the notices in Hazard's "Statistical Register," I., pp. 335, 368 ;
III., p. 173 ; IV., p. 207.   That great results were at once expected from
the new method is shown by an interesting speech of Nicholas Biddle,
ibid., II., p. 230.

ingly high. In 1850–51 the usual reaction set in, prices
went down, production decreased, and the iron-masters
complained.[1] But the natural revival came after a year
or two. Prices rose again ; production increased, and
continued to increase until 1860. Although the duty,
which had been $9 a ton under the act of 1842, was
no more than $3 and $4 under the 24 per cent. rate
which was in force during the years 1858, 1859, and 1860,
and although these were not years of unusual general
activity, the domestic production showed a steady growth.
The country was growing fast, many railroads were in
course of construction, much iron was needed. An un-
diminished home product was consumed, as well as largely
increased imports.

The most significant fact in the iron trade, however, is
to be seen, not in the figures of total production, but in
the shifting from charcoal to anthracite iron. While the
total product remained about the same, the component
elements changed greatly. The production of anthracite

---

[1] The iron-masters admitted that the act of 1846 had been sufficiently
protective when first passed.   But in 1849 and 1850, they began to complain and ask for higher duties.   See " Proceedings of Iron Convention at
Pittsburg (1849)," p. 9 ; " Proceedings of Convention at Albany," pp. 27,
42.   They certainly had a legitimate subject for complaint in the operation
of the *ad valorem* duty, in that it tended to exaggerate the fluctuations of
prices.   When prices abroad were high, the duty was high ; when prices
abroad were low, the duty was low.   Consequently, the price of foreign
iron in the United States, which is the sum of the foreign price and the
duty, fluctuated more widely than the foreign price alone.   This was certainly an evil, especially with an article whose price was liable under any
conditions to vary so much as the price of iron. See the table above, p. 124

iron rose steadily : that of charcoal iron fell as steadily.
The first anthracite furnace was built in 1840. In 1844
there were said to be twenty furnaces, making 65,000 tons
annually.[1] Thence the production rose with hardly an
interruption being

in 1844	.	.	.	.	65,000 gross tons.
" 1846	.	.	.	.	110,000 " "
" 1849	.	.	.	.	115,000 " "
" 1854	.	.	.	.	308,000 net "
" 1855	.	.	.	.	343,000 " "
" 1856	.	.	.	.	394,000 " " [2]

As the anthracite iron production increased, that of charcoal iron decreased. Under the tariff act of 1842, a
large number of new charcoal furnaces had been put up.[3]
Many of these had to be given up under the combined
competition of anthracite and of English iron. Some
maintained themselves by using coke and raw bituminous
coal, in those parts of the country where bituminous coal
was to be had[4]; others disappeared. That at least some

---

[1] See a " Letter of the Philadelphia Coal and Iron Trade to the Committee on Finance " (pamphlet, Philadelphia, 1844).

[2] The figure for 1846 is that given in Taylor, " Statistics of Coal," p.
133. Swank gives the figure for 1846 as 123,000 (gross ?) tons. " Iron in
All Ages," p. 274. The figures for 1849–56 are from Lesley, " Iron
Manufacturers' Guide (1859)," pp. 751,752. Those given by Grosvenor,
" Does Protection Protect ? " p. 225, vary somewhat ; but the differences
are not great.

[3] See the figures in Grosvenor, p. 215. There were built in 1843 9 charcoal furnaces ; in 1844, 23 ; in 1845, 35 ; in 1846, 44 ; in 1847, 34 ; in
1848, 28 ; in 1849, 14.

[4] The use of coke began in the United States about 1850, but was of
little importance until after 1856. The use of raw bituminous coal was introduced about 1850 in the Shenango and Mahoning valleys (on the border

of them should disappear was inevitable. Charcoal iron for general use was a thing of the past; and the effect of the tariff of 1842 was to call into existence a number of furnaces which used antiquated methods, and before long must have been displaced in any event by anthracite furnaces

The use of anthracite not only stimulated the production of pig-iron, but also that of rolled iron and railroad bars. Anthracite was first used in puddling and reheating in 1844 and 1845,[1] and thenceforward rolled iron was made regularly in large quantities. In 1856 the production of rolled iron was nearly 500,000 tons.[2] Iron rails first began to be made while the tariff act of 1842 was in force, though the steps towards making them were taken even before that act put an end to the free admission of English rails.[3] With the decline in railroad building and the

between Pennsylvania and Ohio), where there is suitable coal. Swank, " Iron in All Ages," pp. 281–284. In the " Report of the American Iron and Steel Association for 1876 " (prepared by Swank), the following figures are given of the production of iron with the various kinds of fuel. I have selected a few typical years :

Year.	Anthracite iron.	Charcoal iron.	Bituminous coal and coke iron.	Total.
1854	339,000	342,000	55,000	736,000
1856	443,000	370,000	70,000	883,000
1858	362,000	285,000	58,000	705,000
1860	519,000	278,000	122,000	919,000

The figures here denote net tons.

[1] Speech of A. S. Hewitt, in " Proceedings of Iron Convention at Albany " (1849), p. 54.

[2] Lesley, " Iron Manufacturers' Guide," p. 761.

[3] See a pamphlet, " Observations on the Expediency of Repealing the Act by which Railroad Iron is Released from Duty," 1842. It gives an account of large rolling mills then being erected at Danville, Pennsylvania.

general fall in iron prices, which took place in 1849, many
of the rail mills stopped work.   But the business revived
with the general prosperity which set in early in the decade, and the production of rails steadily increased until
1856. Under the influence of the crisis of 1857 it fell,
but soon rose again, and in 1860 was more than 200,000
tons.[1]

To sum up: The high duty on iron in its various forms
between 1832 and 1841, and again in 1842–46, impeded
importation, retarded for the United States that cheapening of iron which has been one of the most important
factors in the march of improvement in this century, and
maintained in existence costly charcoal furnaces long
after that method had ceased in Great Britain to be in
general use.   The first step towards a vigorous and
healthy growth of the iron industry was in the use of anthracite in 1840.   That step, so far from being promoted
by the high duties, was taken in a time when duties were
on the point of being reduced to the 20 per cent. level.
Hardly had it been taken when the high duties of the
tariff act of 1842 brought about (not indeed alone, but in
conjunction with other causes) a temporary return to the

---

[1] See the figures given in "Report of Iron and Steel Association for
1876," p. 165.   The production of rails is there stated to have been :

In 1849	.	.	.	.	.	.	24,000 tons.
" 1850	.	.	.	.	.	.	44,000 "
" 1854	.	.	.	.	.	.	108,000 "
" 1856	.	.	.	.	.	.	180,000 "
" 1857	.	.	.	.	.	.	162,000 "
" 1860	.	.	.	.	.	.	205,000 "

old charcoal process. A number of new charcoal furnaces
were built, unsuited to the industry of the time and certain to succumb before long. Under the lower duties
from 1846 to 1860, the charcoal production gradually became a less and less important part of the iron industry,
and before the end of the period had been restricted to
those limits within which it could find a permanent
market for the special qualities of its iron.[1] On the other
hand, the lower duties did not prevent a steady growth in
the making of anthracite iron; while the production of
railroad iron and of rolled iron in general, also made possible by the use of anthracite, showed a similar steady
progress. There is no reason to doubt that, had there
been no duty at all, there would yet have been a large
production of anthracite pig- and rolled iron. Meanwhile
the country was rapidly developing, and needed much
iron. The low duties permitted a large importation of
foreign iron, in addition to a large domestic production.
The comparative cheapness and abundance of so important an industrial agent could not have operated otherwise than to promote material prosperity.

We turn now to another industry,—the manufacture of
cotton goods, by far the largest and most important
branch of the textile industry. Here we are met at the

---

[1] Charcoal iron has qualities which cause a certain quantity of it to be in
demand under any circumstances. Since it settled down, about 1860, to its
normal place as a supplement to coal-made iron, the product has steadily
increased with the growing needs of the country. In the years 1863–65 the
annual product was about 240,000 tons. In 1886 it was 460,000 tons.

outset by the fact that, at the beginning of the period
which we are considering, the cotton manufacture was in
the main independent of protection, and not likely to be
much affected, favorably or unfavorably, by changes in
duties. Probably as early as 1824, and almost certainly
by 1832, the industry had reached a firm position, in which
it was able to meet foreign competition on equal terms.[1]
Mr. Nathan Appleton, who was a large owner of cotton
factory stocks, and who was also, in his time, one of the
ablest and most prominent advocates of protective duties,
said in 1833 that at that date coarse cottons could not
have been imported from England if there had been no
duty at all, and that even on many grades of finer goods
competition was little to be feared. In regard to prints,
the American goods were, quality for quality, as cheap as
the English, but might be supplanted, in the absence of
duties, by the poorer and nominally cheaper English
goods,—an argument, often heard in our own day, which
obviously puts the protective system on the ground of
regulating the quality of goods for consumers. The general situation of the cotton manufacture, as described by
Appleton, was one in which duties had ceased to be a
factor of much importance in its development.[2]

---

[1] See the previous essay on "Protection to Young Industries," Part III.,
where an account is given of the history of the cotton manufacture up to
1824.

[2] See Appleton's speech on the Verplanck bill of 1833, "Congressional
Debates," IX., pp. 1216–1217. Compare his remarks in the same volume at p. 1579.

During the extraordinary fluctuations of industry and the gradual reduction of duties which ensued under the compromise tariff of 1833, the business of manufacturing cottons was profitable and expanded, or encountered depression and loss, in sympathy with the industry of the country at large, being influenced chiefly by the expansion of credit and the rise of prices before 1837 and 1839, and the crisis and liquidation that followed those years. Notwithstanding the impending reductions of duty under the Compromise Act, large investments were made in the business in the earlier part of the period. Thus, in 1835–36, the Amoskeag Company began on a large scale its operations in Manchester, N. H.[1] The depression at the close of the decade checked growth for a while, but did not prevent new investments from being made, even before the passage of the act of 1842 settled the tariff uncertainty.[2] The best informed judges said that the causes of increase or decrease of profit had been, as one might expect, the same as those that produced fluctuations in other branches of business; and they made no mention of duties or of tariff.[3] Appleton's account of the

---

[1] Potter, "History of Manchester," p. 552. The Stark Mills were built in 1838, the second Stark Mills in 1839.

[2] Earl, "History of Fall River," pp. 35–37. "From the panic of 1837, which affected every business centre in the country, Fall River seems to have speedily recovered, since within a few years from that date nearly every mill in the place was enlarged, though only one new one was built." *Ibid.*, p. 53.

[3] See the answers from T. G. Cary, treasurer of a Lowell mill, and from Samuel Batchelder to circulars sent out in 1845 by Secretary Walker. Batch-

stage reached by the industry finds confirmation in a careful volume on the cotton manufacture in the United
States, published in 1840 by Robert Montgomery. This
writer's general conclusions are much the same as those
which competent observers reach for our own time.
Money wages were about twice as high in the United
States, but the product per spindle and per loom was
considerably greater. The cotton, in his time, was not so
well mixed, not so thoroughly cleaned, not so well carded
in the United States as in England; but, on the other
hand, the Americans were superior in ordinary power-loom
weaving, as well as in warping and dressing. Elaborate
tables are given of the expenses per unit of product in
both countries, the final result of which, when all things
were considered, showed a difference of three per cent. in
favor of the American manufactures. Calculations of
this kind, which are common enough in discussions of
protective duties, are apt to express inadequately the
multiplicity of circumstances which affect concrete industry; yet they may gauge with fair accuracy the general
conditions, and in this case were made intelligently and
without bias. It is worth noting that Montgomery attrib-
utes the success of the Americans in exporting cottons to

---

elder, our most trustworthy informant on the early history of the cotton
manufacture, writes that " the increase and decrease of profit from 1831 to
1844 have conformed very nearly to the general prosperity of the country."
The circulars and answers are printed in the appendices to Walker's Report. Exec. Doc. 1845–46, vol. II., No. 6. pp. 215, 216, 313.

greater honesty in manufacturing and to the superior quality of their goods.[1]

During the years following the passage of the act of 1842, by which the duties on cottons were increased largely, the manufacturers made high profits. In Secretary Walker's Report, and in other attacks on protective duties, much was made of this circumstance, the high profits being ascribed to the new duties. The protectionists denied the connection, and a lively controversy ensued.[2] The truth seems to be that the case was not different from that usually presented in economic phenomena,—several causes combined to produce a single general effect. The high duties very likely served, in part, to enable a general advance of profits to be maintained for several years. But there was also an increased

---

[1] See " Montgomery's " Cotton Manufacture," pp. 29, 38, 82, 86, 91, 101. The tables of expenses are on pp. 124, 125 ; the remarks on quality of goods, on pp. 130, 194 ; on wages and product, on pp. 118–121, 123. Montgomery was superintendent of the York Factories at Saco, Maine, of which Samuel Batchelder was treasûrer. Allusions to Montgomery's book, and confirmation of some of his conclusions, may be found in Batchelder's " Early Progress of the Cotton Manufacture," p. 80 and following.

At a convention in favor of protection, held in New York in 1842, committees were appointed on various industries. The committee on cottons reported a recommendation to Congress of minimum duties on plain and printed goods, but added that these duties were " more than is necessary for much the largest part of the cotton goods," and that " most of the printed calicoes are now offered to the consumer at lower prices than they could be imported under a tariff for revenue only."

[2] See T. G. Cary, " Results of Manufactures at Lowell," Boston, 1845 : N. Appleton, " Review of Secretary Walker's Report," 1846 ; and the speeches of Rockwell, " Congr. Globe," 1845–46, pp. 1034–1037, and Winthrop, *ibid.*, Appendix, p. 969.

export to China, which proved highly profitable. Moreover, the price of raw cotton was low in these years, lagging behind the advance in the prices of cotton goods; and, as long as this lasted, the manufacturers made large gains. The fact that prosperity was shared by the cotton manufacturers in England shows that other causes than the new tariff must have been at work.

On the other hand, when the act of 1846 was passed. the protectionists predicted disaster [1]; but disaster came not, either for the country at large or for the cotton industry. Throughout the period from 1846 to 1860 the manufacture of cotton grew steadily, affected by the general conditions of trade, but little influenced by the lower duties. Exact figures indicating its fortunes are not to be had, yet we have enough information to enable us to judge of the general trend of events. The number of spindles in use gives the best indication of the growth of cotton manufacturing. We have no trustworthy figures as to the number of spindles in the whole country; but we have figures, collected by a competent and well-informed writer, in regard to Massachusetts. That State has always been the chief seat of the cotton manufacture, and its progress there doubtless indicates what took place in the country at large. The number of spindles in Massachu-

---

[1] Abbott Lawrence predicted in 1849 that " all this [a general crash] will take place in the space of eighteen months from the time this experimental bill goes into operation ; not a specie-paying bank doing business will be found in the United States." " Letters to Rives," p. 12. Appleton made a similar prediction in his " Review of Walker's Report," p. 28.

setts, which was, in round numbers, 340,000 in 1831, had
nearly doubled in 1840, was over 800,000 in 1845, and
was over 1,600,000 in 1860, having again nearly doubled
during the period of low duties.[1] The same signs of
growth and prosperity are seen in the figures of the
consumption of raw cotton in the United States, which,
compiled independently, reach the same general result.
Between the first half of the decade 1840–50, and the
second half of the decade 1850–60, the quantity of raw
cotton used in the mills of the United States about
doubled. The annual consumption, which had been
about 150,000 bales in 1830, rose to an average of more
than 300,000 bales in the early years of the next decade,
and again to one of more than 600,000 bales in the years
1850–54. In the five years immediately preceding the
civil war, the average annual consumption was about

[1] The following figures are given by Samuel Batchelder in a "Report to
the Boston Board of Trade," made in 1860 (published separately ; the essential parts printed also in "Hunt's Merchants' Magazine," xlv., p. 14):

Spindles in Massachusetts :

In 1831	.	.	.	340,000
" 1840	.	.	.	624,500 (other sources make it 665,000).
" 1845	.	.	.	817,500
" 1850	.	.	.	1,288,000
" 1855	.	.	.	1,519,500
" 1860	.	.	.	1,688,500

For New England, and the United States as a whole, Batchelder gives the
following figures, taken from De Bow, for the years 1840 and 1850. They
are not entirely trustworthy, but may be accepted as roughly accurate. We
add the census figures for 1860 :

			Spindles in		
			New England.		United States.
1840	.	.	1,597,000	. .	2,112,000
1850	.	.	2,751,000	. .	3,634,000
1860	.	.	3,859,000	. .	5,236,000

800,000 bales. During these years the consumption of cotton in Great Britain seems to have increased at very nearly the same rate.[1] Such figures indicate that the cotton manufacture was advancing rapidly and steadily. Another sign of its firm position is the steady increase during the same period in the exports of cotton goods, chiefly to China and the East. The value of the cotton goods exported averaged but little over $3,000,000 annually between 1838 and 1843, rose to over $4,000,000 between 1844 and 1849, was nearly $7,000,000 a year between 1851 and 1856, was over $8,000,000 in 1859, and almost touched $11,000,000 in 1860. An industry which regularly exports a large part of its products can hardly be stimulated to any considerable extent by protective duties. No doubt, the absence of high duties had an effect on the range of the industry. It was confined mainly to the production of plain, cheap, staple cotton cloths, and was not extended to the making of finer and "fancy" goods. But, even under the high protective duties of the last fifty years, the bulk of the product has continued to be of the first mentioned kind, and cottons of that grade have been sold, quality for quality, at prices not above those of foreign goods; while comparatively little progress has been made in the manufacture of the finer grades.[2]

---

[1] The reader is referred to the Appendix to the *Quarterly Journal of Economics* for April, 1888, for tables of the consumption of cotton and of the exports of cotton goods.

[2] Batchelder, who was a decided advocate of proctection. wrote in 1861 ⌐

The situation of the woollen manufacture differs in some important respects from that of the cotton manufacture, most noticeably in that it is less favorable as regards the supply of raw material. The maker of cotton goods is sure of securing at home cotton of the best quality at a price below that which his foreign rival must pay. But many qualities of wool cannot be produced to advantage in the United States; while others cannot be grown at all, or at least, notwithstanding very heavy protective duties, never have been grown. Moreover, the raw material, when obtained, is neither so uniform in quality nor so well adapted to treatment by machinery as is the fibre of cotton. Wool is of the most diverse quality, varying from a fine silk-like fibre to a

series of articles for the Boston *Commercial Advertiser*, in which, after comparing the prices and qualities of English and American shirtings, he said : "The inquiry may then be made, What occasion is there for a protective duty ? The answer is : There would be none in the ordinary course of business. But there are sometimes occasions when * * * there has been a great accumulation of goods in the hands of manufacturers abroad, so that, if crowded on their market, it would depress the price of the usual supply of their customers at home. On such occasions, our warehouse system affords the opportunity, at little expense, to send the goods here, where they may be ready to be thrown on the market to be sold," etc.

In Ellison's "Handbook of the Cotton Trade," it is stated, at p. 29 ; "It is believed that, had it not been for the free-trade policy of Great Britain, the manufacturing system of America would at the present time have been much more extensive than it is ; but the spinners and manufacturers of Lancashire can as yet successfully compete with those of Lowell, though for how long a time remains to be seen, for the latter are yearly gaining experience and improving their machinery, so that before long they will be able to compete with the old country, more especially should the executive [*sic*] abolish the present protective system adopted with respect to the import of cotton manufactures." This was written in 1858.

coarse hairy one. A process of careful sorting by hand
must therefore be gone through before manufacture can
begin. In some branches of the industry the qualities of
the fibre, and those of the goods which are to be made
from it, call for more of manual labor, and admit in less
degree of the use of machinery, than is the case with the
cottons; and it is a familiar fact, though one of which the
true meaning has not often been grasped, that a need of
resorting to direct manual labor in large proportion and a
difficulty in substituting machinery, constitute, under conditions of freedom, an obstacle to the profitable prosecution of a branch of industry in the United States. But,
on the other hand, certain qualities of wool are grown to
advantage in the climate of this country and under its
industrial conditions, especially strong merino wools of
good though not fine grade, of comparatively short
staple, adapted for the making of flannels, blankets, and
substantial cloths. At the same time, machinery can be
applied to making these fabrics with less difficulty than
to the manufacture of some finer goods.

Our information in regard to the history of the woollen
manufacture is even more defective than that on iron and
cottons. For the period between 1830 and 1840 we have
no information that is worth any thing. In 1840 the industry was confined to making satinets (a substantial,
inexpensive cloth, not of fine quality), broadcloths, flannels, and blankets.[1] The tariff act of 1842 imposed on

---

[1] See a passage quoted from Wade's "Fibre and Fabric" in the Bureau of
Statistics' 'Report on Wool and Manufactures of Wool." 1887, p. xlvii

woollen goods a duty of 40 per cent., and on wool one of three cents a pound plus 30 per cent. on the value. It is said that during the four years in which these rates were in force a stimulus was giving to the making of finer qualities of broadcloths, the development being aided by evasions of the *ad valorem* duty on wool.[1] The act, however, did not remain in force long enough to make it clear what would have been its permanent effect on the woollen manufacture. Whatever may have been the start made in these few years in making finer woollens, this branch of the industry, as is generally admitted, well-nigh disappeared under the duties of 1846. The tariff of that year imposed a duty of 30 per cent. on woollen goods in general; but flannels and worsteds were admitted at 25 per cent., and blankets at 20 per cent. On wool also the duty was 30 per cent. Under this arrangement of duties,—whether or not in consequence of it,—no development took place in those branches of the manufacture which needed wool that was subject to the 30 per cent. duty. The finest grades of woollens were not made at all. But the manufacture of cloths of ordinary quality (so-called cassimeres and similar goods), and that of blankets and flannels, continued to show a regular growth. The census figures are not of much value as accurate statistics, but there seems to be no reason for doubting that they prove a steady advance in the woollen manufac-

---

[1] Grosvenor. "Does Protection Protect?" p. 147; Introduction to the volume of the "Census of 1860" on Manufactures, p. xxxiii.

ture as a whole.[1] The growth was confined mostly to those branches which used domestic wool; but within these there was not only increase, but development. The methods of manufacture were improved, better machinery was introduced, and new kinds of goods were made.[2] It is a striking fact that the very high protective duties which were imposed during the civil war, and were increased after its close, have not brought the manufacture of woollen cloths to a position substantially different from that which had been attained before 1860. The description of the industry which the spokesman of the Asso-

---

[1] The census figures on the woollen manufacture are :

	Capital. (In million dollars.)	Value of Product.	Hands Employed.
1840	15.7	20.	21,342
1850	26.1	43.5	34,895
1860	30.8	61.9	41,360

The figures for 1850 are exclusive of those relating to blankets ; for 1860 are exclusive of those relating to worsteds.

[2] " Eighteen hundred and fifty saw the success of the Crompton loom at Lowell and Lawrence, on which were made a full line of Scotch plaids in all their beautiful colorings, as well as star twills, half-diamonds. * * * Up to that time fancy cassimeres had been made largely through the Blackstone Valley (in Rhode Island) on the Crompton and Tappet looms, as made by William Crompton. As early as 1846 the Jacquard was used at Woonsocket and Blackstone. From 1850 to 1860 fancy cassimeres made a rapid advance, and the styles ran to extremes far more than they have ever since." Wade's " Fibre and Fabric," as quoted above, p. xlviii.

According to the official "Statistical Information Relating to Certain Branches of Industry in Massachusetts," 1855, at pp. 573–575, woollen goods were made in 1855 in that State as follows :

Broadcloth to the value of	$ 838,000
Cassimeres to the value of	5,015,000
Satinets to the value of	2,709,000
Flannels and blankets to the value of . .	3,126,000
Woollen yarns to the value of	386,000

ciation of Wool Manufacturers gave in 1884 is, in the main, applicable to its state in 1860. "The woollen manufacture of this country * * * is almost wholly absorbed in production for the masses. Nine tenths of our card-wool fabrics are made directly for the ready-made clothing establishments, by means of which most of the laboring people and all the boys are supplied with woollen garments. The manufacture of flannels, blankets, and ordinary knit goods—pure necessaries of life—occupies most of the other mills engaged in working up carded wool."[1]

Some outlying branches of the woollen manufacture, however, showed a striking advance during the period we are considering. The most noteworthy of these is the carpet manufacture, which received a great impetus from the application of newly-invented machinery. The power-loom for weaving ingrain carpets was invented in 1841 by Mr. E. B. Bigelow, and the more complicated loom for weaving Brussels carpets was first perfected by the same inventive genius in 1848.[2] The new machinery at

---

[1] Mr. John L. Hayes, in the "Bulletin of the Association of Wool Manufacturers," vol. xiv., p. 116. Mr. Hayes also states the woollen manufacture to be "capable of producing commodities of the highest luxury,—rich carpets, fine upholsteries, and superfine broadcloths"; but his description of other branches of the industry is similar to that quoted in the text on card-wool goods. "The dress goods manufactured are fabricates almost exclusively for the million, the women of the exclusive and fashionable classes supplying themselves mainly through French importations. The vast carpet manufacture of Philadelphia, larger than in any city of Europe, has its chief occupation in furnishing carpets for the more modest houses."

[2] See the sketch of Mr. Bigelow's career up to 1854, in "Hunt's Merchants Magazine," xxx., pp. 162-170.

once put the manufacture of carpets on a firm basis ; and in its most important branches, the manufacture of ingrain and Brussels carpets, it became independent of aid from protective duties. A similar development took place in the manufacture of woollen hose. The knitting-frame had been invented in England as early as the sixteenth century, but had been worked only by hand. It was first adapted to machinery in the United States in 1831, and was first worked by machinery at Cohoes in New York in 1832. Other inventions followed ; and a prosperous industry developed, which supplied the entire domestic market, and was independent of protective duties.[1] On the other hand, hardly more than a beginning was made before the civil war in the manufacture of worsted goods. In 1860 there were no more than three considerable factories engaged in making worsteds, and the imports largely exceeded the domestic product.[2] Some ex-

---

[1] See the account of the history of the manufacture of knit goods in the "Census of 1860," volume on Manufactures, pp. xxxix.–xlv. Compare the brief sketch by John L. Hayes in his address on "Protection a Boon to Consumers" (Boston, 1867), pp. 9–11. No attempt had been made before 1860, in the United States or elsewhere, to make knit goods of cotton.

[2] See the Introduction to the volume on Manufactures, "Census of 1860," pp. xxxvi.–xxxix.

From the figures of production in the "Census of 1860," and from those of imports in the "Report on Commerce and Navigation" for the fiscal year 1859–60, we have the materials for a comparison of the domestic and the foreign supply of the most important kinds of woollen goods. The figures are :

	Production, 1860.	Imports, 1859–60.
Woollens generally (including flannels, but not blankets, shawls, or yarns)	$43,500,000	$13,350,000
Carpets,	7,860,000	2,200,000
Worsteds	3,700,000	12,300,000

planation of this state of things may be found in the comparatively low duty of 25 per cent. on worsteds under the tariff of 1846. Something was due to the fact that the worsted industry in England not only was long established, but was steadily improving its methods and machinery. But the most important cause, doubtless, was the duty of 30 per cent. on the long-staple combing wool, which then was needed for making worsted goods, and which physical causes have prevented from being grown to any large extent in the United States.

The greatest difference between the woollen industry as it stands to-day and as it stood before 1860 is in the large worsted manufacture of the present, which has grown up almost entirely since the wool and woollens act of 1867. The high duties undoubtedly have been a cause of this development, or at least were so in the beginning; but a further and important cause has been the great improvement in combing machinery, which has rendered it possible to make so-called worsted goods from almost any grade of wool, and has largely done away with the distinction between woollen and worsted goods. The result has been that the worsted makers, as well as the makers of woollens, have been able to use domestic wool; and it is in the production of goods made of such wool that the greatest growth of recent years has taken place.

The tariff act of 1857 reduced the duty on woollens to 24 per cent., but much more than made up for this by admitting wool practically free of duty. Wool costing less than twenty cents at the place of exportation was ad-mitted free, which amounted in effect to the exemption of almost all wool from duty.   Moreover, dyestuffs and other materials were admitted free or at low rates.   The free admission of wool from Canada, under the reciprocity treaty of 1854, had already been in force for three years.[1] The remission of duties on these materials explains the willingness with which the manufacturers in general acceded to the rearrangement of rates in 1857.   In 1860, when the beginnings were made in re-imposing higher protective duties, it was admitted that no demand for such a change came from manufacturers.[2]   The only exception was in the case of the iron-makers of Pennsylvania, who did not share in the benefits of the free list,

---

[1] Large quantities of combing wool were imported from Canada under the reciprocity treaty, and were used in making worsteds and carpets. In 1866, when the treaty was terminated, and high duties had been imposed on wool in general, the manufacturers pleaded hard for the continued free admission of Canada wool, though they were active in securing the general high duties of 1867 on wool and woollens.   But they did not succeed in getting the Canada wools free.   See the "Statement of Facts Relative to Canada Wools and the Manufacture of Worsteds," made by the National Association of Wool Manufacturers, Boston, 1866.

[2] Senator Hunter, who had been most active in bringing about the passage of the act of 1857, said, during the debate on the Morrill bill of 1860. "Have any of the manufacturers come here to complain or to ask for new duties?   If they have, I am not aware of it, with the exception, perhaps, of a petition or two presented early in the session by the Senator from Connecticut.   Is it not notorious that if we were to leave it to the manufacturers of New England themselves, to the manufacturers of hardware, textile fabrics, etc., there would be a large majority against any change?   Do we not know that the woollen manufacture dates its revival from the tariff of 1857, which altered the duties on wool?"   "Congressional Globe," 1859-60, p. 301.   Cp. the note to p. 160, below.

and who opposed the reduction of 1857. So far as the manufacture of woollen goods was concerned, the changes of 1857, as might have been expected, served to stimulate the industry; and it grew and prospered during the years immediately preceding the civil war. A remission of duty on materials obviously operates in the first instance mainly to the advantage of producers and middle-men, and brings benefit to consumers only by a more or less gradual process. The experiment of free wool, with a moderate duty on woollens, was not tried long enough to make certain what would be its final results. It is not impossible that, as is often asserted by the opponents of duties on wool, the free admission of that material would have led in time to a more varied development of the woollen manufacture. On the other hand, it may be, in the case of woollens as in that of cottons, that the conditions in the United States are less favorable for making the finer qualities than for making those cheaper qualities to which the application of machinery is possible in greater degree, and for which, at the same time, the domestic wool is an excellent material. The test of experience under conditions of freedom could alone decide what are the real causes of the comparatively limited range of both of the great textile industries; but it is not improbable that general causes like those just mentioned, rather than the hampering of the supply of wool, account for the condition of the woollen manufacture. However that may be, it seems certain that the practical remission of duty in 1857, whether or no it would in the long run have caused a wide development of the woollen manufacture, gave it for the time being a distinct stimulus; it seems to have had but little, if any, effect on the prices of domestic wool[1]; and it must have tended at the least to cheapen for the consumer goods made in whole or in part of foreign wool.

It would be possible to extend this inquiry farther,[2] but enough has been said for the present purpose. In the main, the changes in duties have had much less effect on the protected industries than is generally supposed. Their growth has been steady and continuous, and seems to have been little stimulated by the high duties of 1842, and little checked by the more moderate duties of 1846 and 1857. Probably the duties of the last-mentioned years, while on their face protective duties, did not have in any important degree the effect of stimulating indus-

---

[1] The price per pound of medium wool, averaged from quarterly quotations, was :

		cts.			cts.
In 1852	. .	38½	In 1856	. .	45
" 1853	. .	53	" 1857	. .	46
" 1854	. .	42½	" 1858	. .	36
" 1855	. .	38	" 1859	. .	47
			" 1860	. .	47½

The prices of other grades moved similarly. The panic of 1857 caused a fall in 1858, but in the following year the old level was recovered. The figures are based on the tables of wool prices in the Bureau of Statistics' "Report on Wool and Manufactures of Wool," 1887, p. 109. The movement of wool prices abroad during these years seems to have been about the same.

[2] In the Introduction to the volume on Manufactures of the "Census of 1860," to which reference has been made before, there is a useful sketch of the history of various branches of manufacture up to that date.

tries that could not have maintained themselves under freedom of trade. They did not operate as strictly protective duties, and did not bring that extra tax on consumers which is the peculiar effect of protective duties. The only industry which presents a marked exception to these general conditions is the manufacture of the cruder forms of iron. In that industry, the conditions of production in the eastern part of the United States were such that the protective duties of 1842 caused a return to old processes, and an enhanced price to the country without a corresponding gain to producers. Even under the rates of 1846 and after the use of anthracite coal, the same effect can be seen, though in less degree.

We often hear it said that any considerable reduction from the scale of duties in the present tariff, whose character and history will be considered in the following pages, would bring about the disappearance of manufacturing industries, or at least a disastrous check to their development. But the experience of the period before 1860 shows that predictions of this sort have little warrant. At present, as before 1860, the great textile manufactures are not dependent to any great extent on protective duties of the kind now imposed. The direction of their growth has been somewhat affected by these duties, yet in a less degree than might have been expected. It is striking that both under the system of high protection which has been maintained since the civil war, and under the more moderate system that preceded it, the cotton and woollen industries have been kept in the main to those goods of common use and large consumption to which the conditions of the United States might be expected to lead them. Very heavy duties have indeed stimulated the manufacture of more expensive goods; and the gradual change in the general economic situation must in any case have had some effect in making the textile industries more diversified. The iron manufacture has advanced by leaps and bounds, chiefly through the development of great natural resources in the heart of the country—hardly touched during the period here under discussion. But even during this period it held its own. Manufactures in general grew and flourished. The extent to which mechanical branches of production have been brought into existence by the protective system has been greatly exaggerated by its advocates; and even the character and direction of their development have been influenced less than, on grounds of general reasoning, might have been expected.

PART II.

TARIFF LEGISLATION, 1861–1909.

———

CHAPTER I.

THE WAR TARIFF.

THE Civil War revolutionized the financial methods of the United States. A new monetary system was created, and tax resources before undreamed of were resorted to at first timorously, in the end with a rigor that hardly knew bounds. The tariff, which had long been the sole source of federal income, was supplemented by a series of extraordinary internal taxes, and was itself called on to yield more revenue and still more. The high duties which the war thus caused to be imposed, at first regarded as temporary, were retained, increased, and systematized, so developing gradually into a system of extreme protection. For many years the tariff was spoken of, and accurately, as " the war tariff,"—a name which faded out of use as the community became accustomed to the new régime, and forgot the various half-hearted and unsuccessful endeavors which were made from time to time toward reduction and reform.

Before the war we had a tariff of duties which, though
not arranged completely or consistently on the
principles of free trade, was yet very moderate
in comparison with the existing system. For
about fifteen years before the Rebellion began, duties
on imports were fixed by the acts of 1846 and 1857.
The act of 1846 had been pássed by the Democratic
party with the avowed intention of putting into operation, as far as was possible, the principles of free
trade. This intention, it is true, was by no means carried out consistently. Purely revenue articles, like tea
and coffee, were admitted free of duty; and on the other
hand, articles like iron and manufactures of iron, paper,
glass, wool, and woollen goods,—in fact most of the important articles with which the protective controversy has
been concerned,—were charged with a duty of thirty per
cent.[1] Other articles again, like steel, copper, lead, were
admitted at a lower duty than this, not for any reasons of
revenue, but because they were not then produced to any
extent within the country, and because protection for
them in consequence was not asked. Protection was by
no means absent from the act of 1846; and the rate of
thirty per cent., which it imposed on the leading articles,
gave no small degree of protection. Nevertheless, the tariff
of 1846 was, in comparison with later tariffs, a moderate
measure; and a return to its rates would have been
considered a great step of reform by those who were op-

The tariff before the war.

---

[1] *Cf.* p. 114, above.

posed to protective duties. The act of 1857 took away still more from the restrictive character of our tariff legislation. Congress, it may be remarked, acted in 1857 with reasonable soberness and impartiality, and without being influenced by political considerations. The maximum protective duty was reduced to twenty-four per cent.; many raw materials were admitted free; and the level of duties on the whole line of manufactured articles was brought down to the lowest point which has been reached in this country since 1815. It is not likely we shall see, for a great many years to come, a nearer approach to the free-trade ideal.

The country accepted the tariff acts of 1846 and 1857, and was satisfied with them. Except in the years immediately following the passage of the former act, when there was some attempt to induce a return to a more rigid protective system, agitation on the tariff ceased almost entirely. There is no doubt that the period from 1846 to 1860 was a time of great material prosperity, interrupted, but not checked, by the crisis of 1857. It would be going too far to assert that this general prosperity was due chiefly to the liberal character of the tariff. Other causes exercised a great and perhaps a predominant influence. But the moderate tariff presumably was one of the elements that contributed to the general welfare. It may be well to add that prosperity was not confined to any part of the country, or to any branches of industry. Manufactures in general continued to flourish; and the reduction of duties which was made in 1857 had the consent and approbation of the main body of the manufacturing class.

The crisis of 1857 had caused a falling off in the revenue from duties. This was made the occasion for a reaction from the liberal policy of 1846 and 1857. In 1861 the Morrill tariff act began a change toward a higher range of duties and a stronger application of protection. The Morrill act is often spoken of as if it were the basis of the present protective system But this is by no means the case. The tariff act of 1861 was passed by the House of Representatives in the session of 1859–60, the session preceding the election of President Lincoln. It was passed, undoubtedly, with the intention of attracting to the Republican party, at the approaching Presidential election, votes in Pennsylvania and other States that had protectionist leanings. In the Senate the tariff bill was not taken up in the same session in which it was passed in the House. Its consideration was postponed, and it was not until the next session—that of 1860–61—that it received the assent of the Senate and became law. It is clear that the Morrill tariff was carried in the House before any serious expectation of war was entertained; and it was accepted by the Senate in the session of 1861 without material change. It therefore forms no part of the financial legislation of the war, which gave rise in time to a series of measures that entirely superseded the Morrill tariff. Indeed, Mr. Morrill and the other supporters of the act of 1861 declared that their intention was simply to restore the rates of 1846. The important change which they proposed to make from the provisions of the tariff of 1846 was to substitute specific for *ad-valorem* duties. Such a change from *ad-valorem* to specific duties is in itself by no means objectionable; but it has usually been made a pretext on the part of protectionists for a considerable increase in the actual duties paid. When protectionists make a change of this kind, they almost invariably make the specific duties higher than the *ad-valorem* duties for which they are supposed to be an equivalent,—a circumstance which has given rise to the common notion, of course unfounded, that there is some essential connection between free trade and *ad-valorem* duties on the one hand, and between protection and specific duties on the other hand. The Morrill tariff formed no exception to the usual course of things in this respect. The specific duties which it established were in many cases considerably above the *ad-valorem* duties of 1846. The most important direct changes made by the act of 1861 were in the increased duties on iron and on wool, by which it was hoped to attach to the Republican party Pennsylvania and some of the Western States. Most of the manufacturing States at this time still stood aloof from the movement toward higher rates.[1]

---

[1] Mr. Rice, of Massachusetts, said in 1860 : " The manufacturer asks no additional protection. He has learned, among other things, that the great-

Hardly had the Morrill tariff act been passed when Fort Sumter was fired on. The Civil War began. The need of additional revenue for carrying on the great struggle was immediately felt; and as early as the extra session of the summer of 1861, additional customs duties were imposed. In the next regular session, in December, 1861, a still further increase of duties was made. From that time till 1865 no session, indeed, hardly a month of any session, passed in which some increase of duties on imports was not made. During the four years of the war every resource was strained for carrying on the great struggle. Probably no country has seen, in so short a time, so extraordinary a mass of financial legislation. A huge national debt was accumulated; the mischievous expedient of an inconvertible paper currency was resorted to; a national banking system unexpectedly arose from the confusion; an enormous system of internal taxation was created; the duties on imports were vastly increased and extended. We are concerned here only with the change in the tariff; yet it must be borne in mind that

---

est evil, next to a ruinous competition from foreign sources, is an excessive protection, which stimulates a like ruinous and irresponsible competition at home,"—*Congress. Globe,* 1859–60, p. 1867. Mr. Sherman said: "When Mr. Stanton says the manufacturers are urging and pressing this bill, he says what he must certainly know is not correct. The manufacturers have asked over and over again to be let alone. The tariff of 1857 is the manufacturers' bill; but the present bill is more beneficial to the agricultural interest than the tariff of 1857."—*Ibid.,* p. 2053. *Cf.* Hunter's Speech, *Ibid.,* p. 3010. In later years Mr. Morrill himself said that the tariff of 1861 "was not asked for, and but coldly welcomed, by manufacturers, who always and justly fear instability."—*Congr. Globe,* 1869–70, p. 3295.

these changes were only a part of the great financial measures which the war called out. Indeed, it is impossible to
understand the meaning of the changes which were made
in the tariff without a knowledge of the other legislation
that accompanied it, and more especially of the extended
system of internal taxation which was adopted at the
same time. To go through the various acts for levying
internal taxes and imposing duties on imports is not necessary in order to make clear the character and bearing of
the legislation of the war. It will be enough to describe
those that are typical and important. The great acts of
1862 and 1864 are typical of the whole course of the war
measures; and the latter is of particular importance,
because it became the foundation of the existing tariff
system.

It was not until 1862 that the country began to appreciate how great must be the efforts necessary to suppress
the Rebellion, and that Congress set to work in earnest to
provide the means for that purpose. Even in 1862 Congress relied more on selling bonds and on issuing paper
money than on immediate taxation. But
two vigorous measures were resorted to for
taxing the people immediately and directly.
The first of these was the internal revenue act of
July 1, 1862. This established a comprehensive system
of excise taxation. Specific taxes were imposed on
the production of iron and steel, coal-oil, paper, leather,
and other articles. A general *ad-valorem* tax was

imposed on other manufactures. In addition, licenses were required in many callings. A general income tax was imposed. Railroad companies, steamboats, express companies were made to pay taxes on their gross receipts. Those who have grown to manhood since the great struggle closed find it difficult to imagine the existence and to appreciate the burden of this heavy and vexatious mass of taxation; for it was entirely swept away within a few years after the end of the war.

The second great measure of taxation to which Congress turned at this time was the tariff act of July 14, 1862. The object of this act, as was stated by Messrs. Morrill and Stevens, who had charge of its passage in the House, was primarily to increase duties only to such an extent as might be necessary in order to offset the internal taxes of the act of July 1st.[1] But although this was the chief object of the act, protective intentions were entertained by those who framed it, and were carried out. Both Messrs. Morrill and Stevens were avowed protectionists, and did not conceal that they meant in many cases to help the home producer. The increase of duties on articles which were made in this country was therefore,

---

[1] Mr. Morrill said, in his speech introducing the tariff bill : " It will be indispensable for us to revise the tariff on foreign imports, so far as it may be seriously disturbed by any internal duties, and to make proper reparation. * * * If we bleed manufacturers, we must see to it that the proper tonic is administered at the same time."—Congr. Globe, 1861–62, p. 1196. Similarly Mr. Stevens said : " We intended to impose an additional duty on imports equal to the tax which had been put on the domestic articles. It was done by way of compensation to domestic manufacturers against foreign importers."—Ibid., p. 2979.

in all cases, at least sufficient to afford the domestic producers compensation for the internal taxes which they had
to pay.   In many cases it was more than sufficient for this
purpose, and brought about a distinct increase of protection.   Had not the internal revenue act been passed,
affording a good reason for some increase of duties; had
not the higher taxation of purely revenue articles, like
tea and coffee, been a justifiable and necessary expedient
for increasing the government income; had not the
increase even of protective duties been quite defensible as
a temporary means for the same end; had not the general
feeling been in favor of vigorous measures for raising the
revenue;—had these conditions not existed, it would have
been very difficult to carry through Congress a measure
like the tariff of 1862.   But, as matters stood, the tariff
was easily passed.   Under cover of the need of revenue
and of the intention to prevent domestic producers from
being unfairly handicapped by the internal taxes, a clear
increase of protection was in many cases brought about.

The war went on; still more revenue was needed.
Gradually Congress became convinced of the necessity of
resorting to still heavier taxation, and of the willingness
of the country to pay all that was necessary to maintain
the Union.   Passing over less important acts, we have to
consider the great measure that was the climax of the
financial legislation of the war.   The three revenue acts
of June 30, 1864, practically form one measure, and that
probably the greatest measure of taxation which the

world has seen. The first of the acts provided for an enormous extension of the internal-tax system; the second for a corresponding increase of the duties on imports; the third authorized a loan of $400,000,000.

The internal revenue act was arranged, as Mr. David A. Wells has said, on the principle of the Irishman at Donnybrook fair; "Whenever you see a head, hit it; whenever you see a commodity, tax it." Every thing was taxed, and taxed heavily. Every ton of pig-iron produced was charged two dollars; every ton of railroad iron three dollars; sugar paid two cents a pound; salt, six cents a hundred-weight. The general tax on all manufactures produced was five per cent. But this tax was repeated on almost every article in different stages of production. Raw cotton, for instance, was taxed two cents a pound; as cloth, it again paid five per cent. Mr. Wells estimated that the government in fact collected between eight and fifteen per cent. on every finished product. Taxes on the gross receipts of railroad, steamboat, telegraph, express, and insurance companies were levied, or were increased where already in existence. The license-tax system was extended to almost every conceivable branch of trade. The income tax was raised to five per cent. on moderate incomes, and to ten per cent. on incomes of more than $10,000.

Internal revenue act, 1864.

Tariff act of 1864. The tariff act of 1864, passed at the same time with the internal revenue act, also brought about a great increase in the rates of taxation. Like the tariff ac of 1862, that of 1864 was introduced, explained, amended, and passed under the management of Mr. Morrill, who was Chairman of the Committee on Ways and Means. That gentleman again stated, as he had done in 1862, that the passage of the tariff act was rendered necessary in order to put domestic producers in the same situation, so far as foreign competition was concerned, as if the internal taxes had not been raised. This was one great object of the new tariff ; and it may have been a good reason for bring ing forward some measure of the kind. But it explains only in part the measure which in fact was proposed and passed. In 1864 the men who were in charge of the national finances were as prompt in taxing heavily as in 1861 they had been slow in taxing at all. Under the pressure of almost unlimited financial need, and with the conviction that a supreme effort was called for, they were willing to tax every possible article at the highest rate that any one had the courage to suggest. They carried this method out to its fullest extent in the tariff act of 1864, as well as in the tax act of that year. At the same time these statesmen were pro tectionists, and did not attempt to conceal their protec tionist leanings. What between their willingness to make every tax and duty as high as possible for the sake of raising revenue, and their belief that high import duties were beneficial to the country, the protectionists had an opportunity such as the country has never before given them. It would be unfair to say that Mr. Morrill, Mr.

Stevens, and the other gentlemen who shaped the revenue laws, consciously used the urgent need of money for the war as a means of carrying out their protectionist theories, or of promoting, through high duties, private ends for themselves or others. But it is certain that their method of treating the revenue problems resulted in a most unexpected and extravagant application of protection, and moreover, made possible a subservience of the public needs to the private gains of individuals such as unfortunately made its appearance in many other branches of the war administration. There was neither time nor disposition to inquire critically into the meaning and effect of any proposed scheme of rates. The easiest and quickest plan was to impose the duties which the domestic producers suggested as necessary for their protection. Not only during the war, but for several years after it, all feeling of opposition to high import duties almost entirely disappeared. The habit of putting on as high rates as any one asked had become so strong that it could hardly be shaken off; and even after the war, almost any increase of duties demanded by domestic producers was readily made. The war had in many ways a bracing and ennobling influence on our national life; but its immediate effect on business affairs, and on all legislation affecting moneyed interests, was demoralizing. The line between public duty and private interests was often lost sight of by legislators. Great fortunes were made by changes in legislation urged and brought about by those who were benefited by them; and the country has seen with sorrow that the honor and honesty of public men did not remain undefiled. The tariff, like other legislation on matters of finance, was affected by these causes. Schemes for money-making were incorporated in it, and were hardly questioned by Congress. When more enlightened and unselfish views began to make their way, and protests were made against the abuses and excessive duties of the war period, these had obtained, as we shall see, too strong a hold to be easily shaken off.

Such were the conditions under which the tariff act of 1864 was passed. As in 1862, three causes were at work: in the first place, the urgent need of revenue for the war; in the next, the wish to offset the internal taxes imposed on domestic producers; and finally, the protectionist leanings of those who managed our financial legislation. These causes made possible a tariff act which in ordinary times would have been summarily rejected. It raised duties greatly and indiscriminately,—so much so, that the average rate on dutiable commodities, which had been 37.2 per cent. under the act of 1862, became 47.06 per cent. under that of 1864. It was in many ways crude and ill-considered; it established protective duties more extreme than had been ventured on in any previous tariff act in our country's history; it contained flagrant abuses, in the shape of duties whose chief effect was to bring money into the pockets of private individuals.

Nothing more clearly illustrates the character of this

piece of legislation, and the circumstances which made its enactment a possibility, than the public history of its passage through Congress. The bill was introduced into the House on June 2d by Mr. Morrill. General debate on it was stopped after one day. The House then proceeded to the consideration of amendments. Almost without exception amendments offered by Mr. Morrill were adopted, and all others were rejected. After two days had been given in this way to the amendments, the House, on June 4th, passed the bill. In the Senate much the same course was followed. The consideration of the bill began on June 16th; it was passed on the following day. That is to say, five days in all were given by the two houses to this act, which was in its effects one of the most important financial measures ever passed in the United States. The bill was accepted as it came from the Committee on Ways and Means, and was passed practically without debate or examination.

This haste was the natural result of the critical stage of affairs and the urgent need of revenue. As in other parts of the legislation of the war period, the recommendations of the Administration and of the party leaders were acted on promptly and with the minimum of debate. Obviously, it was not intended or expected that measures so enacted should become the foundation of a permanent economic policy. Yet in several directions this proved to be the result, and in none more strikingly than in the final outcome of the tariff changes. The legal-tender paper, resorted to as a war measure more distinctly than any other, was retained, it is true; but at least specie payments were resumed, even though after an interval unexpectedly long, and the greatest evils of inconvertible money were done away with. The national-banking system, from the first more clearly designed to be a permanent institution, was also retained, though with changes and vicissitudes not dreamed of at the time of its foundation. The national debt was reduced at a rate unexampled in history. Most of the internal taxes were repealed as fast as possible, leaving only those on spirits and tobacco as permanent parts of the federal fiscal system. The tariff was changed least of all. Some significant modifications in the revenue duties were indeed made, as will be pointed out in the following chapters. But on almost all the articles with which the protective controversy is concerned the rates of the act of 1864 were retained, virtually without change, for twenty years or more; and when changes were finally made, they were undertaken as if these rates were not in any sense exceptional, but were the normal results of an established policy.

The identical duties fixed in 1864 were left in force for a long series of years.[1] When a general revision came to

---

[1] It should be stated that the act of 1864 was not in form a general act, repealing all previous statutes. It left in force, for instance, all provisions of the Morrill tariff of 1861 and of the act of 1862, not specifically affected by its provisions. But it changed so generally the range of import duties, and especially the protective duties, that it had practically the effect of a new general tariff act.

be made, in 1883, they had ceased to be thought of as the results of war legislation. The public, and especially the protected industries, had come to think of them as parts of a permanent policy. Thus habituated to high duties, it was not a difficult step for Congress, under the stress of political contention, to proceed to duties still higher. Hence the war tariff, though from time to time patched, amended, revised, not only remained in force in its important provisions for nearly twenty years, but became in time the basis for an even more stringent application of protection. The steps by which this unexpected transformation in the customs policy of the United States was brought about will be followed in the ensuing chapters.

CHAPTER II.

THE FAILURE TO REDUCE THE TARIFF AFTER THE WAR.

WHEN the war closed, the revenue acts which had been hastily passed during its course constituted a chaotic mass. Congress and the Secretary of the Treasury immediately set to work to bring some order into this chaos, by funding and consolidating the debt, by contracting the paper currency, and by reforming and reducing the internal taxes.[1] The years between 1865 and 1870 are full of discussions and enactments on taxation and finance. On some parts of the financial system, in regard to which there was little disagreement, action was prompt and salutary. The complicated mass of internal taxes was felt to be an evil by all. It bore heavily and vexatiously on the people ; and Congress proceeded to sweep it away with all possible speed. As soon as the immense floating debt had been funded, and the extent of the

[1] Those who wish to get some knowledge of the confused character of the financial legislation called out by the war, are referred to Mr. David A. Wells's excellent essay on "The Recent Financial Experiences of the United States" (1872). Those who wish to study more in detail the course of events after the war should read Mr. Wells's reports as Commissioner of the Revenue, of 1867, 1868, 1869, and 1870.

annual needs of the government became somewhat clear, Congress set to work at repealing and modifying the excise laws. It is not necessary to enumerate the various steps

Abolition of the internal taxes 1866–1872.

by which the internal-tax system was modified. Year after year acts for reducing and abolishing internal taxes were passed. By 1872 all those which had any connection with the subject of our investigation—the protective duties—had disappeared.[1] The taxes on spirits and beer, those on banks, and a few comparatively unimportant taxes on matches, patent medicines, and other articles were retained. But all those taxes which bore heavily on the productive resources of the country—those taxes in compensation for which higher duties had been imposed in 1862 and 1864—were entirely abolished.

Step by step with this removal of the internal taxes, a reduction of import duties should have taken place; at the least, a reduction which would have taken off those additional duties that had been put on in order to offset the internal taxes. This, however, Congress hesitated to undertake. We have seen in the preceding chapter that the opportunity given by the war system of taxation was seized by the protectionists in order to carry out their wishes. It would not be easy to say whether at the time the public men who carried out this legislation meant the new system of import duties to be permanent. Certainly the war methods of finance as a whole were not meant to

---

[1] The most important acts for reducing the internal taxes were those of July 11, 1866; March 2, 1867; March 31, 1868; July 14, 1870; June 6, 1872.

remain in force for an unlimited time. Some parts of the tariff were beyond doubt intended to be merely temporary ; and the reasonable expectation was that the protective duties would sooner or later be overhauled and reduced. Had the question been directly put to almost any public man, whether the tariff system of the war was to be continued, the answer would certainly have been in the negative,—that in due time the import duties were to be lowered.[1] During the years of confusion immediately after the war little was attempted ; but soon a disposition to affect some reform in the incongruous mass of duties began to be shown. Each year schemes for reduction and reform were brought forward. Commissions were appointed, bills were elaborated and considered ; but the reform was put off from year to year. The pressure from the interested domestic producers was strong ; the power of the lobby was great ; the overshadowing problem of reconstruction absorbed the energies of Congress. Gradu-

---

[1] As late as 1870, Mr. Morrill said : " For revenue purposes, and not solely for protection, fifty per cent. in many instances has been added to the tariff [during the war] to enable our home trade to bear the new but indispensable burdens of internal taxation. Already we have relinquished most of such taxes. So far, then, as protection is concerned * * * we might safely remit a percentage of the tariff on a considerable share of our foreign importations. * * * *It is a mistake of the friends of a sound tariff to insist on the extreme rates imposed during the war*, if less will raise the necessary revenue. * * * Whatever percentage of duties was imposed on foreign goods to cover internal taxation on home manufactures, should not now be claimed as the lawful prize of protection, when such taxes have been repealed. There is no longer an equivalent."—*Congress. Globe*, 1869–70, p. 3295. These passages occur at the end of a long speech in favor of the principle of protection.

ally, as the organization of industry in the country adapted itself more closely to the tariff as it was, the feeling that no reform was needed obtained a strong hold. Many industries had grown up, or had been greatly extended, under the influence of the war legislation. As that legislation continued unchanged, still more capital was embarked in establishments whose existence or prosperity was in some degree dependent on its maintenance. All who were connected with establishments of this kind asserted that they would be ruined by any change. The business world in general tends to be favorable to the maintenance of things as they are. The country at large, and especially those parts of it in which the protected industries were concentrated, began to look on the existing state of things as permanent. The extreme protective system, which had been at the first a temporary expedient for aiding in the struggle for the Union, adopted hastily and without any thought of deliberation, gradually became accepted as a permanent institution. From this it was a short step, in order to explain and justify the existing state of things, to set up high protection as a theory and a dogma. The restraint of trade with foreign countries, by means of import duties of forty, fifty, sixty, even a hundred per cent., came to be advocated as a good thing in itself by many who, under normal circumstances, would have thought such a policy preposterous. Ideas of this kind were no longer the exploded errors of a small school of economists; they became the foundation of the policy of a great people. Then the mass of restrictive legislation which had been hurriedly piled up during the war, was strengthened and completed, and made into a firm and consistent edifice. On purely revenue articles, such as are not produced at all in the country, the duties were almost entirely abolished. A few raw materials, it is true, were admitted at low rates, or entirely free of duty. But these were exceptions, made apparently by accident. As a rule, the duties on articles produced in the country, that is, the protective duties, were retained at the war figures, or raised above them. The result was that the tariff gradually became exclusively and distinctly a protective measure ; it included almost all the protective duties put on during the war, added many more to them, and no longer contained the purely revenue duties of the war.

We turn now to a somewhat more detailed account of the process by which the reform of the tariff was prevented. To give a complete account of the various tariff acts which were passed, or of the tariff bills which were pressed without success, is needless. Every session of Congress had its array of tariff acts and tariff bills ; and we may content ourselves with an account of those which are typical of the general course of events. Of the attempts at reform which were made in the years immediately after the war, the fate of the tariff *Unsuccessful* bills of 1867 is characteristic. Two proposals *tariff bill* were then before Congress: one a bill passed *of 1867.* by the House at the previous session ; the other a bill

prepared by Mr. David A. Wells, then Special Commissioner of the Revenue, and heartily approved by
Secretary McCulloch. The great rise in prices and in
money wages in these years, and the industrial embarrassment which followed the war, had caused a demand
for still higher import duties; the House bill had been
framed to answer this demand, and proposed a general
increase.   Mr. Wells recommended a different policy
He had not then become convinced of the truth of the
principles of free trade ; but he had clearly seen that the
indiscriminate protection which the war tariff gave, and
which the House bill proposed to augment, could not be
beneficial.   His bill reduced duties on raw materials, such
as scrap-iron, coal, lumber, hemp, and flax ; and it either
maintained without change or slightly lowered the duties
on most manufactured articles.   A careful rearrangement
was at the same time made in the rates on spices, chemicals, dyes, and dye-woods,—articles of which a careful
and detailed examination is necessary for the determination of duties, and in regard to which the tariff contained
then, as it does now, much that was arbitrary and indefensible.   Mr. Wells's bill, making these reforms, gained
the day over the less liberal House bill.   It was passed by
the Senate, as an amendment to the House bill, by a large
majority (27 to 10).   In the House there was also a majority in its favor; but unfortunately a two-thirds majority was necessary in order to suspend the rules and bring
it before the House.   The vote was 106 to 64 in favor of

the bill; the two-thirds majority was not obtained, and it failed to become law. The result was not only that no general tariff bill was passed at this session, but the course of tariff reform for the future received a regrettable check. Had Mr. Wells's proposals been enacted, it is not unlikely that the events of the next few years would have been very different from what in fact they were. It would be too much to say that these proposals looked forward to still further steps in the way of moderating the protective system, or that their favorable reception showed any distinct tendency against protection. There was at that time no free-trade feeling at all, and Mr. Wells's bill was simply a reform measure from the protectionist point of view. But the vote on it is nevertheless significant of the fact that the extreme and uncompromising protective spirit was not then all-powerful. The bill, it is true, had been modified in a protectionist direction in various ways before it came to be voted on; but the essential reductions and reforms were still contained in it and the votes show that the protectionist feeling was far from being solidified at that time to the extent that it came to be a few years later. Had the bill of 1867 been passed, the character of recent tariff legislation might have been very different. A beginning would have been made in looking at the tariff from a sober point of view, and in reducing duties that were clearly pernicious. The growing habit of looking on the war rates as a permanent system might have been checked, and the attempts at tariff reform in subsequent years would probably have found stronger support and met with less successful opposition. From this time till the tariff act of 1883 was passed, there was no general tariff bill which had so good a chance of being passed. The failure of the attempt of 1867 encouraged the protectionists in fighting for the retention of the war duties wherever they could not secure an increase over and above them ; and in this contest they were, with few exceptions, successful.[1]

Of the legislation that was in fact carried out, the act of Act of 1870. 1870 is a fair example. It was passed in compliance with the demand for a reduction of taxes and for tariff reform, which was at that time especially strong in the West, and was there made alike by Republicans and Democrats.[2] The declared intention of those who framed it and

---

[1] Mr. Wells's bill and the rates proposed in the House bill may be found in his report for 1866-67, pp. 235-290. The principle of "enlightened protection" on which he proceeded is stated on p. 34. At this time Mr. Wells was still a protectionist ; it was not until he prepared his report for 1868-69 that he showed himself fully convinced of the unsoundness of the theory of protection. His able investigations and the matter-of-fact tone of all of his reports gave much weight to his change of opinion, and caused it to strengthen greatly the public feeling in favor of tariff reform.

[2] President Garfield (then Representative) said in 1870 : "After studying the whole subject as carefully as I am able, I am firmly of the opinion that the wisest thing that the protectionists in this House can do is to unite on a moderate reduction of duties on imported articles. * * * If I do not misunderstand the signs of the times, unless we do this ourselves, prudently and wisely, we shall before long be compelled to submit to a violent reduction, made rudely and without discrimination, which will shock, if not shatter, all our protected industries."—Young's Report, p. clxxii. It is worthy of remark that Mr. Garfield had also supported earnestly the unsuccessful bill of 1867. He had appealed to his party to vote so as to make up the two-thirds majority necessary for its consideration, telling them that later

had charge of it in Congress was to reduce taxation. But the reductions made by it were, almost without exception, on purely revenue articles. The duties on tea, coffee, wines sugar, molasses, and spices were lowered. Other articles of the same kind were put on the free list. The only noteworthy reduction in the protective parts of the tariff was in the duty on pig-iron, which went down from $9.00 to $7.00 a ton. On the other hand, a very considerable increase of duties was made on a number of protected articles—on steel rails, on marble, on nickel, and on other articles.[1] We shall have occasion to refer to some of these indefensible exactions in another connection.[2] At present we are concerned only with the reductions of duty which were carried out. Among the protective duties the lowering of that on pig-iron was the only one of importance. This change, indeed, might well have been made at an earlier date, for the internal tax of $2.00 on pig-iron (in compensation for which the tariff rate had been raised to $9.00 in 1864) had been taken off as early as 1866.[3]

The only effort to reform the protective parts of the tariff which had any degree of success, was made in

---

they might "make up their record" by voting against it.—*Congr. Globe*, 1866-67, pp. 1657, 1658.

[1] An increase in the duties on bar-iron was also proposed in the bill as reported by the Committee on Ways and Means; but this, fortunately, was more than could be carried through. See the speeches of Messrs. Brooks (*Congr. Globe*, 1869-70, part 7, appendix, pp. 163-167) and Allison (*ibid.*, p. 192 *et seq.*), which protest against the sham reductions of the bill.

[2] See chapter iii.

[3] See the list of reductions made by the act of 1870 in Young's Report, p. clxxvii.

1872. The tactics of the protectionists in that year illustrate strikingly the manner in which attempts at tariff reform have been frustrated; and the history of the attempt is, from this point of view, so instructive that it may be told somewhat in detail. The situation

Situation in in 1872 was in many ways favorable for tariff
1872. reform. The idea of tax and tariff reform was familiar to the people at large. It was not as yet openly pretended that the protective duties were to remain indefinitely as they had been fixed in the war. The act of 1870 had made a concession by the reduction on pig-iron; further changes of the same kind were expected to follow. Moreover, the feeling in favor of tariff reform was in all these years particularly strong in the West. So strong was it that, as has already been noted, it overrode party differences, and made almost all the Western Congressmen, whether Democrats or Republicans, act in favor of reductions in the tariff. The cause of this state of things is to be found in the economic condition of the country from the end of the war till after the panic of 1873. The prices of manufactured goods were then high, and imports were large. On the other hand, exports were comparatively small and the prices of grain and provisions low. The agricultural population was far from prosperous. The granger movement, and the agitation against the railroads, were one result of the depressed condition of the farmers. Another result was the strong feeling against the tariff, which the farmers

rightly believed to be among the causes of the state of things under which they were suffering.[1] Their representatives in Congress were therefore compelled to take a stand in favor of lowering the protective duties. The Western members being nearly all agreed on this subject, Congress contained a clear majority in favor of a reform in the tariff. Party lines at that time had little influence on the protective controversy, and, although both houses were strongly Republican, a strong disposition showed itself in both in favor of measures for lowering the protective duties.

Added to all this, the state of the finances demanded immediate attention. In 1872, as later in 1883 and in 1890, a redundant revenue compelled Congress to take action of some sort on the tariff as the chief source of federal income. In each of the fiscal years 1870–71 and 1871–72, the surplus revenue, after paying all appropriations and all interest on the public debt, amounted to about $100,000,000, a sum greatly in excess of any requirements of the sinking fund. The government was buying bonds in the open market in order to dispose of the money that was flowing into the treasury vaults.[2]

---

[1] No satisfactory investigation of the period preceding the crisis of 1873 has yet been made. Of the fact that the situation was especially depressing for the agricultural parts of the country, there can be no doubt. The speculative mania and the fictitious prosperity of those years were felt most strikingly in manufactures and railroad building ; exactly why so little effect of this appeared in agriculture has never been clearly explained. The whole period will repay careful economic study.

[2] On account of the low premium on bonds and the high premium on gold,

This being the state of affairs, the Committee on Ways and Means introduced into the House a bill which took decided steps in the direction of tariff
Reform bill in the House.
reform. Mr. Dawes, of Massachusetts, the chairman of the committee, was opposed to the recommendations of the majority of its members, and therefore left the explanation and management of the bill to Mr. Finkelnburg, of Missouri. That gentleman explained that the committee's measure was intended merely to "divest some industries of the superabundant protection which smells of monopoly, and which it was never intended they should enjoy after the war." [1] The bill lopped off something from the protective duties in almost all directions. Pig-iron was to be charged $6.00 instead of $7.00 a ton. The duties on wool and woollens, and those on cottons, were to be reduced by about twenty per cent. Coal, salt, and lumber were subjected to lower duties. Tea and coffee were also to pay less; but the duties on them were not entirely abolished,—a circumstance which it is important to note in connection with subsequent events. The bill still left an ample measure of protection subsisting; but it was clearly intended to bring about an appreciable and permanent reduction of the war duties.

This bill was introduced into the House in April. Before that time another bill had been introduced in the

---

it was cheaper for the government at that time to buy bonds in the open market than to redeem them at par.

[1] See Mr. Finkelnburg's speech, *Congr. Globe*, 1871–72, pp. 2826–?

Senate, by the committee of that body on finance, which also lowered duties, but by no means in so incisive a manner as the House bill. The Senate bill simply proposed to reduce all the protective duties by ten per cent. When the ten per cent. reduction was first suggested, it was strongly opposed by the protected interests, whose representatives, it is hardly necessary to say, were present in full force. They were unwilling to yield even so small a diminution. When, however, the House bill, making much more radical changes, was brought forward with the sanction of a majority of the Committee on Ways and Means, they saw that an obstinate resistance to any change might lead to dangerous results. A change of policy was accordingly determined on. Mr. John L. Hayes, who had been for many years Secretary of the Wool-Manufacturers' Association, and became President of the Tariff Commission of 1882, was at that time in Washington as agent for the wool manufacturers. Mr. Hayes has given an account of the events at Washington in 1872, from which it appears that he was chiefly instrumental in bringing about the adoption of a more far-sighted policy by the protectionists.[1] Mr. Hayes believed it to be more easy to defeat the serious movement in favor of tariff reform by making some slight concessions than by unconditional

Ten per cent. reduction proposed.

Policy of the protectionists.

---

[1] See the speech which Mr. Hayes made, shortly after the close of the session of 1872, at a meeting of the wool manufacturers in Boston ; printed in the *Bulletin of the Wool Manufacturers*, vol. iii., pp. 283–290.

opposition. The woollen manufacturers were first induced
to agree to this policy ; the Pennsylvania iron makers were
next brought over to it; and finally, the whole weight of
the protected interests was made to bear in the same
direction. As a concession to the demand for reform, the
general ten per cent. reduction was to be permitted. With
this, however, was to be joined a sweeping reduction
of the non-protective sources of revenue: the taxes on
whiskey and tobacco were to be lowered, and the tea and
coffee duties were to be entirely abolished.

This plan of action was successfully carried out. An
act for abolishing the duties on tea and coffee was first
passed.[1]   This being disposed of, the general tax and tariff
bill was taken up in the House. The Senate had already
indicated its willingness to act in the manner desired by
the protectionists. It had passed and sent to the House
a bill making the general reduction of ten per cent., and
nothing remained but to get the consent of the House.
But this consent was not easily obtained. A large number of representatives were in favor of a more thorough
and radical reform, and wished for the passage of the bill
prepared by the Ways and Means Committee. But unfortunately the reform forces were divided, and only a
part of them insisted on the Ways and Means bill. The
remainder were willing to accept the ten per cent. reduction, which the protectionists yielded. On the other hand,

---

[1] The House had already passed, at the extra session in the spring of
1871, a bill for admitting tea and coffee free of duty. This bill was now
taken up and passed by the Senate.

the protectionist members were united. Messrs. Kelley and Dawes led them, and succeeded in bringing their whole force to vote in favor of the horizontal reduction. The powerful influence of the Speaker, Mr. Blaine, was also on their side. They finally succeeded in having the original committee bill set aside, and in passing the bill for the ten per cent. reduction. Most of the revenue reformers in the end voted for it, believing it to be the utmost that could be obtained. It must be observed, how-

ever, to their credit, that the " horizontal " re- _{Act of 1872.}

duction of the protective duties was not the only concession to the reform feeling that was made by the act of 1872. It also contained a number of minor but significant changes of duty. The duty on salt was reduced to one half the previous rates; for the feeling against the war-duty on salt, which very clearly resulted in putting so much money into the pockets of the Syracuse and Saginaw producers, was too strong to be resisted. The duty on coal was reduced from $1.25 to 75 cents a ton. Some raw materials, of which hides and paper stock were alone of considerable importance, were admitted free of duty. The free list was also enlarged by putting on it a number of minor articles used by manufacturers. But the important change in the protective duties was the ten per cent. reduction, which applied to all manufactures of cotton, wool, iron, steel, metals in general, paper, glass, and leather,—that is, to all the great protective industries.

It is worth while to dwell for a moment on the abolition

of the duties on tea and coffee ; for this change may fairly be said to have been decisive in fixing the character of our tariff system. The question was whether the reduction of the revenue should be effected by lowering the protective or the non-protective duties. As matters stood in 1872, the removal of the tea and coffee duties prevented a more extended reduction of the protective duties, and, as we shall presently see, eventually left these latter precisely at the point at which they had been before.

The difference in effect between duties on articles like tea and coffee on the one hand, and articles like iron and wool on the other, is easily stated. Both are indirect taxes, reaching the consumer in the shape of higher prices on the commodities he uses. But when a duty is imposed on an article like tea and coffee, the whole increase in price to the consumer is offset by the same amount of revenue received by the government ; whereas when a duty is imposed on an article like iron or wool, the effect is different. In the latter case also the commodity is increased in price to the consumer, and he is thereby taxed. So far as the articles continue to be imported, the increased price, as in the case of tea and coffee, represents revenue received by the government. But when the consumer buys and uses an article of this kind made at home, he must pay an increased price, or tax, quite as much as when he buys the imported article, with the difference that the tax is not paid to the government, but to the home producer. The extra price so received by the home producer does not necessarily, or indeed usually, yield him exceptionally high profits. It is true that in some cases of more or less perfect monopoly he may make, permanently or for a long time, exceptionally high profits ; and in these cases there is ground for saying that the protective system has the effect of robbing Peter to pay Paul. But in the majority of cases, where the conditions of monopoly do not exist, the home producer, while getting a higher price because of the duty, does not make correspondingly high profits. It may cost more, for one reason or another, to make the article at home than it costs to make it abroad, and the duty simply serves to offset this disadvantage of the domestic producer. In not a few cases, while it may cost more to make the article at home than abroad, the duty is greater than the difference in cost. Domestic competition then will cause the price at home to fall to a point less than the foreign price *plus* the duty ; importation will cease ; and yet a virtual tax will still be levied in the shape of prices higher than those which would obtain if there were no duty. Whatever be the details of the working of a protective duty, it is *prima facie* less desirable than a revenue duty, on the simple ground that the tax serves not to yield revenue, but to offset the greater cost of making the commodity at home. Whether the stimulus to domestic production brings other benefits to the community, sufficient to compensate for this disadvantage of protective duties involves the whole problem of the operation of international trade : indeed, the discussion spreads over the entire range of economic principles, and can be settled only by reasoning in which all those principles are taken into account.

The history of the duties on tea and coffee is curious. In the early days of the Republic, when the need of revenue was pressing, they were subjected to duties which for those times were heavy. But in 1830, when the revenue became more than ample, and when there was also a strong feeling in favor of maintaining protective duties, tea, coffee, and cocoa were put on the free list. The situation in 1830 was not unlike that in 1872, except that the feeling through the North in favor of maintaining the protective duties was probably stronger at the earlier date. From 1830 to the Civil War, these revenue articles remained free of duty. The tariff acts of 1846 and 1857, though supposed to be based on revenue principles, made no attempt to secure revenue from this certain and simple source. Protective duties are as certainly taxes as are those on tea and coffee; but in the latter case no domestic producers ask for the retention of the taxes; consequently the revenue duties, unsupported by any strong interest, are easy victims when a curtailment of the national revenue becomes convenient or necessary.

For our present purpose it suffices to point out that the removal of the tea and coffee duties in 1872 served to fix for a long time the character of our legislation on the revenue articles of which they are the type. Step by step, in the various tariff acts passed since the war, all the non-protective duties have been swept away. By far the most important recent legislation in this direction was the removal of the duties on sugar in the act of 1890, a change which, like the removal of the tea and coffee duties in 1872, emphasized the determination of the protectionists to give up the simplest and surest sources of revenue rather than yield an abatement of the protective duties.

To return from this digression to the tariff act of 1872. The free-traders were on the whole satisfied with it ; they thought it a step in the right direction, and the beginning of a process of reform. The protectionists, however, believed that they had won a victory ; and, as events proved, they were right.[1]

It is not within the purpose of this volume to discuss the intrinsic merits of a " horizontal reduction," such as was carried out in the act of 1872. Undoubtedly it is a simple and indiscriminating method of approaching the problem of tariff reform. The objections to it were very prominently brought forward when Mr. Morrison, during the session of 1883–84, proposed to take off ten per cent. from the duties, in exactly the same way that the tariff of 1872 had taken off ten per cent. It is certainly curious that this method, when proposed by Mr. Morrison in 1884, should be vehemently denounced by protectionists

---

[1] Mr. Hayes, in the speech already referred to, spoke of "the grand result of a tariff bill reducing duties fifty-three millions of dollars, and yet leaving the great industries almost intact. The present tariff (of 1872) was made by our friends, in the interest of protection." And again : "A reduction of over fifty millions of dollars, and yet taking only a shaving off from the protection duties."

as crude, vicious, unscientific, and impractical, although, when proposed by Mr. Dawes in 1872, it received their earnest support. There is, however, one objection to such a plan which was hardly mentioned in connection with Mr. Morrison's bill, but was brought out very clearly by the experience of 1872. This is, that a horizontal reduction can very easily be revoked. The reduction made in 1872 was repealed with little difficulty in 1875. After the panic of 1873, imports greatly diminished, and with them the customs revenue. No further thought of tax reduction was entertained; and soon a need of increasing the revenue was felt. In 1875 Congress, as one means to that end, repealed the ten per cent. reduction, and put duties back to where they had been before 1872.[1] The repeal attracted comparatively little attention, and was

Ten per cent. reduction repealed in 1875.

---

[1] It was far from necessary, for revenue purposes, to repeal the ten per cent. clause. Mr. Dawes (who advocated in 1875 the repeal of his own measure of 1872) attempted to show the need of raising the tariff by assuming that a fixed sum of $47,000,000 per year was necessary for the sinking fund,—that the faith of the government was pledged to devoting this sum to the redemption of the debt. But it was very clearly shown that the government never had carried out the sinking-fund provision in any exact way. In some years it bought for the sinking fund much less than the one per cent of the debt which was supposed to be annually redeemed; in other years (notably in 1869–73) it bought much more than this one per cent. The same policy has been followed in recent years. There can be little doubt that the need of providing for the sinking fund was used merely as a excuse for raising the duties. See Mr. Wood's remarks, *Congr. Record* 1874–75, pp. 1187, 1188, and *cf.* Mr. Beck's speech, *ibid.*, pp. 1401, 1402.

It may be noted that in 1875 President Grant and the Secretary of the Treasury recommended, and men like Senators Sherman and Schurz supported, a re-imposition of duties on tea and coffee as the best means of increasing the customs revenues.

carried without great opposition. If a detailed examination of the tariff had been made in 1872, and if duties
had been reduced in that year carefully and with discrimination, it would have been much more difficult in 1875 to
put them back to the old figures. If some of the duties
which are of a particularly exorbitant or burdensome
character had been individually reduced in 1872, public
opinion would not easily have permitted the restitution of
the old rates. But the general ten per cent. reduction,
which touched none of the duties in detail, was repealed
without attracting public attention. The old rates were
restored; and the best opportunity which the country
has had for a considerable modification of the protective
system, slipped by without any permanent result.

Of the attempts at reform which were made between
1875 and 1883, little need be said. Mr. Morrison in 1876,
and Mr. Wood in 1878, introduced tariff bills into the
House. These bills were the occasion of more or less
debate; but there was at no time any probability of
their being enacted.[1] In 1879 the duty on quinine was
abolished entirely,—a measure most beneficial and praise-
worthy in itself, but not of any considerable importance
in the economic history of the country.

Of the tariff act of 1883 we do not purpose speaking in

---

[1] Those who are interested in the details of these measures will find the
bill of 1876 explained in Mr. Morrison's speech, in *Cong. Record*, 1875–1876,
p. 3321. The bill of 1878 was similarly explained by Mr. Wood, *Cong.
Record*, 1877–78, p. 2398. It was at one time supposed that Mr. Wood's
bill might be passed by the House; but the enacting clause was struck out,
after some debate, by a vote of 137 to 114.

this connection. It will be discussed in detail in the con-
cluding pages.

We have now completed our account of the attempts
to reform the tariff which were made between the close of
the Civil War and the general revision of 1883. It is clear
that the duties, as they were imposed in the act of 1864,
were retained substantially without change during the
whole of this period. The non-protective duties were
indeed swept away. A few reductions of protective
duties were made in the acts of 1870 and 1872; but the
great mass of duties imposed on articles which are produced in this country were not touched. It is worth
while to note some of the more important classes of goods
on which the duties levied in 1864 remained in force, and
to compare these duties with the rates of the Morrill
tariff of 1861. The increase which was the result of the
war will appear most plainly from such a comparison. In
the appended table[1] it will be seen that the rates on books,
chinaware, and pottery, cotton goods, linen, hemp, and
jute goods, glass, gloves, bar- and hoop-iron, iron rails,
steel, lead, paper, and silks, were increased by from ten to
thirty per cent. during the war, and that the increase then
made was maintained without the slightest change till
1883. That these great changes, at the time when they
were made, were not intended or expected to be permanent, cannot be denied. An example like that of the
duty on cotton goods shows plainly how the duties were

---

[1] See table II., Appendix.

fixed during the war according to the conditions of the time, and without expectation of their remaining indefinitely in force. The duty on the cheapest grade of cotton tissues had been in 1861 fixed at one cent per yard. During the war the price of cotton rose greatly, and with it the prices of cotton goods. Consequently it is not surprising to find the duty in 1864 to be five cents per yard on this grade of cottons. But shortly after the war, raw cotton fell nearly to its former price; and it does occasion surprise to find that the duty of five cents per yard should have been retained without change till 1883, and even in the act of 1883 retained at a figure much above that of 1861. The duty on cheap cottons happens not to have been particularly burdensome, since goods of this kind are made in this country as cheaply as they can be made abroad. But the retention of the war duty on them, even after it became exorbitantly high, is typical of the way in which duties were retained on other articles on which they were burdensome. Duties which had been imposed during the war, and which had then been made very high, either for reasons of revenue or because of circumstances such as led to the heavy rate on cottons, were retained unchanged after the war ceased. It would be untrue to say that protection did not exist before the great struggle began,—the tariff of 1861, was a distinctly protectionist measure; but it is clear that the extreme protectionist character of our tariff is an indirect and unexpected result of the Civil War.

CHAPTER III.

In the preceding chapter it has been shown how the duties levied during the war failed to be reduced after its close. But in many cases not only has there been a failure to diminish the war rates, but an actual increase over them. We have already noted how the maintenance of the tariff of 1864 brought about gradually a feeling that such a system was a good thing in itself, and desirable as a permanent policy. This feeling, and the fact that Congress and the public had grown accustomed to heavy taxes and high rates, enabled many measures to become law which under normal circumstances would never have been submitted to. In the present chapter we are concerned with the not infrequent instances in which, in obedience to the demands of the protected interests, duties were raised over and above the point, already high, at which they were left when the war closed. The most striking instance of legislation of this kind is to be found in the wool and woollens act of 1867; a measure which is so characteristic of the complications of our tariff, of the remarkable height to which protection has been carried in it, and of the submission of Congress and the people to the demands of domestic manu- Wool and woollen act of 1867. facturers that it deserves to be described in detail. Such a description is the more desirable since the woollen schedule of our tariff is the one which imposes the heaviest and the least defensible burdens on consumers, and at the same time is the most difficult of comprehension for those who have nothing but the mere language of the statute to guide them.

In order to understand the complicated system that now exists, we must go back to the Morrill tariff act of 1861. In that act specific duties on wool were substituted for the *ad-valorem* rates of 1846 and 1857. The cheaper kinds of wool, costing eighteen cents or less per pound, were still admitted at the nominal rate of five per cent. But wool costing between eighteen and twenty-four cents per pound was charged three cents per pound; that costing more than twenty-four cents was charged nine cents per pound. The duties on woollens were increased correspondingly. An *ad-valorem* rate of twenty-five per cent. was levied on them; in addition they paid a specific duty of twelve cents for each pound of cloth. This specific duty was intended merely to compensate the manufacturers for the duty on wool, while the *ad-valorem* rate alone was to yield them any protection. This is the first appearance in our tariff history of the device of exact compensating duties. Compensation for duties on raw materials used by domestic producers had indeed been provided for in previous tariffs; but it was not until the passage of the Morrill act and of its successors that it came to be applied in this distinct manner. As the principle of compensation has been greatly extended since 1861, and is the key to the existing system of woollen duties, it may be well to explain it with some care.

It is evident that a duty on wool must normally cause the price of all wool that is imported to rise by the full extent of the duty. More-over, the duty presumably causes the wool grown at home, of the same grade as that imported, also to rise in price to the full extent of the tax. It is clear that, if foreign wool continues to be imported, such a rise in the price of domestic wool must take place; since wool will not be imported unless the price here is higher, by the amount of the duty, than the price abroad. It may happen, of course, that the tax will prove prohibitory, and that the importation of foreign wool will cease; in which case it is possible that the domestic wool is raised in price by some amount less than the duty, and even possible that it is not raised in price at all. Assuming for the present (and this assumption was made in arranging the compensating system) that domestic wool does rise in price, by the extent of the duty, as compared with foreign wool, it is evident that the American manufacturer, whether using foreign or domestic wool, is compelled to pay more for his raw material than his competitor abroad. This disadvantage it becomes necessary

The compensating system.

to offset by a compensating duty on foreign woollens. In 1861 the duty on wool of the kind chiefly used in this country (costing abroad between ten and twenty-four cents a pound) was three cents a pound. The compensating duty for this was made twelve cents a pound on the woollen cloth, which tacitly assumes that about four pounds of wool are used for each pound of cloth. This specific duty was intended to put the manufacturer in the same situation, as regards foreign competition, as if he got his wool free of duty. The separate *ad-valorem* duty of twenty-five per cent. was then added in order to give protection.

The compensating system was retained in the acts of 1862 and 1864. During the war, it is needless to say, the duties on wool and woollens were considerably raised. They were increased, and to some extent properly increased, to offset the internal taxes and the increased duties on dye-stuffs and other materials; and care was taken, in this as in other instances, that Wool and the increase in the tariff should be sufficient woollen duand more than sufficient to prevent the do- ties of 1864. mestic producer from being unfairly handicapped by the internal taxes. In the final act of 1864 the duties on wool were as follows:

On wool costing 12 cents or less, a duty of 3 cents per pound.
  "   "   "   between 12 and 24 cents, a duty of 6 cents per pound.
  "   "   "   "   24 and 32 cents, a duty of 10 cents per pound,
    plus ten per cent.
On wool costing more than 32 cents, a duty of 12 cents per pound, plus ten per cent.[1]

---

[1] Exactly how this duty on wool of ten per cent. on the value, in addition

The wool chiefly imported and chiefly used by our manufacturers was that of the second class, costing between twelve and twenty-four cents per pound, and paying a duty of six cents. The compensating duty on woollens was therefore raised in 1864 to twenty-four cents per pound of cloth. The *ad-valorem* (protective) duty on woollens had been raised to forty per cent.

During the war the production of wool and woollens had been greatly increased. The check to the manufacture of cotton goods, which resulted from the stoppage of the great source of supply of raw cotton, caused some increase in the demand for woollens. The government's need of large quantities of cloth for army use was also an important cause. After the war, a revolution was threatened. Cotton bade fair to take its former place among textile goods; the government no longer needed its woollens, and threw on the market the large stocks of army clothing which it had on hand. In the hope of warding off the imminent depression of their trade, the wool growers and manufacturers made an effort to obtain still further assistance from the government. A convention of wool growers and manufacturers was held in Syracuse, N. Y., in December, 1865. That both these classes of producers, as a body, understood and supported the views of this meeting, is not at all certain. The mass of wool growers undoubtedly knew

to the specific duty, came to be imposed, the writer has never seen satisfactorily explained. It probably came into the tariff in connection with the discriminating duty of ten per cent. which was imposed on goods imported in the vessels of nations that had no treaty of commerce with us.

nothing of it; they were represented chiefly by a few breeders of sheep. Among the manufacturers, many held aloof
from it when its character became somewhat more plain.
There is good evidence to show that the whole movement
was the work of a few energetic manufacturers of
New England, engaged chiefly in producing carpets and
worsted goods, and of some prominent breeders of sheep.[1]
The fact that the rates of duty, as arranged by the
Syracuse convention, were especially advantageous to
certain manufacturers—namely, those who made carpets,
worsted goods, and blankets,—tends to support this view.
On the surface, however, the movement appeared to be
that of the growers and manufacturers united. The
latter agreed to let the wool producers advance the duty
on the raw material to any point they wished; they under-

---

[1] "This tariff (of 1867) was devised by carpet and blanket makers, who
pretended to be 'The National Woollen Manufacturers' Association,' in
combination with certain persons who raised fine bucks and wished to sell
them at high prices, and who acted in the name of 'The National Wool-
Growers' Association.' * * * A greater farce was never witnessed
* * * Many who took part in the proceedings of 1866, finding that the
Association [of Wool Manufacturers] was used for the convenience of special interests, have since withdrawn."—Harris, "Memorial," pp. 22, 23.

Mr. Harris says elsewhere: "The carpet interest was predominant [in
the Wool Manufacturers' Association]. * * * The President was, and
is now (1871), a large carpet manufacturer; and the Secretary was a very
talented and astute politician, from Washington, chosen by the influence of
the President." And again: "The Association having spent considerable
sums in various ways *peculiar to Washington* (the italics are Mr. Harris's)
increased the annual tax on its members very largely; and at the present
time (1871) it is hopelessly in debt to its President."—"Protective Duties,"
pp. 9, 10; "The Tariff," p. 17. See also "Argument on Foreign Wool
Tariff before Finance Committee of Senate," New York, 1871.

took, by means of the compensating device, to prevent
any injury to themselves from the high duty on the
wool they used.   The tariff schedule which was the result
of this combination was approved by the United States
Revenue Commission.[1]   It was made a part of the unsuccessful tariff bill of 1867, already referred to[2]; and when
that bill failed, it was made law by a separate act, to
whose passage no particular objection seems to have been
made.   The whole course of events forms the most striking example—and such examples are numerous—of the
manner in which, in recent tariff legislation, regard has
been had exclusively to the producer.   Here was an intricate and detailed scheme of duties, prepared by the
producers of the articles to be protected, openly and
avowedly with the intention of giving themselves aid;
and yet this scheme was accepted and enacted by the
National Legislature without any appreciable change from
the rates asked for.[3]

We turn now to examine this act of 1867, whose main
provisions were retained in the acts of 1883 and 1890, and,
after a brief period of radical change under that of 1894,

---

[1] Mr. Stephen Colwell, a disciple of the Carey protectionist school, was
the member of this commission who had charge of the wool and woollens
schedule.   Mr. Wells, who was also a member of the commission, had
nothing to do with this part of the tariff.

[2] *Ante*, p. 21.

[3] The proceedings of the Syracuse convention may be found in full in the
volume of "Transactions of the Wool Manufacturers"; also in "U. S.
Revenue Report, 1866," pp. 360–419.   Mr. Colwell's endorsement of the
scheme is also in "U. S. Revenue Report, 1866," pp. 347–356.   Mr. Wells,
in his report of 1867, sharply criticised the act as passed.

were once more reinstated in the tariff of 1897. In this examination we will follow the statement published in 1866, in explanation of the new schedule, by the Executive Committee of the National Association of Wool Manufacturers.[1] To begin with, the duties on wool were arranged on a new plan. Wool was divided into three classes: carpet, clothing, and combing wool.[2] The first class, carpet wool, corresponded to the cheap wools of the tariff of 1864. The duty was three cents a pound if it cost twelve cents or less, and six cents a pound if it cost more than twelve cents. The other two classes, of clothing and combing wools, are the grades chiefly grown in this country, and therefore are most important to note in connection with the protective controversy. The duties on these were the same for both classes. Clothing and combing wools alike were made to pay as follows:

Act of 1867.
Duty on wool.

Value 32 cents or less, a duty of 10 cents per pound and 11 per cent. *ad valorem.*

Value more than 32 cents, a duty of 12 cents per pound and 10 per cent. *ad valorem.*[3]

---

[1] See " Statement of the Executive Committee of the Wool Manufacturers Association to the U. S. Revenue Commisson," printed in " Transactions," as above ; also printed in " Revenue Report for 1866," pp. 441–460.

[2] Clothing wool is of comparatively short fibre ; it is *carded* as a preparation for spinning ; it is used for making cloths, cassimeres, and the other common woollen fabrics. Combing wool is of longer fibre ; it is *combed* in a combing machine as a preparation for spinning ; and it is used in making worsted goods, and other soft and pliable fabrics.

[3] Here again we have the rather absurd combination of specific and *ad-valorem* duties on wool. In the act of 1867, there is the further complication

Comparing these figures with the rates of 1864, one would not, at first sight, note any great change.   In 1864, wool costing between twenty-four and thirty-two cents had been charged ten cents per pound plus ten per cent. *ad valorem ;* and wool costing more than thirty-two cents had paid twelve cents a pound plus ten per cent.   These seem to be almost exactly the rates of 1867.   But in fact, by the change in classification, a very considerable increase in the duty was brought about.   In 1867 *all* wool costing less than thirty-two cents was made to pay the duty of ten cents per pound and eleven per cent.   In 1864 wool cost-ing (abroad) between eighteen and twenty-four cents had been charged only six cents per pound.   This is the class of wool chiefly grown in the United States, and chiefly imported hither; and it was charged in 1867 with the duty of ten cents and eleven per cent.   With the *ad-valorem* addition, the duty of 1867 amounted to eleven and a half or twelve cents a pound, or about double the duty of 1864.   The consequence was that in reality the duty on that grade of wool which is chiefly used in this country was nearly doubled by the act of 1867 ; and the increase was concealed under a change in classification. The duty on clothing and combing wools, as fixed in

that the *ad-valorem duty* is in the one case ten per cent., in the other eleven per cent.   This difference resulted by accident, as the writer has been in-formed, from the need of complying technically with certain parliamentary rules of the House.   It is hardly necessary to say that this mixture of specific and *ad-valorem* duties on wool has no connection with the compensating system.   The compensating scheme accounts only for the two kinds of duties on *woollen goods.*

1867, has been on the average more than fifty per cent. on the value abroad.

The duty on wool being fixed in this way, that on woollens was arranged on the following *The duty on* plan. It was calculated that four pounds *woollen* of wool (unwashed) were needed to produce *cloths.* a pound of cloth. The duty on wool, as has been explained, amounted to about eleven and one half cents a pound, taking the specific and *ad-valorem* duty together. Each of the four pounds of wool used in making a pound of cloth, paid, if imported, a duty of four times eleven and one half cents, or forty-six cents. If home grown wool was used, the price of this, it was assumed, was equally raised by the duty. The manufacturer in either case paid, for the wool used in making a pound of cloth, forty-six cents more than his foreign competitor. For this disadvantage he must be compensated. Moreover, the manufacturer in the United States, in 1867, paid duties on drugs, dye-stuffs, oils, etc., estimated to amount to two and one half cents per pound of cloth. For this also he must be compensated. In addition he must have interest on the duties advanced by him ; for between the time when he paid the duties on the wool and other materials, and the time when he was reimbursed by the sale of his cloth, he had so much money locked up. Add interest for, say six months, and we get the final total of the duty necessary to compensate the manufacturer for what he has to pay on his raw materials. The account stands :

Duty on 4 pounds of wool at 11½ cents .   .   .   46 cents
" " oils, dye-stuffs, etc. .   .   .   .   2⅛ "
Interest .   .   .   .   4½ "

Total .   .   .   .   .   53 "

Congress did not accept the exact figure set by the woollen makers. It made the compensating duty fifty cents per pound of cloth instead of fifty-three; but this change was evidently of no material importance. The woollen manufacturers got substantially all that they wanted. It will be remembered that in 1864 the compensating specific duty on cloth had been only twenty-four cents per pound.

The *ad-valorem* duty was fixed at thirty-five per cent. The woollen manufacturers said they wanted a "net effective protection" of only twenty-five per cent.[1] This does not seem immoderate. But ten per cent *ad-valorem* was supposed to be necessary to compensate for the internal taxes, which were still imposed in 1867, though abolished very soon after. This ten per cent., added to the desired protection of twenty-five per cent, brought the *ad-valorem*

---

[1] "All manufactures composed wholly or in part of wool or worsted shall be subjected to a duty which shall be equal to twenty-five per cent. net ; *that is,* twenty-five per cent. after reimbursing the amount paid on account of wool, dye-stuffs, and other imported materials, and also the amount paid for the internal revenue tax imposed on manufactures and on the supplies and materials used therefor." Joint Report of Wool Manufacturers and Wool Growers, "Revenue Report, for 1866," p. 430 ; also in "Transactions." The Executive Committee of the Wool Manufacturers' Association said, in 1866 : "Independently of considerations demanding a duty on wool, the wool manufacturers would prefer the total abolition of specific duties, provided they could have all their raw material free, and an actual net protection of twenty-five per cent." Harris, "Memorial," p. 9.

rate to thirty-five per cent. The final duty on woollen cloth was therefore fifty cents per pound and thirty-five per cent. *ad valorem:* of which the fifty cents was compensation for duties on raw materials; ten per cent. was compensation for internal tax; and of the whole accumulated mass only twenty-five per cent. was supposed to give protection to the manufacturer.

This duty was levied on woollen cloths, woollen shawls, and manufactures of wool not otherwise provided for—which included most of the woollen goods then made in this country. On other classes of goods the same system was followed. An *ad-valorem* duty of thirty-five per cent. was imposed in all cases; twenty-five per cent. being intended to be protection, and ten per cent. compensation for internal taxes. The specific duty varied with different goods, but in all cases was supposed merely to offset the import duties on wool and other supplies. For instance, on flannels, blankets, and similar goods, the specific duty varied from fifty cents a pound to twenty cents, being made to decrease on the cheaper qualities of goods, as less wool, or cheaper wool, was used in making a pound of flannel or blanket. The duties on knit goods were the same as those on blankets. On carpets the system was applied with some modification. The specific duty was levied here *by the square yard,* and not by the pound. A calculation was made of the quantity of wool, linen, yarn, dye-stuffs, and other imported articles used for each yard of carpet; the total duties paid on these materials, with interest added as in the case of cloth, gave the com pensating duty per yard of carpet. On this basis, for instance, the specific duty on Brussels carpets was made forty-four cents per yard (the manufacturers had asked for a duty of forty-eight cents); the *ad-valorem* duty of thirty-five per cent. being of course also imposed. In the same way the specific duty on dress goods for women's and children's wear was made from six to eight cents per yard, according to quality. It is evident that the task of making the specific duty exactly compensate for the duties on wool was most complicated in these cases, and that any excess of compensation would here be most difficult of discovery for those not very familiar with the details of the manufacture. As a matter of fact, it is precisely in these schedules of the woollens act that, as we shall see, the "compensating" system was used as a means of securing a high degree of protection for the manufacturer.

These duties, *ad valorem* and specific taken together, have been from fifty to one hundred per cent., and even more, on the cost of the goods. On cloths generally they have been from sixty to seventy per cent. on the value. On blankets and flannels they have been from eighty to one hundred per cent., and have been entirely prohibitory of importation. On dress goods they have been from sixty to seventy per cent.; on Brussels carpets again from sixty to seventy per cent.; and on ingrain carpets from fifty to fifty-five per cent. Yet a net protection of twenty-five per cent. is all that the manufacturers asked for and were intended to have; and the question naturally presents itself, did they not in fact get more than twenty-five per cent.?

The first conclusion that can be drawn from this explanation of the woollens duties is that there was at all events no good reason for the permanent retention of the *ad-valorem* rate of thirty-five per cent. Of that rate ten per cent. was in all cases meant to compensate for the internal taxes. These disappeared entirely within a year or two after the woollens act was passed. Yet the *ad-valorem* rate on woollens remained at thirty-five per cent. without change from 1867 to 1883. Moreover, as the course of the narrative will show, it was steadily raised in later years, from 1883 to 1897, until in the act of 1897 it became as high as fifty-five per cent. There is no more striking illustration of the way in which duties which were imposed in order to offset the internal taxes of the war period, have been retained and have become permanent parts of our tariff system, although the original excuse for their imposition has entirely ceased to exist.

Comment on the *ad-valorem* duty.

It may seem that the retention of the specific duties on woollens was justified, since the duties on wool were not changed. It is true that the duties on dye-stuffs, drugs, and such articles have been abolished or greatly reduced since 1867; but these played no great part in the determina-

Comment on the specific duties.

tion of the specific duty. The duties on wool were not changed till the passage of the act of 1883. There are, however, other grounds for criticising the specific duties on woollens, which have been in fact not merely compensating, but have added, in most cases, a considerable degree of protection to the " net " twenty-five per cent. which the act of 1867 was supposed to give the manfacturers.

The compensating duties, as we have seen, were based on two assumptions : first, that the price of wool, whether foreign or domestic, was increased by the full extent of the duty ; second, that four pounds of wool were used in making a pound of cloth. The first assumption, however, holds good only to a very limited extent. A protective duty does not necessarily cause the price of the protected article to rise by the full extent of the duty. It may be prohibitory ; the importation of the foreign article may entirely cease ; and the domestic article, while its price is raised to some extent, may yet be dearer by an amount less than the duty. This is what has happened with regard to most grades of wool. The commoner grades of wool are raised in this country with comparative ease. The duty on them is prohibitory, and their importation has ceased. Their price, though higher than that of similar wools abroad, is not higher by the full extent of the duty. It is true that the importation of finer grades of clothing and combing wools continues ; and it is possible that the wools of Ohio, Michigan, and other States east of the Mississippi are higher in price, by the full amount of the duty, than similar wools abroad. Even this is not certain; for the wools which continue to be imported are not of precisely the same class as the Ohio and Michigan wools. As a rule, the importations are for exceptional and peculiar purposes, and do not replace or compete with domestic wools. At all events, it is certain that the great mass of wools grown in this country are entirely shielded from foreign competition. Their price is raised above the foreign price of similar material; but raised only by some amount less than the duty. The manufacturer, however, gets a compensating duty in all cases as if his material were dearer, by the full extent of the duty, than that of his foreign competitor. The bulk of the wool used by American manufacturers does not show the full effect of the tariff, and the manufacturers clearly obtain, in the specific duty, more compensation than the higher price of their wool calls for. The result is that this duty, instead of merely preventing the domestic producer from being put at a disadvantage, yields him in most cases a considerable degree of protection, over and above that given by the *ad-valorem* duty.[1]

There is another way in which the compensating duty is excessive. A very large quantity of woollen goods are

---

[1] See the instructive remarks of Mr. John L. Hayes, in *Bulletin Wool Manufacturers* vol. xiii. pp. 98–108. *Cf.* "Tariff Comm. Report," pp. 1782–1785. The production and importation of wool in different parts of the country for a series of years are given in some detail in "Tariff Comm. Report," pp. 2435, 2436.

not made entirely of wool. Cotton, shoddy, and other substitutes are in no inconsiderable part the materials of the clothes worn by the mass of the people. In these goods very much less than four pounds of wool is used in making a pound of cloth, and the specific duty again yields to the manufacturer a large degree of protection.

The second assumption of the compensating system, that four pounds of wool are used in making a pound of cloth, is also open to criticism. The goods in which cotton and shoddy are used clearly do not require so much wool. But it is probable that even with goods made entirely of wool, the calculation of four pounds of unwashed wool for each pound of cloth is very liberal. Wool, unwashed, shrinks very much in the cleaning and scouring which it must receive before it is fit for use ; and the loss by wear and waste in the processes of manufacture is also considerable. The shrinkage in scouring is subject to no definite rule. In some cases wool loses only forty per cent. of its weight in the process, in others as much as seventy-five per cent. The shrinkage in scouring on American wools is rarely more than sixty per cent ; and if to this is added a further loss of twenty-five per cent. in manufacture, there will be needed for a pound of cloth no more than three and one third pounds of wool.[1]

[1] See, as to the loss of wool in scouring, *Quarterly Report Bureau of Statistics,* for quarter ending June 30, 1884, pp. 563–565 ; Harris, " Memorial," p. 11 ; Schoenhof, " Wool and Woollens," p. 10 ; *Bulletin Wool Mf.,* vol. xiii., p. 8. The least loss I have found mentioned is twenty-five per cent. (coarse Ohio), and the highest seventy per cent. (Buenos Ayres wool). Ordinary

With the great majority of goods made in this country, the shrinkage and the loss in manufacture do not amount to more than this. The calculation of four for one is for most American goods a liberal one; and it is evident that the compensating duty, based on this liberal calculation, yields a degree of protection in the same way that it does on goods that contain cotton or shoddy. On the other hand, there are some grades of imported wool on which the shrinkage and loss in manufacture are so great that the compensating duty is not excessive. Some grades of Australian wool, which are imported for manufacturing fine goods and worsteds, are subject to exceptional shrinkage and to exceptional waste in the process of manufacture. Of this class of wool four pounds, and sometimes a little more, are apt to be used for a pound of cloth.[1] In such cases the compensating duty evidently

---

American wool loses between fifty and sixty per cent. in scouring. The loss in weight in manufacturing varies much with the processes, but with care will not exceed twenty-five per cent. With most goods it is less.

If the loss in scouring 100 lbs. of wool is sixty per cent., there remain . . . . . 40 lbs. scoured wool
Deduct twenty-five per cent. for loss in manufacture 10 lbs.

Leaves . . 30 lbs. of cloth,

or 1 lb. of cloth for $3\frac{1}{3}$ lbs. of wool.

If the loss in scouring 100 lbs. of wool is sixty-five per cent. there remain . . . . 35 lbs. scoured wool.
Deduct twenty-five per cent. for loss in manufacture
. . . . $8\frac{3}{4}$ lbs.

Leaves . . 26¼ lbs. of cloth,

or 1 lb. cloth for not quite 4 lbs. of wool.

[1] See the instances given by Mr. Hayes in *Wool Manufacturers' Bulletin*, vol. xii., pp. 4–9. These all refer to Australian wool, which, as Mr. Hayes says elsewhere (*ibid.*, p. 107), is imported in comparatively small quantities for exceptional purposes.

may fail to counterbalance entirely the disadvantage under which the manufacturer labors in the higher price of his raw material; for the wool, being imported into this country, and paying the duty, must be higher in price by the full amount of the duty than the same wool used by the foreign producer. In other words, there are cases where the specific duty is not sufficient to offset the duty on the raw material. It is probable that this fact explains, in part at least, the regular importation of certain dress goods and finer grades of cloths, which continue to come into the country from abroad in face of the very heavy duty. But such cases are exceptional. For most goods made in the United States the compensating duty on the four to one basis is excessive.

One other provision in the act of 1867 may be pointed out, which bears on the calculation of four pounds of wool to one pound of cloth, and at the same time illustrates the spirit in which the act was prepared. It has already been said that the duty on wool is laid on *unwashed* wool; and the compensating duty is fixed on the calculation that it requires four pounds of ˈunwashed wool to make a pound of cloth. The act of 1867 provided that clothing wool, if washed, should pay double duty, and if scoured, treble duty. Similarly combing wool and carpet wool were made to pay treble duty if scoured. But no provision whatever was made as to combing and carpet wools if *washed;* they were admitted at the same rate of duty whether washed or unwashed. This amounted practically to lowering the duty on them. The provision was of no small importance in the case of combing wools; for these always come to market in the washed condition, and would have been regularly subject to double duty if treated as clothing wool was. It was alleged in justification of their more liberal treatment that a double duty on them would have been virtually prohibitory. Very likely this was the case; and, regarded by itself, the arrangement made in the act of 1867 (and retained in all later acts to 1897) was reasonable. But in its train one would have expected a corresponding moderation of the compensatory duties on the goods for which combing wool was used. No such reduction, however, was made; the full compensating duty was imposed; and the *ad-valorem* duty, consequently, was far from indicating the real degree of protection afforded. As it happened, for several years after the act was passed, a turn in fashion brought worsted goods, made with combing wool, into great demand; and during these years certain manufacturers of such goods found their business exceedingly profitable.[1]

If the compensating duty was thus liberal in the case of most woollen goods, and more than liberal in

[1] Under the reciprocity treaty with Canada (1854–1866) wool from that country had been admitted free, and considerable quantities of combing wool had been imported. The loss of this opportunity was one ground why the manufacturers in 1867 were desirous of securing washed wool of this kind without double duty. In 1867–72, there were very heavy imports of combing wool, partly from Canada, mainly from England. In later years, the imports of wool of this class have been small, and the proviso here under discussion has been of minor consequence. Though opposed by the woolgrowers, the admission of washed combing wool at the same rate as unwashed was maintained in all the tariff acts from 1867 to 1897.

the case of worsteds, it was to be expected that other
schedules where a check was more difficult to apply,
would also contain excessive compensation.   The specific
duty on carpets was levied by the yard; that on Brussels carpets, for instance, was forty-four cents a square
yard.   Similarly the specific duty on dress-goods was
levied by the square yard.   That on blankets, flannels,
worsteds, yarns, etc., was fixed by the pound, but was
made to vary from twenty to fifty cents a pound, according to the value of the goods.   The last-mentioned goods,
for instance, paid a duty of twenty cents a pound if worth
forty cents or less a pound; a duty of thirty cents if
worth between forty and sixty cents; and so on.   In
every case, of course, the *ad-valorem* (nominally protective)
rate of thirty-five per cent. was added to the specific
duties.   It is evidently a very complex problem whether
these "compensating" duties represent the exact sum
necessary to offset the increased price of materials due to
the tariff rates on wool, hemp, dye-stuffs, and other
dutiable articles used by manufacturers.   We have seen
that the movement that resulted in the passage of the act
of 1867 was brought about chiefly by the manufacturers
of carpets and worsteds.   These men adjusted the specific
duties, and alone could know with how great accuracy
they attained their object of compensation.   In some instances it was confessed that there was more than compensation in their scheme; this was admitted to be the
case with blankets and dress-goods.   On all goods it is

not to be doubted that a liberal allowance was made in favor of the manufacturers, and that the specific rates gave them a certain amount, sometimes a great amount, of pure and simple protection.

The truth is that the wool and woollens schedule, as it was framed in the act of 1867, and as it remained in the successive modifications of later tariff acts, was in many ways a sham. Nominally it limited the protection for the manufacturer to a clearly defined point, indicated by the *ad-valorem* rate. As a matter of fact, no one could tell how much of the different duties was protective, and how much merely compensating. So complicated was the schedule, and so varying were the conditions of trade and manufacture, that the domestic manufacturer himself found it difficult to say exactly how great a degree of encouragement the government gave him. In some cases the effectual protection might be less than the twenty-five (or thirty-five) per cent. which the tariff was supposed to yield. In the great majority of cases it was very much more than this, and was meant to be more. The whole cumbrous and intricate system—of *ad-valorem* and specific duties, of duties varying according to the weight and the value and the square yard—was adopted largely because it concealed the degree of protection which in fact the act of 1867 gave. Duties that plainly levied taxes of 60, 80, and 100 per cent. would hardly have been suffered by public opinion or enacted by the legislature. Probably few members of Congress under stood the real nature and bearing of the scheme, and no attempt was made to check the calculations of the woollen manufacturers, or to see whether, intentionally or by accident, abuses might not have crept into their proposals.

The most remarkable fact in the history of this piece of legislation was its failure to secure the object which its supporters had in mind. Notwithstanding the very great degree of protection which the manufacturers got, the production of woollen goods proved to be one of the most unsatisfactory and unprofitable of manufacturing occupations. As a rule, a strong protective measure causes domestic producers to obtain, at least for a time, high profits; though under the ordinary circumstances of free competition, profits are sooner or later brought down to the normal level. But in the woollen manufacture even this temporary gain was not secured by the home producers after the act of 1867. A few branches, such as the production of carpets, of blankets, of certain worsted goods, were highly profitable for some years. These were the branches, it will be remembered, in which the compensating duties were most excessive, and the prominent manufacturers engaged in them had done most to secure the passage of the act of 1867. Profits in these branches were in course of time brought down to the usual level, and in many instances below the usual level, by the increase of domestic production and domestic competition.

Manufacturers not benefited by the act.

The manufacture of the great mass of woollen goods, however, was depressed and unprofitable during the years immediately following the act, notwithstanding the speculative activity and seeming prosperity of that time.[1] It has sometimes been said that this was the effect of the act itself; but other causes, such as the cessation of the the war demand and the increasing use of worsted goods in place of woollen goods, probably suffice to account for the unprosperous state of affairs. It has also been said that the lack of diversity in the woollen manufacture of the United States can be traced to those provisions in the act of 1867 by which particularly high protection was given on the common and cheaper goods; the more so since the high duty on wool has tended to hamper the manufacturer in the choice of his material. No doubt it is true that at present the majority of finer woollen goods are imported, and the manufacture in this country is confined mainly to cheaper grades. The situation is not essentially different from that which we have already described as existing before 1860.[2] But here again too much is ascribed, for good or evil, to the tariff. The

---

[1] See an instructive article, by a manufacturer, in "Bulletin Nat. Assoc. Wool Mf.," vol. III., p. 354 (1872). "There is one thing that all who are interested in the manufacture will agree to, that for the last five years [from 1867 to 1872) the business in the aggregate has been depressed, that the profits made during the war have been exhausted mainly, and that it has been extremely difficult during all this time to buy wool and mannfacture it into goods and get a new dollar for an old one."—*Cf.* Mr. Harris' pamphlets, cited above.

[2] See above, p. 147.

limited range of the woollen manufacturer is probably due to deeper causes; in part to the adaptability of the domestic wool for making the woollen goods which form the staples of the American manufacture, in part to the fact that the methods and machinery for those goods are fitted to our economic conditions. The causes, in fact, are probably analogous to those which have confined the cotton manufacture within a limited range. But, on the other hand, it is clear that the act of 1867 has not been successful as a protective measure; it has not stimulated the woollen industry to any noticeable degree, nor has it greatly affected the character or extent of the imports. So far as the wool-growers are concerned, it has not prevented the price of wool from declining in the United States, in sympathy with the decline elsewhere; nor has it prevented the shifting of wool-growing from the heart of the country to the western plains, where wool is raised under conditions like those of Australia and the Argentine Republic. The manufacture probably would have been, on the whole and in the long run, more satisfactory to those engaged in it if they had had free wool and if woollens had been charged with no more than the protection of 25 per cent. which the act of 1867 was supposed to give.[1] Some establishments, no doubt, have arisen which could not continue under such a system, and for these temporary provisions should be made if the present duties are swept away.

---

[1] There is a voluminous literature on the wool and woollens duties. The original scheme was discussed in Mr. Wells's "Report for 1866–67," pp.

The woollens act of 1867 has been discussed somewhat at length because it is the most striking illustration of the manner in which protective duties were advanced after the war at the request of domestic producers. There are not a few other cases in which an increase of duties beyond the level reached during the war was made. After the woollens act, perhaps the most remarkable is the copper act of 1869. Before that year the duty on copper ore had been five per cent., that on copper in bars and ingots had been two and a half cents per pound. Under the very low duty on copper ore a large industry had grown up in Boston and Baltimore. Ore was imported from Chili, and was smelted and refined in these cities. But during the years immediately preceding 1869 the great copper mines of Lake Superior had begun to be worked on a considerable scale. These mines are among the richest sources of copper in the world, and under normal circum-

Copper act of 1869.

50, 60. Further attacks on the scheme will be found in Mr. Wells's " Report for 1869-70," pp. xcii–cv ; Wells, " Wool and the Tariff " (1873) ; Harris, " Memorial to Committee on Ways and Means " (1872) ; Schoenhof, " Wool and Woollens " (1883). On the other side a steady advocacy of the compound system will be found in the *Bulletin of the Association of Wool Manufacturers*, to which reference will be frequently made in the following pages. Mr. Wells's remarks in 1870 are criticised in the *Bulletin*, vol. ii., pp. 19–34 ; the changes made in the compound system in 1883 are defended in vol. xiii., pp. 1–13, 89–128 ; and the changes of 1890, in vol. xx. Compare also the " Examination of the Statements in the Report of the Revenue Commissioner," House Rep., 41st Cong., 2d session, Report No. 72 ; the " Tariff Commission Report of 1882," pp. 2240–2247, 2411–2440 ; and the references given on p. 296, *note*, in this volume. Statistics are collected in the *Wool Book* (1893), published by the Wool-Manufacturers' Association, and in the volume on *Wool and Manufactures of Wool* (1894), issued by the Bureau of Statistics. Treasury Department.

stances would supply the United States with this metal more cheaply and abundantly than any other country; yet by virtue of our tariff policy these very mines caused us for many years to pay more for our copper than any other country. The increased production from these mines, with other circumstances, had caused copper to fall in price in 1867 and 1868; and their owners came before Congress and asked for an increase of duties. Copper ore was to pay three cents for each pound of pure copper, equal to twenty-five or thirty per cent., in place of the previous duty of five per cent.; and ingot copper was to pay five cents per pound, instead of two and a half cents. The bill making these changes was passed by both houses. President Johnson refused to sign it, and sent in a veto message, which bore marks of having been composed by other hands than his own. But the President was then perhaps the most unpopular man in the country; Congress had got a habit of overriding his vetoes, and the copper bill was passed in both Houses by the necessary two-thirds vote, and became law.[1] The effect of the higher duty was to accelerate the closing of the smelting establish-

---

[1] The veto message is in *Congress. Record*, 1868–69, p. 1460. It was written by Mr. David A. Wells, as that gentleman has informed the writer. The character of the bill was made clear enough in the course of the debate, at well as by the veto message. See Brooks's speech, *ibid.*, p. 1462. The manner in which this bill, and others of the same kind, were carried through Congress is illustrated by some almost naive remarks of Mr. Frelinghuysen : " My sympathies are with this bill, as they always are for any tariff bill. I confess, however, that I do not like this system of legislation, picking out first wool, then copper, then other articles, and leaving the general manufacturing interests without that protection to which they are entitled, and thus dividing the strength which those great interests ought to have. By'

ments which had treated imported ores, and to aid the domestic producers of copper in pocketing large profits. The displacement of the imported copper by the Lake Superior product would have come in any case; for, as events proved, the sources of supply in this country were rich enough not only to oust foreign competitors at home, but soon to invade the market abroad. With the aid of the duty, the mining companies were able to form a combination which fixed the price of copper within the country at a higher price than that ruling abroad. When it was impossible to dispose of the entire product within the country, large quantities were sent abroad and sold at whatever price could be got,—lower in any case than the domestic price. The great profits secured by those who were shrewd and fortunate in developing the mines were doubtless due in the main to the unsurpassed richness of the copper deposits. But they were increased by the copper duty of 1869; and thus for a series of years the great natural resources of the country became a cause not of abundance and cheapness, but of curtailment of supply and dearness.[1]

Still another instance of the increase of duties since the war is to be found in the case of steel rails. Before 1870 steel rails had been charged with duty under the head of

---

still, if a bill is introduced which gives protection to copper, trusting to the magnanimity of the Representatives from the West who have wool and copper protected, I should probably vote for the bill."—*Ibid.*, p. 161.

[1] On the effect of the copper act, see Mr. Wells' Essay, already referred to, in the Cobden Club series, pp. 518–521. *Cf.* the "Report of the Tariff Comm.," pp. 2554–2577. On later developments in the copper industry see the present author's *Some Aspects of the Tariff Question*, ch. xi.

"manufacturers of steel not otherwise provided for," and
Steel rails, as such had paid forty-five per cent. The
1870. tariff act of 1870 changed this to a specific
duty of 1¼ cents per pound, or $28 per gross ton.
At the time, the change caused an increase, but no
very great increase, in the duty. The Bessemer process
of making steel had hardly begun to be used in 1870,
and the price of steel rails at that time in England
was about $50 per ton. The *ad-valorem* rate of forty-
five per cent., calculated on this price, would make the
duty $22.50 per ton, or not very much less than the duty
of $28 per ton imposed by the act of 1870. Between
1870 and 1873, the price of steel rails advanced in England, and the specific duty of $28 imposed in the former
year was not higher than the *ad-valorem* rate of forty-five
per cent. would have been. But after 1873 the prices of
Bessemer steel and of steel rails steadily went down. As
they did so, the specific duty became heavier in proportion to the price. By 1877 the average price of steel rails
in England was only a little over $31 per ton; and since
1877 the English price has not on the average been so
high as $28 per ton. The duty of $28, which this country
imposed, therefore became equivalent to more than one
hundred per cent on the foreign price. The result of this
exorbitant duty was an enormous gain to the producers of
steel rails in the United States. The patent for the use of
the Bessemer process was owned by a comparatively small
number of companies; and these companies, aided by a

patent at home and protected by an enormous duty against foreign competitors, were enabled for a time to obtain exceedingly high prices for steel rails. During the great demand for railroad materials which began on the revival of business in 1879, and continued for several years thereafter, the prices of steel rails were advanced so high that English rails were imported into this country even though paying the duty of one hundred per cent. During this time the price in England was on the average in 1880 about $36 per ton, and in 1881 about $31 per ton. In this country during the same years the price averaged $67 and $61 per ton. That is, consumers in this country were compelled to pay twice as much for steel rails as they paid in England. Any thing which increases the cost of railroad-building tends to increase the cost of transportation; and a tax of this kind eventually comes out of the pockets of the people in the shape of higher railroad-charges for carrying freight and passengers. The domestic producers of steel rails secured enormous profits, of one hundred per cent. and more on their capital, during these years. These profits, as is always the case, caused a great extension of production. The men who had made so much money out of Bessemer steel in 1879–81 put this money very largely into establishments for making more steel. New works were erected in all parts of the country. At the same time the demand fell off in consequence of the check to railroad-building; and the increased supply, joined to the small demand, caused prices here to fall almost to the English rates. But during the years of speculation and railroad-building the tariff had yielded great gains to makers of steel rails; and popular feeling against this state of things was so strong that in 1883 Congress felt compelled, as we shall see, to make a considerable reduction in the duty.[1]

Still another case, and one which bears some resemblance to the woollen act of 1867, is to be found in the change of the duty on marble, which was made in 1870. The duty on marble had been put in 1864 at fifty cents per cubic foot, and twenty per cent. in addition. This, it may be remarked, is one of the not infrequent cases in which our tariff has imposed, and still imposes, both *ad-valorem* and specific duties on the same article. No compensating principle, such as is found in the woollen schedule, explains most of these mixed duties; and it is hard to find any good reason for retaining them, and giving the customs authorities the task of assessing the duty both on value of the article and on its weight or measure. The cause of their retention, there can be little doubt, is that they serve to conceal the real extent of the duties imposed. The duty on marble, for instance, had been thirty per cent. in 1861, and had been raised to forty per

Marble, 1864 and 1870.

---

[1] The effect of the steel-rail duty is discussed more in detail in Mr. J. Schoenhof's "Destructive Influence of the Tariff," ch. vii. On the profits made by the manufacturers, see Mr. A. S. Hewitt's speech in Congress, May 16, 1882, *Congress. Record*, pp. 3980–83. On later developments, J refer to *Some Aspects of the Tariff Question*. Part III. especially ch. xii.

cent. in 1862. The mixed duty put on in 1864 was equivalent to eighty per cent. and more.[1] A direct increase of the duty from forty to eighty per cent. would hardly have been ventured on; but the adoption of the mixed duty veiled the change which was in fact made. One would have supposed that this rate of eighty per cent. would have sufficed even for the most ardent supporter of home industries; but in 1870 a still further increase was brought about. It was then enacted that marble sawed into slabs of a thickness of two inches or less should pay twenty-five cents for each superficial square foot, and thirty per cent. in addition; slabs between two and three inches thick should pay thirty-five cents per square foot, and thirty per cent.; slabs between three and four inches thick should pay forty-five cents per square foot, and thirty per cent.; and so on in proportion. Marble more than six inches thick paid at the old rate of fifty cents per cubic foot, and twenty per cent. It is evident that the change made in the duty on marble in slabs caused a great increase. The duty on the thinnest slabs (two inches or less in thickness) became $1.50 per cubic foot, and thirty per cent. in addition; this same

---

[1] The duty of 1864 was fixed, as Mr. Morrill then explained, in accordance with an arrangement made between the importing merchants and "the gentlemen in Washington in the marble-quarry interest." The latter were Mr. Morrill's constituents. It did not seem to occur to that gentleman that the persons who were to pay for the marble should be regarded at all. Originally Mr. Morrill had even proposed a duty of seventy-five cents per cubic yard, with twenty per cent. in addition. See *Congr. Globe*, 1863–64, pp. 2746-2747.

marble had hitherto been admitted at fifty cents per cubic foot, and twenty per cent. The new rates of 1870 were equivalent to between 100 and 150 per cent. on the value, and proved to be practically prohibitive. The effect of the marble duty and of the change made in it in 1870 can be understood only by those who know the circumstances under which marble is produced and imported in this country. The only marble imported, and that which alone is affected by the duty, is fine marble used for ornamental purposes in mantel-pieces, furniture, grave-stones, etc. Such marble comes into use very largely in the shape of slabs of a few inches in thickness. The marble is imported, notwithstanding the heavy duty, from Italy, whence it is brought cheaply by ships that have taken out grain and other bulky cargoes. It is produced in the United States in a single district in Vermont. The owners of the marble quarries in this district had their product raised in price almost to the extent of the duty of 80 or 150 per cent. The result was to make these quarries very valuable pieces of property, and to put very handsome profits into the pockets of their owners; profits which represent practically so much money which Congress ordered those who used ornamental marble to pay over to the quarry-owners.[1]

Wool and woollens, copper, steel rails, marble, which we have now considered, are sufficient examples of the man-

---

[1] In regard to the duty on marble, see " Tariff Commission Report," pp. 227, 1560, 1648.

ner in which duties, already raised to high figures during the war, were still further increased after the war, for the benefit of the domestic producers. Other instances could be given in which an equal disregard Other of the consumer and taxpayer has been examples, shown. The duty on flax, the raw material flax, nickel. of a manufacture not over-prosperous, had been $15 per ton in 1864; in 1870 it was raised to $20 on undressed flax, and to $40 on dressed flax. Nickel had been admitted free of duty in 1861, and had paid only fifteen per cent. by the act of 1864. In 1870 the duty was sudenly made thirty cents per pound, or about forty per cent. on the value. Nickel, like marble, is produced in only one locality in this country. There exists a single nickel mine, in Pennsylvania, owned by a well-known advocate of protection, and, with the aid of the tariff, this mine, doubtless, has yielded the owner very handsome returns.[1] Examples need not be multiplied. Enough has

---

[1] Mr. Joseph Wharton, of Philadelphia, is the owner of the nickel-mine, and has appeared frequently before Congressional Committees in advocacy of this duty and of others. See the "Tariff Commission Report," pp. 201–204. A heated controversy on this subject was raised by Mr. Wharton's pamphlet, "The Duty on Nickel" (Philadelphia: 1883), with which may be compared the remarks of Mr. D. A. Wells, in the *Princeton Review*, July, 1883, pp. 8–11.

In the years after 1870, the nickel situation was affected, first, by the discovery of rich mines in New Caledonia, controlled by a French Company; and next, about 1889, by the discovery of a rich mine in Canada. The Pennsylvania mine seems to have shown signs of exhaustion, and its owner advocated the admission of nickel ore and matte at a low rate of duty, with the retention of the duty on nickel itself for the protection of the works which had been put up to refine the Pennsylvania nickel. See the statements of Mr.

been said to show how the increase of duties of which the war was the immediate occasion, continued after the war had ceased.

The retention of the high duties of the war is to be explained by the pressure of other problems, the fear of infringing on vested rights and interests, the powerful opposition which is always met in withdrawing public bounty when once it has been conferred. To explain the additions to the protective system made after the war, by measures like the woollens act of 1867 and the copper act of 1869, some regard must also be had to the influence of private interests in Congress. The details of these acts, and of other acts passed since the war, have undoubtedly been settled in large part by men who had a direct pecuniary interest in securing an increase of the duties. It is highly improbable that bribery, direct or indirect, was ever used to affect tariff legislation. But it may be fairly said that a general laxity of opinion on the duties of public men enabled provisions to find their way into tariff legislation which could not have been carried through in a more healthy state of affairs. The demoralization has shown itself quite as strikingly in other parts of federal legislation as in tariff matters; it has shown itself most strikingly of all in some State legislatures and in municipal administration. During the period immediately after the war, the state of things was probably

---

Wharton and others in the Senate " Tariff Testimony " of 1888–89, pp. 1347–64, and in the House " Report on the Revision of the Tariff," 1890 pp. 1153-1161.

worse than at any other time in our history. The redundant currency promoted speculation and gambling; jobs were plenty and lobbyists strong; some legislators thought it not improper to become "interested" in enterprises which their votes might affect, and few Congressmen hesitated to advocate measures that would put money in the pockets of influential constituents. Conditions of this sort account largely for the higher duties of the years after the war. It cannot be said that there was any consistent policy or sustained public opinion in favor of extending the protective system.

CHAPTER IV.

THE TARIFF ACT OF 1883.

THE tariff act of 1883 made the first general revision since the Civil War, apart from the abortive horizontal reduction of 1872. After the crisis of 1873, little or nothing was heard about the tariff. Currency questions came into prominence during the period of depression. The successful resumption of specie payments in 1879, and the revival of prosperity which set in at the same time, finally diverted public attention from the monetary situation; and the same set of causes contributed to centre attention once more on the tariff system. The revival of activity in 1879 and the years following caused a great increase in imports, and so a great increase in the customs revenue. For several years after 1879, the surplus revenue was on the average over a hundred millions annually. The redundant revenue compelled a revision of the customs duties, and it was inevitable that not only the financial but the economic aspects of the tariff should once more become prominent.

The connection between tariff legislation and the state of the revenue has indeed been almost constant in our history. In 1842 an empty treasury was followed by the passage of a high protective tariff. In 1857 an overflowing revenue caused a reduction of the duties. In 1861 the Morrill tariff was passed, partly in order to make good a deficit. During the war the need of money led to the act of 1864. The ten per cent. reduction of 1872 was called out largely by the redundant revenue; its abolition in 1875 was excused by the falling off in the government income. The protection- *Agitation on the tariff renewed.* ist acts of 1824 and 1828 and the so-called revenue act of 1846, stand practically alone as general measures little affected by the state of the revenue at the time. Since the Civil War, the financial situation has usually given the occasion for changes in the tariff rates; and this is true of the act of 1883, as well as of the acts of 1890 and 1897.

In 1882 Congress passed an act for the appointment of a Tariff Commission, which was to report at the next session of Congress what changes it thought desirable. The majority in Congress *Tariff Commission of 1882.* then was protectionist, and of the gentlemen appointed by the President on this commission a majority were advocates of high protection; while no member could be said to represent that part of the public which believed a reduction of the protective duties to be desirable. Mr. John L. Hayes, the secretary of the Wool Manufacturers' Association, was president of the commission. Its report was laid before Congress at the beginning of the session of 1882–83. At first no action on this report or on the tariff seemed likely to be taken; for the House, in which rev- enue bills must originate, was unable to agree on any

bill. But the House having passed a bill for the reduction of some of the internal taxes, the Senate tacked
to this bill, as an amendment, a tariff bill, based, in
the main, on the recommendations of the Tariff Commission. When this bill came before the House the
protectionists again succeeded, as in 1872, in obtaining a
parliamentary victory. By an adroit manœuvre they managed to have it referred to a conference committee.[1] In
this committee the details of the tariff act were finally settled ; for the bill, as reported to the Senate and House by
the conferees of the two bodies, was passed by
them and became law. The object of the ma-   Act of 1883 ;
nœuvre was to check the reduction of duties as   how passed.
it appeared in the Senate bill; and this object was attained. The changes made by the conference committees
were, as a rule, in a protectionist direction. The duties

---

[1] This manœuvre was a curious example of the manner in which the rules
of Congress are manipulated in order to affect legislation. A two-thirds vote,
by the existing rules, was required to bring the Senate bill before the House.
A two-thirds majority in favor of the bill could not be obtained ; though it
was probable that on a direct vote a majority in its favor could have been got.
The protectionists wished to have the bill referred to a conference committee, which would probably act in the direction desired by them. For this
purpose a resolution was introduced by Mr. Reed, of Maine, providing for
a new rule of the House, by which a bare majority was to have power to
take up a bill amended by the Senate for the purpose of non-concurrence in
the Senate amendments, *but not for the purpose of concurrence.* By the passage of this rule a majority of the House could take up the tariff bill, and
then refuse to concur in the Senate amendments ; but under this rule the
amendments could not be concurred in. There was, consequently, no
possibility of passing the tariff bill in the shape in which it came from the
Senate. The bill had to be referred to a conference committee ; and in
that committee, as the text states, the details of the bill were settled. The
Reed rule, though made a permanent rule of the House, was passed merely
in order to attain this object.

on a number of articles were raised by the committee above the rates of the Senate bill, and even above the rates which the House had shown a willingness to accept. The consequence was that the tariff act, as finally passed, contained a much less degree of reduction than the original Senate bill; and it was passed in the Senate only by a strict party vote of 32 to 31, while the original Senate bill had been passed by a vote of 42 to 19.[1]

In taking up the provisions of the act of 1883, it will be best to consider first those cases in which an increase in the duties was made. Changes of this sort were made in a considerable number of cases, and are significant of the general character of the measure. To begin with, the duties on certain classes of woollen goods were raised.

[1] Mr. Morrison, in 1884, said: "The office and duty of a conference committee is to adjust the difference between two disagreeing houses. This House had decided that bar-iron of the middle class should pay $20 a ton; the Senate that it was to pay $20.16 a ton. The gentlemen of the conference committee reconciled this difference—how? By raising bar-iron [of this class] above both House and Senate to $22.40. The Tariff Commission reported that the tariff on iron ore should be 50 cents a ton. The Senate said it should be 50 cents a ton. The House said it should be 50 cents a ton. Gentlemen of the conference committee reconciled the agreement of the House, Senate, and Tariff Commission into a disagreement, and made the duty on iron ore 75 cents a ton. The gentlemen of the conference did a similar service for the great corporation of corporations, the Iron and Steel Association, by giving it a tax of $17 on steel rails, which the House had fixed at $15 and the Senate at $15.68 per ton." Quoted in Nelson's "Unjust Tariff Law," pp. 22, 23. *Cf.* remarks to the same effect by Senator Beck, who was a member of the conference committee.—*Cong. Record*, 1883–84, p. 2786.

The conferrees for the Senate were Messrs. Morrill, Sherman, Aldrich, Bayard, and Beck; for the House, Messrs. Kelley, McKinley, Haskell, Randall, and Carlisle. All but three (Bayard, Beck, and Carlisle) were strong protectionists.

On most woollens the figures were lowered ; though, as
will be seen, the reduction in these cases was not such as
to bring any benefit to consumers.   But on certain classes
of woollens, on which a reduction of duty, if made, would
have been of real importance, the duties were advanced.
This was the case with dress goods made wholly of wool.
Under the act of 1867 such goods had paid a maximum
duty of eight cents per yard and forty per cent.   The
forty per cent. rate on these goods had already been above
the general *ad-valorem* duty of thirty-five per cent. established by the act of 1867.   Nevertheless the act of 1883
increased the duty on these goods to nine cents a yard
and forty per cent.   The Tariff Commission had even
recommended twelve cents a yard and forty per cent.
Goods of this class were, and still are, the largest single
item in the importations of woollens into the United
States.   They are made to no very great extent by the
domestic manufacturers.   The new duty was intended to
enable the latter to engage profitably in making them ;
since the old duty, though it amounted in all to more
than sixty-five per cent. on the value of the imports, had
not sufficed for this purpose.   The increase in the specific
duty was not supposed to be necessary to give more
effective compensation for the wool duty ; in fact, as
we shall see, the duty on wool was slightly lowered, so
that the compensating duty, if changed at all, should have
gone down.   The new duty was a concession to the demand of the manufacturers for still further protection.

---

[1] The Tariff Commission, in its "Report" (p. 31), said : " The new clause
in relation to all-wool merino goods is a new provision, and has in view the

It did not attain its object; all-wool dress goods continued to be imported, and few, if any, were made at home; and in time a still further increase of duty was asked, and at last was granted in the tariff act of 1890.

Next to dress goods, such as were discussed in the preceding paragraph, the class of woollens of which the importations were largest were the finer grades of cloths and cassimeres. The importation of these went on steadily in large quantities. Their production was carried on in this country only to a limited extent. It is not surprising, therefore, to find here also a rise of the rates in the act of 1883. Cloths were divided into two classes: those costing more and those costing less than eighty cents per pound. The latter, costing less than eighty cents, were admitted, as before, at an *ad-valorem* duty of thirty-five per cent. But the former, costing more than eighty cents per pound, were made to pay forty per cent. The specific compensating duty was reduced somewhat in both cases, in connection with the lower duties on wool, which will presently be discussed; but the *ad-valorem* rate, that which is avowedly protective, was increased. This increase also did not have the desired effect; importations continued in large volume; and here again a further advance in duties was asked and obtained in 1890.

A change of almost the same kind was made in the

introduction of fabrics never yet successfully made in this country. Many of these goods constitute staple fabrics * * * and their manufacture would be a desirable acquisition to our national industry." The duties of the act of 1883 on wool and woollens were discussed in detail by Mr. Hayes in *Bulletin Wool Mf.*, xiii. 1-13, 89-128.

duties on cotton goods.   Here also the duty was lowered
on the common grades of goods ; and on these grades the
reduction was again a purely nominal one.   But on other
grades of cotton goods, whose importation still continued,
and on which a decrease in the duty would have caused
some lowering of prices and relief from taxation, there
was no reduction, but an increase.   The duty on cotton
hosiery, embroideries, trimmings, laces, insertings, had
been thirty-five per cent. under the old law.   In the act
of 1883 it was made forty per cent.   The duty of thirty-
five per cent. had been imposed during the war, in 1864,
at a time when raw cotton was taxed, and the manufactured cotton also paid a heavy internal tax.   This rate had
remained unchanged from 1864 till 1883, notwithstanding
the abolition of the internal taxes.   The importance of
the new duty of forty per cent. is clear only when we
know that imports of cottons consist chiefly of goods of
the class on which the duty is raised.   About two thirds
of the cottons imported became subject to the increased
duty.

The process by which the protective system has gradually been brought to include almost every article, whatever its character, whose production in the country is
possible, is illustrated by the history of the duty on iron
ore.   This most raw of raw materials had paid in 1861 a
duty of ten per cent. as an unenumerated article; and the
rate had not been changed during the war, since the article was not one likely to be imported or to yield revenue.
In 1870, when the protective principle, as we have seen,

was applied with greater strictness in various directions, the duty was raised to twenty per cent. In later years iron ore began to be imported in considerable quantities, especially from Spain; and the duty was raised in 1883 to seventy-five cents per ton, or about thirty-five per cent. on the value.

Still another instance of the advance of duties in the new act was in the rates on certain manufactures of steel.

Steel. Here, as has so often happened, the increase was concealed under what was in appearance merely a change in classification. The duties on steel ingots, bars, sheets, and coils had been, until 1883, those fixed in the tariff of 1864,—from two and one quarter cents to three and one half cents per pound, varying with the value of the steel. The act of 1883 reduced these duties slightly, making them from two to three and a quarter cents per pound. But previous to 1883 "steel, in forms not otherwise specified," had been admitted at a duty of thirty per cent. Under this provision, which had been in force since 1864, a number of articles, like cogged ingots, rods, piston-rods, steamer shafts, and so on, had paid only thirty per cent. The act of 1883, however, specificially enumerated these and other articles, and put them in the same schedule with steel ingots and bars,— that is, compelled them to pay a duty of from two to three and a quarter cents a pound. The effect was a considerable rise in the duties on the newly enumerated articles.

These examples indicate the mode and the extent in which the protective system was extended in the act of

1883. As a rule, duties were advanced on protected articles
of which importations continued in considerable volume.
The advance was by no means universal, being affected,
as our tariff legislation so often has been, by the haphazard manner in which the details of the measure were
finally settled.   But it was made in so large a number of
important cases as to give the act a distinctly protectionist
flavor.   Such extensions of the protective system probably were not at that time expected or desired by the
public.   The Tariff Commission had been given the task
of revising the tariff "judiciously."   The rates recommended by it were declared to effect a general reduction
of twenty per cent. or more, and the declared object of
the leaders in the dominant party was to make a reform
in the tariff system.   Reform then was still understood to
mean reduction, and real reduction, in the protective
duties; and an actual increase in rates, such as we have
seen on cottons, woollens, and other articles, was no part of
what the public expected or the act professed to do.   In
truth, these changes were made in good part without plan
or consistency, as so many details have been settled in our
statutes: a result inevitable from the absence, in our
system, of concentrated responsibility for the details of
legislation.   Some advances were proposed by the Tariff
Commission, others by the House and Senate Committees; some by amendments in the House, others by
amendments in the Senate; not a few, as was noted
above, were finally settled in the Conference Committee.
In many cases, they were half concealed by changes in

classification, or coupled with reductions of other articles in the same schedules. Had a separate bill been brought forward, proposing the higher duties contained in the act. it certainly could not have passed.

We may turn now to an examination of the cases in which duties were reduced in 1883.

The schedules in the tariff which have the greatest effect on the welfare of the country are those fixing the duties on iron and wool; and to these we will first give our attention. The change in the duty on wool was sufficiently simple. The *ad-valorem* rate was taken off. The duty of 1867, it will be remembered, had been, on wools costing less than thirty-two cents, ten cents per pound plus eleven per cent. *ad valorem*, and, on wools costing more than thirty-two cents, twelve cents per pound plus ten per cent. *ad valorem*. These *ad-valorem* rates of eleven and ten per cent. were taken off, and the rates left simply at ten and twelve cents per pound. In regard to the greater part of the wools raised in the United States, this reduction was purely nominal. It left the duty on the cheaper grades of wool, raised in Texas and in the Territories, at a point where it was still entirely prohibitory. So far as concerns the higher grades of wools, such as are raised in Ohio and neighboring States, the reduction was real, though so small in amount that it practically left the situation unchanged.[1] On carpet wools the duty was

---

[1] The duty in the act of 1883 was ten cents on wool costing *thirty* cents or less, and twelve cents on that costing more than thirty cents. The change (in the line of division, according to value) from thirty-two to thirty cents was not without importance ; and, as far as it went, it evidently tended to neutralize the reduction. See the *Bulletin Wool Mf.*, xiii., 11, 109.

reduced from the former rates of six and three cents a pound, to five and two and a half cents. These wools are practically not raised in the United States at all ; and the reduction on them was again real, though slight.

On the whole, the changes in the duty on this raw material indicated a desire to make concessions to the opponents of protection. Greater reductions would probably have been made but for the fear of arousing among the wool growers a feeling of opposition to the protective system as a whole. Little can be said in favor of the duty on wool ; and even on strictly protectionist grounds much can be said against it. Notwithstanding the cumbrous machinery of compensating duties, it undoubtedly has a hampering influence on the wool manufacture, and has been one factor, though perhaps not the most important, in confining this industry to the limited range that is so often complained of. As a tax on raw materials, it tends to bear with heavier weight than would be the case with the same duty on a finished product ; since it is advanced again and again by the wool dealer, the manufacturer, the cloth dealer, the tailor, each of whom must have a greater profit in proportion to the greater amount of capital which the wool duty and the higher price of wool make it necessary for him to employ. So strong and so clear are the objections to duties of this kind that hardly another civilized country, whatever its general policy, attempts to protect wool.[1]

---

[1] Not only England, but countries like France, Germany, Austria, Italy which have applied protective duties in recent years, admit wool free

Moreover, the reduction of a duty of this kind can take place with exceptional ease. Wool is not produced, as a rule, in large quantities, by persons who devote themselves exclusively to this as a business. It is mainly produced by farmers, whose chief income comes from other sources, and on whom a reduction of duty and a fall of price would fall with comparatively little weight. In the Western States and Territories, it is true, wool is grown on large sheep ranches, by producers with whom it is not a subsidiary business. But the qualities of wool grown there are least affected by the duty. While the price of Territory wools is probably higher than the price of similar wools abroad, it is by no means higher by the full extent of the duty. The argument for the consideration of vested interests is consequently less strong than in the case of manufactures in which a large plant is invested, and where the interests of a large body of workmen are involved in the retention of things as they are.

We turn now to the reductions of duty on woollen goods, which would naturally follow the lower duty on wool. It has been seen that the *ad-valorem*, or protective, duty was not decreased at all, and Woollens. that on the finer classes of woollens it was increased from thirty-five to forty per cent. But the specific, or compensating, duty was reduced from fifty cents to thirty-five cents a pound. The woollens duty of 1883 was thirty-five cents a pound and thirty-five per cent. on goods costing less than eighty cents per pound, and thirty-five cents and forty per cent. on goods costing more than eighty cents. The lowering of the specific duty was in part called for by the reduction of the duty on wool; but the decrease was somewhat larger than the reduced duty on the raw material made necessary. The compensating duty in the new act was fixed on the assumption that no more than three and one half pounds of wool are used in making a pound of cloth; whereas the act of 1867, it will be remembered, was framed on the basis of four pounds of wool to the pound of cloth. This may be called a tacit confession that the compensating duty of 1867 had been excessive; and the new arrangement took away some of the protection which was formerly given by the specific duty. But the changes were more nominal than real. So far as the finer grades of woollens were concerned, it was more than offset by the increase in the *ad-valorem* duty from thirty-five to forty per cent. So far as the cheaper grades of woollens were concerned, it had no real effect. The duty on these was prohibitory before, and it remained prohibitory. Such a change has no effect on trade or prices, and brings no benefit to consumers. Precisely similar is the state of things in regard to flannels, blankets, and similar goods. On these also the specific duty was reduced, on the cheapest grades from a rate of twenty cents a pound to rates of ten and twelve cents. But the new rates were still high enough to shut out importation, and brought about no change beyond that of the figures on the statute-book.[1]

[1] Complaint was made that the act of 1883 reduced the duties on goods more than the duties on wool   ~ Hayes's articles in *Bulletin*

Changes of precisely this kind are to be found in other parts of the act of 1883. The rates on the cheap grades of cotton goods, for instance, show a considerable reduction. On the lowest class of unprinted goods the duty had been five cents per yard ; it was made two and one half cents. But the old duty had for many years ceased to have any appreciable effect on the prices of cotton goods. The common grades of cottons can be made, as a rule, as cheaply in this country as anywhere in the world ; in fact, some of them are regularly exported in large quantities. If the duty on such cottons were entirely abolished, it is probable that they could not be imported ; and it is certain that a very small duty would suffice to shut out from our market all foreign competitors in them. Under these circumstances a reduction of duty like that of 1883 could be of no effect whatever. The same holds good of almost all the various reductions in the specific duties on plain and printed cotton goods.

Cottons.

Wool Mf., vol. xiii. This was certainly the case with worsted goods, which were admitted at specific duties not sufficient to compensate for the duties on wool. The mistake in adjusting these duties was made by Mr. Hayes himself, in the bill framed by the Tariff Commission. It led to a long struggle on the part of the manufacturers to get a construction of the act of 1883 making worsteds dutiable as woollens. The Democratic administration of 1885–89 refused to adopt such a construction ; the Republican administration in 1889 did so, but the courts, when a case was tried before them, promptly decided that the remedy was not to be found by misconstruing the statute ; and in 1890 a special act was passed, in advance of the general tariff act of that year, making worsteds dutiable as woollens. A good brief statement of this episode is in the *Report of the Secretary of the Treasury for 1887*, p. 35. The *Bulletin Wool Mf.* is full of it from 1886 to 1889, and a detailed account of the last steps in 1889 is in vol. xx. The special act is in 26 *Statutes at Large*, 105.

These changes also were nominal. On the other hand, in the case of the finer cotton goods, laces, and trimmings, on which a lowering of the rates would have been of real effect, there was, as we have seen, no decrease, but an increase.

The duty on pig-iron was reduced from $7.00 to $6.72 a ton. This change was insignificant, hardly two per cent. on the foreign price of iron. A greater could have been made without danger of any disturbance of the iron trade. The same was the case with the reduction on bar-iron, which, on the ordinary grade, lowered the duty from one cent a pound to eight tenths of a cent. The reduction still left the duty high enough to prevent any lowering of prices and any effect on trade. The duties on the various forms of manufactured iron—hoop, band, sheet, plate iron—went down in much the same way. The reductions were slight in all cases, and often merely nominal. In general, the new rates on iron and its manufactures were such as to have no appreciable effect on the trade and welfare of the country.

The duty on steel rails showed a considerable reduction. The old rate had been $28 a ton; the new one was $17. If this change had been made four or five years earlier, it would have been of much practical importance; but when made, it had no effect whatever. It has already been said that, after the enormous profits made by the steel-rail makers in 1879–1881, the production in this country was greatly increased. At the same time the demand from the railroads fell off, and the huge quantities which the mills were able to turn out, could be disposed of, if at all, only at prices greatly reduced. The consequence was that the price of rails, which in 1880 was higher than the English price by the full extent of the duty of $28, fell rapidly after 1881, and brought the American price in 1885 to a point but little above the English. The new duty of 1883 was under these circumstances still prohibitory. In 1887, when a revival of railway building set in, the price of rails again went up. It is probable that at this time, when there was an active demand for rails, the decline of the duty to $17 was of real effect, preventing the American price from rising as high as it would have gone if the old duty had been retained. But the demand fell off quickly after 1887: the American price fell correspondingly, and soon became higher than the English price by an amount much less than the duty of $17. With the possible exception of the year 1887, the duty of $17 was as much a prohibitory one as the old duty of $28 had been, and the reduction on the whole was as much nominal as those in other parts of the iron schedule.

Analogous in its effects to the reduction on steel rails was that on copper. The duty on this article went down from five cents, the rate imposed in 1869, to four cents a pound. The duty on copper had enured to the benefit of the owners of the copper mines of Lake Superior, aiding them to combine and fix the price of copper without fear of competition from abroad. The great profits of their mines caused them steadily to increase their product; and although much of their surplus was disposed of abroad, at prices lower than those demanded at home, the growing supply caused the domestic price slowly to fall. The discovery of large deposits of copper, in latter years, in Montana and Arizona, and the shipment to market of a great deal of copper from these sources, broke for a while the monopoly of the Lake Superior combination, and caused the price to go down still farther. Importation of copper in any considerable quantities ceased many years ago. The steady increase in the domestic supply brought the price to a point but little above the foreign price. The maintenance of the duty still enabled the combined copper producers at times to secure a higher price than they could have got without the duty; but under ordinary conditions the enormous quantities of copper yielded by the mines compelled a price to be accepted virtually as low as the foreign price.

The cases of copper and steel rails are sometimes referred to as successful applications of protection to young industries. On the surface, the object of such protection seems here to have been obtained. That the price of these articles fell after the duty was imposed, indeed proves nothing; for their prices fell the world over. But their prices fell faster than in foreign countries, and fell nearly, if not quite, to the foreign level; and a price as low as the foreign price, or lower, is the object sought by protection to young industries. This result, however, was not the consequence, in the case of copper certainly, of any stimulus given by the duty to improved methods of production. It was the result of the extraordinary richness of the copper mines, whose discovery and use was not affected by the duty, and would have brought the price down even sooner had it not been for the duty. The duty, so far from stimulating the fall in price, checked it. Much the same is true of steel rails. To be sure, here there seems to have been some stimulus to invention, and some advance by American works over the processes in use abroad ; but in the main the decline in the price of rails has been due to improvements common to all countries, to the discovery of rich beds of iron ore on Lake Superior, and not least to the decline in the cost of transporting and bringing together the coal and ore for making the Bessemer iron,—factors not perceptibly affected by the duty.

Other reductions in the act of 1883 may be briefly noted. The duty on marble was fixed at sixty-five cents per cubic foot on rough marble, and at $1.10 per cubic foot on marble sawed, dressed, and in slabs. This was a slight decrease from the compound duties discussed in the preceding chapter.[1] The duty on nickel was put at fifteen cents a pound, in place of the previous duty of twenty and thirty cents a pound. Practically all the nickel imported had come in at the duty

Other reductions.

---

[1] See p. 224.

of twenty cents; consequently the reduction was less considerable than it appeared at first sight to be. A change of greater importance was the reduction of the duty on silks from sixty to fifty per cent. In part, it is true, this was again a merely nominal change, many silk goods being as effectually kept out by a duty of fifty per cent. as by one of sixty. But a large quantity of silks were steadily imported; on these, and on goods of the same sort made in the country, the lowering of the duty meant a real decline in the burden of taxation.[1] The reduction of 1883 was as great as could have been expected, and was in marked contrast with the advances made in the duties on finer cotton and woollen goods. The same contrast appears in the reduction of the duty on finer linens from forty to thirty-five per cent. On a considerable number of other articles also reductions were made; the reductions being usually slight, yet sufficient in number to indicate a disposition to concede something to those who called for a curtailment of the protective duties.

The duties on a number of agricultural or mainly agricultural products, such as beef and pork, hams and bacon, lard, cheese, butter, wheat, corn, and oats were left unchanged in the act of 1883. The duty on barley was somewhat lowered at the request of the brewers of beer; and that on rice also was slightly reduced. But almost all of these products were

Wheat, corn, etc.

---

[1] On the history of the silk manufacture and on the new questions that arose in later years, I refer to *Some Aspects of the Tariff Question,* chapters xiv., xv., xvi.

charged with the same rates as in previous years. It is needless to say that the duties on them have no effect whatever, except to an insignificant extent on the local trade across the Canadian border. The duties were left unchanged in order to maintain the fiction that the agricultural population secured through them a share of the benefits of protection. The reductions in this schedule, on barley and on rice, affected almost the only products on which the duties in fact were of any advantage to the agricultural producer or of any disadvantage to the consumer. In this regard, as in others, there was a sharp contrast between the legislation of 1883 and that which followed it in 1890 and 1897.

Enough has been said of the details of the act of 1883. Its general character cannot be easily described ; in truth, it can hardly be said to have any general character. On the whole, it may be fairly described as a half-hearted attempt on the part of those wishing to maintain a system of high protection, to make some concession to a public demand for a more moderate tariff system.[1] Some duties were increased, some lowered ; nor was any consistent policy followed. Some raw materials, like

---

[1] Mr. John L. Hayes, the President of the Tariff Commission, writing more particularly of the new duties on wool and woollens, said, shortly after the passage of the act : " Reduction in itself was by no means desirable to us ; it was a concession to public sentiment, a bending of the top and branches to the wind of public opinion to save the trunk of the protective system. In a word, the object was *protection through reduction.* We were willing to concede only to save the essentials both of the wool and woollens tariff. * * * We wanted the tariff to be made by our friends."—*Bulletin Wool Mf.*, xiii., 94

wool and pig-iron, were admitted at slightly lower rates;
others, like iron ore, were charged with higher rates.
The same incongruities appear in the duties on more
finished goods ; though as to these it may be said that
the reductions were generally nominal, rarely of real effect.
Looking at the tariff system as a whole, it retained, substantially unchanged, the high level of duties reached
during and after the Civil War.   No new line of policy
was entered on, in one direction or the other ; and it
remained for the act of 1890, the next step in our tariff
history, to begin a sharp and unmistakable movement in
the direction of still higher protection.   That measure will
be the subject of the next chapter.

CHAPTER V.

THE TARIFF ACT OF 1890.

AFTER the passage of the tariff act of 1883 few persons would have expected, for a long series of years, a further extension of the protective system. Nevertheless, a marked increase of duties was made, within a few years, in the act of 1890, familiarly known as the McKinley tariff act: a measure which marks a new phase in our tariff history and in the protective controversy.

In the years immediately succeeding the passage of the act of 1883, several unsuccessful attempts were made to amend it.[1] In 1884, Mr. Morrison, of Illinois, introduced a bill by which a general reduction of twenty per cent., and the entire remission of duties on iron ore, coal, lumber, and other articles, were proposed. Mr. Morrison may have been moved to advocate the plan of a "horizontal" reduction by the example which had been set in 1872; and doubtless he was also influenced by the circumstance that the protectionists themselves had arranged the details of the act of 1883, and could not complain of disproportionate reductions, or of a disturbance of relative rates,

---

[1] An account of these attempts is given by Mr. O. H. Perry in the *Quarterly Journal of Economics* for October, 1887, vol. ii., pp. 69–79.

under a plan which affected all articles equally. Nevertheless, the proposal met with vehement opposition not
only from the Republicans, but from a strong minority in
Mr. Morrison's own party. It was disposed of on May 6,
1884, by a vote (156 to 151) striking out its enacting
clause. Two years later, in the Forty-ninth Congress, a
similar disposition was made of another bill introduced
by Morrison. The proposal of 1886, however, was different from that of 1884, in that it made detailed changes in
the duties. Lumber, salt, wool, hemp, flax, and other
articles were put on the free list ; the duty on woollens
was made thirty-five per cent., the specific duties on woollens being removed with the duties on wool; and reductions were proposed on cottons and on sugar. The bill
never was discussed in Congress, for Mr. Morrison's
motion to proceed to its consideration was defeated by a
vote of 157 to 140, and during the rest of the session no
further attempt was made to take it up. Early in the
next session, in December, 1886, a motion was again made
to proceed to the consideration of revenue bills, and again
was defeated.[1]

With the session of 1887–88, however, the tariff controversy entered on a new phase. President Cleveland's

---

[1] Some other measures of less significance were also introduced in these
years, such as a bill of 1884, to restore the duties of 1867 on wool, which
was defeated by a close vote of 126 to 119, and bills introduced by Messrs.
Randall and Hiscock in 1886. Mr. Randall's bill proposed the removal of
internal taxes on tobacco, fruit brandies, and spirits used in the arts, entire
remission of duties on lumber, jute butts, and a few minor articles, and a
slight reduction of some other duties. Mr. Hiscock's bill proposed similar
changes in the internal taxes, and a large reduction of the duty on sugar,

annual message to Congress, in December, 1887, was de, voted entirely to the tariff, and urged vigorously a general reduction of duties, and more especially the removal of duties on raw materials. Mr. Cleveland's decided and outspoken attitude had the effect of committing his party unreservedly to a policy of opposition to the existing protective system, and so of making this question more distinctly a party matter than it had been at any time since the Civil War. It is true that in the campaign of 1884 the Republicans had put forward the tariff question as the main issue on which they wished to stand before the country ; but in that year the personal qualifications of Mr. Blaine for the Presidency played an important part in the election, which therefore could not be said to turn simply on the tariff issue. Moreover, within the Democratic party there was then an active minority opposed to the policy of tariff reduction favored by most of the Democrats. This minority had been strong enough to defeat Mr. Morrison's tariff bill of 1884. On the measure of that year, while 151 Democrats voted in the affirmative, 41 voted in the negative, and, with the aid of a compact Republican vote in the negative, put an end to the bill. The strength of this element in the Democratic party had declined somewhat in later years ; but in December, 1886, at the opening of the short session 1886–87,

with a bounty to American sugar-makers. Both of these bills, which indicated the manner in which the protectionists tried to grapple with the problem of reducing the revenue, were referred to the Committee of Ways and Means, and, not being reported from that body, never came to a vote in the House.

26 Democrats out of 169 voting were still recorded in opposition to the tariff reform measure then under consideration.[1]   In the new Congress, whose first session opened with Mr. Cleveland's message on the tariff, the situation was changed.   The Mills bill, so-called, prepared during that session, was passed by the Democrats in the House distinctly as a party measure ; out of 169 Democrats voting all but four voted for it.   The Republicans were as unanimous in voting against it, and, by way of counter manifesto, prepared in the Senate, where they had a majority, a bill for changing the tariff system in the direction of further protection.   The position of both parties was in this way sharply defined, and in the campaign of 1888 the tariff question was the issue squarely presented.

Neither the Senate bill prepared by the Republicans, nor the Mills bill prepared in the House by the Democrats, was expected to reach the stage of enactment. Both served simply to give concrete expression to the principles of the two parties.   The Mills bill reduced the duty on pig-iron to $6.00 a ton, fixed the duties on cottons at 35 or 40 per cent. (all specific duties on cottons being abolished), and made reductions of a similar sort, not often great in themselves, but significant in principle, on other manufactures.   The incisive changes were on raw materials.   Hemp, flax, lumber were to be admitted free.   Most important of all, wool was put on the free

---

[1] Tables on the votes, by States, on the bills considered between 1883 and 1887 will be found in Mr. Perry's article in the *Quarterly Journal of Economics*, just referred to.

list ; a change naturally accompanied by the proposal to
abolish the specific or compensating duties on woollen
goods.   The Senate bill, on the other hand, proposed
distinctly a further extension of the protective system.
A considerable number of duties were raised, especially
on manufactures of which imports continued in large
volume, like finer cottons and woollens.   On a few
articles concessions were made, as in the free admission
of jute, and a small reduction of the duty on steel rails.
In the crucial case of wool, the Senate bill provided for a
slight increase above the rates of 1883, both on clothing
and carpet wools, and for a corresponding advance in the
specific duties on woollens ; these changes being accompanied in some cases by an increase in the *ad-valorem*
duties on these goods.

The victory of the Republicans in 1888, and the election
of President Harrison, were the results of the issue thus
placed before the voters.   The election was won by a
narrow margin, and was affected by certain factors which
stood apart from the main issue.   The independent
voters had been disappointed with some phases of President Cleveland's administration of the civil service, and
many who had voted for him in 1884, did not do so in
1888.   In New York, whose vote was practically decisive,
political intrigues helped to turn the scale. On the whole,
however, the Republicans held their own, and even made
gains, throughout the country, on the tariff issue ; and
they might fairly consider the result a popular verdict in
favor of the system of protection.   But their opposition

to the policy of lower duties, emphasized by President Cleveland, had led them not only to champion the existing system, but to advocate its further extension, by an increase of duties in various directions. This they had proposed in the Senate bill of 1888, and had pledged themselves to effect in the debates of the campaign. Accordingly when the Congress then elected met for the session of 1889–90, the Republican majority in the House proceeded to pass a measure which finally became the tariff act of 1890. This measure may fairly be said to be the direct result of Mr. Cleveland's tariff message of 1887. The Republicans, in resisting the doctrine of that message, were led by logical necessity to the opposite doctrine of higher duties, and felt compelled, for the sake of party consistency and political prestige, to pass a tariff measure of some sort. Notwithstanding grave misgivings on the part of some of their leaders, especially those from the northwest, the act known popularly as the McKinley bill was pushed through after long and wearisome debates, and finally became law in October, 1890. To some of the details of this important measure we may now turn.[1]

The wool and woollens schedule had become the most important and most sharply debated part of the tariff system, and the changes made in it by the act of 1890 deserve careful attention. On wool, the division into three classes, clothing, combing, and carpet wool, was

---

[1] An excellent account of the legislative history of the act of 1890, and also of the acts of 1894 and 1897, is given in Stanwood's *American Tariff Controversy,* vol. ii., chapters 16, 17, 18.

retained, and the changes in duty were in the main significant from their direction rather than from their amount.
The duties on clothing and combing wool, it will be
remembered, had been slightly lowered in 1883 ; they were
slightly raised in 1890. That on clothing wool went up from
ten to eleven cents per pound ; on combing wool from
ten to twelve cents. The change was meant to put the
wool duties where they had been before 1883, and to
placate certain malcontents who ascribed a fall in the
price of wool to the reduction of duty of that year. The
decline in price was undoubtedly due to other causes, and
indeed was much greater than could have been accounted
for by the slight reduction of 1883 ; while the change in
duty in 1890 was too small to have any serious effect
beyond emphasizing the determination of the Republicans to yield nothing on this part of the protective system.
So far as the difference in rate between clothing and
combing wool goes (eleven cents on the one, twelve on
the other), it is difficult to see what was gained. The
distinction between the two classes is largely nominal,
many kinds of wool being available either for carding or
for combing, and the difference in the duties was in any
case too slight to have any appreciable effect. Apparently, it served simply to cause needless complication in
administering the collection of duties.

On carpet wools, a more radical change was adopted,
more radical at least in form. As has been observed
elsewhere, the conditions in regard to carpet wool are
peculiar. Practically no **wool** of this grade is grown in

the United States. It is of a coarse quality grown **mainly**
in countries like Asia Minor, India, Russia, and the Argentine Republic, from which it is imported into the
United States in large quantities. The reason why it is
not grown in advanced communities like the United
States, Australia, England, France, Germany, is very
simple. With the same labor and attention required for
carpet wool, the grower in civilized communities, by care
and intelligence in the breeding and management of sheep,
can secure a better quality of wool, commanding a higher
price; accordingly he confines himself to the more profitable sorts. The demand for an increase in the duty on
carpet wool was based on a suspicion that wool, properly
belonging to the clothing or combing class, had been entered as carpet wool, and so had escaped the higher duty.
Probably some part of the imported carpet wool is in
fact used in making cloths; but the fraction is small, and
can have no appreciable effect on the price of domestic
clothing wool. The endeavor to increase the duty naturally was opposed by the carpet manufacturers, and led
to an acrimonious discussion in the committee-rooms between them and the advocates of the supposed interests
of the farmers. The result in the McKinley act was a
compromise. The carpet-wool duty was made *ad valorem* instead of specific, varying from thirty-two per **cent.**
to fifty per cent.; the change to the *ad-valorem* method
being intended to make the duty adjust itself automatically to the quality and value of the wool.[1]   Obviously

----

[1] The change in duty is most easily explained by putting together the
rates under the acts of 1883 and 1890.

the cnange in one respect was objectionable : it brought
with it the temptations to fraud and undervaluation which
are inevitable under *ad-valorem* duties.   With it there
went some other provisions which made the new duties
more rigorous than they seem to be on their face.   Thus,
if any carpet wool should be improved at all by an admixture of merino or English blood, it became dutiable
as clothing or combing wool.   If any bale stated by the
importer to be dutiable under one class, contained any
wool of another class, the whole bale was dutiable at the
highest rate.   If any wool had been sorted or increased
in value by the rejection of any part of the original fleece,
it was subject to double duty.   Some of these provisions
were framed in ambiguous language, giving occasion foi
troublesome lit:gation and uncertainty as to the real effect
of the legislation.   But all were objectionable to those
who imported and used carpet wool, and emphasized the
policy of keeping that article within the protective system.   Yet if there is any article as to which that system
does not attain its object, it is carpet wool.   None is
grown in the country, and none is likely to be ; it is a
raw material for an important manufacture ; its free admission would harm no vested interest.

Turning now to the duties on manufactures of wool,

In 1883 carpet wool,
   if worth 12 cents or less per pound, paid **2½ cents.**
      "   more than 12 cents,   "   5   "
In 1890 carpet wool,
   if worth 13 cents or less per pound, paid **32 per cent.** *ad valorem.*
      "   more than 13 cents,   "   50   "   "   "
Most carpet wool is worth ten cents a pound or more ; consequently the
new *ad-valorem* rates meant, in almost all cases, an increase on the ~~duty.~~

we find a further development in the direction taken in
1883; namely, a development toward greater complications in the already complicated scheme of duties built up
in the act of 1867. It will be remembered that in 1883
the duty on woollen cloths proper, the central point in the
wool and woollens schedule, had been changed from the
uniform rate fixed in 1867 to rates varying with the value
of the goods. In the act of 1890 the policy of varying
rates was advanced still further. The mode in which
these duties developed cannot be better exhibited than
in tabular form, thus:

DUTIES ON WOOLLEN CLOTHS.

IN 1867,	IN 1883,	IN 1890.
50 cents per lb., plus 35 per cent.	(1) If worth 80 cents or less per lb., 35 cents per lb., plus 35 per cent. (2) If worth more than 80 cents per lb., 35 cents per lb., plus 40 per cent.	(1) If worth 30 cents or less per pound, 33 cents per lb. plus 40 per cent. (2) If worth between 30 and 40 cents per lb., 38½ cents per lb., plus 40 per cent. (3) If worth more than 40 cents per lb., 44 cents per lb., plus 50 per cent.

It will be seen that the act of 1890 reduced slightly the
specific duty on the cheapest woollens, those costing 30
cents or less per pound. This is another tacit admission,
similar to that made in the act of 1883, that on cheap goods
the old compensating duty had been excessive. The
ad-valorem rate on these goods was raised to forty per cent.
No pretence was now made of limiting the net protection
supposed to be given by the *ad-valorem* duty, to that mod-

erate rate of twenty-five per cent. which had been the nominal object of the original compound scheme of 1867. On
the second class of goods, costing between 30 and 40 cents
a pound, there was an increase over the rates of 1883 both
in the specific and in the *ad-valorem* duties. Finally, on
the third class under the new act, woollens costing over
40 cents, the increase in duties was marked : the specific
duty was 44 cents a pound, and the *ad-valorem* duty went
up to fifty per cent. On ready-made clothing the duties
were higher still, being fixed at 49½ cents a pound, plus
sixty per cent.

There are two features in this rearrangement of the
duties on woollens which call for comment. In the first
place, the compensating duty on the cheaper goods was
on the face of it made excessive. Thus, on goods valued
at between 30 and 40 cents a pound the compensating
duty was fixed at 38½ cents. The compensation was simply for the rise in the price of wool used by the American
manufacturers, due to our duty on imported wool. This
extra expense to the domestic manufacturer, in the higher
price of wool, was assumed, by the terms of the act, to be
as great as the total cost of making the same woollen
goods for the foreign manufacturer,—wool, wages, and
everything else. But the foreign goods were valued at
between 30 and 40 cents a pound, which means that they
cost about so much ; while the duty which compensated
the American producer was 38½ cents a pound. As will
be presently explained, this extraordinary compensating
duty was more nominal than real, since no classes of

goods to which it would apply are likely to be imported. But it was none the less an anomaly.

The second feature to be noted is connected with the first. It is the new dividing point in the valuation and classification of woollen cloths : the maximum duty being no longer on goods worth over 80 cents per pound, but on goods worth over 40 cents. The change obviously served to increase the duties more than would appear at first sight ; since goods worth between 40 and 80 cents now paid not the lowest, but the highest duty. The effect of the new classification in fact was that all cloths imported must pay the highest rate. The imports of woollens are chiefly of the finer qualities. When the act of 1883 was passed, it was probably expected that few woollens of the lower class then provided for (namely, those worth less than 80 cents per pound) would be imported. In the first years after 1883, this was the case. But as time went on, a growing proportion of woollens came in at the lower value and the correspondingly lower duty ; until in 1889 a good part of the cloths imported were classified at the lower rate. This unexpected development was due partly to a decline in the price of wool after 1883 ; partly to improvements in manufacturing which made it possible to produce goods more cheaply ; and partly, no doubt, to the temptation to make goods, and perhaps also undervalue them at the custom-house, in such manner as to bring them in at the lower rate of duty. At all events, the act of 1890 was so arranged as to put an end to this importation of woollens at the lower end of the schedule. To all intents and purposes it has made

all woollen goods likely to be imported at all, subject to
the maximum rate of duty.[1]

Next we may consider the duties on women's and
children's dress goods. The duties on these had already
been raised in 1883 above the rates of 1867; in 1890 they
were further raised. As in the case of cloths for men's
wear, the increase took place partly by direct advance in
the rates, partly by a shifting of the classification. The
compensating duty on these goods, it will be remembered,
had been from the first arranged by the yard, and not by
the pound. The changes in duty can again be best presented in tabular form.

DUTIES ON DRESS GOODS.

IN 1883.	IN 1890.
(1) Worth 20 cents a yard or less: duty, 5 cents a yard, plus 35 per cent.	(1) Cotton warp, worth 15 cents a yard or less: duty, 7 cents a yard, plus 40 per cent.
(2) Worth over 20 cents a yard: duty, 7 cents a yard, plus 40 per cent.	(2) Cotton warp, worth over 15 cents a yard: duty, 8 cents a yard, plus 50 per cent.
(3) Made wholly of wool: duty, 9 cents a yard, plus 40 per cent.	(3) If the warp contains any wool: duty, 12 cents a yard, plus 50 per cent.

[1] The imports of woollen cloths during the period in which the act of 1883 was in force were as follows (the figures denote thousands of dollars):

	Worth 80 cents or less.	Worth over 80 cents.
Fiscal Year 1884,	$243,000	$12,974,000
" 1885,	213,000	9,867,000
" 1886,	314,000	9,151,000
" 1887,	713,000	9,309,000
" 1888,	1,073,000	9,778,000
" 1889,	1,125,000	8,133,000

During that part of the fiscal year 1890-91, when the duties of the act of
1890 were in force, the imports of woollen cloths were,

The specific duty on the lowest class went from 5 cents to 7; the *ad-valorem* duty from 35 to 40 per cent. In the middle class the rates advanced from 7 to 8 cents, and from 40 to 50 per cent. The line of division by value went down from 20 to 15 cents, so that a larger proportion of the goods come in under the middle duty of 8 cents plus 50 per cent. On the third class, the rates went up in similar proportions,—from 9 to 12 cents, and from 40 to 50 per cent. One other effective change was made, indicated in the tabular statement, but deserving more detailed description. In 1883 the third class, in which the duties were highest, included goods made wholly of wool, and these only. In 1890, certain goods of mixed materials were transferred to it. The first two classes included, in 1890, fabrics "of which the warp consists *wholly* of cotton or other vegetable material." Consequently the third class included such as have a warp containing any fraction of wool; and these mixed goods, as well as goods made entirely of wool, become subject to the new maximum duty of 12 cents per yard, plus 50 per cent.

The changes on dress goods were undoubtedly those of greatest practical effect in the wool and woollens schedule.

---

(1) valued at 30 cents or less per pound	. . . .	$1,248
(2) valued at between 30 and 40 cents	. . . . .	49,925
(3) valued at over 40 cents	. . . . . .	6,303,500

Practically all were valued at over 40 cents, and so paid the maximum rate of 44 cents per pound, plus 50 per cent. Reduced to an *ad-valorem* equivalent, this was a duty of about 92 per cent. On the few goods of the second class imported (worth between 30 and 40 cents) the duty was 143 per cent.

The importation of these goods into the United States was enormous: having ranged between fifteen and twenty millions of dollars' worth annually in the years since the act of 1883. It was natural that those who held to the principle of protection should endeavor to check them. There had been a tendency, similar to that noted in the case of woollen cloths, though not so marked, for a growing importation of the cheaper goods (valued at less than 20 cents a yard under the act of 1883); and this contributed to the change in valuation and description in the new act. By the act of 1890, these fabrics were subjected in almost all cases to the maximum duty, equivalent to over one hundred per cent. on their foreign value.[1] It was surprising that imports continued in face of a duty so very high; yet continue they did, indicating that not only the imported fabrics, but the domestic fabrics of the same sorts, were raised in price for the consumer by the full extent of the duty. The explanation of the steady inflow of these goods, and the inability of the American manu-

---

[1] In that part of the fiscal year 1890–91 in which the new duties were in force, the imports of the three classes of dress goods were:

  (1) valued at 15 cents or less (duty 7 cents plus 40 per cent.) $768,000
  (2) valued at more than 15 cents (duty 8 cents plus 50 per cent.)   845,000
  (3) if the warp contains any wool (duty 12 cents plus 50 per cent.) $5,281,000

On goods of the third class, the duties collected were $5,423,000, making 103 per cent. of their value.

It should be noted that dress goods exceeding a certain weight (four ounces a square yard) are treated like men's woollens and are subjected to the maximum duty on these,—44 cents a pound plus 50 per cent.

For a statement of the grounds from the protectionist point of view, for these very high duties, see an article by Mr. William Whitman, in the *Bulletin of the Wool Manufacturers*, vol. xx., pp. 283–304.

factturers to supplant them, is probably to be found largely
in the peculiarities of their manufacture, and the difficulty
of adapting it to American conditions. Of course, with
duties high enough, anything can be made in the United
States; and the higher duties of 1890, increased still further as they were in 1897, served to stimulate effectively
the manufacture of fine woollens and dress goods.

In other parts of the wool and woollens schedule there
were similar changes. Some of the higher duties were
merely nominal. Thus the duty on ingrain carpets, which
had been 12 cents a yard plus 30 per cent. in 1883, went
up to 19 cents plus 40 per cent.; that on Brussels carpets,
from 30 cents plus 30 per cent. to 44 cents plus 40 per
cent. The duty on these had been prohibitory before;
the changes served simply to make them more prohibitory,
and were of no practical effect whatsoever. Other changes
were, like the higher duties on dress goods, of real importance, such as the increase in the duties on knit goods
and underwear. Of these the imports also were considerable, and a change in duties consequently had a material
effect on industry and prices. The patience of the reader
would be needlessly taxed by a further consideration of
these details. Enough has been said to indicate the
character of the wool and woollens schedule of the act of
1890; we may pass to other parts of the measure.

Among textiles cotton goods come next in importance
to woollens in our tariff system. On the cheaper grades
of cotton cloths, the duties, which had already been
reduced in 1883, were still further lowered. Thus, on

the cheapest grade of unbleached cottons, the duty decreased from $2\frac{1}{2}$ to 2 cents a yard. These, however, are goods which are manufactured in the United States as cheaply as in foreign countries, and which we are more likely to export than import. The duties were and are nominal, and the change went no further than a revision of certain unimportant figures in the statutes. On goods whose importation had continued under the act of 1883, and on which the duties had been of real importance, the changes were in the other direction. On the highest grade of cotton prints, the duty went up from 6 to $6\frac{3}{4}$ cents a yard ; with the further proviso that goods valued at over 15 cents a yard, on which the duty had before been 40 per cent., now became subject to one of 45 per cent. In the drag-net clause, fixing the duty on cotton manufactures not elsewhere provided for, the old rate of 35 per cent. was replaced with one of 50 per cent. Some duties were changed from *ad-valorem* to specific with the effect of raising them materially. Thus, on cotton cords and braids, the former rate of 35 per cent. became one of 35 cents per pound, equivalent to about 60 per cent. The most striking change, however, was in the case of knit goods and stockings. On cotton stockings, the act of 1883 had collected a uniform rate of 40 per cent. This was replaced in 1890 by a complicated system of graded duties, partly specific and partly *ad-valorem*, and varying with the assessed value of the goods. The new rates can again be best described by a statement in tabular form :

If the value is 60c. or less a dozen, the duty is 20c. a dozen, plus 20 per ct.

"	"	betw. 60c. & $2.00	"	"	"	50c.	"	"	30 " "
"	"	betw. $2.00 " $4.00	"	"	"	75c.	"	"	40 " "
"	"	over $4.00	"	"	"	$1.00	"	"	40 " "

Knit goods of cotton, and more particularly cotton stockings, are imported in large amounts, the annual value of the imports having been hitherto between six and eight millions. Most of these were of the second class in the schedule just given, dutiable at 50 cents a dozen plus 30 per cent.,—equivalent, on the average, to about 70 per cent. on the value. The raw material here is cheaper in the United States than abroad, and it is surprising that so heavy a duty should have been considered necessary to encourage the domestic manufacture. The explanation of the continued large imports is apparently to be found in part in a great advance in foreign methods of production, due to the newly invented or newly improved machinery, the use of which has not yet been introduced into this country. In part the explanation lies doubtless in the fact that the finer cotton stockings are made on knitting frames with a large use of hand labor. At all events, the changes just noted present as extreme a case of the application of protection as is to be found in our legislation.

On linen goods, of which only the coarsest qualities have been made in the country, the finer being all obtained by importation, the duty went up from 35 to 50 per cent. Linen laces and embroideries were advanced from 30 to 60 per cent. On silks the general duty remained as before, at 50 per cent.: on silk laces

and embroideries it went up to 60 per cent. Plush
goods of all sorts, whether made of silk, cotton, or wool,
were subjected to very high rates. A complicated scheme
of duties was adopted, partly specific and partly *ad-valorem*, and varying with the value of the goods; the system
being similar in its construction to that already described
as to cotton hose, and bringing about duties of 60 and
70 per cent. on the value. The imports of velvets,
plushes, and similar goods, were heavy, and the domestic
production was inconsiderable; the rates stood for another
determined effort to establish a new manufacture under
the shelter of very high duties.[1]

One general characteristic of the McKinley act may
here be discussed. It was the great development of the
method of minimum valuations and minimum duties
substantially similar to that adopted in the tariff act of
1828. This mode of grading the duties was adopted not
only in the cases described in the preceding pages—woollen
cloths, dress goods, cotton stockings, velvets and plushes—
but in other cases also, such as blankets and flannels, boiler
and plate iron, penknives and table-knives, shotguns, and
pistols.[2] On some of these articles the minimum system had
already been adopted in earlier acts; on others it was newly
adopted in 1890. The object apparently was to avoid an
ad-valorem duty, and yet to secure an adaptation of the rate
of duty to the value of the article. But, in doing this

---

[1] The provisions as to velvets and similar fabrics are in sections 350 and
411 of the act.

[2] See sections 138, 165, 167, 170, 393.

the fundamental difficulty of *ad-valorem* duties—-the temptation to undervaluation—is met, as was pointed out in the discussion of the act of 1828, in aggravated form.[1] The foreign manufacturer is tempted to make goods so as to bring their value near the minimum points, and the importer is tempted to undervalue them. No doubt another object sought in the minimum system, in 1890 as in 1828, was to conceal the real extent and weight of the duties imposed : a result the more likely to be attained where the duties are not only graded by valuation, but are also mixed specific and *ad-valorem* duties.

The duties on iron and steel would have been thought, in 1870, and even in 1880, the most important parts of the protective system. But in recent years the enormous development of the iron industry in the heart of the country has materially changed the situation. The bulk of the iron in the country is now made of ore mined on the shore of Lake Superior, smelted with bituminous coal mined west of the Appalachian chain. Pennsylvania also contributes its ore, and there has been a striking development of iron-making in the South. Iron smelted with anthracite coal, which played so important a part in our industrial history in the period from 1850 to 1870, has wellnigh disappeared.[2] Most of the production now takes place far from the seaboard, and the greater part of the producers of pig-iron can disregard foreign competition. A lowering of the duty

---

[1] See pp. 93, 103, above.

[2] Compare what is said below, at pp. 299–302, and the references there given, as to the recent history of the iron manufacture.

on pig-iron to $6.00, the rate which was proposed in the Mills bill of 1888, would have had no appreciable effect in any quarter. The effect of a complete abolition of the duty would be confined mainly to the sea-board districts. These are for all practical purposes nearer to England than they are to the central States, which are now the seat of the greatest domestic production of iron. In the McKinley act, no change in the duty on pig-iron was proposed, and it remained at the old rate, $6.72 a ton.

The situation is much the same in regard to iron ore. The duty on ore is significant only in regard to those grades which contain little phosphorus, and are therefore available for the making of steel by the Bessemer process. The great rich beds of Bessemer ore on the shore of Lake Superior, having easy water communication with the heart of the country, can supply the larger part of the smelters more cheaply than foreign ore could. This ore has made its way far to the eastward, and has been used by establishments very near the sea-board, which, but for the duty, would be likely to use more or less of foreign ore. The eastern establishments which make steel must get their Bessemer ore either by long railway haul from the West, or by importing it subject to duty. Large works have already been established on the Atlantic coast, using ore from rich deposits in Cuba, and therefore desirous of getting ore free.[1] Notwithstanding a strong endeavor from these producers to secure a remission of the duty, it

[1] In later years, not only Bessemer ores, but others also, have become important among the Cuban deposits.

remained in the McKinley act at the old rate, seventy-five cents a ton.

On steel rails the duty was reduced to six-tenths of a cent a pound, or $13.44 a gross ton. This reduction was of the same sort as that made in 1883 : it left the duty still at a prohibitory rate. The steady advance in the iron and steel manufacture in the United States, the growth of the West, the discovery of rich sources of iron and coal, above all, the enormous decline in the cost of bringing these materials together, due to the cheapening of railway rates, reduced the price of steel rails as well as of other manufactures of iron. As the figures given in the Appendix show, the price still remained higher in the United States than in England. But cost of transportation from the sea-board to the interior is such that even in the absence of the duty, steel rails would be imported only to supply railways near tide-water. In the main, the steel-rail duty has done its work, for good or ill : it is no longer of great economic importance. The same remark may be made of the duty on copper, which went down in the act of 1890 to 1¼ cents a pound. Copper would not be imported in any event ; its price at ordinary times is not higher in this country than it is abroad ; a duty serves only to make it possible for the combination of copper producers, in occasional times of exceptional demand, to keep up the price above the foreign price.

A different aspect of the tariff of 1890 appeared in the rise in the duty on tin-plates. This article had never been produced in this country, and had never been subjected to duties comparable to those on other manufactures of iron. In 1862 a duty of twenty-five per cent. had been imposed, and had been retained until 1872, when, at the time of the general reduction of that year, it was lowered to fifteen per cent.[1] In 1875, when the general reduction of 1872 was repealed, the rate was changed to a specific duty of $1\frac{1}{10}$ cents a pound, equivalent to about twenty per cent. at the prices then ruling. But this change did not have any effect in stimulating domestic production, and in 1883 the duty was reduced to one cent a pound, equivalent, at the prices of 1883, to an *ad-valorem* rate of about thirty per cent. At that rate the importations had been very large, twenty millions of dollars and more a year, and the domestic production had been *nil*. The question presented itself squarely whether a further and great extension of the protective system should be made. Those who believed that system to be wise, naturally maintained that this article had been unfairly singled out for a specially low rate of duty; and in the act of 1890 a duty of $2\frac{2}{10}$ cents a pound, equivalent to about seventy per cent., was imposed. The continuance of this duty, however, was made subject to a curious condition, unprecedented in our tariff legislation: that after the year 1897, tin-plates should be

---

[1] See pages 182–185 above. The language of the acts of 1862 and 1875 was not entirely clear, and in 1878 an attempt was made to have tin-plates classified under another head in the tariff schedules, and so subjected to a higher duty. But Secretary Sherman maintained the interpretation of the statutes which had been followed since 1862, and the duties were collected as stated in the text. See a letter of Secretary Sherman's in the " Tariff Commission Report " of 1882, p. 208.

admitted free of duty, unless the domestic production
for some one year before that date should have equalled
one third of the importations during any one of the years
between 1890 and 1896.   In other words, the permanent
maintenance of the duty was made conditional on a substantial increase of the domestic production.   Obviously,
so long as there was no domestic production, the duty
had been merely a revenue duty,—an indirect tax of the
simplest type, not of the best sort doubtless, but substantially similar in its effects to duties on tea or coffee.
The alternative now presented was that it should either
become a protective duty, with the peculiar effects flow-
ing from such, or that it should cease to be a tax
at all.[1]

As to agricultural products, there were some innocuous
changes, and some of real importance.   The duty on
wheat went up from twenty to twenty-five cents a bushel,
and that on Indian corn from ten to fifteen cents;
changes which obviously could be of no consequence
whatever.   Equally insignificant in their general effects
were the higher duties on potatoes and eggs, which might
possibly have some slight effect in checking the border
trade between Canada and the Northern States, but in
the main must be of petty character.   Among changes of
greater importance was an increase of the duty on barley

---

[1] The duty remained in force; the increase in domestic production did
take place.   But this was due chiefly to the greater cheapness of the steel
sheets which, when coated with tin, are known as tin-plates.   On the
causes of this change, see *Some Aspects of the Tariff Question*, ch. xii., p.
170.

from ten to thirty cents a bushel; a change meant to protect the farmers of some Northern States against Canadian barley. Oddly enough, the duty on rice, which, like barley, is imported in considerable quantities, was slightly reduced. On another set of agricultural products there were some changes in the direction of higher duties; namely, on textile materials like hemp and flax. On flax the duty was increased from $20 to $22.40 a ton; on dressed flax, from $40 to $67.20 a ton. On undressed hemp the duty remained unchanged; on dressed hemp it went up from $25 to $50 a ton.[1] Notwithstanding some attempts to get encouragement for the production of jute in the Southern States, that tropical commodity, which we import largely, was relieved from the former duty and admitted free.

We may now turn to another phase of the act of 1890, the remission of the duty on sugar, which was important in its effects on the financial situation, and in its connection with the reciprocity provisions of the act. The duty on sugar had been in the main a revenue duty; for nine tenths of the consumption was still supplied by importation. Only one tenth of the sugar was made at home, almost exclusively in the sugar-cane district of Louisiana; on this alone could the distinctive effects of a protective duty be felt. Substantially, therefore, the sugar duty presented the same questions as were presented by the

---

[1] The duties on hemp and flax (reduced in 1894, and raised again in 1897 and 1909; abolished in 1913 and re-imposed in 1922), have been of little effect. For some discussions of the economic problems involved see the *Quarterly Journal of Economics*, vol. iii., p. 260; vol. xxxi., p. 500.

tea and coffee duties in 1872.[1] At the same time, the receipts from sugar were very large. They formed the most important single item in the revenue from customs, and in the period immediately preceding 1890 were on the average about fifty-five millions a year. In that period the United States were embarrassed by a large surplus in the revenue, the situation in this respect being again similar to that in 1870–72. At the same time the duty on sugar, averaging about two cents a pound on the grades chiefly imported, was high, considered simply as a tax and without regard to its connection with the general financial and economic situation. The Mills bill of 1888 had proposed a reduction of about fifteen per cent. ; the Senate bill of the same year proposed to cut the rate to about one half that then in force. There was general agreement that some reduction should be made.

The McKinley act went further : it admitted all raw sugar free. On refined sugar a duty of one half cent per pound was retained, by way of protecting the domestic sugar refiners. This duty was open to the objection of playing into the hands of the Sugar Trust, which had just reached the stage of controlling practically the entire sugar refining of the country. Undoubtedly it did ; but the previous tariff system, by making the duty on refined sugar higher than that on raw sugar, had done the same ; and the act of 1890 left the situation as it was, simply maintaining for good or ill a policy as to the sugar refiners which had been followed for a generation or more.

---

[1] See above, pp. 186–180

With the free admission of raw sugar came a bounty to the domestic sugar producers at the rate of the former duty, two cents a pound. There would have been an obvious inconsistency in leaving the sugar producers to their fate, at a time when other domestic producers were receiving increased protection. Moreover, there was a disposition to assist and stimulate the production of sugar in other ways, especially from beets. The bounty was accordingly given, at the rate of two cents a pound, on all domestic sugar, for the period from July 1, 1891, to July 1, 1905. Such a change in one sense is immaterial to the domestic sugar producer. He must sell his sugar at a lower price, but gets a bounty which makes up the loss. But so far as ease of collection goes, the bounty clearly is less advantageous than the duty was. The benefit of the duty came to him without trouble, in the shape of a higher price. The benefit of the bounty he can secure only by a process, somewhat troublesome and not unattended with expense, of filing descriptions and statements at government offices, securing licenses, and submitting to the regulations which the government must of necessity prescribe to prevent fraudulent use of the bounty provisions.

So far as the financial object in view was concerned, the sections on sugar accomplished their object. Indeed, perhaps they more than accomplished it. The remission of the duty cut off fifty or sixty millions of revenue; the bounty called for an extra expenditure of six or eight millions. The act also reduced the internal tax on tobacco from eight cents to six cents a pound; and the same Con gress that passed it increased the appropriations in several directions, especially for more liberal pension payments. It would certainly have been wiser financial policy to be content with a reduction of the sugar duty such as was proposed in the Senate bill of 1888–89. Those who opposed the protective system on principle naturally objected to the financial effects of the sugar remission on still another ground—it left the hands of Congress less free to deal with the more distinctly protective duties. Such duties as those on wool and woollens, lumber, iron ore, and similar materials, are more burdensome in character than was the sugar duty; but the remission of these taxes is much more difficult in the face of a deficit than of a surplus.

The complete remission of the duty on sugar was undoubtedly determined on as a means of gaining popularity for the new tariff act in the West, where the higher duties on manufactured articles might be difficult to present in an attractive light. The same object was had in view in another set of provisions, closely connected with the new sugar schedule,—the reciprocity provisions. The trend of public opinion on the tariff bill, while it was under discussion in the House, made some of the Republican leaders uneasy as to its effects on the party prospects in the West; and this feeling was strong with Mr. Blaine, not the least shrewd of the Republican leaders. The bill had passed the House of Representatives without the reciprocity provisions; they were inserted at the last moment in the Senate, almost under pressure from Mr

Blaine and those who shared his views. The effect of these provisions was to give the President power to impose by proclamation certain duties on sugar, molasses, tea, coffee, and hides, if he considered that any country exporting these commodities to the United States " imposes duties or other exactions on the agricultural or other products of the United States, which, in view of the free introduction of sugar, molasses, tea, coffee, and hides into the United States, he may deem to be reciprocally unjust or unreasonable." [1]

This particular mode of reciprocal engagement has a distinct economic advantage over the ordinary form of reciprocity. The ordinary form consists in the simple remission of duties to a favored country, duties remaining on goods coming from countries not favored. Such a remission is likely not to redound to the advantage of the domestic consumer. Unless the favored country can easily supply the whole market, or other countries are quickly admitted to the lower duties, prices are not affected, and the foreign producer reaps the whole benefit of the remission. The United States has had one conspicuous illustration of the workings of reciprocity of this sort, in the treaty of 1876 with the Hawaiian Islands. Under that treaty, sugar was admitted free from the islands; but they were far from being able to supply all the sugar consumed; other sugar was imported, paying duty; the

---

[1] The duties authorized under these conditions were: on coffee, three cents a pound; on tea, ten cents a pound; on hides, one and a half cents a pound; on the grades of raw sugar chiefly imported, a trifle over one cent per pound,—about one half the duty which was in force before 1890.

price remained as high as before, and the Hawaiian planters reaped the benefit of the remission.[1]   But the re-imposition of duties on articles coming from a particular country, if it leaves enough of other countries in the field, not paying duty, to supply the domestic consumption, brings a pressure to bear on the enemy without injuring the consumers at home.   It is true that if one of the countries on whose goods duties were re-imposed, should supply a very large part of our consumption, the result would not be so innocuous.   If, for example, the duty of three cents a pound were imposed on coffee from Brazil, all coffee would go up in price, not only that from Brazil, but that from other countries; and the producers from other countries would gain three cents a pound on their coffee, which the consumers in the United States would pay.   But it was not probable that the power given by the reciprocity provisions would ever be exercised in a case of this sort.   The simple threat of re-imposing duties would usually be relied on as a means of securing concessions from other countries.

Concessions so obtained may or may not be advantageous to the countries making them ; and they may or may not be of real importance and advantage to the United States.   The countries from which concessions were asked were chiefly the South American countries.   So far as agricultural commodities imported into them from the United States were concerned, a lowering of duties meant lower prices to the South American consumers, and

---

[1] On the Hawaiian treaty and the general sugar situation see *Some aspects of the Tariff Question*, Part II., chs. iv., v., vi., vii.

very probably an enlarged demand for such commodities sent from the United States. Grain, flour, provisions, are sent to these countries by the United States alone, and a remission of duties on them operates as a remission of the duty on English tin-plate would operate in the United States: it is practically a complete remission. Such changes bring about a real reduction of the burdens of taxation, and a real enlargement of the international division of labor.

But if the South American countries lower their duties on manufactured goods from the United States, the result may be different. Many of these goods are not made as cheaply in the United States as in European countries; as to others, the United States might not be able to supply the whole consumption of the country which gave it favors. Under such conditions, the lower duties would not mean lower prices to the South American consumer. The United States would then be in much the same relation to them, as the Hawaiian Islands were to the United States under the reciprocity treaty of 1876. Concessions of this sort, however, which do not redound to the ultimate advantage of the communities giving them, are not likely long to remain preferential. Sooner or later, they are likely to be granted to all comers. The experience of European countries under commercial treaties, especially under the net-work of treaties which spread over Europe after the conclusion of the treaty of 1860 between England and France, shows that a remission of duty in favor of one country soon is extended to others, and becomes practically equivalent to a general lowering of the customs scale. This was likely to be the outcome of any concessions secured to the United States from South American countries under the reciprocity provisions; a result no doubt advantageous to all concerned, but less peculiarly advantageous to the United States than more limited concessions would have been.[1]

As a whole, the tariff act of 1890 presented to the American people without disguise the question whether

---

[1] In the course of 1892, treaties were concluded with the following countries: Great Britain, for Jamaica, Trinidad, Barbadoes, and British Guiana; Spain, for Cuba and Porto Rico; Salvador; the Dominican Republic; Nicaragua; Honduras; Guatemala; and Brazil. The remissions or reductions of duty secured by these treaties were chiefly on agricultural articles and others produced abundantly and cheaply in the United States. Duties were imposed under the authority conferred by the reciprocity section, on sugar, tea, coffee, hides, coming from Venezuela, Colombia, and Hayti. The only country of considerable importance among these was Venezuela, which usually sends to this country about one tenth of the coffee imported.

With Germany, an arrangement was made by which the United States got the benefit of the slightly lower rates of duty conceded by Germany to Austria and Hungary by the treaties of 1892 with these countries. With France, a similar arrangement was made, by which American commodities were admitted at the minimum tariff of the French legislation of 1892.

All these arrangements came to an end with the tariff of 1894. The act of that year, it is true, contained a saving clause by which the reciprocity treaties were to remain in force "except where inconsistent with the provisions of this act." But as the act admitted tea and coffee free unconditionally, and imposed a duty of forty per cent. on all sugar, its provisions were necessarily inconsistent. The duty reimposed on sugar deprived the United States of the chief *quid pro quo* which had been available under the act of 1890,—the maintenance of the free admission of sugar. An account of the whole episode is given in Laughlin and Willis's "Reciprocity," chs. VI., VII., VIII.; and an analysis of the working of the treaty with Brazil, the largest of the South American countries, in an article by L. Hutchinson, *Political Science Quarterly*, vol. XVIII., June, 1903.

they wished a large extension of the protective system beyond the point to which it had developed by the legislation of the war period. The act of 1883, as we have seen, did indeed raise not a few of the protective duties; but other duties it lowered, and the advances were neither so great nor so conspicuously put forward as in the act of 1890. A retention of the existing state of things, such as on the whole the act of 1883 amounted to, might be urged on the ground that vested interests should not be disturbed, and that the inevitable disadvantages of any far-reaching change would outweigh any ultimate gain. The act of 1890 boldly proposed something more: a radical extension of the protective system. The question of principle never was so squarely presented.

CHAPTER VI.

THE TARIFF ACT OF 1894.

THE question of principle which was presented to the American people by the tariff act of 1890 was answered with remarkable promptness, and, to all appearances, in unmistakable terms. Immediately after the passage of the act, the party which had thus espoused the extreme protective policy suffered a crushing defeat; and, after two years of discussion and deliberation, the verdict at the polls was again overwhelmingly against it. The McKinley tariff had become law in October of 1890. In November, the Congressional elections were held, and the Republicans were defeated as they had never been defeated before. In the new Congress which was to succeed that which had passed the act of 1890, they secured only one quarter of the Representatives; their opponents outnumbered them three to one. Even States like Massachusetts, Ohio, Illinois, Michigan, long supposed to be stanchly Republican, returned Democratic majorities. The tariff question, which had been uppermost in public debate at this election, was again uppermost, two years later, in the election of 1892. President Cleveland, who had made the tariff question the political issue of the day, was once more nominated by the Democrats ; and President Harrison was renominated by the Republicans. Again the result was a triumph for the Democrats, whose candidate received nearly twice as many electoral votes as his opponent. Again a row of Western States joined the ranks of the Democrats,—Indiana, Illinois, Wisconsin ; while Ohio was retained on the Republican side by a slender majority of a bare thousand votes. The Congressional elections, while less dramatically one-sided than those of 1890, told substantially the same story. The Democrats had an overwhelming majority in the House ; and in the Senate, as the elections in the various State legislatures were gradually held, they secured a working majority. The result was to assure them of full control of all branches of the federal legislature in the Fifty-third Congress, for the term of 1893–95.[1]

The Democrats, twice victorious, might fairly claim an emphatic declaration of the people in favor of their policy. How clear the popular verdict may really have been, is as

---

[1] For convenience of reference, the strength of the two parties in Congress in 1889–95 is here summarily stated :

	House.		Senate.	
	Republicans.	Democrats.	Republicans.	Democrats.
51st Congress, 1889–91,	166	159	39	37
52d Congress, 1891–93,	88	236	47	39
53d Congress, 1893–95,	126	220	38	44

In addition to the 44 Democrats and 38 Republicans in the Senate of the 53d Congress, there were three Populists. These might be expected ordinarily to vote with the Democrats on tariff questions ; but their support could not be implicitly relied on.

difficult to say as it must always be to interpret the meaning of a general election. The demoralization of the civil service, the scandals which that demoralization is sure to bring on every administration, the usual reaction of public favor, defections to the Populist Party—all these played their part. On the tariff itself, there was little in public discussion to indicate that the true questions at issue were fairly before the popular mind. A vague uneasiness about trusts and monopolies, which the protective duties were supposed to promote, clearly had much effect in strengthening the hands both of Democrats and of Populists; and the comparatively simple questions which at bottom are involved in the protective controversy were obscured by a cloud of talk about pauper wages and monopolist manufacturers, British free trade and American patriotism. Yet the tariff certainly had been squarely presented as the issue in these compaigns, and the Democrats were justified in acting on the theory that the popular will had declared itself against the policy of high protection.

But the enthusiasm which the victory at first aroused among the Democrats was dampened almost at once by the events of the extra session of the summer of 1893. The silver question had not been at issue between the parties in 1892. President Cleveland had repeatedly declared himself to be opposed to the policy of enlarging the silver currency. The Republicans also, even though they had tried to placate the silver element by passing the silver purchase act of 1890, had none the less declared themselves in favor of keeping the silver issues at par with gold. But the silver question, pushed aside by the tariff question in 1890–92, came suddenly to the front in 1893, when the commercial crisis, ascribed (with sufficient reason) to the excessive issues of silver currency, compelled action on the financial situation. President Cleveland called an extra session, for the one purpose of repealing the silver purchase act and discontinuing silver coinage and silver issues. The strong element in his party which was in favor of the free coinage of silver fought this proposal, vigorously in the House, desperately in the Senate. The administration succeeded ; its policy was carried out ; the silver purchases were brought to an end. But the bitter struggle within the ranks of the Democrats did much to shatter their cohesion, and to deprive them of that spirit of determination in their own ranks, and that respect and prestige in the community, which are secured by a united and single-minded party.

Another factor that weakened the effect of the victories of 1890 and 1892 was the narrow Democratic majority in the Senate. The slowness with which, under our political system, the composition of the Senate responds to changes in the popular vote, is shown by the precarious hold which the dominant party had in that body. In the House, with a majority of nearly two to one, it could proceed without regard to discontent or dissent on the part of a fraction of its own members. But in the Senate the defection of a very few among the majority would destroy its control of legislation. As it happened, for one reason or another there was danger of such defections. Some Democratic Senators were half-hearted on the general question of tariff reduction; others came from States which had strong interest in particular duties,—especially the Louisiana Senators. Old quarrels and bickerings, dating back to President Cleveland's first administration, and due chiefly to petty squabbles over appointments to office, caused still others to take a spiteful pleasure in blocking the movement for tariff reform which the President had so much at heart. The administration made some endeavor, both during the extra session of 1893 and during this regular session, to restore unity and discipline, and to bring all the Senators to the support of the party policy, by putting offices at the disposal of the sulky few. But this move availed little. It threw back for the time being the all-important cause of reform in the machinery of the government; and yet did little or nothing to remove the difficulties that arose from the narrow and uncertain majority in the Senate. Thus, for one cause and another, there was danger of defection in that body, and a need, based on more or less serious grounds, of conciliation and of careful management; a need which, as it turned out, had a great and unexpected effect on the final shape of the tariff act.

Such were the political conditions under which the regular session of 1893–94 began. At the extra session of 1893, no attempt had been made to deal with the tariff; but the committees had been arranged, and among them the Committee of Ways and Means, which had thus

been able to begin its preparations at an early date.
Progress with the tariff bill was accordingly easy in the
House. The committee reported its bill as early as
December 19. That bill proposed some important remissions of duty, and in all directions made considerable
reductions; not enough, indeed, to make it a revolutionary measure, yet enough to bring about, if enacted, a real
and unmistakable change in the general tariff policy of
the United States. Its specific provisions will be more
conveniently discussed as we follow one by one the different phases of the proposed legislation, and the final
outcome of the whole. The House acted with reasonable promptness: the bill was passed on February 1, substantially in the shape given it by the party leaders on
the Ways and Means Committee.

Matters went more slowly in the Senate. There the
finance committee did not report the bill until March 20,
and then with many and important amendments. The
changes were all in the same direction,—toward moderating the reductions, and taking the edge off the measure as passed by the House. When the bill came from
the committee to the Senate, still further amendments of
the same sort were added. Hence when, after long
delays, it was finally passed by the Senate, on July 3, it
was a very different measure, in spirit and in details, from
that which had been passed by the House.

The House and Senate disagreeing, the bill went to a
conference committee. Almost without exception, during the last thirty-five years, the details of tariff bills have

been finally adjusted in such committees; and it was **to** be expected that in this case, as in others, the act as passed would be half-way between the House bill and the Senate bill. This expectation was disappointed. In the Senate the bill there had been passed by a vote of thirty-nine to thirty-four, and among the thirty-nine were two or three Populist Senators who owed no allegiance to the Democratic Party. The votes of all the Democratic Senators were felt to be necessary for its final passage. Several among them insisted on amendments admitted to be distasteful to the mass of their party associates; and the close balance of parties in the Senate enabled them to command the situation. President Cleveland's letter to Mr. Wilson, the chairman of the House Committee of Ways and Means, urging resistance to the Senate amendments, had no effect beyond that of making clear to the country what were his own views. Whether better management in the Senate would have secured a result more in consonance with the party pledges and principles is not easy to say : beyond question, the leadership of the Democrats in the upper branch was lamentably unskilful. In the end, the House accepted all the amendments of the upper body, and the bill as shaped in the Senate became the act of 1894. President Cleveland signified his justifiable discontent with its provisions by permitting it to become law without his signature. It finally went into effect on August 28.

So much as to the immediate history of the act. We may proceed now to consider its main provisions.

First and foremost was the removal of the duty on wool, and with it an entire change in the duties on woollen goods. Wool and woollens had been for years the central part in the protective system. The change here was an important—almost revolutionary one; and it may be remarked at once that in the whole act no other articles of large importance were thus incisively dealt with.

Free wool was important in its political and in its economic aspects. The duty on wool had been the most significant feature in the policy of all-inclusive protection which the Republicans had emphasized in the McKinley act of 1890. It had been almost the only article through which protection could be promised and given to agricultural voters. There were duties, to be sure, on wheat, corn, and meats—articles which were continuously exported and obviously could not be affected by an import duty. But wool was imported, and was really affected by the duty; and it could be fairly maintained that here the farmers got some share of the benefits of the protective system. Moreover, some of the central States of the country, like Ohio, where there was much wool-growing, were closely divided in politics. Here the wool duty played a prominent part; and it required some courage among the Democrats to present themselves squarely on the platform of free wool.

In its economic aspects the removal of the duty on wool was important as a crucial application of the principle of free raw materials. In that advocacy of protection which has gained the most respectable hearing from serious students of economics,—the advocacy, namely, of what goes by the names of developing protection, educational protection, protection to young industries,—it has usually been explained that crude materials are beyond the scope of the protective policy. Even in the political arguments which we often hear from German writers of the present time, and in which national dependence and self-sufficiency play a large part, the line has usually been drawn against the inclusion of articles of this sort in the protective régime. The desire to encourage the manufacture of woollens has probably been quite as effective as these more theoretical considerations in preventing the extension of the protective policy to wool, even in the countries which in late years have gone so far in the direction of protection. At all events, no country of advanced civilization has maintained any duty on this material, and the retention of such a duty in the United States was perhaps the most characteristic feature of our protective system. President Cleveland had specifically advocated the free admission of wool in his message of 1887; the Democrats had put it on the free list in the Mills Bill, in which they outlined their policy in 1888; the Republicans had emphasized their adherence to the opposite policy by increasing the duty on wool in the McKinley act. Now, at last, it went on the free list.

Equally great, at least in form, was the change in the duties on woollen goods. Here the curious system of compound duties was completely swept away. Its history and development, from the first germs in 1861 to the

elaborate rates in the tariff act of 1890, have been sufficiently detailed in the preceding chapters. No part of
the tariff was more intricate ; in none was it more difficult
to ascertain the real degree of net protection finally given
the manufacturers ; in none were the duties higher. In
place of these old complex rates a simple system of *ad-
valorem* duties was established. In the bill as passed by
the House the rate (on the important classes of woollen
goods) was made forty per cent. in the first year, with a
reduction of one per cent. each year for five years, until
eventually a definitive rate of thirty-five per cent. should
be reached. But among the many changes made by the
Senate was the adoption of a much more conservative
policy as to woollens, and a considerable advance beyond
the House rates. The rate was fixed at fifty per cent.,
once for all, on the more important classes of goods.
Certain cheaper sorts of blankets and flannels, it is true,
were subject to no more than twenty-five per cent. ; and
the cheapest kinds of fabrics for men's and women's
wear were to pay but forty per cent. But, as in former
tariff acts, these lower rates were applicable only to goods
which had not been imported in the past, and would not
be imported under the new rates. On all men's clothes
and women's dress-goods which were valued at more than
50 cents a pound,—that is, on practically the whole mass
of such articles really subject to foreign competition,—
and on all manufactures of wool not specially provided
for, the *ad-valorem* duty was that of the McKinley act,—
fifty per cent. Similarly, on the important classes of

carpets, while the old specific or compensating duty disappeared, the *ad-valorem* duty was left at forty per cent.
In general, the higher *ad-valorem* rates established by the
tariff act of 1890 remained untouched: the change on
woollen goods was limited to a simplification of the system of duties by the abolition of those specific rates
which had previously been levied as an offset to the
duties on the raw material.

Theoretically, therefore, the manufacturers of woollen
goods lost nothing by the change. They were treated, in
the act as finally passed, with marked tenderness: a tenderness further emphasized by the fact that, while wool
was admitted free at once, the new duties on woollens
did not go into effect until January 1, 1895. For a season they thus got their material free, yet had the benefit
of the old duties on their goods. Practically, however,
even with this aid toward adjusting themselves to the
new conditions, the manufacturers had to face a trying
period of transition. We have seen, in the preceding
chapters, that the specific duties on woollens, though
nominally a simple offset for the increased price of wool
due to the duty on that material, contained in many
cases a large amount of disguised protection. This was
lost under the new system. Even where the case was
different, and where the specific duties had done no more
than to compensate, the gain from the abolition of the
duties on wool did not inure to the manufacturers by any
automatic process. They had to learn to take advantage
of the lower price at which they could buy the imported

wool, now free; and only by taking full advantage of it could they be in a position to meet the competition of the foreign makers, whose products were coming in at the simple *ad-valorem* duty on woollens.   To do this, the domestic manufacturers, long confined to the use of domestic wool and of a very small range of foreign wool, had to learn to adjust or improve their machinery, to use new qualities of wool, and to make new kinds of cloths. The advocates of the remission of the duty on the raw materials had always maintained that the change would vivify the woollen manufacture, widen its range, and increase its prosperity.   On the other hand, among the manufacturers and their representatives, there had been a natural aversion to the abandonment of a system, however complicated and confused, to which the industry had been compelled to accommodate itself by a quarter-century of legislation.   What the final outcome would be, could appear only after a considerable trial of the new system, continued over some years at least.   But the general public had not been trained by either side in the controversy to await the results with any patience.   The protectionists had predicted immediate disaster; their opponents immediate prosperity.   This mode of dealing with controverted questions is perhaps inevitable in popular discussion: certainly the *post hoc, propter hoc* argument has been applied to the protective controversy, both in its larger aspects and in its relation to particular industries, with astonishing readiness.   No critical observer could expect the change in the duties on wool and woollens to show its real effects in one season, or in several seasons, or to work out its results without more or less uneasiness and embarrassment for the domestic producers. That its ultimate result—considering how tenderly the manufacturers were dealt with in the act of 1894—would be harmful to the woollen industry as a whole, seems highly improbable. So far as the general question of protection was concerned, the wool and woollen schedule in the act of 1894, while it made a sharp break with the past, in putting on the free list at least one important raw material, evidently left the principle of protection, as applied to manufacturers, absolutely untouched, and affected the operations of the woollen manufacturers no more than was inevitable in view of the radical policy followed with regard to wool.[1]

On other textile materials and products the changes in duties were by comparison unimportant. On most manufactures of cotton there was some change, but in few cases an effective change. On some of the cheaper grades there was on the surface a considerable reduction. Thus the cheapest class of unbleached and unprinted cotton goods became subject to a duty of one cent per yard, in place of the old duty of two and one-half cents. But these

---

[1] For some consideration in detail of the effects of the old system on wool and woollens, see an article by the present writer in *Quarterly Journal of Economics* for October, 1893; a criticism of this article by Mr. S. N. D. North in the *Bulletin of the Wool Manufacturers*, for December, 1893; and a discussion at large in *Some Aspects of the Tariff Question*, ch. xx.

goods are made as cheaply in the United States as in foreign countries, if not more cheaply ; they would not be imported in any event; and the change in duties was merely nominal.   On finer cotton goods, more than likely to be imported, the changes in rates were not great. Where the duty had been fifty per cent. in 1890, it became forty per cent. in 1894; where it had been forty per cent., it became thirty-five per cent.   On knit goods there was a more considerable reduction, at least as compared with the rates of 1890.   These goods, as we have seen, had been subject in 1890 to a complicated series of mixed specific and *ad-valorem* duties.   They were now subject to a simple duty of fifty per cent.   This, while a reduction from the rates established in 1890, was higher than the duty in force before that date.   Here, as in not a few other cases, the reform movement of 1894, as checked and pruned in the Senate, did not even succeed in wiping out all the effects of the extreme protective movement that preceded it.

Silk manufactures, on which the protective duties of the last generation had very important effects, were hardly touched.   The duties on some silks went down from sixty to fifty per cent., on others from fifty to forty-five per cent. The changes were hardly worth mentioning. Much the same was the case with linens. Dressed flax was admitted at 1½ cents per pound, just half the duty of 1890. Manufactures of flax were admitted at reductions of duty very similar to those just noted as to silks. Since virtually no linens of finer quality were (or are) produced in this country, and those of coarser quality were as effectually shielded by the new duty as by the old, matters remained very much as they had been. One change was an exception. Bagging of jute, flax, or hemp, for grain or cotton, was admitted free of duty—a direct concession to the farmers and planters.

Next we may turn to the duties on minerals and mineral products. Here the articles to which public attention was chiefly given were coal and iron ore. These are by no means the most important articles in the tariff schedule relating to minerals and metallic products; but they are emphatically raw materials, the question of principle in dealing with such was hotly raised as to them. The two houses of Congress here disagreed sharply: the House put both articles on the free list, while the Senate insisted on the retention of duties, even though reduced duties. The dispute drew to this part of the tariff system a share of public attention disproportionate to the real industrial significance of the duties, and brought into full relief the failure of the act as finally passed to carry out with steady consistency the Democratic Party policy.

Free coal would be of some consequence on the north Atlantic coast and on the Pacific coast. Both districts happen to be far from the domestic sources of supply, and comparatively near to mines across the border. The Pacific coast got coal from British Columbia and from Australia, and felt the duty on coal as an undesirable burden. But with few manufactures, and a mild climate, the burden was not a serious one. In New England, essentially a manufacturing community, the case might be different. Some Canadian mines are geographically a bit nearer than the mines of West Virginia and Virginia which feel their competition. It was a question, to be sure, how serious that competition would be, how good the quality of the Canadian coal would prove, how effectively the transportation of this coal could be organized. But it was difficult to give any good reason for not allowing New England every opportunity for cheapening its supply of coal. The opposition to the repeal of the duty was a clear and simple case of an attempt of certain producers to make a levy on consumers. Coal had been made free by the House; the act left it subject to a duty of forty cents per ton. The old rate had been seventy-five cents. The amendment made by the Senate was felt in all quarters to mean a conspicuous failure to carry out consistently the program of the Democratic Party.

The result was similar with the duty on iron ore. The essential facts as to the working of this duty have already been stated.[1] Here too the question of duty or no duty was immaterial so far as the great bulk of domestic production and consumption was concerned. The question was simply whether certain iron and steel establishments near the seaboard should get their iron ore free, or should be induced by a duty to buy domestic ore produced at a distance. Directly, the issue was between the great corporations which mined the ore in the West, and the other great corporations which had iron and steel plants on or

[1] See above, p. 271

near the Atlantic seaboard. It might be argued, indeed, that this was the only issue. In view of the long series of producers and middlemen whose operations must inter-vene before the finished product of industry can reach the consumer, still more in view of the hindrances to unfet-tered competition among the middlemen, it might be plau-sibly maintained that not only the immediate question, but the ultimate question, was between two sets of producers, not between the producers and the public. But here, as on many other questions, it is safe to proceed on the general ground that the wider the sources of supply and the cheaper the raw materials of production, the greater the chances that the benefits will filter through the layers of middle-men, and that the public as consumers will eventually gain. Hence, so far as any question of principle was concerned, everything was in favor of free ore. Arguments as to the development of struggling industries or the fostering of na-tional independence could not be to the point; since the great bulk of our iron ore, and the great bulk of our iron and steel, were sure to be produced within the country under any circumstances. The fate of the iron-ore duty was the same as that of the coal duty. The House repealed it; the Senate restored the duty, but at forty cents instead of seventy-five cents per ton. Again the principle of free raw materials was set aside.

The duty on pig iron was brought down in the act from $6.72 to $4 a ton. In the House of Representatives the duty had been made twenty per cent., which would have meant a much more considerable reduction on most qualities of iron. Twenty years earlier, even ten years earlier, such a change as was proposed by the House would have been of great importance: even that enacted would have been of moment. As matters stand in the closing years of the century, the reduction did not signify much. The production of crude iron advanced at an enormous rate after 1880. With the discovery of new sources of supply, with improvements in production and transportation, the great bulk of the iron would be produced at home, even if there were no duties at all. Some parts of the Atlantic and Pacific seaboards, which are distant from the domestic centres of production, would import iron, if free of duty, rather than buy it at home. But in the main, the days in which the duty on pig iron could exercise very wide reaching effects, were gone by. The change made in 1894 encountered little opposition, because it could be no longer of great effect.

The duty on steel rails, that old bone of contention, was lowered from $13.44 to $7.84 a ton. From 1883 to 1894, each tariff act had taken a slice from this duty: each time in such manner that no direct effect was felt on prices, the decline in the duty following and not preceding the decline in prices. The steady fall in the prices of iron and steel products during the past generation has been due to a variety of causes. Partly they have been of world-wide operation, bringing about a tendency to lower iron prices in all countries; partly they have been of special effect in this country, in the discovery of new sources of supply, and their utilization through great improvements in transportation.   No small factor has been the remarkable application of American enterprise, invention, and engineering skill to the production on a vast scale of Bessemer ore, Bessemer iron, and Bessemer steel. Through it all, the prices of steel and of steel rails have been steadily higher than they would have been without a duty ; and the tariff system has contributed to the maintenance of monopoly profits.   The lowering of the duty on steel rails in 1894, like the earlier reductions, had no immediate results, the duty being still left at the prohibitory point. But, as in the case of previous reduction, the lower rate set a limit to possible future advance in prices.   Nothing could have been lost, and something would probably have been gained, by a more incisive change.[1]

On one other much disputed article a change was made, of greater practical importance than in the case of steel rails, but again of less extent than might have been expected.   The duty on tin-plate was reduced to exactly one-half that which had been levied in the act of 1890: it had been $2\frac{2}{5}$ cents per pound, and it was made $1\frac{1}{5}$ cents. The reduced duty is still higher than that in force before 1890; so that here again the legislation of that year was allowed to leave its mark on the statute-book.

In most of these cases specific duties were retained by the Senate, in place of the *ad-valorem* duties which had been adopted by the House.   In some cases, it is true,

---

[1] I have given an extended description of the growth of the iron indus- try since 1870, and an analysis of the working of protection, in *Some Aspects of the Tariff Question*, Part III.

the Senate simply raised the *ad-valorem* rates which the
House proposed; and here the outcome was usually a
substantial reduction from the old specific rates. Thus
the duties on chains, guns, and some sorts of cutlery remained in *ad-valorem* form, and were considerably lowered.
The general retention of specific duties by the Senate was
among the changes which most disappointed the advocates of lower duties; and this for the simple reason that
it was made the occasion for higher rates than had been
proposed in the other form. So far as the direct question
of administrative advantage goes, everything speaks in
favor of specific duties; and our tariff reformers have
usually been curiously blind to the difficulties inevitable
in the collection of *ad-valorem* duties. But these latter
have the unquestionable advantage of telling their own
tale. What the meaning and effect of a specific duty is,
can often be known only to a few persons familiar with
the details of some minute branch of trade. In fixing
them, the legislator necessarily seeks the advice of experts, who are likely enough to have wishes and interests
opposed to those of the public. Wittingly and unwit-
tingly, these duties have often been arranged in a manner
to promote the interests of particular enterprises, and so
to justify the charge that they tax the many for the benefit of the few. Hence the natural repugnance of those
who are opposed to the principle of protection; hence
their disappointment when the comparatively simple
scheme of *ad-valorem* duties adopted in the House was
transformed by the Senate into a system of specific

duties intricate, bewildering, and not unfairly open to
suspicion.

Among other manufactured articles, earthen-ware and
china-ware were dealt with least tenderly. Here it is somewhat surprising to find a real and effective change in the
duty. Finer qualities of china-ware went down from sixty
to thirty-five per cent., the cheaper qualities from fifty to
thirty per cent.   The finer qualities had always been
imported in very considerable quantities; it was very
possible that under the reduced duty large quantities of
the cheaper grades might also be imported.[1] On what
principle these articles should have been selected for
special reduction, it is difficult to say; but certainly there
was here a substantial change. Glassware of all sorts
remained very much as it was.

Questions in many ways different from those which
arose with regard to manufactures and raw materials,
were presented by the duty on sugar. That article came
into sudden and surprising prominence in the debates of
1894. It is true that it had played an important part in
1890, when the remission of duty on raw sugar had been
an essential part of the general policy of the McKinley
tariff act.   But attention had then been given mainly to
the burden which the tax on raw sugar imposed on consumers, and to the benefits which its remission would
bring to them. In 1894, however, the tax on refined
sugar, and its effect on the sugar-refining industry,

---

[1] See what is said of earthen-ware and china-ware in my paper in the
Quarterly Journal of Economics, vol. iii., p. 286.

received the greater share of attention. This change in
the point of view was due to the fact that between the
two dates the monopoly conditions in the refining of sugar
had become a matter of common knowledge. Hence
the question of protection as fostering monopoly was
brought home to the public, uneasy at best at the development apparently on all sides of combinations and
trusts.

The sugar duty, in its various forms, involved a great
variety of economic and social questions. That on raw
sugar involved both fiscal questions and questions as to
the social effects of taxation. That on refined sugar presented at once a phase of the protective controversy and
a phase of the new and portentous problem of monopoly
combinations. It will be advantageous to consider sepa-
artely the very different questions presented by the two
parts of the sugar tax.

The reasons for and against a duty on raw sugar in 1894
may be summarized thus. In favor of the duty it was to be
said that it would yield at once a large, certain, steady revenue. Some increase in the revenue was agreed on all
hands to be necessary. No one change in the McKinley
act had done so much to upset the federal budget as the
removal of the duty on sugar, and no one change was so
certain to bring an additional revenue as the re-imposition
of this tax. In view of the position of the federal Treasury as the holder of the metallic reserve for virtually all
the paper money outstanding, it was of prime importance
to put it in a secure financial position.

Next, while the sugar duty is a tax, it was in 1894 (setting aside the comparatively small domestic production of sugar) a simple tax, bringing none of the diversion of domestic industry and none of the ulterior consequences which flow from protective duties. It is commonly asserted by Protectionists that a remission of revenue duties, like those on tea, coffee, and sugar, is in a peculiar sense a remission of taxation ; the implication being that protective duties on commodities made at home are not really taxes, but in some roundabout way are pure gain. It would be the part of courage and honesty for those opposed to protection to act on the ground that, while both alike are taxes, the revenue duties are the less burdensome and the less harmful of the two. They should, therefore, where opportunity arises, maintain revenue duties boldly and remit protective duties freely. As between duties on raw wool, coal, and iron ore on the one hand, and a duty on sugar on the other, the party opposed to the principle of protection should unhesitatingly have chosen the latter.

Thirdly, the Louisiana sugar producers were fairly entitled to some consideration. Unlike wool-growing, their industry involved a considerable plant ; and it offered no easy opportunity for a change to something else. An immediate abolition of the duty, or of the equivalent bounty which had been granted in 1890, would unquestionably work hardship to them. In view of the tenderness with which most of the protected industries were treated, they might reasonably complain of any sudden and unconditional withdrawal of the aid which they had had for generations.

The strong argument against the duty on raw sugar is that which bears against almost all indirect taxes productive of a large revenue. To be productive, such taxes must be imposed on articles of wide consumption; and articles of wide consumption are always of the sort consumed proportionately more by the poor than by the rich. The tax is socially unjust. The full weight of this objection can be fairly judged, to be sure, only on a consideration of the incidence of an entire system of taxation,— in the present case, not only of the federal taxes, but of the State and local taxes as well. It might conceivably be maintained that the State and local taxes, which are chiefly direct, serve to offset the injustice of an indirect tax like the sugar duty. They are levied in the first instance chiefly on the well-to-do; and though their ultimate incidence is in the highest degree complex, it is at least doubtful whether they bear with proportional weight on those classes in the population which would be most affected by a duty on sugar. It is probable, too, that other parts of the tariff schedule, notably the duties on textiles, bear most heavily on commodities consumed by the richer classes. But a comprehensive inquiry of this sort would almost certainly fail of a satisfactory conclusion; and it is inevitable that Congress should have an eye solely to the federal taxes which are under its control. Here there is the clear social injustice of a sugar duty, considered *per se*. Add to this its visible and unmistak able payment by consumers, and the pressure against **it** in a democratic community becomes formidable.

The conflict between sober counsels in favor of the productive revenue duty, and popular suspicion of its effects in aggravating inequalities in taxation and so in the distribution of wealth, was emphasized by the income tax proposal. Obviously the income tax, which was made a part of the tariff act of 1894, was precisely what the sugar duty was not. The revenue from it was uncertain in amount, and in any case would come in but slowly, affording no prompt relief to the Treasury. Moreover, levied as it was only on incomes exceeding $4000 a year, it was a tax on the rich alone, and thus precisely the opposite in social effect from the sugar tax. The income tax was popular in the South and West, where it was most strongly felt that the burden of taxation did not bear sufficiently on the rich, and where the strength of the Treasury was a matter of indifference, not to say hostility; while the sugar tax (barring the exceptional case of Louisiana) was strongly opposed in those regions.

Curiously enough, the outcome of the action of Congress was that both of these taxes were put into operation. In the bill as passed by the House, sugar had been made free, and the bounty abolished. But in the Senate the two Louisiana Senators were among those whose votes were needed if the tariff bill was to pass that branch, and they insisted on some concession to their constituency. The Administration, anxious for a substantial balance in the right direction at the Treasury, also brought its influence to bear in favor of the sugar duty. Consequently it was inserted by the Senate; while the income tax, which in the House had been in a manner a substitute for it, was also retained in the Senate. Later, the decision of the Supreme Court as to the unconstitutionality of the income tax as levied by the act, wiped out that part of the measure, and left the duty on raw sugar without an offset, to the bitter disappointment of those who had opposed both this tax in itself and the tax on refined sugar which it brought in its train.

As it became law, the act imposed a duty on raw sugar of forty per cent. *ad valorem.* The bounty of 1890 was abolished. The new duty was equivalent roughly to one cent a pound, or about one-half the duty in force before 1890, and one-half the bounty granted in that year. Its *ad-valorem* form was peculiar. Never before, except under the general policy of *ad-valorem* rates in the acts of 1846 and 1857, had sugar been subjected to any other than a specific duty. The form now adopted served to cut a Gordian knot: it was a short cut out of the difficulties which were met in the endeavor to arrange varying rates on different grades of raw sugar in such manner as to satisfy both the Treasury officials, the sugar producers, and the refiners. It connects itself with the discussion of the extra rate on refined sugar: to which we may now turn.

The salient facts as to the sugar refiners and their relations to the tariff system were simple and familiar. Sugar refining had been, almost as a matter of course, within

the protective pale, and had been aided by a duty on refined higher than that on raw sugar. The policy of discriminating in this way in favor of the domestic refiners
would probably not have been questioned, except in the
matter of degree, had it not been for the development of
monopoly conditions in the industry by the formation of
the Sugar Trust, which later grew to be the American
Sugar Refining Company, still popularly known as the
Trust. This put a new phase on the matter in the public
eye, the more so as the sugar combination had been one of
the first among the trusts, and had been more prominently
before the community than any other. The more ardent
free-traders have always contended that protective duties
are the chief cause of combinations and monopolies, or
trusts. It needs no great acquaintance with economic
history, and no great skill in general reasoning, to show
that the tendency to combination has deeper causes than
protective legislation, and presents problems more complicated, and in their social importance more weighty,
than those involved in the tariff controversy. But it is
undoubtedly true that in some cases the drift toward
monopoly conditions has been promoted by favoring
duties. Sugar refining happened to be a case of monopoly familiar to all the world ; the monopoly in this case
had in fact been both easier to bring about and a source
of greater profit, because of the protective duty ; while
the nature of the article made a tax in favor of the monopoly producer particularly odious.

With all sugar free, whether raw or refined, the American refiner would be at some slight disadvantage, since freights would amount to a trifle more on raw sugar than on the less bulky refined sugar which might have been imported from foreign quarters. But this disadvantage would be insignificant. Hence when the House passed the tariff bill with both raw and refined sugar free of duty, it practically left the refining monopoly to stand on its own legs, neither helped nor substantially hindered by the tariff. When, however, a duty on sugar was resolved on in the Senate, the difficult question at once was raised how to adjust the rate on refined sugar to that on the crude form. A level duty, at the same rate on raw and on refined, would put the refiners to some real disadvantage. From 100 pounds of raw sugar something less (95 to 98) of refined sugar is obtained, and a level duty would operate distinctly to the advantage of the foreign refiner. Hence, if a revenue duty were imposed on raw sugar, and if it were desired to treat the refiners with absolute indifference, a slight additional duty should be put on refined. Exactly how great this additional duty should fairly be, it was not easy to calculate. The data for the calculation must come chiefly from the refiners; and any figures furnished by them must be received with caution. But a very small difference would suffice to prevent refiners from having any ground for complaint. If a duty of one cent a pound were put upon raw sugar, an additional duty of one-twentieth of a cent would be ample to offset the loss in weight on refined sugar made from the dutiable raw sugar.

Naturally, the sugar refiners wanted something more than bare equality. They wanted a continuance of the favors which the legislature had granted them for generations in the past. In 1890, when raw sugar had been admitted free, refined sugar had been subjected to a duty of one-half a cent per pound. It is probable that the processes of refining are carried on at least as cheaply in the United States as in any foreign country, and that even without any protection at all the sugar-refining industry could maintain itself, and the sugar monopoly make handsome profits. With a barrier against foreign competitors such as the tariff of 1890 gave, the profits were enormous. It was inevitable that great efforts should be made to preserve them.

Briefly, the changes which the sugar schedule underwent during the session were as follows. In the tariff bill as first reported to the House by the Committee of Ways and Means, raw sugar was left free, and a duty of one-quarter of a cent per pound was put on refined sugar. In other words, the largess given to the monopoly by the act of 1890 was to be reduced one-half. In the House, however, the feeling was in favor of a more radical change. The provision for a duty on refined sugar was struck out; and all sugar, raw and refined, was put on the free list, so depriving the trust of all legislative favors. In the Senate, the finance committee amended the sugar schedule by imposing specific duties on raw sugar, roughly at the rate of one cent per pound, with an additional duty of one-eighth of one cent per pound on refined sugar. The duty on raw sugar was inserted partly to gain revenue, partly to secure the votes of the Louisiana Senators for the bill. But when final action came to be taken in the Senate, still another change was made. The duty on raw sugar was changed from specific to *ad valorem*, and was made forty per cent. Over and above this, the duty of one-eighth of one cent on refined sugar was retained. Still further, a provision which had been introduced into the tariff act of 1890 was also retained, by which an extra duty of one-tenth of a cent per pound was imposed on refined sugar coming from countries that gave an export bounty. In this form the sugar schedule was passed by the Senate, had finally to be accepted by the House, and so became law. The final outcome was more than satisfactory to the Sugar Trust. There was the duty of one-eighth of a cent on refined sugar; and there was an extra one-tenth of a cent on refined sugar coming from those continental countries, especially Germany, which give an export bounty, and whose competition was alone to be seriously dreaded. The *ad-valorem* form of the duty was also advantageous, bearing as it did less heavily on lower grades of sugar than on higher.[1] On the whole, the re-

---

[1] *Ad-valorem* duties are assessed on the value of the imported commodities at the time and place of purchase. Raw sugar comes largely from distant countries, or from countries with which transportation is not highly organized, as from Cuba, Java, Brazil, and the Hawaiian Islands. The value at the place of purchase is comparatively low, and freight is comparatively high. On the other hand, refined sugar would be imported, if at all, only from the more advanced European countries. Freight charges from these are low, and the value at the time and place of purchase does not differ very greatly from the value at the American ports. Virtually, therefore, the *ad-*

fining monopoly, while it lost something, came out of the struggle victorious, and was left in little less secure control over the trade under the act of 1894 than under the act of 1890.

Much was said during the session and after the session of influences brought to bear by the trust on certain Senators. An investigation held during the course of the session brought out some facts freely suspected before, and not creditable to our political life. It was admitted that the trust had made contributions to the chests of both political parties, although nominally to the State organizations only. No bargains are ever made in these too familiar cases, but it is expected and understood that what is called " fair consideration " will be given to the interests of the obliging donor. It was proved also that some Senators had speculated in sugar stock. No protest as to the absence of connection between such dealings and the legislator's vote can save them from the taint of dishonor. It would appear also that the success of the trust was promoted by the position of the Louisiana Senators, who were anxious to secure a duty on raw sugar, and who seem to have entered into some sort of bargain for supporting the higher duty on refined sugar in exchange for aid to their own efforts.

In any case it is clear that the sort of manipulation by which the refiners succeeded in retaining their favors from

valorem duty is less heavy on raw sugar than on the refined, and so yields to the refining monopoly an advantage, not easy to calculate, yet probably substantial. It is certain that this form of duty was advocated by the representatives of the trust—in itself a reasonable ground for suspicion.

the tariff was possible only because of the narrow majority which the Democrats had in the Senate. Where one or two votes would have sufficed to block the whole measure, the opportunity for dishonest or selfish pressure on legislation was easy. It is possible to bribe or convince or entangle a few legislators, and so bring them to throw to the winds party consistency and public justice ; but fortunately our conditions are not so corrupt as to make it possible to bribe a whole party or overturn a strong majority. In the House, where the Democratic majority was greater, the manipulation of sugar duties was impossible. It was in the Senate, where a change of one or two votes meant failure to the whole measure, that the unsavory result was achieved.

No part of the tariff legislation of 1894 was more disappointing to those who were earnest in their advocacy of tariff reform than the outcome of the sugar imbroglio. None, too, did more to damage the prestige of the Democrats. They had posed as the champions of the public against the monopoly ; yet the trust had conquered. It is true that the extra duty on refined sugar—the part of the schedule which alone was of real advantage to the trust—was less than it had been in 1890, and that the public in reality was better off than it had been before. But the intricacies of the case were too complicated to be readily understood by the average voter. The imposition of any duty at all on sugar was probably thought to be a surrender to the trust. The revenue tax on raw sugar, fairly open to objection on grounds of social injustice, was supposed in many quarters to be much more objectionable, —to be levied *in toto* for the benefit of the monopolists. The effect of a simple sweeping away of all duties on sugar, whether raw or refined, would have been transparent to the popular mind ; but the impression left by the long and unsuccessful struggle, and the complicated outcome, was mainly that the promises of the Democrats had not been kept.

No doubt the strong feeling which the surrender to the sugar monopoly aroused rested largely on a blind opposition to combinations in general, and to the corporations which are supposed, rightly or wrongly, to have a monopoly position. Whether the tendency to combination is to be welcomed or regretted, has not often been soberly considered by the American public. The usual assumption is that it is an unquestionable evil, to be fought in every way by legislation. That disposition which shows itself, both among the welcomers of socialism and among many critical economists, to accept combinations and consolidations and to use them as instruments of social reform, finds hardly an echo in the United States. Doubtless the popular instinct here is right. The drift to consolidation and monopoly presents problems with which a democratic community can deal only under great disadvantages. To regulate it, to use it, to secure from it the possible benefits, requires a degree of nicety and consistency in legislation which our American communities could reach only by slow and arduous steps. Legislation to check consolidation may be unwise, and probably is futile ; but legislation directed to encourage it, still more legislation to augment the profits of a monopoly, is surely of the worst.

The revulsion against the extreme protective system which showed itself in the elections of 1890 and 1892 was probably in a large degree a consequence of the popular feeling just described. While the essential question as to protective duties is comparatively simple, the intricate reasoning which is needed to follow the effects of such duties into all the ramifications of international and domestic trade can have but little influence on the average citizen. He reasons from few premises, and is affected by simple catch-words. The outcry against trusts and monopolies, though in fact it describes an exception rather than the normal working of protective duties, was probably the most effective argument in bringing about the public verdict against the McKinley act. It is expressive of the general feeling of unrest as to the power of great corporations, the growth of plutocracy, the gulf between the few very rich and the masses of comparatively poor, which is becoming a stronger and stronger political force, and is destined in the future to have larger and larger effect on legislation.

It is clear that the new tariff act made no deep-reaching change in the character of our tariff legislation. The one exception was the removal of the duty on wool. Barring this, there was simply a moderation of the protective duties. A slice was taken off here, a shaving there; but the essentially protective character remained.

This would have been the case even had the Wilson Bill, as originally proposed to the House or as passed by that body, become law. That less anxiously conservative measure was of course alleged by its opponents to portend ruin to American manufacturers and prostration to American labor. In fact, while it might have affected some industries, it would have caused no considerable disturbance of industry and no considerable rearrangement of the productive forces of the nation. The act as finally passed was even less potent for good or for evil. In not a few cases, the duties, while lower than those enacted in the McKinley act of 1890, were still higher than under the tariff act of 1883. As far as it went, it began a policy of lower duties; but most of the steps in this direction were feeble and faltering.

Whether such a measure be good or bad, must be decided in the main on general principles. To follow out its influence on the prosperity of the community requires time for the observation of effects, and great skill and caution in the interpretation of industrial phenomena. Even had the new legislation been much more drastic, its final effects on general welfare could have shown themselves only after the lapse of a considerable period, and then might easily have been concealed or obscured by the operation of other causes. To judge a very moderate measure like that of 1894 by its visible fruits is so difficult as to touch the bounds of the impossible. The effects on any particular industry,—which are but a fragmentary bit of evidence as to the promotion of general prosperity.—

are sufficiently difficult to trace. We have seen how the one radical change made by the act, in abolishing the duty on wool, required time to show how it might affect the wool and woollen industry. Even after the lapse of time, there could hardly be such an unmistakable result one way or the other as to prevent doubt and dispute. When all the evidence on this point was in, it could still be of little avail toward answering the fundamental question,—whether the productive forces of the community were applied to better effect with a low tariff than without it.

But the general public has been taught to expect immediate, almost magical effects. Both parties in the protective controversy have preached the same gospel, and made the same promises. For high duties and for low duties alike it has been claimed that they would convert depression into prosperity. This has been the case, in more or less degree, throughout our tariff history; and the inevitable disappointment with the expectations so raised has had its effect in bringing about the vacillations in public feeling and the frequent changes in policy. The act of 1894 was defended and attacked on the same superficial grounds; and it happened to suffer from the contingencies of the moment. It went into effect shortly after an acute commercial crisis, and in the worst stage of a period of severe depression. The crisis and the depression, were due, in this case as in all others, to a long and complex set of causes, some of them still obscure even to the best informed and most skilled observers.

That the tariff act played any serious part in bringing them about, would not be maintained by any cool and competent critic. But the great mass of the public judged otherwise. The act had been followed by hard times; at best, it had done nothing to remedy them. Half-hearted in its provisions, unlucky in the time of its enactment, it could make no warm friends, and earn no general approval.

Thus, whether in its effects on legislation or on public opinion, the movement for tariff reform from 1887 to 1894 was in its outcome disappointing. The decisive victories in the elections of 1890 and 1892 had led the free-traders to form high hopes: the real beginning of the long deferred reform seemed at last at hand. But the victorious party was soon split by internal dissensions. With the acute crisis of 1893 and the growing accentuation of differing opinions on the currency, that issue forced itself forward. The session of 1893–94, as it progressed, witnessed slackened enthusiasm, inept leadership, and an inglorious result. President Cleveland's action in permitting the new tariff act to become law without his signature, put the final stamp of indifference and disappointment on the measure.

CHAPTER VII.

THE TARIFF ACT OF 1897.

AT the time of the passage of the tariff act of 1894 nothing seemed more improbable than an early return to the policy of high and all-embracing protection. That policy, as embodied in the act of 1890, had met with apparently unquestionable rebukes at the polls in 1890 and 1892. Nor was there anything in the legislation of 1894 to invite a reaction. As we have seen, the act of that year, so far from being radical, had been, with the single exception of the free admission of wool, anxiously conservative. Once it was passed, the community heaved a sigh of relief and dared to hope that from this quarter at least there would be for a space no further cause of industrial uncertainty and disturbance.

If this reasonable expectation was disappointed, the explanation is to be found, not in any demonstrable change in public feeling, but in the complete overturn in the general political situation. Suddenly and unexpectedly, the tariff was shoved aside as the party issue, and the currency took its place. The stormy session of 1893, in which the silver-purchase act of 1890 had been repealed, foreshadowed the coming change; the commercial crisis of 1893, and the years of depression which followed,

completed it with surprising quickness.   Ever since the
demoralizing days of the excessive paper issues of the
civil war, periods of depression have favored the growth
of the party of cheap money.   The free-silver party, now
the party of cheap money, found its hold strengthening
in the South and West, and finally captured the Democratic organization.   In the South, always the main
seat of the political strength of the Democrats, the tariff
question had for some time been holding its dominant
place largely as a matter of tradition.   The opposition
to protection had been inherited from the political tenets
of *ante-bellum* days, and the tariff issue was easily displaced by the new and burning question.   The majority
of the Democrats of the new generation were won to the
free-silver side; the old leaders were contemptuously discarded; the political centre of gravity suddenly shifted
The Democrats being pledged defiantly to one side, the
Republicans had no choice but to take the other.   Thus
the election of 1896 turned directly on the question of
the free coinage of silver.   The popular verdict was clear
on that question, and on that only.

It was not to be expected, however, that the Republican party would desert its old faith, or turn suddenly
with whole and single heart to the new issue forced upon
it.   For years—almost for generations—the Republicans
had been fencing and compromising on the various phases
which the currency question from time to time assumed.
Moreover, the depression which set in after the crisis of
1893 made an opportunity for the apostles of high pro-

tection as well as for those of free silver. Both parties
in the newspaper tariff controversy of 1890–94 had predicted a general rush of prosperity, the one from high
duties, the other from low duties. As the years succeeding 1893 grew blacker and blacker, the stanch protectionists had the opportunity to cry: " We told you so; let us
return to the policy of prosperity." In the early part of
1896, before the silver question had forced itself to the
front, the Republicans had resolved to stake the issue once
more on protection; and it had accordingly been settled
that Mr. McKinley was to be the party candidate for the
Presidency. What might have been the outcome of a
campaign in which the tariff was the single issue cannot
be said; though the general conditions at the moment
certainly were favorable to the party not in power. Fate
willed it that the campaign centred on silver. But here,
after all, the Republicans were on the defensive. As to
the currency, they undertook only to maintain the *status
quo;* while on the tariff, though it might be in the background during the campaign, they had resolved to take
the offensive, and had engaged to legislate afresh at the
first opportunity.

This difference in disposition as to the two problems
became more pronounced when the smoke of battle
cleared away, and the next move was in order. While
the popular and electoral votes had been clearly for the
Republicans, the complexion of the national legislature
was not so altered as to give them a free hand on the
currency. In the Senate they had no controlling major-

ity without the aid of silver votes. On the currency
question the party, as such, could do nothing,—certainly
nothing without dissension and recrimination. But on
the tariff question something could be done at once.

The occasion for action was the more urgent because
of the state of the finances. For several years there had
been a deficit in the current operations of the Treasury.
The first fiscal year in which the balance had been on the
wrong side was 1893–94; and then followed several years
similarly unfortunate.[1] The very circumstance that the
deficit appeared, and indeed had been most serious, while
the tariff act of 1890 was still in force, indicated that it was
due, not to the particular provisions of the act of 1890 or
of its successor of 1894, but to the general industrial conditions of the period after 1893. The great crisis of 1893,
itself the result of a complexity of causes, among which
reckless monetary legislation was the chief, had been followed, as such revulsions must be, by a sharp falling-off in
the imports and a consequent heavy decline in the customs
revenue. The deficit which resulted was often alleged to
be due to specially inadequate legislation in 1894. The

[1] Fiscal Year.	Ordinary Revenue.	Expendi- tures.		
1892–93	461.7	459.4	2.3	Surplus
1893–94	372.8	442.6	69.8	Deficit.
1894–95	390.4	433.2	42.8	"
1895–96	409.5	434.7	25.2	"
1896–97	430.4	448.4	18.0	"

The figures indicate millions of dollars. The deficit really began to appear in the second half-year of the fiscal year 1892–93; but the receipts in
the first half-year had been large, so that this fiscal year as a whole showed
a small surplus.

act of 1894 had indeed failed to make rigorously careful provision for the needed revenue; but the same had been the case with the act of 1890, and was again the case, as we shall presently see, with that of 1897. The looseness of our federal legislation, so far as careful calculation of income and outgo is concerned, is an old and familiar phenomenon, the result partly of general political conditions and partly of the reliance on so variable a source of revenue as protective customs duties. But in partisan discussion, much was made of the failure of the act of 1894 to yield the revenue needed at the time; and at all events some measure of relief for the Treasury was called for.

Hence President McKinley, in calling the extra session of 1897, asked Congress to deal solely with the import duties and the revenue. The two questions of industrial policy and of legislation for revenue ought, indeed, to be considered separately. But in the history of tariff legislation in the United States, as in that of most other countries, they have been constantly interwoven; and so they were in this case. What with the undeniable need of revenue, the comparative ease with which party strength could be consolidated on the question of protection, the old predilection of all the leading spirits among the Republicans for that issue, and the clearly expressed wish of the President, the tariff at the extra session received exclusive consideration. Thus the first fruits of the election of 1896 were legislation, not on the question which had been uppermost in the campaign, but on the tariff question, on which no clear and unequivocal evidence of popular feeling had been secured.

The legislative history of the measure was instructive, and in some respects showed striking contrasts with that of its predecessor of 1894. In the House the bill was reported by the Committee on Ways and Means as early as March 18th, within three days after the session began. This extraordinary promptness was made possible by methods that paid scant respect to the letter of the law. Strictly, so long as the new Congress had not met, no one was authorized to take any steps towards legislation at its hands. But, long before this, it was settled that Mr. Reed was to be once more Speaker, and he was able to intimate that the existing Committee on Ways and Means was to remain substantially unchanged in the next Congress; and, during the hold-over session of 1896–97, that committee accordingly was at work on the tariff bill, and was able to present it to the new Congress immediately on its assembling. Mr. Dingley, already chairman of the committee in the Fifty-fourth Congress (1895–97), was again to be chairman for the next; and his name was attached in popular discussion to the new measure which he was able to present with such celerity.

The action of the House was as prompt as that of its committee. Within less than two weeks, on March 31st, the bill was passed. Only a comparatively small part of it had been considered in the House: no more than twenty-two of the one hundred and sixty-three pages were taken up for discussion. In the main, the committee scheme was adopted as it stood, being accepted once for all as the party measure and passed under the pressure of rigid party discipline. The whole procedure was doubtless not in accord with the theory of legislation after debate and discussion. But it was not without its good side also. It served to concentrate responsibility, to prevent haphazard amendment, to check in some measure the log-rolling and the give-and-take which beset all legislation involving a great variety of interests. Under the iron rule of Speaker Reed, the House gave the session to the enactment of a deliberately planned tariff bill, and to that only.

In the Senate progress was slower, and the course of events showed greater vacillation. The bill, referred at once to the Senate Committee on Finance, was reported after a month, on May 8th, with important amendments. There was an attempt to impose some purely revenue duties; and, as to the protective duties, the tendency was towards lower rates than in the House bill, though on certain articles, such as wool of low grade, hides, and others (of which more will be said presently), the drift was the other way. The Senate, however, paid much less respect than the House to the recommendations of the committee in charge. In the course of two months, from May 4th to July 7th, it went over the tariff bill item by item, amending without restraint, often in a perfunctory manner, and not infrequently with the outcome settled by the accident of attendance on the particular day; on the whole, with a tendency to retain the higher rates of the House bill. As passed finally by the Senate on July 7th, the bill, though it contained some 872 amendments, followed the plan of the House Committee rather than that of the Senate Committee. As usual, it went to a Conference Committee. In the various compromises and adjustments in the Senate and in the Conference Committee there was little sign of the deliberate plan and method which the House had shown, and the details of the act were settled in no less haphazard fashion than has been the case with other tariff measures. As patched up by the Conference Committee, the bill was promptly passed by both branches of Congress, and became law on July 24th.

In what manner these political conditions affected the character of the act will appear from a consideration of the more important specific changes.

First and foremost was the re-imposition of the duties on wool. As the repeal of these duties had been the one important change made by the act of 1894, so their restoration was the salient feature in the act of 1897. On clothing and combing wool the precise rates which had been imposed in the tariff act of 1890 were restored. Clothing wool was subjected once more to a duty of eleven cents a pound, combing wool to one of twelve cents. On carpet wool there were new graded duties, heavier than any ever before levied. If its value was twelve cents a pound or less, the duty was four cents; if over twelve cents, the duty was seven cents.

In 1894, when the duties on wool were removed, the

general expectation alike of the advocates and opponents of protection was that this change had come to stay. The political and economic probabilities in 1894 were such as to justify the expectation. The astonishing growth of all manufactures, uninterrupted before and after that date, made it certain that the United States under any tariff conditions would be a great manufacturing country, and seemed to warrant the belief that the desire for freedom in the use of materials would become stronger, the prospect of an expanding foreign trade more tempting, the demand for protection to domestic industries less insistent. The need of foreign wool for clothing the people of the United States and the inadequacy of the domestic supply were clear then, and indeed became more clear in the intervening years. In the woollen manufacturing industry itself it was to be expected with confidence that, once the transition to free wool accomplished, the manufacturers would oppose a return to the old *régime*. And, as it proved, the manufacturers expressed themselves in terms surprisingly strong on the disadvantages, from their point of view, of a return to the wool duties.[1] If, nevertheless, the change was made, the explanation is to be found mainly in the unexpected turn of the political wheel.

---

[1] " Never until he had experience under free wool did the manufacturer realize the full extent of the disadvantages he suffers by reason of the wool duty, and the impossibility, by any compensating duty, of fully offsetting these disadvantages." So much was said in the statement made before the Ways and Means Committee by the secretary of the Wool-Manufacturers' Association. *Bulletin of the Wool Manufacturers*, March, 1897. p. 84.

Wool is the article as to which it can be said with greatest truth and greatest plausibility that the farmer gets his share of the largesses of protection. It is true that in 1892 the farmers of Ohio and of other central States seemed to show that they were indifferent to the attraction; for in that year a whole row of central States had voted against the party of protection, and in Ohio itself the victory of that party had been so narrow as to be equivalent to a defeat. It is true also that the main effects of the duty on wool would certainly be to stimulate the activity and increase the profits of the large wool-growers in the thinly settled trans-Missouri region, rather than to benefit substantially the farmers proper.[1] But the determination to give evidence of fostering care for the farming interest was too strong to be affected

---

[1] In a formal communication to the Ways and Means Committee the Wool-Manufacturers' Association used the following language : '' The real explanation of these extraordinary demands lies in the fact that the wool-growers of the Middle West find themselves in need of protection against their American competitors west of the Mississippi River. It was not the imports under the McKinley law, but the cheaper-grown wools of the Far West, which made wool-growing relatively unprofitable on the high-priced lands of Ohio, Michigan, Pennsylvania. Every further expansion of the ranch industry must increase the effects of this competition. An enormous tariff on wool, such as is proposed, would overstimulate this ranch industry, by its promise of excessive profits, and would thus still farther increase the difficulties of the Middle-West farmer.'' *Bulletin of the Wool-Manufacturers*, June, 1897, p. 133. The wool-growers had at first asked a duty of fifteen cents a pound on clothing and combing wool, and finally had proposed, as an ''ultimatum,'' twelve cents. The manufacturers had offered to join in recommending duties of eight and ten cents (graded by value) on clothing wool, and of nine and eleven cents on combing wool. In the act the growers got substantially their ultimatum,—eleven cents on clothing wool, twelve cents on combing wool.

by such considerations. The silver party had posed ostentatiously as the special friend of the debtor and the farmer. The Republicans, having pushed forward the tariff as their first strong card, must needs do something for the farmer; and heavy duties on wool were the natural result, consistent at once with the established party policy and with the long-continued and earnest contention of President McKinley himself.

One other part of the wool duties served to show how the general political complications affected the terms of the tariff act. The duties on carpet wool, as has already been noted, were made higher than ever before. In the House the rates of the act of 1890 had been retained; but in the Senate new and higher rates were inserted, and, though somewhat pruned down in the Conference Committee, were retained in the act. They were de. manded by the Senators from some States in the far West, especially from Idaho and Montana. These Senators, though Republican, were on the silver side in the monetary controversy, and so by no means in complete accord with their associates. They needed to be placated; and they succeeded in getting higher duties on the cheap carpet wools, on the plea of encouragement for the comparatively coarse clothing wool of their ranches. It had been shown time and again, on the very principles of protection, that carpet wools were not grown in the country, and that those imported did not affect to any appreciable extent the market for domestic wool. But the Western Senators. who held the balance of power, were able none the less to secure this concession to their demands. It deserves to be noted, on the other hand, that the Senate had been disposed to lower the duties on clothing and combing wool. The Finance Committee had proposed rates of eight and nine cents a pound, and the Senate itself had voted rates of ten and eleven cents; the reduction being due to the influence of the manufacturers, who were opposed to the high duties not only because of the price added on the raw material, but also because of the still higher duties on their own products which would be entailed.[1] But in the Conference Committee the House rates of eleven cents on clothing wool and twelve cents on combing wool were restored, and so appeared on the statute book.

The same complications that led to the high duty on carpet wool brought about a duty on hides. This rawest of raw materials had been on the free list for just a quarter of a century, since 1872, when the duty of the war days had been repealed. It would have remained free of tax if the Republicans had been able to carry out the policy favored by the great majority of their own number. But here, again, the Senators from the ranch-

---

[1] " It is not pleasant for the American wool manufacturer to be told that the average *ad-valorem* rate upon woollen goods, under the tariff of 1890, was 98 per cent. It does not particularly help the case from the consumer's point of view to reply that the actual protective duty accorded him under that law did not exceed 45 per cent. The public looks at the fact—98 per cent." So spoke the Secretary of the Wool-Manufacturers' Association to the House Committee. *Bulletin of the Wool Manufacturers*, March, 1897, p. 83. None the less, the manufacturers in 1897 secured, and presumably asked for, an increase of the protective (*i. e., ad-valorem*) duty on woollens to 55 per cent.,—a rate higher than any imposed before.

ing States were able to dictate terms. In the House bill, hides had still remained on the free list. In the Senate a duty of 20 per cent. was tacked on. The rate was reduced to 15 per cent. in the Conference Committee, and so remained in the act.

The restored duties on wool necessarily brought in their train the old system of high compensating duties on woollens. Once more we find the bewildering combination of *ad-valorem* duties for protection and specific duties to compensate for the charges on the raw material. In the main, the result was a restoration of the rates of the act of 1890.[1] There was some upward movement almost all along the line; and the *ad-valorem* duty alone, on the classes of fabrics which are most largely imported, crept up to 55 per cent. Just thirty years before, in 1867, when the system of compound duties on woollens was first carefully worked out, it rested on the assumption that a "net" protection of 25 per cent. was to be secured. But the *ad-valorem* rate, designed to give this net protection, had advanced steadily in the acts of 1883 and 1890, and in the act of 1897 reached 55 per cent.!

---

[1] The drift of the changes from the rates of 1890 is shown by the following figures as to the two classes of goods most largely imported :

DUTIES ON WOOLLEN CLOTHS.

1890.	1897.
(1) If worth 30 cents or less per pound, 33 cents per pound plus 40 per cent.	(1) If worth 40 cents or less per pound, 33 cents per pound plus 50 per cent.
(2) If worth between 30 and 40 cents per pound, 38½ cents per pound plus 40 per cent.	

The experiment of free wool and of moderated (though but slightly moderated) duties on woollens, was thus tried under the act of 1894 for three short years, and these, moreover, years of great general depression. As has been already said, even under normal business conditions the transition from the system of high duties must have been for a while disturbing and trying, and the full effects of the change, alike for consumers and producers, could not have worked themselves out for several years.[1]

(3) If worth more than 40 cents per pound, 44 cents per pound plus 50 per cent.	(2) If worth between 40 and 70 cents per pound, 44 cents per pound plus 50 per cent.
	(3) If worth over 70 cents per pound, 44 cents per pound plus 55 per cent.

DUTIES ON DRESS GOODS.

1890.	1897.
(1) Cotton warp, worth 15 cents a yard or less, 7 cents a yard plus 40 per cent.	(1) and (2) the same; but with the proviso that the *ad-valorem* duty shall be 55 per cent. if the value is over 70 cents per pound.
(2) Cotton warp worth more than 15 cents a yard, 8 cents a yard plus 50 per cent.	
(3) If the warp has any wool, 12 cents a yard plus 50 per cent.	(3) If the warp has any wool, 11 cents per yard plus 50 per cent.; but with the proviso that the *ad-valorem* duty shall be 55 per cent. if the value exceeds 70 cents per pound.

It will be observed that, under the act of 1897, on dress goods (of which some $20,000,000 worth was imported in 1896), the customs officers must ascertain, first, whether the warp consists "wholly of cotton or other vegetable material"; if so, whether the goods are worth more or less than 7 cents a yard; if not, whether they are worth more or less than 70 cents a pound. All these circumstances affect the rate of duty, and obviously increase the difficulties of administration and the opportunities for evasion.

[1] See above, pp. 294–296.

While the manufacturers had cheaper wool and unlimited choice in the use of it, they had to learn to avail themselves of this advantage. The wool-growers, especially in the central districts, had to face a fall in the price of wool, and had hardly time to make the change (more or less inevitable under any conditions) of raising sheep for mutton rather than for wool. As it happened, all this distressing transition was made the more trying because it took place in a period when all industry was depressed. Just as the general revulsion of the years 1893–97 was ascribed by the protectionists to the tariff act of 1894, so the special difficulties of the wool manufacturers and wool-growers were ascribed to that measure, and here with some show of reason. Given a reasonable time, with general economical conditions of a normal sort, and it is more than probable that the new *régime* in the wool industry would have won its way to general acceptance But the experiment of free wool and of simple duties on woollens was tried for too short a time to prove the wisdom of the change.[1]

On cotton goods the general tendency was to impose duties lower than those of 1890. This was indicated by the drag-net rate, on manufactures of cotton not otherwise provided for, which had been fifty per cent. in 1890, and was 45 per cent. in 1897. There was, again, as in

---

[1] On the episode of 1894–97, and indeed on the whole history of wool-growing from the earliest times to 1908, by far the best investigation is that of Professor C. W. Wright, *Wool-growing and the Tariff*, published in the Harvard Economic Studies (1910).

1890, a rigorously elaborate system of combined specific and *ad-valorem* duties on certain sorts of goods selected for especially heavy rates, such as cotton stockings and hose, and plushes, velvets, corduroys.[1] In the main, the cotton manufacturers held aloof from the new measure. The rates of the act of 1894 had been not unsatisfactory to them; and they may have feared some such policy in regard to their material as befell the wool manufacturers. In fact, the Senate, in the course of its tortuous amendments, inserted in the bill (apparently somewhat to its own surprise) a duty on raw cotton, designed to check the importation of certain kinds of Egyptian cotton whose fibre fits it for some special uses. But here no political complication within the Republican party bolstered up the change; and this proviso, absurd enough, but no more absurd than those relating to carpet wool and to hides, disappeared in the Conference Committee.

On two large classes of textile goods new and distinctly higher duties were imposed,—on silks and linens. The duties on silks present a remarkable case of the unexpected extension of the protective system. From the time of the

---

[1] Compare pp. 267–269 above, where the duties on these articles under the act of 1890 are referred to. The same objectionable method of specific duties, graded by value, was applied in the act of 1897, and in general with higher rates; thus by paragraphs 315, 318, 319, 386 of the act of 1897. On cotton hose, to give a single example, the lowest classes (*i. e.*, the cheapest goods) and the rates on them were:

Class.	Duty.
In 1890—Value 60c. or less per dozen	20c. a dozen plus 20%
In 1897—Value $1 or less per dozen	50c. a dozen plus 15%

Clearly, the duty of 1897 was very much higher than that of 1890 had been.

civil war, silks had been subject to heavy *ad-valorem* duties—60 per cent. from 1864 to 1883, and 50 per cent. from 1883 to 1897. These duties had caused a great silk-manufacturing industry to grow up, with results that were in some respects surprising, and might perhaps be cited as showing the possibility of successful application of protection to young industries. But the measure of apparent success thus attained, and the degree of protection thus afforded, did not satisfy the manufacturers or the dominant protectionists. An increasing competition from silk goods produced in Japan was feared, the spectre of " cheap labor " being invoked once more. Moreover, the fraud and undervaluation inevitable under any high *ad-valorem* duty had long suggested the desirability of arranging some schedule of specific duties on silks. Unquestionably the administration of the *ad-valorem* duty had been unsatisfactory, and the rates of 50 and 60 per cent. had been less effective in checking imports than they would have been without the almost systematic undervaluations by consignees and agents. On the other hand, the difficulties of framing a schedule of specific duties were great, and indeed had hitherto been thought insuperable. In view of the greatly varying qualities of the goods, and the difficulty of grading them by any external marks, duties by the pound or yard would be too high on the cheaper goods, disproportionately low on the dearer. The act of 1897 boldly attempted to grapple with the difficulties of the case, and for the first time imposed specific duties on silks. The

mode of gradation was to levy the duties according to
the amount of pure silk contained in the goods. The
duties were fixed by the pound, being lowest on goods
containing a small proportion of pure silk, and rising as
that proportion became larger; with the proviso that in
no case should the duty be less than 50 per cent. This
plan brought about an unquestionable increase in the
rates, especially on the cheaper silks. How great the increase was, could be judged only by a person minutely
conversant with the trade, and might be difficult to calculate in advance even by such a person. On the other
hand, it was doubtful whether the administrative difficulties encountered under the high *ad-valorem* duties of
previous acts would not appear in full force under this
one. The exact determination of the percentage in
weight of pure silk in any given piece of so-called silk
goods could hardly be an easy matter. Yet this had to
be precisely ascertained for the satisfactory administration of the duties of 1897. Thus, the duty on certain
kinds of silks was $1.30 per pound, if they contained 45
per cent. in weight of silk; but advanced suddenly to
$2.25, if they contained more than 45 per cent. The
same sort of gradation, bringing sudden great changes
in duty as an obscure dividing line was crossed, ran
through the whole schedule; and the temptation to false
statement at the hands of the importer would seem to be
as great as the difficulty of detection at the hands of the
customs examiner. Both in the high range of rates and
in the attempt at rigorous enforcement the new act here

went far beyond the act of 1890, making a new and important advance in the application of extreme protection.[1]

On linens another step of the same kind was taken, specific duties being substituted here also for *ad-valorem*. In 1890, the *ad-valorem* rate on linens had been raised to 50 per cent., to be reduced in 1894 to 35 per cent. In 1897, a compound system was adopted: specific duties imposed with *ad-valorem* supplements, such as had already been tried on cotton hose, velvets, and other fabrics. Linens were graded somewhat as cottons had been graded since 1861, according to the fineness of the goods as indicated by the number of threads to the square inch. If the number of threads was sixty or less per square inch, the duty was one and three fourths

---

[1] The important part of the silk schedule in the act of 1897 is paragraph 387, which fixed the duties on " woven silk fabrics in the piece, not specially provided for." The same rates are applicable, under section 388, to silk handkerchiefs. The method of grading is exemplified by the following summary statement of some of the rates first enumerated.

Duties on silk piece goods :

(1) containing 20% or less in weight of silk, if in the gum......$0.50 per lb.

          if dyed in the piece .60   "

(2) containing 20 to 30% in weight of silk, if in the gum...... .65   "

          if dyed in the piece .80   "

(3) containing 30 to 45% in weight of silk, if in the gum...... .90   "

          if dyed in the piece 1.10   "

(4) containing 30% or less in weight of silk, if dyed in the

      thread or yarn, black............................... .75   "

          other color........................ .90   "

(5) containing 30 to 45% in weight of silk, if dyed in the thread

      or yarn, black................................... 1.10   "

          other color............................ 1.30   "

So the schedule goes on, the duties advancing by stages as the per cent. in weight of silk becomes greater, as the goods are dyed in the thread or yarn,

cents a square yard; if the threads were between sixty and one hundred and twenty, the duty was two and three fourths cents; and so on,—plus 30 per cent. *ad-valorem* duty in all cases. But finer linen goods, unless otherwise specially provided for, were treated leniently. If the weight was small (less than four and one half ounces per yard), the duty was but 35 per cent. On the other hand, linen laces, or articles trimmed with lace or embroidery, were dutiable at 60 per cent.,—an advance at 10 per cent. over the rate of 1890. The new specific duties on linens were expected to induce some cotton mills to turn to cheaper grades of linens, such as towel cloth; but the general conditions of the manufacture of finer linens made it doubtful here, as in the case of finer silks and woollens, whether the imported fabrics would be supplanted.

---

as the goods are "weighted in dyeing so as to exceed the original weight of the raw silk," and so on. Goods of lighter weight (less than $1\frac{1}{3}$ ounces per yard) are subject to still higher duties; those of lightest weight ($\frac{1}{3}$ ounce per yard or less), to the highest duty of all, the maximum being $4.50 per pound.

It deserves to be noticed that the woollen manufacturers, confronted with the undervaluation problem under the *ad-valorem* duties on woollens, found it impossible to frame a scheme of specific duties. A special committee from their number, which attempted to devise such a scheme, found that "a wholly specific schedule is impossible, because of the thousands of variations—in weave, in texture, in materials, in finish—which distinguish woollen goods from those of all other textile manufactures." See *Bulletin of the Wool Manufacturers*, March, 1897, p. 72. In the tariff bill as passed by the House the duties on woollens (over and above the compensating duty) had been made partly *ad valorem* and partly specific with gradations by value. But this additional complication in the woollens schedule was struck out in the Senate.

It was inevitable, under the political conditions of the session, that in this schedule something should again be attempted for the farmer; and, accordingly, we find a substantial duty on flax. The rate of the act of 1890 was restored,—three cents a pound on prepared flax, in place of the rate of one and one half cents imposed by the act of 1894. Here, too, no appreciable economic change was likely to result. Bagging for cotton, which had been admitted free under the act of 1894, was subjected to a duty, but a lower duty than that of 1890: the rate being $\frac{6}{10}$ cent per square yard in 1897, as compared with $1\frac{6}{10}$ cents in 1890. This compromise may also be regarded as making some concession to the planter of the South.

On chinaware the rates of 1890 were restored. The duty on the finer qualities which are chiefly imported had been lowered to 35 per cent. in 1894, and was now once more put at 60 per cent. On glassware, also, the general *ad-valorem* rate, which had been reduced to 35 per cent. in 1894, was again fixed at 45 per cent., as in 1890. Similarly the specific duties on the cheaper grades of window-glass and plate-glass, which had been lowered in 1894, were raised to the figures of 1890; though on some of the more expensive kinds of plate-glass the lower rates of 1894, being still sufficient to prevent importation, were left substantially unchanged.

The metal schedules in the act of 1897 showed in the main a striking contrast with the textile schedules. Important advances of duty were made on many textiles.

and in some cases rates went considerably higher even
than those of 1890.   But on most metals, and especially
on iron and steel, duties were left very much as they had
been in 1894.   Indeed, Mr. Dingley, in introducing the
bill in the House, said that, " the iron and steel schedule,
except as to some advanced products, had not been
changed from the present law, because this schedule
seemed to be one of the two of the present law [the
other being the cottons schedule] which are differentiated
from most of the others, and made in the main protective."   Hence we find, as in the act of 1894, iron
ore subject to duty at forty cents a ton, and pig iron
at four dollars a ton.   On steel rails also there was no
change from the comparatively moderate rate of 1894; it
remained $7.84 per ton.   On coal there was a compromise
rate.   The duty had been seventy-five cents a ton in
1890, and forty cents in 1894; it was now fixed at sixty-
seven cents.

On the other hand, as to certain manufactures of iron
and steel farther advanced beyond the crude stage, there
was a return to rates very similar to those of 1890.
Thus, on pocket cutlery, razors, guns, we find once more
the system of combined *ad-valorem* and specific duties,
graded according to the value of the article.   It is not
easy to unravel the meaning and probable effects of the
complicated duties imposed in these cases; but it is clear
that they were framed with a view to imposing a very
high barrier to imports, and yet were arranged on the
system, vicious from the administrative point of view, of

bringing sudden changes in duty as a given point in ap-
praised value is passed.[1]

Some other items in the metal schedule deserve notice.
Copper remained on the free list, where it had been put
in 1894. Already in 1890 the duty had been reduced to
one and one fourths cents per pound. As the copper
mines, almost alone among the great enterprises of the
country, had been enjoying uninterrupted prosperity,
even during the period of depression, and had been exporting their product on a great scale, no one cared a
straw for the duty. For good or ill the copper duty had
worked out all its effects years before. On the other
hand, the duties on lead and on lead ore went up to the
point at which they stood in 1890. Here we have once
more the signs of concession to the silver Republicans

---

[1] Pocket cutlery supplies a good example of the methods applied in the
acts of 1890 and 1897 to the articles here mentioned. The rates of duty
were :

1890.

Class.	Duty.
(1) Value (per dozen) 50 cents or less.	12 cents (per dozen) plus 50 per cent.
(2) Value 50 cents @ $1.50.	50 cents plus 50 per cent.
(3) Value $1.50 @ $3.00.	$1.00 plus 50 per cent.
(4) Value over $3.00.	$2.00 plus 50 per cent.

1897.

Class.	Duty.
(a) Value (per dozen) 40 cents or less.	40 per cent.
(1) Value 40 @ 50 cents.	12 cents plus 40 per cent.
(2) Value 50 cents @ $1.25.	60 cents plus 40 per cent.
(3) Value $1.25 @ $3.00 per dozen.	$1.20 plus 40 per cent.
(4) Value over $3.00.	$2.40 plus 40 per cent.

It will be seen that on the cheapest knives there was a reduction in duty as
compared with 1890 ; while on the higher classes, and especially on the sec-

of the far West.   A considerable importation from
Mexico of ores bearing both lead and silver had brought
some competition with American mines yielding the
same metals — competition which could not well be
helped as to the silver, since that would find its way to
the international market in any case, but which could be
impeded so far as the domestic market for lead was concerned.   Accordingly there was a substantial duty on
lead, and on lead-bearing ore in proportion to the lead
contained.[1]

In general, the duties in the metal schedule ceased
to excite controversy, and even to arouse attention.
Whether or no as a result of the application of the protective system, the iron and steel industry had in fact

---

ond, there was an increase.   The most effective change was that by which
the line of classification by value was shifted from $1.50 to $1.25,—a shift
which caused many goods to come under class 3 in 1897 which were in class
2 in 1890, and so caused a great advance in the duty chargeable.   It may
be noted incidentally that the figure of $1.50, to mark the dividing line be-
tween classes 1 and 2, had been retained both in the House bill and in the
Senate bill : the change to $1.25 was made at the last moment in the Con-
ference Committee.   It needs only a glance at the duties under these classes
in 1897 to show how great will be the temptation to manufacture knives, and
to juggle with their value, in such manner as to bring them below the dividing line of $1.25.   The same vicious method of grading the duties on pocket
knives had been followed in the act of 1894, though with somewhat lower
rates.   In 1890 and 1897 (not in 1894) the method was also applied to
razors, table-knives, and guns, and in 1897 to shears and scissors.   The
pertinent paragraphs of the act of 1897 are numbers 153 to 158

[1] The duties from 1890 to 1897 were :

	Lead ore, per pound of lead contained.	Lead per pound.
1890	$1\frac{1}{2}$ cents.	2 cents.
1894	$\frac{3}{4}$ cent.	1 cent.
1897	$1\frac{1}{2}$ cents.	$2\frac{1}{8}$ cents.

passed the period of tutelage, and had become not only independent of aid, but a formidable competitor in the markets of the world. The extraordinary development of this industry during the period between 1870 and 1895 is one of the most remarkable chapters in the remarkable economic history of our century. The discovery of the wonderful beds of iron ore on Lake Superior; the fever-ish development of the coal deposits of the middle West; the amazing cheapening of transportation by water and rail; the bold prosecution of mining, transportation, manu-facturing, not only on a great scale, but on a scale fairly to be called gigantic—all these revolutionized the con-ditions of production. They called for resource and genius in the captains of industry; enabled the bold, capable, and perhaps unscrupulous to accumulate fortunes that rouse the uneasy wonder of the world; and gave rise to new social conditions and grave social problems. Some-thing of the same sort happened in the growth of copper mining; though here the richness of the natural resources counted far more, and the situation in general was more simple. Among the forces which were at work in these industries, protective duties probably counted for much less than is often supposed. An eagle eye in divining possibilities, boldness and resource in developing them, skill and invention in designing the most effective mechani-cal appliances,—these forces of character and of brains, developed by the pressure of competition in a strenuous community, and applied under highly favoring natural conditions, explain the prodigious advance.

The forces which so completely changed the situation of the iron and steel industry were most actively at work through the decade from 1880 to 1890. By 1890 they had worked out their effects on such a scale as to command general attention. In that year, for the first time, the production of pig iron in the United States exceeded that of Great Britain. The enormous output, and the cheapened cost, must soon have brought a sharp fall in prices. The crisis of 1893, and the depression which followed, precipitated the fall, and soon, as is the common effect of such revulsions, intensified it. Prices of all the crude forms of iron and steel went down to the foreign level and even below it. After a long period of gradual but rapid change, the results of the new conditions in the industry now suddenly worked themselves out. Not only was the domestic market fully supplied, but the beginnings of an export movement appeared. Imports of the cruder forms of iron and steel ceased entirely; and the more highly manufactured forms which continued to be brought in were mainly " specialties," made by unusual processes or affected by exceptional conditions.

Perhaps the most striking consequence of these changed conditions was the new situation as to steel rails. With the aid of cheaper pig iron, and by means of improved methods, rails were made as cheaply as in Great Britain, if not more cheaply. The combination which had succeeded for so many years in keeping the price of rails above the normal point, was still able to hold together for some years after 1893. But the stress of continued depression, slackened demand, and sharper rivalry, finally caused it to give way in 1897, and the price of rails dropped abruptly. The duty imposed in the act of 1897 ($6.72 per ton) was nominal; for domestic prices were as low as foreign. Doubtless, in the future, such a duty, like those of former acts, might facilitate another combination and another period of inflated prices. But for the time, steel rails were exported, not imported, and at all events the period when protection could be said in any sense to be needed had clearly passed.

Another consequence of the changed conditions in the iron and steel industry was that the duty on tin plate, a bone of contention under the act of 1890, was disposed of, with little debate, by the imposition of a comparatively moderate duty. The higher duty on that article in the act of 1890 (2$\frac{1}{5}$ cents per pound) had been advocated by protectionists and attacked by their opponents with equal bitterness. Yet the reduction in 1894 (to 1$\frac{1}{5}$ cents) had aroused little comment; while in 1897, with the protectionists in full command, it was raised to no more than 1$\frac{1}{2}$ cents, again with little comment. In the intervening period the prices of the steel sheets from which tin plates are made (tin plates being simply sheets of steel coated with tin) had fallen in the United States in sympathy with the prices of all forms of iron and steel; and this not only absolutely, but as compared

with the prices of similar articles in Great Britain
Hence even the duty of 1894 was as effective for the
purposes of promoting the manufacture of this particular
article, as had been the higher duty of 1890; while that
of 1897 which was a trifle higher than that of 1894, was
more than sufficient to maintain the protectionist support for the industry. The episode was certainly a
curious one. The much-contested duty of 1890 went
into effect just at a time when the general development
of the iron and steel industry was preparing the way for
the immediate effectiveness of the duty in stimulating domestic production; while the rapid fall in iron and steel
prices after 1890, and especially after 1893, enabled the
tin plate manufacture to hold its own, after a brief space,
with a much lower duty than it had so insistently demanded in 1890.

A part of the act which aroused much public attention
and which had an important bearing on its financial yield
was the sugar schedule—the duties on sugar, raw and
refined. It will be remembered that the act of 1890 had
admitted raw sugar free, while that of 1894 had imposed
a duty of 40 per cent. *ad valorem*. This *ad-valorem* rate
had produced a revenue much smaller than had been expected, and, indeed, smaller than might reasonably have
been expected. Notwithstanding the insurrection in
Cuba and the curtailment of supplies from that source,
the price of raw sugar had maintained its downward tendency; and the duty of 40 per cent. had been equivalent
in 1896 to less than one cent a pound. In the act of

1897 the duty was made specific, and was practically doubled. Beginning with a rate of one cent a pound on sugar tested to contain 75 per cent., it advanced by stages until on sugar testing 95 per cent. (the usual content of commercial raw sugar) it reached 1.65 cents per pound. The higher rate thus imposed was certain to yield a considerable increase of revenue. Much was said also of the protection now afforded to the beet sugar industry of the West. That industry, however, was still of small dimensions and uncertain future. The protection now extended to it, moreover, was no greater than had been given by the sugar duty, even higher than that of 1897, which had existed from the close of the civil war to 1890. No doubt the changed conditions of agriculture and of the methods of beet sugar manufacture might cause the same duty to have a greater effect at the close of the century than during the earlier period. But this effect could come but slowly, and for many years the sugar duty would not fail to yield a handsome revenue to the Treasury; while at the same time it enabled the protectionist party to pose once more as the faithful friend of the farmer.

On refined sugar, the duty was made 1.95 cents per pound, which, as compared with raw sugar testing 100 per cent., left a protection for the domestic refiner,—*i. e.*, for the Sugar "Trust,"—of one eighth of one cent a pound. Some intricate calculation would be necessary to make out whether this "differential" for the refining interest was more or less than in the act of 1894; but, having

regard to the effect of the substitution of specific for *ad-
valorem* duties, the Trust was no more favored by the act
of 1897 than by its predecessor, and even somewhat less
favored.[1] The changes which this part of the tariff act
underwent in the two Houses are not without significance. In the bill as reported to the House of Representatives by its committee, and as passed by the House,
the initial rate on the crudest sugar (up to 75 degrees)
was the same as that finally enacted, one cent; but the
rate of progression was slower (.03 cent for each degree instead of .035), and the final duty on the important
classes of raw sugar in consequence somewhat less. The
so-called differential, or protection to the refiners, was
one eighth of a cent per pound. In the Senate there
was an attempt at serious amendment. The influence of
the Sugar Trust in the Senate had long been great. How
secured, whether through party contributions, entangling

---

[1] The rates of 1897 were:

On raw sugar testing up to 75 degrees................	1	cent per lb.
For each additional degree.........................	$\frac{35}{1000}$	" "
Hence raw sugar testing 95 degrees pays.............	1.65	" "
And raw sugar testing 100 degrees pays..............	1.825	" "
Refined sugar pays................................	1.95	" "
Leaving a difference between the refined sugar rate and that on raw sugar at the 100 degree rate of........	.125	" "

In regard to sugar coming from countries paying an export bounty, the
act of 1897 made a change from the methods of 1890 and 1894, when a fixed
additional duty of $\frac{1}{10}$ cent per pound had been imposed on bounty-fed
sugar. It was now provided in general terms (in section 5 of the act of
1897) that on any article on which a foreign country paid an export bounty,
an additional duty should be imposed " equal to the net amount of such
bounty or grant "; the Secretary of the Treasury being required to ascertain
this amount in each case.

alliance, or coarse bribery, the public could not know; but
certainly great, as the course of legislation in that body
demonstrated. The Senate Finance Committee reported
an entirely new scheme of sugar duties, partly specific
and partly *ad valorem*, complicated in its effects, and
difficult to explain except as a means of making concessions under disguise to the refiners. But here, as on
other points, the Senate treated its committee with scant
respect, threw over the whole new scheme, and re-inserted
the rates of the House bill on raw sugar, but with an increased differential, amounting to one fifth of a cent, on
refined sugar. So the bill went to the Conference Committee, with the differential alone in doubt. What debates and discussions went on in that committee is not
publicly known. It is one of the curious results of our
legislative methods that the decisive steps are often
taken in star chamber fashion. But it was credibly reported that the sugar schedule was the sticking-point,—
that on this schedule, and this only, each branch was
obstinate for its own figures. Finally, the Senate gave
way. By slightly increasing the duty on raw sugar, and
leaving that on refined at the point fixed by the Senate,
the House secured virtually the retention of the *status
quo* as to the differential in favor of the Sugar Trust.
The result certainly was in striking contrast to that of
1894. Then, too, there was a struggle between the
House and the Senate on the protection of the Trust,—
not indeed on that alone, but on that conspicuously.
Then the House had proposed to wipe out all duties

and so all protection; while the Senate had proposed a
substantial largess to the Trust.   After a struggle much
longer than that of 1897, the House had given way, and
its leaders had been compelled to make a mortifying
concession to an unpopular policy.   The outcome in
1897 was, it is true, in substance not different.   The
differential was the same under the act of 1897 as it had
been under that of 1894; and the increase in the duty on
raw sugar once more enabled the refining monopoly, as
the one large importer, to make an extra profit, temporary but handsome, by heavy imports hurried in before
the new act went into force.   But the moral effect was
very different.   The House in 1897 had adopted the
plan of leaving things as they were, and had successfully
resisted the effort of the refining monopoly to secure
more.   The result was due mainly to greater party cohesion and more rigid party discipline, enforced by the
genial despotism of the autocratic Speaker of the
House.

The tariff act of 1894 had repealed the provisions as to
reciprocity in the act of 1890, and had rendered nugatory
such parts of the treaties made under the earlier act as
were inconsistent with the provisions of its successor.[1] The
act of 1897 now revived the policy of reciprocity, and in
some ways even endeavored to enlarge the scope of the
reciprocity provisions.[2]   One of its sections recited, in
almost the exact phraseology of the act of 1890, that the

[1] Section 71 of the act of 1894.
[2] Sections 3 and 4 of the act of 1897.

President, if satisfied that other countries imposed duties
that were "reciprocally unequal and unreasonable," might
suspend the free admission of certain specified articles—
tea, coffee, tonka beans, and vanilla beans—and that
these articles should thereupon be subject to duty, coffee
at three cents a pound, tea at ten cents, and so on.   The
act of 1890 had held out the threat of duties as to some
other important articles—sugar and hides.   But these
could not now be easily used for the reciprocity clauses,
being dutiable in any case.   Tonka beans and vanilla
beans, even though imported mainly from the tropical
parts of South America, were hardly weighty substitutes.

Quite different in purpose, and designed to reach
countries of the same rank in power and civilization as
the United States, were some provisions which contemplated not fresh duties, but a reduction of those imposed
by the new act.   In the first place the President was
authorized, "after securing reciprocal and reasonable
concessions," to suspend certain duties, and to replace
them by duties somewhat lower.   The articles on which
reductions could thus be made were argol (crude tartar),
brandies, champagne, wines, paintings, and statuary.
The country aimed at was France.   The higher duties
on silks in the new act would especially affect this
country, and might tempt her to reprisals.   Her system
of maximum and minimum duties, adopted in 1892, was
expressly devised as a means of securing concessions in
commercial negotiations.   Now the United States followed suit, and arranged her own system of duties in

such manner that concessions were provided for in advance.

More important in its scope, but so limited as regards time and conditions as to promise little practical result, was the next section, which contemplated commercial treaties for general reductions of duties. The President was authorized to conclude treaties providing for reductions of duty, up to 20 per cent., on any and every article. But the treaties must be made within two years after the passage of the act; the reductions could be arranged only through a period not exceeding five years; and the treaties must be ratified by the Senate, and further "approved by Congress," that is, by the House as well as by the Senate. The other reciprocity arrangements, described in the preceding paragraphs, did not need the consent even of the Senate. The arrangement for a possible general reduction of duties by 20 per cent. was not contained in the House bill, but was inserted by the Senate in the course of its amendments. Restricted as it was, the chance of its leading to any change in the rates of duty was of the slightest.[1]

An important aspect of the new act, and one much discussed, was its fiscal yield. Designed to give protection to domestic industries, it was expected also to bring to the Treasury a much-needed increase of revenue. This combination of industrial and fiscal policy is too common

---

[1] Under the first described of these reciprocity plans, commercial agreements were soon reached with France, Germany, Italy, and Portugal. No treaties of the second sort were ever made.

in the history of the United States, as indeed in that of other countries, to have aroused much comment. Yet it was certainly unfortunate that so little attention was given to the simple question of revenue, without regard to protection or free trade. Additional taxes on beer or on tobacco (not to mention duties on tea and coffee), even though so moderate in rate as to have been little noticed and easily born by consumers, would have yielded a large, steady, and easily collected revenue. Proposals for taxes of this sort were indeed made by the Senate Finance Committee; but most of them were struck out by the Senate itself, and hardly a trace remained in the act as passed. A slight increase in the tax on cigarettes and a modification of certain rebates in the taxes on beer alone remained as simply fiscal measures. Barring these minor changes, protective duties, and these only, were relied on to convert the deficit into a surplus.

There was much heated discussion immediately after the passage of the act as to its effect on the public finances; it being predicted with equal confidence that it would fail to secure the desired revenue, and that it would convert the deficit into a surplus. It was certainly to be expected that,—once the heavy imports rushed in just before the passage of the act were out of the way,—the increased duties on sugar, on wool and woollens, and on other articles, would swell the revenue considerably. But how much? On this subject the only thing certain was that the financial effect was entirely uncertain. All calculations as to the fiscal results of

such customs legislation as the United States undertook
in 1883, in 1890, in 1894, and in 1897, rest simply on
guesswork.   Supposing the imports to remain the same
as in some previous year, it is possible to state what a
given rate of duty will yield; but no one can foretell with
any approach to accuracy what the imports will be.
This is more particularly the case with imports of protected articles, and so with the revenue derived from
them.   Such an article as sugar, indeed, once the rate of
duty is fixed, yields a fairly regular amount.   Barring
sugar, we have in the main dutiable imports that fluctuate
greatly and unexpectedly from year to year.   Even with
rates unchanged, it is impossible to know in advance
with any degree of certainty what the revenue will be.
In times of activity imports tend to rise, and the revenue
swells; in times of depression they tend to fall, and the
revenue shrinks.   He who could foretell the oscillation of
the industrial tides would have something on which to
base an estimate of the direction at least, if not of the
rate, in the movement of the national revenues.   But
even for the most experienced observer and under stable
rates of duty, there must always be a large margin of uncertainty in estimates of the future tariff revenue.   With
rates much changed, no estimate can be more than a
guess.

The discussions as to the revenue to be expected from
the act of 1897 served to bring into vivid relief not only
the haphazard character of our fiscal methods, but the
need of reform in the general financial and monetary

system. One of the arguments urged in favor of its
passage was that an increase of revenue was necessary in
order to enable the Treasury to fulfill its obligations for
the maintenance of gold payments; and it was even
maintained that a surplus was the one thing needful to
bring about a sound and stable monetary situation. No
doubt, as things had stood ever since the resumption of
specie payments in 1879, it was not only desirable on
grounds of every-day prudence that the revenue should
at least equal the expenditure, but this was important
for the monetary responsibilities which had been imposed
on the Treasury of the United States. It was clear, however, that a continuing surplus, and the unfailing avoid-
ance of a deficit, were not to be expected. A large
accumulated surplus tempts to reckless expenditure, as it
did in 1890; while the inevitable periods of depression
recurrently cut down the revenue, and make occasional
years of deficit more than probable. It was unfortunate
that the questions of protection to domestic industries
and of revenue for the government should be interwined.

This source of difficulty, which had so much affected
tariff legislation in 1894 as well as in 1897, was removed in
1900, when the gold standard act reorganized the Treasury
and set aside the reserve fund of 150 millions for the
security of the paper money. Thereby the monetary
system was made independent of fluctuations in the
general revenue. The question of protection and free
trade still remained complicated with the revenue problem of the government; and this was inevitable, as

long as customs duties were so largely relied on for meeting the national expenses. But the monetary problem at least was finally separated from the fiscal problem.

The tariff of 1897, like that of 1890, was the outcome of an aggressive spirit of protection. As in 1890, much was said of the " verdict of the people " in favor of the protective policy. Yet the election of 1896 turned on the silver question; and the Democrats in 1894 certainly had much more solid ground for maintaining that the popular verdict had been against high-handed protection than the Republicans in 1897 that it had been in favor of such a policy. Given the political complications of 1896–97, it was no doubt inevitable that a measure imposing higher duties should come. But the act of 1897 pushed protection in several directions farther than ever before, and farther than the political situation fairly justified. It disheartened many who had supported the Republicans on the money issue in 1896; and even good party members, loyal to the general policy of protection, doubted whether that policy had not now been carried too far.

The new and unexpected turn thus given the tariff history of the United States was the more regrettable because the general trend of the country's development made a liberal policy at once easier and more inviting. The closing years of the century found new economic conditions, which must become of greater and greater consequence for our customs policy as the next century is seen to open a new era. The United States is a great manufacturing country; not only this, but one in which the bulk of the manufacturing industries is no longer seriously dependent on protection. The changes in the metal industries, to which reference was made in the preceding pages, are not only important in themselves, but are of far-reaching consequence for the general industrial future of the United States. Iron and steel, on which the material civilization of the modern world rests, are produced more abundantly than anywhere else, and at least as cheaply,—soon, if not yet, will be produced more cheaply. With the wide diffusion of a high degree of mechanical ingenuity, of enterprise, of intelligence and education, it is certain that the United States will be, and will remain, a great manufacturing country. The protective system will be of less and less consequence. The deep-working causes which underlie the international division of labor will indeed still operate, the United States will still find her advantages greater in some directions than in others, and the ingenuity of legislators will still find opportunity to direct manufacturing industry into channels which would not otherwise be sought. But the absolute effect, still more the proportional effect, of such legislation on the industrial development of the country will diminish. The division of labor within the country will become more and more important, while international trade will be confined more and more to what may be called specialties in manufactured commodities, and articles whose site of production is determined mainly by climate.   Not only sugar (for the present), tea, coffee, and the like, but wool also belong in the class last mentioned, as to which climatic causes dominate; and the duties on wool, with those on woollens in their train, are thus the most potent in bringing a substantial interference with the course of international trade. But, on the whole, protective duties, however important they may be in this detail or that, cannot seriously affect the general course of industrial growth, and will affect it less and less as time goes on.   In any case, the question for the future will be, even more than it has been in the past, not whether the United States shall be a manufacturing country, but in what directions her manufactures shall grow,—whether in those where aid and protection against foreign competition are constantly sought, or in those where natural resources and mechanical skill enable foreign competition not only to be met, but to be overcome on its own ground.

CHAPTER VIII.

THE TARIFF ACT OF 1909.

THE tariff act of 1897 proved the longest-lived of the general tariff acts of the United States. Its nearest rival was the act of 1846, which remained undisturbed for eleven years. That of 1897 remained in force for twelve years.

This comparative stability was the result of various causes. The fact that the Republican party, which passed the Dingley act, was in power continuously during the twelve years from 1897 to 1909, naturally made changes less likely. But the tariff act of 1846 also remained unchanged, notwithstanding a great political shift, for a period nearly as long; for, as will be remembered, the protectionist whigs came into power in 1849, and remained in control till 1853. Political stability hence would not seem to be essential to tariff stability. More important, doubtless, was widespread prosperity. This followed the enactment of the Dingley act, and was ascribed to it by the protectionists. Prosperity as widespread had followed the act of 1846. In the earlier case, as in the later, the country was naturally content with matters as they stood, not being prompted by industrial or financial troubles to the trial of a remedy through changed import duties.

But most important was the fact that at both periods other great problems pressed for solution. After 1846, the slavery question came more and more to the fore, and prevented the tariff from being a commanding public issue. After 1897, the questions of industrial combination—trusts, railways, monopolies—served to divert attention from the tariff. At both times, the public (or the politicians) were right, in concentrating discussion on the matters most important. Slavery signified much more than the tariff, during the generation preceding the Civil War. Industrial combination signified much more in the opening years of the twentieth century; for here was and is the great problem for the future.

It was this very attention to a different subject, however, which at the later date compelled action on the tariff once more. The tariff was felt to need overhauling because it was believed, rightly or wrongly, to promote combinations, or at all events to increase the profits in great protected industries. The huge fortunes acquired in some protected industries, the Carnegie fortune most conspicuously of all, brought the feeling against monopolies and trusts to bear against the high duties. As has already been said,[1] the trend toward combination is essentially a consequence of increasing large-scale production. But it has been intensified in some cases by protection, and the profits of some " trusts " have been greatly swelled. The two things—trusts and the tariff—are much associated in the public mind, and hostility to the combinations

---

[1] See pages 310, 316.

has bred hostility to extreme protection. Hence the Republican party in its campaign platform of 1908 gave a promise of revising the tariff; and its candidate, soon to become President Taft, pledged his efforts to secure a revision—"revision" being understood on all hands to mean primarily reduction.

The Republican platform contained a new version of the principle on which protection was to proceed: paraded, to be sure, as the "true" or "long-established" Republican doctrine, but, nevertheless, in its precision of statement substantially new. The doctrine was laid down as follows: "In all protective legislation the true principle of protection is best maintained by the imposition of such duties as will equal the difference between the cost of production at home and abroad, together with a reasonable profit to American industries."

This notion, very little heard of before,[1] played a surprisingly large part in the discussions of 1908–09, and was hailed in many quarters as the definitive solution of the tariff question. It has an engaging appearance of moderation; yet it leads logically to the most extreme results. It seems to say,—no favors, no undue protection, nothing but equalization of conditions. Yet little acumen is needed to see that, carried out consistently, it means simple prohibition and complete stoppage of foreign trade.

Anything in the world can be made within a country

---

[1] The Republican platform of 1904 had a similar phrase: "The measure of protection should always at least equal the difference in cost of production at home and abroad." This seems to be the first platform statement of the "true principle"; but very little attention was given it in 1904.

if the producer is assured of "cost of production together with reasonable profits." In a familiar passage of the *Wealth of Nations*, Adam Smith remarked that "by means of glasses, hotbeds, and hot walls, very good grapes can be raised in Scotland, and very good wine can be made of them at about thirty times the expence for which at least equally good can be brought from foreign countries."[1] In the same vein, it may be said that very good pineapples can be grown in Maine, if only a duty be imposed sufficient to equalize cost of production between the growers in Maine and those in more favored climes. Tea, coffee, cocoa, raw silk, and hemp,—any quantity of things that are now imported can be grown in the United States provided only that a duty high enough be imposed. No doubt it will be said that these things are not "fitted" for our natural conditions, and that duties should not be "unreasonably" high. But the difference is simply one of degree. Sometimes a moderate duty may be called for in order to "equalize cost of production," sometimes a very high duty. Consistently and thoroughly applied, the "true principle" means that duties shall be high enough to cause anything and everything to be made within the country, and international trade to cease.[2]

---

[1] *Wealth of Nations*, book iv., ch. ii.; vol. i., p. 423, Cannan edition.

[2] Unflinching application of "the true principle" was not often advocated, but the following extract from the *Congressional Record* (May 17, 1909, p. 2182) indicates that the foremost protectionist leader was willing to go all lengths.

Mr. ALDRICH.   Assuming that the price fixed by the reports is the correct one, if it costs 10 cents to produce a razor in Germany and 20 cents in the United States, it will **require** 100 per cent. duty to equalize the conditions

On the other hand, the "true principle," consistently analyzed, means simply that the more disadvantageous it is for a country to carry on an industry, the more desperate should be the effort to cause the industry to be established. Of course the term "cost of production" is used, in these discussions, in the sense of the money advances that must be made by the employing capitalists. The more labor that must be employed at current wages to get a given article to market, the larger these money advances become. In other words, they are large because (for whatever reason) much labor is required per unit of product; that is, because the efficiency of labor is low. One of the most familiar facts of industry, though one most commonly forgotten in the protective controversy, is that high money wages do *not* necessarily mean high prices of the things produced. When labor is effective, high wages and low prices go together. Obviously the community is prosperous precisely in proportion as this combination exists,—high wages and low prices. But where labor is ineffective, there, if money wages be high, high prices will ensue. The more of high-priced labor that must be employed in order to produce a given article, the higher will

in the two countries. . . . And so far as I am concerned, I shall have nc hesitancy in voting for a duty which will equalize the conditions.

Mr. BAILEY. The Senator from Rhode Island would vote unhesitatingly for a duty of 300 per cent.

Mr. ALDRICH. If it was necessary——

Mr. BAILEY. If he thought it was necessary.

Mr. ALDRICH. Certainly. If it was necessary to equalize the conditions, and to give the American producer a fair chance for competition, other things being equal, of course, I would vote for 300 per cent. as cheerfully as I would for 50."

be its "cost of production," and the higher must be the duties in order to "equalize cost of production at home and abroad."

All the current notions on this topic among the staunch protectionists rest on the belief that high wages (high money wages, that is,—few go beyond this phase of the problem) cannot be maintained in our American community unless there be protection against the commodities made by cheaper labor abroad. And this belief rests on the notion that high wages necessarily mean high prices.[1] The truth is that a high general level of real wages is the outcome of high general efficiency of labor. Given such efficiency, it would continue, tariff or no tariff. But this seems to the protectionists an incredible proposition. The verdict of the economists, though practically unanimous against the protectionist belief, has no visible effect in overthrowing it. That high wages are due to the tariff, and cannot be kept high without high duties, has been dinned in the ears of the public so persistently that it has become for the average man an article of faith. To connect high wages with the effectiveness and productiveness of labor; to consider whether it is worth while to direct labor into industries where it is not effective; to reflect what it really means to "equalize" a high domestic cost of production with a lower foreign cost; in fact, to reason carefully and consistently on the tariff question,—all this,

---

[1] For a more extended discussion of these general questions I refer the reader to my volume on *Free Trade, the Tariff, and Reciprocity*, ch. iv., "Wages and Prices in Relation to International Trade," and ch. vii., "Cost of Production and the Tariff."

unfortunately, is almost unknown. The average employer and the average laborer alike accept the familiar catch-words and fallacies: let us stimulate employment, make demand for labor, create the home market, equalize cost of production, preserve American industries and the American standard of living.

None the less, the attention given to this "true principle" was significant of some concession to those who believed that protection had been carried too far. There was an uneasy feeling that duties had been *more* than sufficient to "equalize," and that they brought *more* than "a reasonable profit" to American producers. As every one conversant with our tariff system knows, they were often excessive in this sense. They were higher than was necessary to enable the domestic producers to hold their own. A vast number of the duties were simply prohibitory. Many were innocuous as well as prohibitory, —mere nominal imposts, on articles produced as cheaply within the country as without, and not importable under any conditions. Such were the duties on wheat, corn, cattle and meat, and other agricultural products,—dust in the farmer's eyes. Such too were the duties on cheaper cotton goods, on boots and shoes, and many other manufactured articles. On still others the rates, while so high as to prohibit importation, were not nominal: cost of production might be higher in the United States than abroad, yet only a little higher, so that the duties went beyond the point of mere "equalizing." Such for example was the case with certain grades of woollens and silks. In the absence of any importation of competing goods (the woollens and silks that continued to be imported were mainly special articles, different from the domestic textiles) it was difficult to calculate just how far any equalizing duty at all might be needed, on the basis of "the true principle." But it is certain that existing rates were much more than equalizing.[1]

A disposition to scan duties critically according to their conformity to the "true principle" was shown by the Ways and Means Committee of the House, in which the consideration of the tariff measure began. The chairman of that committee, Mr. Payne, though a staunch protectionist, was not a fanatical one. On sundry schedules the inquiries of the Committee, under his leadership, were directed toward a comparison of domestic and foreign cost, and a comparison again of the difference in cost with the rates of duty.[2] It is true that inquiries of this sort, conducted in

---

[1] Senator Aldrich, on introducing the Conference Report which settled the details of the tariff act of 1909 (see below, p. 376), said · "If there are any prohibitive duties in this bill, if there are any duties that are excessive along the lines I have laid down [the true principle], I do not know it. I do not believe there are any duties levied in this bill that are excessive or are prohibitory." *Congr. Record*, vol. 44, p. 5305. This could be nothing but bravado.

[2] Mr. Payne's attitude is indicated in the following passage from his speech introducing the bill:

" Some gentlemen think in order to be protectionists that after they have found out the difference between the cost of production here and the cost abroad they ought to put on double that difference by way of a tariff rate, and they are willing to vote for such a provision in the bill, and if crowded they will go to three times that amount. I do not believe that such a man is a good friend of protection. I believe we should fix these duties as nearly as we can at the difference between the cost here and the cost abroad, and not after we have decided what that difference is, double it, add 100 per cent. to it. . . . He is the better friend to protection who tries to keep

hearings before Congressional Committees, can lead to no accurate results. The persons who appear as witnesses are almost invariably interested producers, and the figures and statistics presented by them are of very doubtful value. Any one who looks over the reports of these hearings must observe how vague and obviously exaggerated are the recurring statements about wages and cost of production. If accurate information on these matters were desired, the effective method would be to engage agents or "experts," say from the Bureau of the Census or the Bureau of Corporations, and give them a year or two in which to make careful investigation. Even so, in view of the variations of cost of production in different establishments, and the difficulty of selecting the representative firms, it may be questioned how far usable results could be got. At all events, no such systematic procedure was thought of. The usual array of indiscriminate figures was presented and printed, with a natural tendency on the part of the protectionists to accept without question statements indicating that their "true principle" could be maintained only by keeping duties very high.[1]

---

the rates reasonably protective to the people engaged in the industry." *Congr. Record*, p. 7.

It should be noted, to Mr. Payne's credit, that his speech introducing the tariff bill was a very careful one, explaining with much detail the changes proposed. In this fullness of detail it was in marked contrast with the flamboyant and empty speeches with which Messrs. McKinley and Dingley introduced in the House the tariff bills of 1890 and 1897.

[1] The hearings of 1908–09 before the Ways and Means Committee were prolonged, and contained, in addition to the usual mass of irrelevant and

The hearings before the House Committee led to a curious and instructive episode. It is significant of the trend of international competition that the rivals most frequently held up as menacing by the petitioners for higher duties were the Germans, not, as in the hearings of earlier periods, the English. The statements in regard to wages in Germany were so loose and exaggerated that the Germans were led, both by pride and by a hope of affecting the course of legislation here, to take notice of them. Their government referred the printed hearings to various firms in Germany. A whole sheaf of comments and memoranda from such sources was transmitted by the German Foreign Office to our Department of State, and by this to the Senate. They reached the Senate Committee on Finance early in April, and slumbered there for a month. In May some of the so-called "insurgent" Senators asked for them, and they were ordered to be printed. But they were not printed or published until August, after the adjournment of Congress. It was said, in explanation of the delay, that the government printing-office was so busy as to be unable to bring them out earlier. But this was a flimsy pretext. Anything that Congress

---

useless matter, much material valuable for the student of economics. They were printed, too, with more care than had been shown on previous occasions, in eight volumes, arranged by topics, and well indexed.

There were no hearings before the Senate, though there were unreported "conferences" between the members of the Senate Finance Committee and persons interested in the duties. Senator Aldrich, in discussing various details, referred to figures as to cost of production presented to his Committee by domestic producers ; but such figures, not subject even to the test of publicity, had still less weight than those presented to the House Committee.

really wanted was supplied with exemplary promptness. The truth was that the ruling spirits in the Senate did not wish the information to be put at the disposal of opponents. For this they had good ground. The figures given by American producers as to wages in Germany, and other figures supposed to prove differences in cost of production, were shown to be virtually worthless, and not a little instructive information was given on the general aspects of tariff rivalry. But probed and sifted information was not desired by the Republican leaders, or at least by those who guided the course of action in the Senate. Any sort of vague and exaggerated statement as to wages and cost was readily accepted, and made the occasion for a drastic application of the sanctified "true principle." [1]

Two sets of reductions in duties engaged the special attention of the House Committee: on iron and steel, and on certain raw materials. The conspicuous position of the Steel Corporation compelled attention to the former. To the point of removal of the iron and steel duties the Committee would not go; but some reductions were proposed. The raw materials most discussed were coal, lumber, iron ore, hides. These the Committee proposed to admit free of duty. As to the fate of these proposals more will be said presently.

On the other hand, some advances in duty were frankly proposed, usually on the ground that the "true principle" called for them. The duties on mercerized cottons—fab-

---

[1] The German reports were finally printed as Senate Document No. 68, Part 2, 61st Congress, 1st session.

rics treated by a process which gives them a silk-like sheen —were advanced, because of " the additional labor and the difference in the cost of labor." The duties on women's gloves and on certain sorts of hosiery were similarly increased. Other advances could be less easily defended on grounds of this sort, and were the obvious result of pressure from some geographical district, or from some legislator who had to be placated. Zinc ore, previously free, was subjected to duty because the people of the Missouri zinc mining district insisted on their share in the benefits of protection. The duty on split peas was increased,— a petty matter, worth noting only because of the explanation of the change,—on " the personal knowledge and evidence of a member of the House who knows all about the business."[1] The duties on some fruits—figs, prunes, lemons—were raised, as a sop to the California members. There were other instances of this sort—advances of rates proposed because some member of the Committee had a constituent who was interested in a particular article, or because the Committee felt it necessary to make sure of the vote of a given region. None the less, the House bill made significant reductions: none of revolutionary character, or likely to have serious economic effects, yet indicative of a disposition to bring about some " real " revision.

No great changes from the Committee's rates were made in the House itself. Notwithstanding active debate, and a vigorous attempt by interested representatives to retain

---

[1] I quote from Mr. Payne's speech introducing the bill, *Congr. Record.* vol. 44, p. 9.

duties as against the proposed extension of the free list, the bill passed by the House was substantially that prepared by the Committee. On the hotly debated items of coal, hides, iron ore, the Committee was sustained: they were left on the free list. On lumber, the leaders could not hold the House; a duty was retained, but at half the existing rate.

In the Senate the course of events was different. In most of the tariff acts of the previous generation, the influence of the Senate on legislation had been greater than that of the House, and had been exercised in favor of higher duties. The greater influence of the Senate was the natural result of its smaller size, its compactness, and the longer term of its members. That this influence should be exercised so often in the direction of higher duties, has been ascribed to the greater subservience of Senators to large monied interests. There is truth in the charge. In legislation on other subjects also, especially during the contest over railway legislation, it appeared that the Senate was, if not the stronghold, at least the stronger hold of those corporations and industries whose money-making might be affected by legislation. But so far as the tariff was concerned, another circumstance was at least equally important in explaining the ultra-protectionism of the Senate. Each State is equally represented. Montana and West Virginia have as many votes as New York and Iowa. The Senators from a thinly populated State have disproportionate power in fighting for duties that are for the interest of their constituents, or are supposed to be. Geographical

representation in the Senate, as well as the relation between the individual members resulting from senatorial
courtesy in confirming appointments,[1] is thus peculiarly
favorable to log-rolling. The votes of small dissatisfied
States cannot be ignored, as they can in the House.
Washington, Idaho, Montana, Wyoming, West Virginia,
will easily combine in favor of duties on coal and on
hides, and together constitute a formidable phalanx.
The strictly manufacturing States, such as Massachusetts
and Pennsylvania, feel it necessary to conciliate such a
group, and to let them have duties on their local products,
in order to secure their adhesion to the general protectionist scheme. The log-rolling process, as has been said
by President Lowell, is the great evil of democratic
government; and that evil nowhere appears more conspicuously than in the dealings of a body like the American
Senate with tariff legislation.

Nevertheless, there was a vigorous protest from within
the ranks of the Republican party. The Senators from
some of the great agricultural States of the Middle West—
Wisconsin, Iowa, Nebraska, Minnesota—stood staunchly
for reductions in duties. Their constituencies, more strongly than any other part of the country, felt hostility to real
and supposed monopolies. They represented the healthy
uprising against monied domination, the resolution to
grapple with the great social and industrial problems of
the twentieth century. No doubt the tariff was less

---

[1] Compare the extract given below (p. 379, note), from Mr. Payne's
remarks as to the duty on hides in 1807

closely connected with those problems than they and their representatives supposed. A combination and monopoly were smelled behind every high duty, even though (as in the case of the cotton manufacture) the conditions clearly were not those of monopoly. No doubt, too, there was the usual half-heartedness and inconsistency in their attitude on the general question. They were taunted with being unfaithful to their party and even (after the common question-begging way of the fanatical protectionists) with being enemies to their country and allies of designing foreigners. To this they replied that they were the true and faithful and reasonable protectionists. Even these critics never planted themselves on any ground of clear-cut principle. They simply represented a strong feeling of unrest and discontent, which the leaders in the Senate disregarded on the tariff as on other questions.

The combination of local interests in the Senate was made the more effective by the leadership of Senator Aldrich. Senator Aldrich, unlike the House leader, was a protectionist of the most unflinching type. At the same time he had had long experience and was exceptionally well informed on tariff details. His influence went far to account for the amendments made in the Senate. These were no less than 847 in number; many of them, to be sure, merely on matters of form and phraseology, but over half of substantial importance. Their drift was upwards. The much debated raw materials, iron ore, hides, coal, were again made subject to duties; the duty on lumber was raised above the rate fixed in the House.

The duties' on cotton goods, hosiery, and other manufactures were advanced. Many of the changes substituted specific for ad valorem duties, or shifted the dividing line in the progression of specific duties. Just what such changes mean is often difficult for even the most expert to ascertain.[1] It is tolerably certain that, made under such auspices, they would tend in general to tighten the extreme protective system, and were likely to embody "jokers,"—new rates of real importance, advantageous to particular producers, and concealed in the endless details.

So the bill went to a Conference Committee, and there, as usual, its details were finally settled. The Conference Committee consisted of eight members from each house, five Republicans and three Democrats. The Democrats were put on the Committee only *pro forma*. The ten Republicans from the two houses got together by themselves, and came to an agreement, against which the six Democrats simply registered the stock partisan protest. Such has been the procedure with all the tariff legislation of the last generation. What passed in the Conference Committee can only be guessed, but guessed with some certainty: weary sessions, hurried procedure, give and take, insistence by this or that member among the ten on some duty in which he is particularly inter-

---

[1] "Some of these amendments I have studied diligently, and I am not able to say to-day whether they raise or lower the rates, and have not been able to determine yet with the aid of gentlemen who are experts on this subject."—Mr. Payne, in the brief House debate on the Senate amendments, *Congr. Record*, p. 4168

ested. Irresponsibility in legislation reaches its acme.[1]

In one respect a new influence was brought to bear on the Conference Committee, and a new responsibility was assumed. The administration suddenly brought pressure to bear in favor of the House rates, or rather in favor of lower rates all around. President Taft had pledged his party, during the campaign, to undertake a revision of the tariff downward; and it had been given out, apparently on good authority, that he would veto a bill that failed to carry out the pledge. During the long debates in both houses, he had abstained from any serious effort to influence the course of legislation. But at the very last stage—it is not certain whether from a sudden change of tactics, or in pursuance of a policy kept till then deliberately in the background—he took the position of titular head of the party, and urged reductions in duties. His outspoken attitude strengthened the moderate element, and finally brought about a measure less stultifying in view of his own pledges than had seemed possible when the bill first went to the Conference Committee.

---

[1] The following episode will serve as illustration. The duty on shingles had been 30 cents per thousand in 1897. The Senate proposed to raise it to 50 cents a thousand, and this higher rate was finally enacted. Mr. Payne gave the following account of what took place in the Conference Committee: "This 20 cents a thousand on shingles * * * was most strenuously insisted on. Any of you gentlemen who have been on Committees of Conference know how those things are. Senator So-and-So wants something and must have something. Finally I told them I was willing, in this great trade on the lumber schedule, involving millions of dollars, to throw in a jack-knife like shingles, and gave them the rate of 50 cents. * * * They claimed it was absolutely essential to the business. I never could see it in that light, but was in favor of the rate of the Dingley bill."—*Congr. Record*, p. 4698.

The most hotly disputed single item was the duty on hides. These had been free of duty from 1872 to 1897. In 1897 they had been subjected to a duty of fifteen per cent., on the insistent demand of the representatives of the grazing States, especially Montana.[1] The House passed the bill of 1909 with hides free; the Senate, again at the insistence of the grazing States, proposed to restore the duty of fifteen per cent. Instead of a compromise, in the shape of a reduced rate, such as might have been expected to result from this disagreement, complete abolition of the duty was finally secured. This victory of good sense was clearly due to President Taft, and constituted the one conspicuous fulfilment of his pledge to bring about really lowered duties.

On any but the most extreme protectionist principles, there is no excuse for a duty on hides. There can be nothing in the nature of protection to young industries— no prospect of ultimate cheapening through a stimulus to improved domestic production. Even the "true" principle of equalized cost of production could not be applied to a by-product of a flourishing export industry. Nor were any arguments of this sort presented in favor of the duty. The case was put frankly on the ground of give and take; if everything is to be protected, why not hides?[2] And on this ground, the ranching representatives

---

[1] The duty of 1897 applied only to cattle hides. Calf-skins, goat-skins, sheep-skins, horse-hides, and the like continued throughout to be free of duty.

[2] Mr. Payne gave the following account of the way in which the duty on hides came to be imposed in 1897 :

had a case. If imports are bad *per se*, and domestic supply is good *per se*, why should hides be free when wool, hemp, flax, lumber, ore, remained dutiable?

It happened, too, that the duty on hides had not been, like so many on crude products, of limited effect. The imports were a considerable portion of the total supply, and the imported and domestic hides came in competition in the same market.[1] The case was one where the protective duty had its full effect: the price of the whole domestic supply, as well as of that imported, was raised by the amount of the duty. It is striking that a country in which cattle-raising has been largely carried on, and from which meat-products have been largely exported, should have imported quantities of hides. The demand for this joint product, or "by-product," is relatively great in the

---

"When the Dingley bill came before the House, reported by the Committee, it was reported with free hides, and I saw a number of gentlemen on this [the Republican] side of the House, and a number of gentlemen on the other side of the House, led by Jerry Simpson of Kansas, voting for a duty on hides. He was a little more frank than some of these modern-day tariff-for-revenue people. He said he wanted to get his share. He did not believe in a duty on hides, but he wanted to get his share. * * * It went over into the Senate. We did not have a Republican majority in the Senate in those days, but we did have a majority of those who claimed to be protectionists, and one of these protectionists of populistic tendencies would not vote for the bill unless it carried a duty on hides, and the Senate accommodated him. *That is one of the courtesies of the Senate when any member wants something done.*"—*Congr. Record*, p. 21.

[1] In an elaborate statement compiled by the Census Bureau, on "Imports, Exports, and Domestic Manufactures," the following figures were given as to cattle hides:

	Pounds	*Values*
Imports (1904–5)	111 mill.	14.5 mill. dollars.
Domestic Product (1904)	456 mill.	44.2 mill. dollars.

United States. No satisfactory substitute has been found for leather, whether for footwear, harness, belting, or the other manifold uses ; and our prosperous and well-equipped population calls for great quantities of it.

Other raw materials were treated in more gingerly fashion, and the original proposal for admitting them free was not carried out. Coal, which the House had proposed to admit free, was finally subjected in the act to a duty of 45 cents a ton, in place of the 1897 rate of 67 cents. Iron ore, which also the House had proposed to make free, was made dutiable at 15 cents, in place of 40 cents. It has already been noted that the proposal for free admission of lumber, made by the Ways and Means Committee, could not be carried even through the House. The duty there was set, on the lowest grade, at $1.00 (per thousand feet); the Senate proposed $1.50; the act finally made the rate $1.25, in place of the 1897 rate of $2.00.

On wood-pulp and printing paper a long struggle led finally to no change as regards pulp, and on printing paper to but a slight reduction. The situation was complicated by bickering with Canada, from which came a considerable part of the supply of the raw material, pulp-wood (the round logs). Pulp-wood had always been admitted free ; nor was any change on this score contemplated or made. The Canadians wished to manufacture their own raw material ; hence one of their provinces (Ontario) prohibited the export of the logs, and another (Quebec) established what was virtually an export duty.[1] Both in the United

---

[1] The Quebec legislation consisted in reducing the royalty for wood cut on

States and in Canada, more particularly in the former, there was protest against the wastage of the spruce forests; and in the United States there were also charges of trust manipulation of the price of paper. A special Congressional Committee, appointed at an earlier date, had recommended, after elaborate investigation, that the duties on paper be lowered and that pulp be admitted free; both changes to be conditional on the repeal by Canada of her restrictive legislation. In the tariff act as passed these recommendations were followed, though the reduction in the paper duty was made less by the Senate than had been provided by the House. Both the House and Senate bills, and the act as passed, provided for additional duties on pulp, and on paper also, if the Canadian regulations should stand. The expectation seems to have been that the Canadians would yield, especially as they were to be threatened also by a general increase of duties under the maximum and minimum clause of the tariff act.[1] But our legislators had reckoned wrong. Canada refused to budge. She had sought for two decades after the termination (in 1866) of the old reciprocity treaty to reëstablish friendly commercial relations with the United States. Her offers had been steadily and almost ostentatiously repulsed.[2] The "National Policy" of protection, adopted in Canada at the outset largely by

---

crown lands, ordinarily 65 cents a cord, to 40 cents a cord if the wood were manufactured within the province. Both in Quebec and Ontario wood cut on crown lands alone was affected

[1] See below, p. 403.

[2] See Mr. Edward Porritt's *Sixty Years of Protection in Canada*. ch. iii.

way of retaliation, had been gradually made stronger and more sweeping. By 1909 it had such a firm hold that there was no thought of submitting to what seemed a bullying attitude on the part of the United States. No change in the restrictions on pulp-wood was offered. Consequently the conditional relaxations of our own duties on pulp and paper never went into effect.[1]

As to all the changes on materials, there is a question how far reductions or remissions will redound merely to the advantage of the manufacturer or middleman, how far to that of the "ultimate consumer." Free hides, it was said, would benefit only the tanners or the shoemakers, but the price of shoes would not be affected. The answer obviously is that the case is the same with every cause lessening the price of materials,—improved processes, better transportation, and what not. The final result in

---

[1] The duty on wood-pulp remained, as it had been in 1897, $\frac{1}{12}$ cent a pound, plus an additional duty equal to the Canadian export charge.

The duties on printing paper in 1897 and 1909 were (on the lowest class, —they were graded) as follows :

Duty of 1897	Duty of 1909
$6.00 per net ton, ordinary duty	$3.75 per net ton, ordinary duty
.50 additional duty because of Quebec export charge	2.00 " " retaliatory duty
	.35 " " additional duty because of Quebec export tax
$6.50 total duty	$6.10 total duty

The retaliatory and additional duties were levied only on pulp and paper made from timber cut on the crown lands of the restricting Provinces ; not on all imports coming from Canada.

The Congressional Committee, referred to in the text, printed an enormous mass of testimony on the pulp and paper situation, and prefaced it with an excellent summary report.

cheapening consumers' goods may come slowly and halt-
ingly ; but so long as there is effective competition among
the several series of producers and middlemen, and so
long as there is a cheapening of the materials for all those
engaged in supplying a given market, the legislator may
feel safe in providing for free materials.

No doubt the cheapening of materials sometimes affects
only a part of the market. Lower duties on coal and
lumber, or their free admission, have but a limited range
of influence. Free coal, as has already been said,[1] would
be of some advantage to coal-users in New England and
the extreme Northwest ; though in both districts the possible consequences were much exaggerated both by advocates and opponents. Free lumber would lead to slightly
larger importation from Canada along the eastern frontier,
but probably to none of any moment in the Northwest.
It would check a bit, even if only a bit, the wastage of our
own forests, and in so far was clearly sound policy. Not a
few Southern representatives voted for the retention of
the duty on lumber, and their votes turned the scale in
its favor. Yet, both because of geographical limitation
of competition and because of the different quality of
Southern lumber, the duty was of no real consequence for
their constituents. The attitude both of constituents and
representatives illustrated the state of veritable funk concerning lower duties (not to mention free trade) which had
been induced by the constant shouting about safeguarding
American industries against pauper labor. Iron ore (on

---

[1] See p. 298.

which the duty was reduced from 40 to 15 cents a ton)
presented a case where the effect of lowered duties was even
more limited.[1]   All that can be said is that in some degree
competition would be promoted, and some better opportunity given for the development of the iron-making
industry of the Eastern region.

On iron and steel the process, begun in 1890,[2] of reducing duties no longer of any effect, was carried a step
further.   The rates were lowered along the whole range,
as will be seen from the following typical figures:

	Duty of 1897	Duty of 1909
Pig iron	$4.00 ton	$2.50 ton
Scrap iron and steel	4.00 "	1.00 "
Steel Ingots (lowest class)	6.72 "	3.92 "
Steel Rails	7.84 '	3.92 "
Tin Plate	1½ c. a pound	1⅛ c. a pound

Nobody supposed that these changes were of any consequence.   The time had gone by when the duties on
crude iron and steel had any considerable effect.   The
"true principle," if rigorously applied to the vast inte-
grated enterprises which now constituted the representative
firm in iron-making, would have led to the complete repeal
of all these duties.

A word may be said with regard to steel rails, which
had played so important a part in the tariff history of
earlier years.   As I have shown in detail elsewhere,[3]

---

[1] See p. 271.

[2] See pp. 272, 300, 342.   Compare also what is said below, at p. 402,
note, of the increase in 1909 of the duty on structural steel.

[3] See *Some Aspects of the Tariff Question*, p. 140.

prices in the United States were, after 1897, on the whole lower than prices in England. Imports virtually ceased, being limited to sporadic cases of special shapes or out-of-the-way shipments. The duty might have been the occasion for a rise in American prices during years of active demand, such as were those from 1900 to 1906. Yet in fact the price was singularly constant,—it was $28.00 a ton uniformly from 1902 on. This steady price was the result of a combination between the various rail-makers. The general policy of the great Steel Corporation, which produced more than half of the rails, and was dominant in the "gentlemen's agreement" that settled the price, was to mitigate fluctuations in iron and steel, and keep the industry on a more even keel than in previous times. The situation may be fairly adduced as illustrating the possible benefits of combination in making the course of trade less haphazard. In the case of steel rails this policy was more successful than with other iron products, because the railways themselves had largely passed the stage of speculative and fluctuating construction, and consequently called for more regular supplies of rails. At all events, the price of rails remained steady for a long series of years. It must be said, too, that the price was not only steady, but moderate. Very likely, even at this moderate price, profits were good; but at all events, the price was not usually higher than the price abroad, and in most years even lower; and profits were not made higher by protection. To repeat what was said before, the iron and steel duties, for good or ill, had done their work. They

25

no longer played an important part in the tariff controversy, and were no longer of any considerable economic
consequence.[1]

With the free admission of hides came reductions in
duties on corresponding manufactures,—on leather from
20 per cent. to 5 per cent., on shoes from 25 per cent. to
10, on harness and saddlery from 35 per cent. to 20.   These
reductions were insisted on by the ranching representatives,
with a touch of vindictiveness, as the counterpart of free
hides, and were somewhat grudgingly accepted by the
representatives of the leather and shoe districts. Here
again no one supposed that any real changes would ensue
from the lowered duties. Tanning and shoemaking are
among the industries in which American labor is applied
with resource and advantage, in which high wages and
low prices are made possible by efficiency and ingenuity,
and in which there are exports, not imports. The hesita-
tion in acceding to the reduced duties arose chiefly from
that pusillanimity about foreign competition which per-
vades almost the whole manufacturing community.

In the case of shoes, of which the exports are considerable, it was said that not only American shoes were being
exported, but American shoe-machinery also, and that
after a time, when foreigners had learned to use this
machinery, their lower wages would enable them to send
cheaper shoes back to the United States. Of course it is

---

[1] The steel-rail situation should be considered in connection with the
general development of the iron manufacture. See what is said above,
pp. 301, 344, and *Some Aspects of the Tariff Question*, chs. ix., x., xii.

true that, for any American manufacturing industry subject to possible foreign competition, the price of independence is unceasing progress. To hold its own, and to pay current high wages, it must not only have the lead, but keep the lead. It must continue to advance steadily, with new ways and better processes, as fast as competitors adopt its established improvements. The history of industry, and especially that of English industry in its long contest with foreign rivals, indicates that probably it can keep the lead. Imitative competitors usually remain in the rear. They are constantly left behind by those whose ways they copy. Certainly there is nothing to indicate that a different result has appeared or is impending as to those American manufactures which had long reached the stage of independence and of export, such as sewing-machines, tools and hardware, agricultural implements, electrical apparatus, and these very boots and shoes.

As had been the case with all the tariff acts since the Civil War, that of 1909 brought advances in the duties as well as reductions. Some of these advances were made in good faith for the purpose of getting more revenue; some were for the purpose of rectifying real or supposed errors or inconsistencies in previous acts; and some were intended, openly or with subterfuges, to give additional protection.

On cotton goods advances were made both for rectification of old duties and for the imposition of new. In some cases unexpected interpretations by the courts of the language of the act of 1897 had caused very low duties on certain cotton textiles. A few changes, prepared for the purpose of making these rates about the same in range as those on other goods, were not unreasonable, and indeed, from the point of view even of a moderate protectionist, were imperative.[1] Other changes were made, however, with the avowed purpose of promoting some domestic industry and adding to the sweep of the protective system.[2] The duty on mercerized cottons, already referred to, was advanced by imposing an extra cent per yard on goods treated by this process. The duties on certain grades of cotton hosiery—seamless or fashioned hose—were advanced, chiefly on the cheaper grades.[3] A minor item, but one which caused some discussion, was the duty on razors, in which a very considerable increase was made.[4] By far the most important and systematic advance was that in the silk schedule. It will

---

[1] These changes were explained by Senator Aldrich, *Congr. Record*, p. 2847 *seq.* An analogous change was made on pocket knives; parts (unassembled) being made dutiable at the same rates as completed knives.

[2] For a careful analysis of the changes on cottons, see a brief article by Mr. M. T. Copeland in the *Quarterly Journal of Economics*, Feb., 1910. p. 422; and one by Mr. S. M. Evans, in the *Journal of Political Economy*, December, 1910, on "The Making of a Tariff Law."

[3] The rates on seamless—fashioned or shaped—cotton hose stood thus in the acts of 1897 and 1909:

Classification	Duty of 1897	Duty of 1909
Value up to $1.00 a dozen	$ .50 c. a dozen, plus 15%	$ .70 c. a dozen, plus 15%
" $1.00 @ 1.50 " "	.60 " " "	.85 " " "
" $1.50 @ 2.00 " "	.70 " " "	.90 " " "
" $2.00 @ 3.00 " "	1.20 " " "	1.20 " " "
" $3.00 @ 5.00 " "	2.00 " " "	2.00 " " "
" over $5.00 " "	55%	55%

It will be seen that the increase was solely in the specific duties on the lower classes, and had most effect on the cheaper goods within each class,

[4] The changes on razors were as follows. The specific duties throughout were, per dozen:

be remembered that in 1897 an elaborate system of specific
duties on silks had been substituted for the previous ad
valorem rates.[1] In 1909 the House left unchanged the
specific duties as fixed in 1897; but the Senate completely overhauled them. The silk schedule, intricate
before, became more intricate than ever, and only a person
well versed in the trade could make out the meaning and
probable effect of the changes. But it was clear on the
face of it that the specific duties were advanced throughout and that they replaced more and more the ad valorem
duties,—a change no doubt of probable administrative
advantage, but the pretext in this act, as so often before,
for a substantial increase in the effective rates. It is noteworthy that neither in 1897 nor in 1909 was there any but
the slightest explanation of the new silk duties. In 1897,
when Mr. Dingley introduced the House bill containing
them, he did not refer to this schedule.[2] In 1909 they
appeared for the first time in the Senate bill. There were
no public hearings before the Senate Committee, and the
new silk duties, like the new cotton duties, were the
result of private conferences with the domestic producers,
perhaps also with customs officials. They were not
mentioned, or barely mentioned, when the Senate's bill

Act of 1897	Act of 1909
Value up to $1.50, duty 50 c. plus 15%	Value up to $1.00, duty 35%
" $1.50 to 3.00, " $1.00 plus 15%	" $1.00 to 1 50, " .72 plus 35%
	" $1.50 to 2.00, " $1.20 plus 35%
	" $2 00 to 3.00, " $1.44 plus 35%
" over $3.00, " $1.75 plus 20%	over $3.00, " $1.80 plus 35%

[1] See p. 337.

[2] There was, however, in 1897, much debate on the silk duties by the
Senate. See Mason, *The American Silk Industry*, p. 89.

was reported. Nor was much said about them in the debates. The intricacy of the schedule, and the difficulty of making out its meaning, may account for this lack of discussion. It is certain that a systematic increase was made in a series of duties already very high.[1]

Both as to cottons and silks, the advances in duty were defended on the ground that the articles were luxuries, and therefore properly subject to high rates for revenue purposes. It is true that the changes affected chiefly the finer grades of both textiles. But the avowed object of those who secured the new rates was to check the imports and promote domestic production, not to secure a revenue from the imports. The defence of the new rates on this ground was an afterthought. It is not improbable that

---

[1] One illustration will indicate the nature of the changes in the silk duties. In 1897 the duties on silk piece goods weighing $1\frac{1}{3}$ to 8 ounces square yard, had been arranged in classes, the duty being so much on goods containing 20% and less of silk, more on goods containing 20% to 30% silk, still more if containing 30 to 45% of silk ; then further differentiated according as they were or were not dyed or printed. In 1909 a new classification was made. Light-weight goods, $1\frac{1}{3}$ to $2\frac{1}{2}$ ounces per square yard, were set apart, and subjected to higher duties; those weighing more ($2\frac{1}{2}$ to 8 ounces) were also subjected to higher duties, though not in the same degree as the light-weight goods. The following were the changes on the cheapest goods, containing the least percentage of silk :

1897	1909
Containing up to 20% of silk, weighing $1\frac{1}{3}$ to 8 oz. per yard, in the gum............duty 50 c. lb. dyed or printed etc.... " 60 c. lb.	Containing up to 20% silk, weighing $1\frac{1}{3}$ to $2\frac{1}{2}$ oz. per yard, in the gum............70 c. lb. dyed or printed etc....85 c. lb. The same, weighing $2\frac{1}{2}$ to 8 oz. per yard in the gum...........$57\frac{1}{2}$ c. lb. dyed or printed etc....80 c. lb.

Similar advances were made on all the classes, the duties rising as the percentage of silk became greater, and being throughout higher than the duties of 1897.

on the first imposition of higher duties, the revenue will increase, imports continuing. But as domestic products take the place of the imports, the revenue dwindles. Protection and revenue are inconsistent objects; the more effective the protection (and the main object of the changes on cottons and silks was to make it more effective) the more certain the loss of revenue.

All these were cases in which duties already very high were put up still another notch. The question arises, why should imports have continued to pour in notwithstanding the previous heavy duties, and why should such extreme rates have been demanded by the domestic producers? I suspect that the answer is the same in all these cases. It is that the commodities are made by methods not adapted to American ways of efficiency. In this country manufacturing efficiency comes by the use of highly-developed machinery, continuous operation, standardized processes, and interchangeable parts. Where methods of this kind can be employed, the American employer can pay high wages and yet sell at low prices; very likely he can export. Where he uses much direct labor and few labor-saving appliances, where he tries to make few goods of any pattern, he cannot compete with the countries of low wages and handicraft efficiency. Just why the American machine-using ways should be applied with success in some directions and should fail in others, is often difficult to explain, and indeed constitutes one of the most intricate problems in industrial history. The young-industries argument may sometimes apply   The very introduction of the new branch into the country may turn invention in that direction and bring about the development of labor-saving processes. But the fact that extremely high duties are demanded is *prima facie* an indication that the field is not a promising one for this sort of development.

At all events, in all these cases of duties shoved higher and higher, great cost of direct labor was urged,—of course with the usual exaggeration and the usual jeremiads about the cheap labor of foreign countries. The seamless stockings on which duties were raised were of the kind not knitted complete by the marvellous self-acting machinery of the modern knitting frame. They must be finished and shaped by hand; and this fact probably explained why they continued to be imported. Mercerized cottons, as one of the advocates of the duty said with emphasis,[1] called for an unusual amount of labor, and therefore—on the "true principle"—for an unusually high duty. On silks, the duties were highest, and the importations at the same time most likely to continue, in case of the very cheap and the very dear classes of goods. The same was the case with many articles of hardware, such as pocketknives. In both instances it was the medium-grade goods, used and made in large quantities, that gave scope for machinery and standardized processes.

It hardly need be said that no one explanation can fit all the complications of industry. The continuance of importations in the face of high duties sometimes is due

---

[1] See the speech of Senator Lodge, June 1; pp. 12, 13 of the separate pamphlet reprint of this speech.

to the simple fact that foreign producers are technically in advance, and the demand for still higher duties is made because the domestic producers have failed to keep abreast of them.   While protection in the United States has not usually caused slackening of progress, it has in some cases done so.   This is one of the most important questions of fact in regard to the increase or retention of a particular duty, but one which received no attention in the talk about cost of production and the "true principle." Razors, for example, seemed to be made by more effective methods in Germany than in this country; although, as to the modern safety razor, the reverse was the case.   In chemical products and dyes the Germans certainly had the lead, and higher duties seemed to be simply props for the industrially inefficient.[1]

On two of the most important schedules in the tariff virtually no changes at all were made.   The wool and woollen duties were left intact, except for a reduction in the duty on wool tops, and a slight reduction on yarns and dress goods.[2]   Of these minor changes, only that af-

---

[1] The House proposed to raise the duty on coal-tar colors from 30 to 35 per cent., but in the act it was finally left at 30 per cent.   Mr. Payne, in advocating the House rate, was compelled to admit: "I am sorry to have to confess it, but the truth is that the chemists in Germany beat the world. . . . Some enterprising men here wanted to go into the business. . . .   But the Germans came in here and dumped colors in the market, and as often as our people succeeded in making the color and putting it on the market, the Germans came in and sold cheaper colors, or an equal color at a less price."

[2] The ad valorem duty on the cheaper grade of yarns was reduced from 40% to 35%, and the ad valorem duties on cotton-warp dress goods were also lowered by 5 per cent.   The specific duties on these articles remained unchanged.   The reductions bore in both cases on grades of goods not

fecting tops caused discussion. Wool tops are fibre in a stage toward yarn, intermediate between combing and spinning. They had been subjected to very high duties in previous acts under an omnibus clause (as wool " partly advanced in manufacture "), and attention had been directed to them by some published correspondence of 1897 between Mr. Whitman, the President of the Wool Manufacturers' Association, and the then Secretary of the Association, Mr. North.[1] Mr. Whitman, who was the head of the one great mill making tops for other spinners, desired in 1897 the retention of the duty on this product as well as the increase of duties on other products of the mill. He was aided in securing them by the fact that the Association Secretary, Mr. North, served also as confidential clerk of the Senate Finance Committee. The whole situation was one too familiar in our tariff history : the details of legislation had been virtually arranged by persons having a direct pecuniary interest in the outcome, and having also the closest relations with the legislators controlling the outcome. Even though there was no corruption—and there is no ground for suspecting anything more than generous contributions to party chests—the outcome was much the same as if there had been corruption. It illustrates once more how radically bad was the method by which the details of our tariff legislation were settled.

imported because the duties had been prohibitory ; the changes signified nothing. On tops, which had before come in under a high drag-net rate, a considerable reduction was made both in the specific and ad valorem duties; but the rate still remained high enough to be prohibitory.

[1] This correspondence can be found in the Hearings before the Committee on Ways and Means, vol. v., p. 5492.

No one ventured a word in criticism of the principle of a duty on raw wool. Some woollen manufacturers asked for a change in the method of assessing it, advocating an ad valorem duty, or one based on the varying shrinkage of the wool. They made out a strong case in favor of such a change. But the leading spirits in Congress were afraid to touch the complicated wool and woollens schedule. The duties on wool had enormous political strength. They were supposed to give the farmer a share of the benefits of protection, though in fact the beneficiaries were the ranchers of the Far West. To tamper with them would have endangered the allegiance to the wonder-working protective system in a section always disposed to be restive under it. So the duties on wool, and with them the huge structure of compensating and protecting duties on woollens, remained untouched.

Similarly the duties on sugar were left virtually untouched. A slight concession was made on one point where, as in the case of tops, unfavorable comment happened to be made at the time of the tariff debate. That point was the "differential," or extra duty on refined sugar, which operates as protection to the sugar refiners. Here there was a reduction from 12½ cents per hundred pounds to 7½ cents per hundred pounds. The American Sugar Refining Company, or "trust," happened to be in the public eye for other reasons, and this change in duty was among the consequences. As the situation stood in 1909, it was of no effect. The trust was in a less commanding position than it had been in previous years, and competition had cut down the margin between the price of raw sugar and refined. The differential of 7½ cents per hundred weight now quite satisfied the refiners. Moreover, new managers had assumed control of the trust, and nothing was heard of any attempt at influence on legislation.

The duty on raw sugar—by far the most important part of the sugar schedule—remained in every detail as it had been fixed in 1897.[1] Here the champions of the farmers were once more in evidence. The domestic production of beet-sugar had made great strides since 1897, and had become important among the sources of supply. Most of this beet-sugar came from the arid and semi-arid States, like Colorado, Utah, California; but, among the strictly agricultural States, Michigan also was a considerable producer. The domestic beet-sugar growers were the vehement opponents of any reduction in the rate of duty, and made much of high cost of production, as regards beets for the farmers and sugar for the manufacturers. The truth seemed to be that in a State like Michigan beet-sugar making could not be carried on without a tariff prop; while farther west, especially in a State like Colorado, it needed none. The Michigan sugar people had embarked in the business under the direct encouragement of the government. The Department of Agriculture had been preaching beet-sugar, in season and out of season. for appropriate regions and for inappropriate: not unnaturally the growers were almost ferocious in their opposition to the proposal for reducing the duty on sugar. In face

[1] See pp. 349–350 for a statement of the duty of 1897

of their opposition, things were left *in statu quo*.

One change of some importance was made in the sugar schedule. It was provided that raw sugar, not exceeding 300,000 tons, should be admitted free of duty from the Philippine Islands. The imports from the islands had never reached this amount; the limitation was due to a fear on the part of the domestic sugar producers that there might be at some future time much greater imports. For the time being, the proviso meant that all Philippine sugar was to come in free. Some such concession to this dependency had long been urged by President Taft. The feeling in favor of it rested in good part on a confused notion, fostered by much of the ultra-protectionist talk, that a duty brings a burden on the foreign producer, not on the domestic consumer. It was urged that we should not treat the Philippine producers as foreigners, by maintaining what was supposed to be a burden on them. In fact, the concession meant not that a burden was removed, but that a virtual subsidy was granted.

The duty on sugar, which until 1890, and indeed until 1897, had been chiefly a revenue duty,[1] had become a protective duty of wide effect, and in some ways of unusual effect.

---

[1] See the discussion of it from this point of view, p. 305. The beet-sugar question is an interesting and important one, closely connected with questions of agricultural development. See articles by H. C. Taylor in the *Annals of the American Academy of Social and Political Science*, vol. xxii. (1903), p. 179, and by G. W. Shaw in the *Journal of Political Economy*, June, 1903, p. 334; my own discussion in *Some Aspects of the Tariff Question*, ch. vii; and R. G. Blakey's monograph *The United States Beet-Sugar Industry and the Tariff* (1912). (Note continued on p. 398.)

As has already been said with regard to the remission of duty on Hawaiian sugar,[1] a partial remission redounds to the advantage of the favored producer, not of the domestic consumer. Ordinarily a duty brings a burden on the domestic consumer, and its remission therefore ordinarily brings relief to him. But a partial remission means a loss of revenue for the Treasury, no relief for the consumer, and a virtual bounty to the exempted producer. This consequence had not been unforeseen when the Hawaiian treaty was made, in 1876; but it had been supposed that but a small amount of sugar would be produced in the islands. In fact, the product, under the stimulus of the bounty, increased by leaps and bounds and became an important part of our total supply.   This sort of favoritism, already important as to Hawaii, was made permanent after the Spanish War and was greatly extended. The Hawaiian remission, which formerly rested on the treaty with the islands, became definitive after their annexation to the United States in 1898. Imports from Porto Rico, of which sugar was the most important, were made free of duty in 1901. The same treatment was now extended by the tariff act of 1909 to Philippine sugar. It is only a matter of phraseology whether we say that the protective system was extended by this process to Hawaii, Porto Rico, and the Philippines, or that a bounty was given to the producers in these regions.   The

---

The American Sugar Refining Co. (the trust) had made large purchases of stock in the various beet-sugar factories, and hence was quite content that the duty on raw sugar should stand.

[1] See p. 279.

substantial fact was that the American consumer continued to pay the full tax on sugar, in the form of a higher price, and that the benefit of the remission went to the various favored producers.

With those various remissions, and the growth of the domestic beet-sugar industry, the sugar duty came to be distinctly a protective duty. In 1890, it had been still in the main a revenue duty. By 1909, only one half of the sugar consumed continued to be dutiable, the other half being free of tax; but the price of the whole was raised by the full amount of the tax. Such is the characteristic situation with a protective duty.

Still another complication in the sugar situation arose from the treaty of 1903 with Cuba, by which Cuban sugar was admitted at a reduced duty,—at twenty per cent. off, or four-fifths of the full duty. That arrangement, as well as the rate of the duty, was left unchanged by the tariff act of 1909. So long as other foreign countries sent in sugar, and paid the whole duty on it, the price of the total supply was raised by that full amount. Cuban sugar producers then got the benefit of the twenty per cent. off, precisely as those in Porto Rico and Hawaii got the benefit of entire remission. Until 1909, it may be remarked, the Philippine sugar producers had been in the same situation as the Cubans; their product till then had come in with twenty-five per cent. off, or at three-fourths of the full duty. The Cuban sugar crop had been for many years the largest single item in the sugar supply of the United States. With a favoring climate. ready access to

market, the stimulus of lowered duty, and peaceful conditions in the island, it grew rapidly.   Foreign full-duty
sugar had been almost crowded out by the time of the
passage of the act of 1909, and, barring accidents, was
likely to be crowded out completely before many years.
When this stage was reached, the effective duty would be
that on Cuban sugar,—four-fifths of the full rate.   The
special advantages to Cuban sugar would then disappear
and the bounty or protection to the various favored producers—in Hawaii, Porto Rico, Philippines, Louisiana,
the beet-sugar States—would be at four-fifths of the
nominal tariff rate.[1]

To return now to the provisions of the act of 1909.
Here, as in previous tariffs, there were so-called "jokers,"
—obscure changes, working to the advantage of particular individuals, and concealed amid the endless details

---

[1] For a more detailed discussion of this aspect of the sugar question,
I refer the reader to my discussion of the sugar situation at large in
Some Aspects of the Tariff Question, Part II.

The great changes which took place between 1890 and 1908 in the
sources of sugar supply, and consequently in the effects of the duty, are
shown by the following figures:

SUGAR SUPPLY AND REVENUE FROM SUGAR DUTY, 1890 AND 1908
Fiscal Year, 1889-90

Supply (million lbs.)		Revenue (million dollars)	
Free of tax:			
Domestic Cane......... 301		....	
Domestic Beet......... 8		....	
Hawaiian............... 243		....	
Total free of tax...............	652	....	
Duty-paying....................	2,607	Total revenue..................	54.0
Total supply...................	3,259	....	54.0

(For the figures of 1908, see p. 401, note.)

The process is a familiar one. A constituent, or friend,
or contributor to the party campaign expenses, gets the
ear of an influential Congressman or Senator, and proposes
an increase in the duty on an article which he produces
or wishes to produce. If his sponsor is high in the party
councils—above all, if a member of the House Committee
on Ways and Means or the Senate Committee on Finance,
—the log-rolling method almost ensures enactment of the
increased duty. Where such changes concern important
articles, like cottons, woollens, silks, hosiery, there is
usually some public discussion and at least *pro forma*
justification. But where minor articles are to be affected,

Fiscal Year, 1907–08

Supply *(million lbs.)*		Revenue *(million dollars)*	
Free of tax:			
Domestic Cane.........	773	....	
Domestic Beet..........	927	....	
Hawaiian...............1,078		....	
Porto Rico.............	469	....	
Total free of tax...............	3,247	....	
Taxed at reduced rate:			
Philippine (75% of full			
duty)...............	29	....	.3
Cuban (80% of full duty)	2,462	....	32.2
Total at reduced tax...........	2,491	....	32.5
Paying full duty...............	1,045	....	17.4
Total supply....................	6,783	Total revenue..................	49.9

It will be seen that in 1890 one-sixth only of the sugar was free and five-
sixths paid the full duty. In 1908, on the other hand, one-half the sugar
was not taxed at all, one-third paid partial duty, one-sixth only paid full
duty. Consequently, though the consumption was doubled by 1908, the
revenue remained (very nearly) the same as in 1890. Yet the consumers in
1908 paid virtually as high a tax per pound as in 1890, and paid twice as
much in the aggregate; since all sugar, whether free, or partially dutiable,
or dutiable at the full rate, was raised in price by the amount of that full
rate.

the new rates are quietly put through without check or
scrutiny.   In the act of 1909, this was particularly the
case in the Senate, since the Finance Committee of that
body gave no public hearings and, among its own members, naturally carried senatorial courtesy to the limit.
Thus the duty on some nippers and pliers was quietly
advanced, for the benefit of a single manufacturer in New
York,—in this case under the sponsorship of the Vice-
President.   The duty on cheap cotton gloves, such as are
used by policemen, the militia, and the army for parade
occasions, was virtually doubled, there being a projector
who succeeded in getting the ear of a New England
Senator.[1]   The duty on horn combs was raised from thirty
to fifty per cent.   The duty on woven fabrics of asbestos
was raised in similar degree.   Although, as already stated,
the duties on iron and steel in most of their crude forms
were reduced, the rate on structural steel was advanced,
by the quiet insertion, in the Senate, of a clause whose
effect was not at all apparent on first inspection.[2]   Every

---

[1] This duty (paragraph 328 in the tariff schedule of 1909) was a typical
case of the " joker."   The previous rate had been fifty per cent.   The new
rate was, when valued under $6.00 per dozen, 50 cents per dozen, plus 40 per
cent.; valued over $6.00 per dozen, 50 per cent.   This did not seem on the
face of it a marked increase.   But the gloves which it was designed to reach
were the cheap sort, worth abroad about $1.00 per dozen; on these the duty
was practically doubled.   The device was familiar in the tariff legislation of
the period ; compare p. 269, above.   See also p. 443, below.

[2] Paragraph 121 of the act reads thus : " Beams, girders, . . . together
with all other structural shapes of iron or steel, *not assembled or manufactured, or advanced beyond hammering, rolling, or casting,* valued at $\frac{9}{10}$ cent
per pound or less, [duty] $\frac{1}{10}$ cent per pound ; valued above $\frac{9}{10}$ cent per
pound, $\frac{4}{10}$ cent per pound."   The duty in 1897 had been $\frac{5}{10}$ cent per pound ;
hence there was apparently a decrease in duty.   But the language of the

one conversant with our tariff history knows that such items have been too common. But it was hardly to be expected that they should appear in a tariff act supposed to be in fulfilment of a pledge for downward revision.

A new set of provisions appeared in the maximum and minimum arrangement. They were very simple. The stated tariff rates were declared to constitute the minimum tariff of the United States. To these rates 25 per cent. was to be added,—25 per cent. not of the rates, but 25 per cent. of the value of the articles imported,—on goods coming from countries which "unduly discriminate" against the United States. This undue discrimination might be either "in the way of tariff rates or provisions, trade or other regulations, charges, exactions, or in any other manner," or by export bounty or export duty [1] or prohibition upon

---

paragraph (otherwise identical with that of the corresponding paragraph of 1897) was amended by the insertion of the words in italics. There was no mention, in any other part of the act, of structural steel that *is* "assembled or manufactured or advanced"; hence this became dutiable, under the dragnet clause, as a manufacture of iron and steel not specially provided for,—namely, at 45% ad valorem. This meant a marked increase.

Like other sorts of iron and steel, structural steel was not likely to be imported in ordinary times. But on an unusual press of demand, there had been imports in New York and at other places easily reached by ocean steamers. There was evidence of an international compact, as to steel rails, structural steel, and other products, for dividing the field between the American steel makers (primarily the Steel Corporation) and their foreign rivals, especially the German *Stahlwerksverband*. The increased duty on structural steel clinched the compact as to that article, by keeping the foreigners out of the American market. I have given some details regarding these "jokers," in *Free Trade, the Tariff and Reciprocity*, ch. ix., "How Tariffs should not be made."

[1] The provision in regard to export duties, by which they might become the ground for levying the maximum tariff, was neither in the House bill nor in the Senate bill. "The words 'or imposes no export duty' were

export. The minimum tariff plus this 25 per cent. constituted the maximum tariff. After March 31, 1910, the maximum tariff was to be applied unless the President had been satisfied that there was "no undue discrimination" against the United States. If so satisfied, he might by proclamation admit goods from a given country at the minimum tariff rates. The administration of the maximum and minimum system was thus put entirely in the hands of the President.

Fortunately, every endeavor was made by President Taft, and in the end with success, to prevent an application of the maximum tariff. By April 1, 1910, he was able to declare himself satisfied that there was no "undue" discrimination against the United States by any country whatever, and the "minimum" rates, that is, the tariff duties really meant to be in force, were universally applied. Negotiations with Germany and France led to some relaxations of their duties and regulations as to American products; and, in true mercantilist spirit, these were held forth as great gains to American industry, and inferentially as causes of detriment to the foreign countries concerned. Negotiations with Canada led to but the slightest concessions. That country refused, as already stated,[1] to modify her regulations as to wood pulp, or to make any

---

inserted in conference, and I believe were inserted at the suggestion of a few paper manufacturers in order to impose the maximum tariff on paper coming from the Province of Quebec." Mr. Mann, *Congr. Record*, p. 4732. I do not know what grounds there may be for this suspicion. Compare note to p. 382, note, above.

[1] See p. 382.

changes of moment in her general tariff system. Some minor changes were secured, which enabled the Administration to make a respectable show of having gained something in the way of lower duties; and a tariff war, which at one time seemed probable, was averted. In view of the unmistakably critical temper of the country as to the general Republican policy and not least as to the tariff, it would have been politically almost suicidal to increase duties against any important country by the 25% rate of the maximum tariff. Add to this the sincere wish of President Taft and his associates to prevent any such increase, and the application of the minimum rates was almost a foregone conclusion.

The section providing for the maximum and minimum arrangement contained at the end a curious clause,[1] which seemed, strictly construed, to relate solely to that arrangement, but has been construed to have a wider bearing. During the session there was talk, especially among the advocates of downward revision, of the desirability of a Tariff Commission. Some persons went so far as to suggest a Commission which should be entrusted by Congress with the power of fixing the tariff rates, and readjusting them from time to time "according to conditions"; a scheme obviously impracticable. But there was much to be said in favor of creating a body with powers of investigation. Hearings before Congressional Committees, as

---

[1] It read thus: "To secure information to assist the President in the discharge of the duties imposed upon him by this section, and the officers of the government in the administration of the customs laws, the President is hereby authorized to employ such persons as may be required."

has been said,[1] are most unsatisfactory sources of information. And there is need of information. The endeavor
to apply the "true principle" (of equalizing costs of production), while far from being a solution of the real problems underlying the tariff controversy, is of importance
in reference to vested interests and the disturbance of
existing adjustments. It is important, too, toward ascertaining how far monopolies are getting excessive profits
under the shelter of "unduly" high duties. On all such
topics sifted and accurate information is called for. A
permanent body of competent persons can do much toward
clarifying public opinion and promoting careful legislation. The proposal for a tariff board having functions
of this sort was welcome to the Administration, but very
unwelcome to the extreme protectionists. The clause
inserted in the maximum and minimum section was one
of those ambiguous compromises, so common in our legislation, whose outcome depends on the spirit in which
they are construed. Its language seemed to refer only to
the matter of foreign discrimination. But the board appointed under this authority was directed, while giving
attention first of all to the administration of the maximum
and minimum rates, to gather information on the tariff
generally, with reference to the domestic situation as well
as the foreign. The declared policy of the Administration
was to use the board as a sort of Tariff Commission: an
indication that the act of 1909 was not regarded in this

[1] See p. 369.

quarter, as it was among the extreme protectionists, as "settling" the tariff question.[1]

The reciprocity arrangements provided for by the act of 1897 disappeared entirely. The sections relating to reciprocity in that act were expressly repealed, and the President was given authority to terminate all agreements made under them. As these reciprocity agreements never had been of any substantial importance, their repeal was of little significance, except as indicative of the disappearance of any intention to deal with tariff questions in this way.

In sum, the act of 1909 brought no essential change in our tariff system. It still left an extremely high scheme of rates, and still showed an extremely intolerant attitude on foreign trade. The one change of appreciable importance was the abolition of the duty on hides. As an offset to this were the increased duties on cottons and silks, and on a number of minor articles. Most disappointing was the mode in which the subject was dealt with. There was the same pressure from persons engaged in industries subject to foreign competition, the same willingness to accede to their demands without critical scanning. In the House, under the leadership of Mr. Payne, there was an endeavor both to maintain publicity and to prevent such concealed items. In the Senate, things went in star-

[1] President Taft's declaration in regard to the tariff board was made in his speech at Winona, Minn., in October, 1909. Professor H. C. Emery was made chairman of the board. The urgency appropriation act of 1909 appropriated money for its expenses, for one year only. A further and enlarged appropriation (of $250,000 a year) was secured for its work in 1910.

chamber fashion, and the familiar process of log-rolling and manipulation was once again to be seen. The act as finally passed brought no real breach in the tariff wall, and no downward revision of any serious consequence.

None the less, a somewhat different spirit from that of 1890 or of 1897 was shown in 1909. Though the act as a whole brought no considerable downward revision, it was less aggressively protectionist than the previous Republican measures. The increases of duty were more furtive, the reductions were more loudly proclaimed. The extreme advocates of protection were on the defensive. There was unmistakable evidence in Congress and in the community of opposition to a further upward movement. High-water mark apparently had been reached, and there was reason to expect that the tide, no longer moving upward, might thereafter begin to recede.

CHAPTER IX.

THE TARIFF ACT OF 1913.

THE closing sentences of the preceding chapter were written in 1910, in the edition of this book which was published shortly after the passage of the tariff act of 1909. The course of events soon confirmed the forecast then made. In the Congressional elections of the autumn of 1910 the Republicans suffered a defeat as decisive, even though not quite so overwhelming, as that which twenty years earlier had followed the passage of the McKinley tariff act of 1890. At both elections, in 1910 as well as in 1890, there was virtually no other question than the tariff on which the parties differed ; and it would seem to have been shown once more that when this issue presented itself without complication from others, the popular verdict was against the stubborn maintenance of a rigid protective policy.

Beyond question, the industrial conditions of the moment contributed also to the Republican defeat. Depression had followed the crisis of 1907, and had continued after the passage of the tariff of 1909. During the extraordinary decade of activity and prosperity which followed the tariff of 1897 (no doubt a deceptive prosperity, in part seeming as much as real), the Republicans had vaunted theirs as the party of good times, and had ascribed all the country's blessings to the wonder-working policy of protection.   It was inevitable that, when collapse and depression came, the Republicans should in turn be held responsible, since they had assumed the credit for all preceding converse experiences.   They were hoist by their own petard.

The particular form commonly taken by the indictments against the Republicans for bad times was that of holding them and their tariff policy responsible for the rise in the cost of living.   On this question, as on the connection between tariffs and prosperity, a sensible person trained in economics would have to make his reservations.   The rise in prices during the opening decade of the century was world wide.   Its main cause, in the judgment of almost all the economists, was the immense increase in the output and supply of gold.   The tariff doubtless kept the prices of some commodities higher in the United States than elsewhere; but they had been kept higher under the duties of earlier periods also,—by the tariffs of 1890 and 1897.   It was not proved, or susceptible of proof, that the tariff was the cause of the continuing rise in all prices throughout these years.[1]

---

[1] In saying this, I would not deny the theoretic probability that a system of protection will bring about a rise in general prices and incomes (a fall in the value of money) that goes on for some time after its inception.   But the changes made by the tariff of 1897 hardly caused any such disturbance of international trade as to warrant the conclusion that the course of prices was sensibly affected by this factor.   On the general reasoning, see J. S. Mill's *Principles of Political Economy*, book v., ch. iv., §6, and Taussig, *International Trade*, ch. 13, pp. 141–148.

The particular phase of rising prices which most aroused comment and bitterness was that in articles of food, especially breadstuffs and meats. For this, too, the tariff was in no considerable degree responsible. Special causes were at work to raise the higher prices of some necessaries: in part temporary crop conditions, and, probably more important, the permanent force of steadily increasing pressure upon land that was no longer super-abundant. But, just as the Republicans had reasoned *post hoc ergo propter* when they ascribed all prosperity to their protective tariff, so the Democrats now reasoned with at least equal speciousness when they ascribed not only depression but the high cost of living to that same tariff. For many years luck had been with the party of protection. The luck turned after 1907, and it was natural, nay inevitable, that their opponents should take all tactical advantages of the new turn of events.

Much the same is to be said of the relation between the tariff and monopolies. As has already been remarked [1] the combination problem, though it touches the tariff problem, is by no means identical with it, or to be solved by tariff legislation. But the feeling was strong that trusts had been aided by the tariff, if not created by it. That they had been aided could not be gainsaid. The way in which the tariff had been dealt with in 1909,— the conspicuous pressure from large corporations and the spectacle of manipulation of rates at the behest of domes-

---

[1] See pp. 310, 316, above.

tic producers,—strengthened the impression that the "interests" looked in this direction for support. The part played by protection in establishing and maintaining the combinations was much over-stated; but there was enough of truth in the charge that they were benefited by the tariff to make this also an effective campaign argument.

Under the influence of these different causes, the Republicans went down to defeat in the Congressional elections of 1910, and to nothing less than rout in the Presidential election of 1912. No doubt their collapse in the latter year was due largely to the split within their own ranks which ensued after the candidacy of ex-President Roosevelt for nomination and the formation of the new Progressive party. Yet few unbiased observers would have questioned that even without this defection the Republicans in 1910–12 had little prospect of victory. The disaffection with the party and its leaders, made clear in the Congressional elections of 1910, had shown no signs of abating. The day of the Democrats had come.[1]

---

[1] The strength of the parties in Congress was as follows:

61st Congress, 1909–1911 (that which passed the tariff act of 1909):
House, 214 Republicans   Senate, 60 Republicans
     175 Democrats   32 Democrats

62d Congress (1911–1913):
House, 228 Democrats   Senate, 51 Republicans
     165 Republicans   43 Democrats
       1 Socialist

63d Congress, 1913–1915 (that which passed the tariff act of 1913):
House, 286 Democrats   Senate, 51 Democrats
     122 Republicans,   44 Republicans
      21 Progressives, Progres-   1 Progressive
         sive Republicans, and
         Independents

During the sixty-second Congress (1911–13) the Democrats had a majority in the House only. The Senate was
still controlled by the Republicans. Consequently there
was much pulling and hauling, and posing for electioneer-
ing effect; but no legislation on the tariff, and no prospect
of any. The Democrats in the House passed bills which
they knew the Senate would not entertain; the Senate made
amendments which it was certain the House would reject.
After their defeat of 1910 the Republicans could no longer
take an attitude of uncompromising refusal to make reductions. But they maintained, and no one with more insistence than President Taft, that Congress should wait until
the Tariff Board had reported; thus only could a "scientific"
revision be accomplished.[1] The Democrats in the House
naturally looked on this contention as a mere pretext for
delay, and pushed ahead with proposals of their own. They
passed bills for lowering greatly the duties on cottons, and
on wool and woollens; and they passed a "farmers' free
list" bill, which indicated what element in the electorate
they were determined to bid for. The circumstance that
in the Senate there were Republicans with Progressive
leanings, who had already shown in 1909 a spirit of revolt
on the tariff question,[2] caused some among these bills—
on wool and woollens, and on iron and steel—to run the
gauntlet of the Senate: patched up and compromised
measures, in reality satisfactory to no one. But as all

---

[1] Compare what is said of the Tariff Board below, p. 424.
[2] See p. 376, above.

hands expected, these came to nothing, being either vetoed by President Taft or lost in Conference Committee. The real struggle, it was felt, would come in the next ensuing election; the decision must be in the hands of a Congress in which one party or the other had control throughout.

To this general do-nothing attitude there was one exception. President Taft's Administration concluded in 1910 a reciprocity treaty with Canada which required by its terms the approval of both houses of Congress. The treaty portended no serious industrial consequences. It proposed to admit free of duty into both countries certain agricultural products and a few raw materials, such as wheat, lumber, wood-pulp. It was bitterly opposed by the extreme protectionists; and the proposed free admission of wheat and the like products was once again made the occasion for dangling before the farmer his supposed concern in this part of the protective system. Nevertheless, the bill for approving the treaty was carried not only in the House but in the Senate also; though in the latter body with a resulting dissension among the already divided Republicans that foreshadowed the coming split in the party. But after having been carried through in the United States, the treaty, to every one's surprise, was defeated in Canada. The Liberal party there, which had agreed to it and championed it, was overthrown by the opposing Conservatives at an election in which the treaty was the sole issue. In previous years, especially in the last two decades of the nineteenth century, the

Canadians had been more than willing to enter into closer trade relations with the United states. But various causes had led to a change of feeling: not only the repeated and almost insolent rejection of their overtures by our unrelenting protectionists, and the consequent adoption of a " national " policy of their own, but the great impetus to prosperity from the growth of the Canadian Northwest. Some flighty utterances by American public men, during the debates on this side the border, alluding to the treaty as a step toward ultimate annexation, offended the growing feelings of independence and pride, which at best made the popularity of the measure uncertain. At all events, defeated the treaty was in Canada ; and thus the one tariff measure which the Taft Administration had made its own and had carried through in the teeth of angry opposition came to naught.

The 63d Congress (1913–1915) was completely controlled by the Democrats. In the House their majority was overwhelming ; and even in the slow-changing Senate they were sure of control. President Wilson, as was to be expected, called an extra session almost immediately, and the tariff was at once taken in hand. A bill for general revision had already been elaborated by the House Committee of Ways and Means during the hold-over session which ended in March, 1913. This became the basis of a new bill, which was passed promptly by the House (May 8). In the Senate progress was slower ; there were wearisome and fruitless debates in an all-summer session; and not until the close of September did the Senate pass it. The act became a law October 3, and went into effect at once.[1]

Both in the House and Senate the Democrats showed remarkable party cohesion, in striking contrast with the dissensions of the distracted Republicans, and in equal contrast with the dissensions which the Democrats themselves had experienced at the time of the previous tariff-reduction measure (1894).[2] Party caucuses of the Democrats voted on the bills as prepared by the House and Senate committees; the influence of tradition and leadership was exerted, with success, to hold the party members to the program settled by the majority within their own ranks. To this success the attitude of the Administration contributed most effectively. President Wilson had quietly but unhesitatingly assumed leadership, and secured a hold on his associates and followers which astonished friend and enemy. Luck was again with the Democrats. They had an able leader in the House, in Mr. Underwood, the Chairman of the Ways and Means Committee; they had a brilliant party chief in the President. They were able to march straight to their goal.

---

[1] It was provided, however, that wool should not become free of duty until Dec. 1, 1913; that the reductions on woollens should not take effect until Jan. 1, 1914; and that the first change on sugar (see p. 425, below) should not take effect until March 1, 1914. The postponements enabled importers and manufacturers of these important articles to adjust themselves more easily to the new conditions.

[2] Compare pp. 286-288, above.

Notwithstanding this steadiness and unity of action, the tariff act still showed the influence of our cumbrous two-chamber system. The Senate made many amendments to the House bill ; and at the last moment a quantity of details had to be settled in the hurried meetings of a Conference Committee.[1] It is to be said, however, that the conflicting amendments and eventual compromises gave little evidence, if indeed any at all, of the sort of manipulation which had affected the details of the tariff acts of 1890, 1897, and 1909. Persons interested in maintaining or increasing this or that rate of duty got but cold comfort. The Senate amendments were usually in the direction of lowering the House rates ; among other changes they made some considerable additions to the free list. If there were " jokers," they were the result not of design but of ignorance or inattention. Errors and inconsistencies there were. Such will always remain as long as there is no concentration of responsibility for the details of

---

[1] For example, the bill as passed by the House provided for a discount of 5 per cent. when goods were imported in American vessels. The question was raised whether such a proviso was not in violation of commercial treaties with various countries ; accordingly the Senate struck it out. In the Conference Committee it was again inserted, but with an additional clause that it should not " abrogate, impair, or affect " the provisions of any treaty. . Just what the provision signified, with this clause added, seems not to have been considered. It appeared that almost all countries, and especially the great carrying countries (Great Britain, Germany, Holland) had treaties providing against discrimination ; and the Treasury Department ruled that in view of these treaty conditions the clause was inoperative. The Supreme Court finally held that the entire clause was invalid because of the conflict with the treaties.

legislation; and there can be no concentration so long as two legislative bodies are each free to patch every measure.

Some aspects of the debates on the act, and some questions of principle raised by the debates, may first receive attention.

The new principle of which most was made by the advocates of the act was that of a "competitive tariff." In 1909, it will be remembered, the Republicans had professed to act on quite a different principle,—that of equalizing cost of production. These two were set forth by both sides as starting from opposite poles in the tariff controversy. And yet, impartially considered, and assuming consistent application, they would seem to come to very much the same thing. The notion underlying equalization of cost of production is that of enabling the domestic producer to compete on even terms with the foreign producer. This would seem to be essentially the notion of a "competitive tariff." It is true that in the Republican statements of the principle of equalization, something was said of a "reasonable profit" to the domestic producer; whereas the Democrats, when explaining what was meant by a "competitive tariff," pooh-poohed reasonable profits, and intimated that the competition should be such as to cut down domestic profits, and perhaps wipe out some of them. Yet a reasonable profit is obviously to be considered among the normal expenses of production, even though it be not so reckoned under the usual methods of cost accounting. A "competitive tariff" would

seem to be one under which domestic and foreign producers can compete in such manner that both should get
reasonable profits. Fairly and consistently applied, therefore, the principle of a competitive tariff cannot be said
to differ in essentials from that of a tariff equalizing cost
of production.

In discussing the tariff act of 1909, I have already
pointed out the obvious fact that universal equalization
of cost of production means universal application of
protection.[1] The principle of a " competitive tariff " perhaps does not go quite so far, especially if applied with a
less generous reckoning of the domestic producer's expenses. None the less, under that principle also duties
should be made high on commodities produced in the
United States under disadvantageous conditions, and
therefore at heavy expense. The notion of the " competitive tariff " is no less inconsistent with the principle of free
trade than is the rival one. Under consistent free trade,
the competition between the foreign producer and the
domestic producer would not be a weighted one, with
handicaps in favor of the domestic producer; it would be
quite an even one. The principle of a " competitive
tariff " would seem to mean merely that protection should
not be unnecessarily high, yet high enough to ensure the
maintenance of domestic production.

Another phrase much used in the debates of 1913 was
that of a " legitimate " industry. No legitimate industry,

[1] See p. 363, above.

it was said, would be endangered. What is an illegitimate industry? one that cannot maintain itself without
some sort of legislative prop? or one that has lost the
right to a prop because of the methods by which its
promoters have sought to influence legislation in the
past? or one that has secured unusual profits through
monopoly or semi-monopoly? Perhaps the phrase refers
to industries which could hold their own under a comparatively moderate scale of duties, but rules out industries depending upon a range of duties distinctly high.
Or it may mean that vested industries should not be
disturbed,—industries established on the supposition that
the policy of protection, maintained for so many years,
would be continued indefinitely. Hardly any intimation
was given that an industry was illegitimate merely
because dependent on protection. Neither phrase—
"legitimate" industries or "competitive" industries—was
used in such a way as to commit its advocates either to
the abolition of protection or to a consistent application
of free trade.

All such catchwords, however, are less important in
their strict and consistent meaning than in what they
imply to the average voter. Their implications were by
no means the same. They suggested very different points
of view. The Republicans, when they professed to be
desirous of merely equalizing costs of production, made
it clear that they meant duties to be kept amply high
enough to leave the domestic producer in command of

the situation. The Democrats, when they spoke of competition, meant that duties should be kept below the point of prohibition. The Republicans wished to make sure of keeping imports out; the Democrats wished to make sure of letting some in. And further, the Democrats, however they might speak of competitive rates and legitimate industries, reserved the alternative, where political or economic expediency prompted it, of throwing these principles to the winds and of fixing duties quite without regard to competition or legitimacy.

None the less, there was occasional discussion that implied the essential free trade reasoning. "Legitimate" industries were sometimes described as those economically legitimate; that is, such as could hold their own without protection. From still another point of view the illegitimacy of protection as such was implied. The House leader, Mr. Underwood, in a widely circulated speech,[1] presented some estimates of the taxes which the consumer paid under the tariff, and reckoned among these the amounts paid in the form of higher prices on commodities produced at home. Calculations of this kind call for the greatest caution. There were but few commodities,—sugar and wool might be instanced,—for which it could be figured out with any accuracy how great was the rise in price which the duties caused, and how great was the total burden on the consumer if both domestic output

---

[1] The speech was made in the House, April 23, 1913, and circulated in pamphlet form.

and imports were considered. In most cases figures of
this sort rest on guesswork.   Such, for example, was the
case with calculations of the total burden from the duties
on cottons, silks, woollens, glassware, manufactures of
iron.   This much, however, is to be said : one who parades
such figures uses the essential argument for free trade.
He can hardly admit the stock protectionist pleas, under
which it is not admitted for a moment that there is a real
tax on the consumer, still less a net loss to him, because of
higher prices of commodities produced within the country.
One who argues after this fashion would seem not to be
able to use the principle of a " competitive tariff," which
assumes a partition of the market between the domestic producer and the foreign; or at the most he can use it only as
a sort of stop-gap, a rough-and-ready expedient for keeping
duties within the bounds set by regard for vested interests.

Perhaps no topic brought into clearer light the mode
in which the two parties approached the tariff question
than that of the expediency of maintaining a tariff board.
Unless the principle of free trade is to be sweepingly and
consistently applied, there is ground for detailed inquiry
on the facts of each particular industry.   Under free
trade, such inquiry is superfluous.   All that needs then
to be done is to treat the imported and domestic supply
on the same terms : either tax both at the same rate, or
free both from taxes, and let the results of completely
equal competition work themselves out.   But this drastic
treatment no one proposed, at least for immediate general

application. Now if the basis of adjustment was to be
that of making conditions competitive, or that of equalizing
cost, or that of regarding most established industries as
legitimate,—on any such basis the question in each particular case must arise, what precise rate of duty brings
about the desired adjustment? Hence the Republicans
had much to say about the need of an expert board of
investigators and the recklessness of disturbing the
foundations of industry without painstaking examination.
That the Ways and Means Committee of the House, or
the Finance Committee of the Senate, was not in position
to make such investigations was now freely admitted by
the Republicans. They did not deny their own sins of the
past in this regard, but urged improvement for the present
and the future. There was much complaint that the Democratic Ways and Means Committee had proceeded rough-
shod, arrived at duties by guesswork, and fixed rates on
materials and half-finished commodities that were inconsistent with rates upon finished or nearly finished commodities.
The new tariff, it was said, was not a "scientific" tariff.

In this there was not a little truth. The duties were
in fact settled in more or less rough and ready fashion.
Doubtless the exact rates in many cases were the results
of compromise, not of any close calculation or accurate
information. Beyond question the same sort of thing had
gone on in previous years, and even more flagrantly.
But the Republicans could maintain that since 1909 the
Tariff Board had been at work and had shown the possi-

bility of more deliberate and discriminating procedure.[1]
And yet the Democrats could not be seriously expected
to pay much attention to this demand for prolonged
preparation and expert examination. In the first place,
the Tariff Board was a Republican device. However excellent its work,—and no competent observer would deny
that it had thrown much needed light on the industries
which it investigated,—a flavor of partisanship remained.
The very fact of its being a Republican product caused
the Democrats to turn their backs on it. More important,
however, was the circumstance that detailed and elaborate inquiry necessarily meant delay. The Democrats
were not to be blamed for believing that, however unbiased the members of the Tariff Board might have been,
and however excellent their work, the real object of the
Republican leaders who championed the Board was to
stave off early action and perhaps give a chance for the
political situation once more to take a turn in their favor.
Postponement of action by the Democrats until the re-

---

[1] The Tariff Board (see pp. 405–407) made three reports : (1) On the
Pulp and News-Print Paper Industry, 1911 ; (2) On Wool and Manufactures of Wool, 4 volumes, 1912 ; (3) On Cotton Manufactures, 2 volumes,
1912. It published also in 1912 a Glossary (explanatory and statistical
list) on the chemical schedule.

These publications contain a mass of information of high value for the
study of industrial history as well as for that of the tariff. Yet it can not
be said that they influenced seriously the tariff legislation of 1913. Some
Republicans in 1911–13 made at least a show of proposing changes based on
the Board's investigations ; but the Democrats used them to no considerable
extent. The Board came to an end in 1912 through the failure of Congress (that is of the Democrats in the House) to make appropriations for it.

sults of an expert board's inquiries should be at hand was to give up their golden opportunity. They had control for the first time in many years of all branches of the national legislature,—not only the House and the Presidency, but even the Senate. Their time had come, and to have waited would have been politically suicidal.[1]

Among the changes in duties made in the act of 1913 by far the most conspicuous and important were those on sugar and wool. Both were admitted free; wool at once, and sugar after an interval of two and a half years.

The duty on sugar under the acts of 1897 and 1909, it will be remembered, had been one and two-thirds cents. The duty became one and one-quarter cents a pound, until May 1, 1916; after that date all sugar to be admitted free. The transitional duty of one and one-quarter cents a pound remained subject to the reduction of 20 per cent. for sugar from Cuba.

There were some clear advantages in the course thus

---

[1] Something which might possibly be equivalent to the work of the Tariff Board was provided in one of the closing paragraphs of the act of 1913 (Section IV, Paragraph R) under which "The President shall cause to be ascertained each year, the amount of imports and exports of the articles enumerated in the various paragraphs in section one of this act and cause an estimate to be made of the amount of the domestic production and consumption of said articles, and where it is ascertained that the imports under any paragraph amount to less than 5 per cent. of the domestic consumption of the articles enumerated he shall advise the Congress as to the facts and his conclusions by special message, if deemed important in the public interest." The notion of a competitive tariff seems to underlie the provision. Nothing is said about cost of production, which played so large a part in the instructions to the old Tariff Board and in its investigations.

taken. In the first place, the sugar duty contributed heavily to the customs revenue. The income tax, which was expected to make up for loss in the customs revenue, would almost certainly require time for working out its full yield. The temporary retention of the sugar duty eased the process of fiscal rearrangement. Second, the sugar producers were given time for readjustment to new conditions. The production of raw sugar, whether cane or beet, is in these modern days a manufacturing industry almost as much as an extractive one. The abolition of the sugar duty presented squarely the problem of vested interests in an industry with a large investment of fixed capital. In all such cases there is good ground for postponed reductions.

It is difficult to see how anything could be said in favor of free sugar on the principle of a competitive tariff. or on that of attacking only the "illegitimate" industries. So far as raw sugar is concerned, there had been steady competition between the domestic producers, as well as between them and the foreign producers. The imports of sugar had always been large. The production of cane sugar and beet sugar within the United States was as legitimate as could be the case with any highly protected industry. The abolition of the duty could be defended with consistency only on the ground that a cheap supply from abroad is better than a dear supply at home. This is the gist of the principle of free trade.

As it happened, the final step contemplated in 1916 was

never taken. When that date came, the political situation had changed. In the mid-term elections of 1914 the Democrats had lost their overwhelming majority in Congress; and though still in control, they could no longer ignore the strenuous faction in their own ranks who fought against free sugar. Moreover both parties, Republicans as well as Democrats, were fencing for position in the coming presidential election. Hence there was no longer unfaltering support of the policy inaugurated in 1913. An amending act of 1916 provided for the retention of the sugar duty at the rate of $1\frac{1}{4}$ cents a pound (1 cent a pound on Cuban sugar); and so it remained until the passage of the tariff act of 1922.

What has been said of free sugar holds for the complete and immediate abolition of the duty on wool. In their tariff bills of 1911 and 1912, the Democrats had not ventured to go so far. It had been proposed to leave the duty on wool at 20 per cent. Through the influence of President Wilson, the bolder step was taken of admitting it free once for all. It will be remembered that this had been the one radical change made in the ill-starred tariff act of 1894.[1] In urging the same step in 1913, President Wilson showed the unhesitating courage which won the respect of his opponents no less than of his friends. It happened that the juncture was favorable for the change. A sweeping reduction, perhaps amounting to complete

---

[1] See p. 291, above.

abolition, had been on the cards for so many months that
the market had adjusted itself to the prospect, and the price
of wool had been for some time on a free wool basis.

Here again none of the current formulas were applicable in justification of so sweeping a change,—neither those
of the Democrats nor those of the Republicans. The
Republican formula about equalizing cost of production
had indeed been shown to be quite impossible of application. The excellent report of the Tariff Board had
made it clear that the expense of producing wool under
the ordinary farming conditions was impossible of any
precise demarcation, and that even for wool produced
under ranching conditions cost varied so much in different regions as to make the equalization formula useless.[1]
The principle of a competitive tariff was quite as unserviceable. The wool duty had for many years been competitive; that is, the imports had been continuous, and
had tended to grow. So far as revenue was concerned,
complete abolition unmistakably meant a fiscal loss. Nor
could it be said that wool growing was an illegitimate
industry, except from the free trade point of view. A
clear decision seems to have been made against even the
veiled and apologetic arguments or protection.

The necessary corollary of free wool was the abolition
of the compensating (specific) duties upon woollen goods.

---

[1] See the Tariff Board's *Report on Wool and Manufactures of Wool*
(1912); especially vol. i., pp. 10–11, and vol. ii., p. 376. *Cf.*, my comments on that Report in *Free Trade, the Tariff and Reciprocity*, ch. viii.

They went by the board, as they had gone in 1894. Only the *ad valorem* duties upon woollen goods were retained; and these were substantially reduced. It will be recalled that the *ad valorem* duties of 1897 and 1909 had been, upon most goods, 50 and 55 per cent. Even in 1894, the duty on woollens had been left, on the more important classes of goods, as high as 50 per cent. On almost all of the woollen fabrics concerning which controversy had been waged the rate now was reduced to 35 per cent. Yarns remained dutiable at 20 per cent., tops at 15 per cent. The rates on carpets ranged from 20 to 35 per cent. The 35 per cent. rate thus established was that of the original compensating act of 1867.[1]

Nominally, the reduction in protection on woollens was solely in the reduced *ad valorem* rate only. In fact, however, the abolition of the specific compensating duties meant a further reduction of protection. As was well-known to every one who had given attention to the complexities of Schedule K, these compensating duties had given not a little concealed protection. They had been more than enough to accomplish their nominal object. that of simply offsetting the influence of the wool duty in raising the domestic price of wool. This additional concealed protection had not been in the main the consequence, as was so often charged, of deliberate plotting or manipulation. It had been the result of gradual and in some respects unexpected changes in the development of

---

[1] See p. 204. above

the industry.[1]   Whatever the process by which the result
had been brought about, the duties on woollen goods,
reckoning together both the specific compensating duty
and the supposedly protective *ad valorem* duty, had become extremely high.   They had ranged as high as 100
per cent. on the few goods that continued to be imported,
and were equivalent to 140 or 150 per cent. on most
foreign goods, which naturally did not continue to be imported in face of these prohibitive rates.

Here was a great decline in rates,—from 100 per cent.
or more, to 35 per cent. or less,—leading the public to
expect a marked fall in prices.   But it was quite certain
that the effect of the change would not be so great as if—
this is often assumed in popular discussion—every cut in
duty necessarily brought a corresponding change in price
The duties on woollens, to repeat, had been in the main pro
hibitory.   Domestic woollens had the field to themselves,
and competition among the domestic makers kept the
prices of most goods within the range fixed by expenses
of production within the country.   Those expenses of production were unquestionably made higher because the raw
material, wool, was raised in price by the duty.   In what
degree the strictly manufacturing expenses also were
higher than in foreign countries was extremely difficult to

---

[1] On the concealed protection from the compensating duties, see the
Tariff Board's Report, vol. i., pp. 124, 133, 147, and numerous other passages.   In at least one instance, that of the duty on rugs, the compensating
figure seems to have been raised by deliberate manipulation ; see p. 184 of
the Report.

make out. If the 35 per cent. duty simply offset higher manufacturing expenses within the country, the change made in the woollen duties could prove but nominal, sub-stituting a sufficiently effective protecting duty for a needlessly high and prohibitory one.

It would seem that in this case the Democrats strove to apply the competitive principle. The inquiries of the defunct Tariff Board, and some further calculations based upon them, indicated that a duty of 35 per cent. would correspond roughly to the difference in expenses of pro-duction between American and foreign manufacturers.[1]

The duty of 1913 might then be expected to enable the domestic producers to hold their own. But the differ-ences were great between the various classes of goods. It was to be expected that some woollens, especially those of the cheap and medium grades, would continue to be manufactured within the country under the new con-ditions; while others, of finer quality, would be imported in larger amounts, displacing to some unpredictable extent the domestic goods. Predictions of universal disaster, such as many protectionists uttered (largely in the vain hope of staving off the reductions), would not be verified. But the outcome necessarily had to remain uncertain for some years. Time must be allowed for the operation of legislation of this kind. The act of 1894, as has already

---

[1] See the excellent article by Mr. W. S. Culbertson, in the *American Economic Review*, March, 1913, which summarized the results of the Tariff Board's investigations and added some valuable calculations of his own.

been said,[1] had not been left in force long enough to make clear the consequences of the similar changes then made. Only if the provisions of the act of 1913 were allowed to work out their effects for a considerable period, under normal and settled conditions, could it be seen what would be the effects on the domestic industry; and this sort of test, as will be shown in the next chapter, was never applied.

On cotton goods the reductions were not dissimilar in character and in effect from those in the *ad valorem* rates on woollens. The changes on the statute book were great. But in this case also the consequences in trade and industry were likely to be much less considerable than in the figures.

The rate on the lowest counts of cotton yarns was but 5 per cent. On the cheapest grade of unprinted and unbleached cotton cloths, it was $7\frac{1}{2}$ per cent. For finer grades, the rates rose progressively, the highest on yarns being 25 per cent., and on plain cloths $27\frac{1}{2}$ per cent. An additional duty of $2\frac{1}{2}$ per cent. was imposed in all cases on cloths bleached, dyed, printed, or mercerized. The maximum duty on cloths was thus 30 per cent. On ordinary hosiery, the rate was 20 per cent.; but on hosiery fashioned and shaped, comparatively high duties were retained,—40 per cent. if the value was 70 cents per dozen or less, 50 per cent. if the value exceeded 70 cents. This was one of the comparatively few cases in which the much-abused fence system (abrupt steps in the rate of

---

[1] See p. 334, above.

duty, when goods get beyond a given value point) was retained. Cotton knit goods, in general, were dutiable at 30 per cent., and the drag-net clause (" manufactures of cotton not specially provided for") had 30 per cent. Cotton gloves, which had been affected by one of the " jokers" of 1909,[1] were dutiable at 35 per cent.

These figures, to repeat, made very radical changes from those previously on the statute book. But, to repeat once more, on most of the goods the reduction was but nominal. The cheaper grades of cottons are produced in the United States as cheaply as in any country. Barring occasional specialties, no such goods are imported. They are exported from the United States, not imported. Goods of medium grade, though not exported, would hardly be imported in considerable quantities even under complete free trade; and the *ad valorem* duties imposed in 1913 continued to keep the domestic market securely in the hands of the American manufacturers. It was the finer grades of goods that were most likely to be affected. The importation of these had continued even in face of the previous high duties, and was likely to be stimulated by the lower rates. It was these also which had been most affected by the specific duties of the earlier tariff acts. The adjustment of the specific duties had been undertaken at the behest of the domestic manufacturers, or at all events at their suggestion, and had been so devised as to impede most

[1] See p. 402, above.

effectively the competition of the foreign manufacturers.
No doubt in most of these cases the duties were needlessly high.   They were prohibitory, as they were in the
case of most woollen goods ; and the continuing importations consisted largely of specialties which held their own
in the market notwithstanding prices much enhanced by
the duties.   In the case of the finer cotton goods, as in
that of the finer woollen goods, there was likely to be
some displacement of domestic products by foreign.

All the duties on cotton goods were now assessed by
value.   Except for the retention of a remnant of the
fence system in the hosiery duties, not a specific rate
appeared in the entire schedule.   This radical change
was made the occasion for severe criticism, on the
familiar ground that *ad valorem* duties tempt to undervaluation and fraud.   The criticism was not without
basis ; and yet the adoption of the *ad valorem* system
was almost inevitable.   It was in no small part the result
of abuses in the previous adjustment of the specific
duties.   The cotton schedule had been a highly intricate one, with duties varying according to the count
of threads per square inch, the number of yards to the
pound, the bleaching, coloring, and staining, and finally
with a most elaborate fence system of value points.   Just
what the whole intricate array signified could be known
only to persons conversant with every detail of the
industry ; that is, chiefly to the manufacturers themselves.
It was more than suspected that the manufacturers, in

their suggestions to the friendly legislators of former days, had manipulated the rates in such manner as to secure not only high protection, but higher protection than would have been granted if the significance of the rates had been fully understood. Charges of this sort, though doubtless exaggerated, were not without foundation. In the act of 1909 itself, which had professed to reduce duties, some changes had been made, and more had been attempted, for increasing the intricate specific duties in a fashion not straightforward.[1] In view of this familiar situation it was to be expected that the Democrats should cut loose once for all from the specific system, and sub-stitute *ad valorem* duties, which tell their tale on their face. Moreover, the temptation to undervaluation was not likely to be considerable under duties as moderate as most of those in the cotton schedule of 1913. This temptation becomes progressively greater as duties be-come higher, and is least when duties are low. Although no hard and fast rule can be laid down, it is probable that duties of 30 per cent. *ad valorem* can be collected on goods of a standard sort as honestly and efficiently as elaborate specific duties. The danger point in these matters seems to be reached with duties as high as 40 per cent., certainly with duties as high as 50 per cent. It is naturally greatest for goods not of a standard character, whose current market prices are difficult to check. It happens that cottons precisely of this kind

---

[1] See the reference given above, p. 388, note 2.

had been subject to *ad valorem* duties in the tariff acts of former years. As regards these, the difficulties were made less rather than greater, since the *ad valorem* rate was lowered; while on the goods formerly subject to specific duties, neither the rate nor the character of the goods was such as to make the system unworkable.

The duties on silks were readjusted on the same principle as those on cottons. *Ad valorem* duties were substituted throughout for specific. The general rate on silk fabrics was made 45 per cent.; on velvets and plushes, 50 per cent. In the Senate, amendments were inserted retaining (though with some reductions) the previous system of rates by the pound. But the House refused to concur in these amendments and the act as finally passed swept away almost every specific duty in the silk schedule.

In this case also the abolition of specific duties was due in large part to a feeling of suspicion concerning their intent and real effect. The highly complex system adopted in 1897, and retained in 1909, had been devised nominally by the customs officials, but at the least with the advice and concurrence of the manufacturers. The plea which had been advanced for the change from *ad valorem* to specific rates was that thus only could undervaluation and fraud be prevented. Beyond doubt undervaluation had been common and sometimes flagrant. Beyond doubt, also, it was lessened after 1897; though by no means entirely prevented, since under the drag-net clause a considerable part of the imports still remained subject to an *ad valorem* duty.[1] On the other hand, so intricate was the classification, so fine and minute were the lines of gradation in the specific duties so troublesome was it to check inaccurate and ever fraudulent statements, so difficult to find competent supervisors at the meager salaries offered by the government, that the working of the new system seems to have proved in practice not greatly superior to that of the old. But these administrative difficulties were not decisive in bringing about the complete return to the old *ad valorem* plan. It was tolerably certain that the elaborate specific duties contained some "jokers"; and any readjustment of them, calling of necessity for advice from the same persons that had planned them at the outset, was likely still to retain jokers. The certain method of getting rid of this wretched adjunct of the tariff legislation of previous years was to maintain *ad valorem* duties throughout.

The rates on silk fabrics were left comparatively high; on most goods 45 per cent. The reductions were by no means so great as those on cottons and woollens. This remained true, even after making allowance for the circumstance that a duty of 45 per cent. is much more likely to be shaved by undervaluation than is one of 30 per cent.; making allowance, too, for the further

---

[1] All silks on which the specific duties did not amount to as much as 45 % or 50% (the rates varied on different goods) had been left dutiable in 1897 and 1909 at these *ad-valorem* rates as minima —See what is said on the silk duties, above, pp. 248, 337.

circumstance that the unusual variety in silk fabrics makes it difficult to check importers' statements of market value and impedes the detection of undervaluations. The silk manufacturers got off easily. The explanation apparently is that silks were regarded as luxuries, and therefore properly subject to duties higher than on other textiles. It need hardly be said that if taxes on luxuries are to be imposed on strict revenue principles, and with the design of reaching persons who can well afford to pay, they should be imposed upon the domestic article as well as upon the foreign. To fix a customs duty, for purposes of revenue, at a point so high as greatly to impede importation, almost to prohibit it, is obviously stultifying. There is ground for suspecting that something precisely of this sort was done in 1913, in the case of the silk duties. The rates remained prohibitory on most silks. A lower range of rates would probably have yielded more revenue, and would have been more in accord with the competitive principle.

The silk manufacture, as it happens, had reached the stage where there was good ground, on other than bare revenue principles, for a reduction of duties. It had had for half a century an unusually high degree of protection. It had grown with extraordinary rapidity to very great dimensions. Its character had been entirely changed. The development was not only quantitative but qualitative. It may present a case—

I am not convinced that it does, but at least the possibility is present—of successful protection to young industries. The duties had become prohibitory on most silk goods, as they had on woollens. The rates could have been reduced much more without disturbance to the bulk of the industry. The time would seem to have come for application of at least some approach to the final test in the young-industry argument,—an incisive reduction of duties, in order to ascertain whether the industry leaned less on protection than when first supported and had made progress toward eventual independence.

Another schedule upon which the reduction of duty was less than might have been expected was that on pottery and earthenware. Here also duties were left comparatively high, apparently on fiscal grounds. The changes in rates on the significant articles were as follows:

	Act of 1909	Act of 1913
Earthenware and crockery, not colored or ornamented . .	55%	35%
Crockery, colored or ornamented .	60%	40%
China and porcelain ware, not colored or ornamented . .	55%	50%
China and porcelain ware, colored or ornamented...............	60%	55%

The cheaper grades, classed as earthenware and crockery (whether plain or ornamented), were largely produced in the United States. Though the imports were not inconsiderable, the domestic manufacturers in the main held the field. The case was the reverse with the finer grades,—china and porcelain ware,—on which it will be seen that high duties were retained. These were chiefly imported, and might be fairly regarded as articles of luxury. The duties on them being mainly revenue duties, there was no reason why they should not be left comparatively high. No doubt the problem of under-valuation remained. It had been the occasion of much trouble in the past, and might not improbably continue to be so in the future. On earthenware and crockery proper, where the duties were left at 35 and 40 per cent., the situation was different. These were distinctly pro-tective duties, and moreover so high on many grades as to be prohibitory. On the competitive or fiscal principle, it would seem that, like the silk duties, they might have been lowered even more than was done.

The duties on iron and steel caused comparatively little debate, as had been the case in 1909. It had become more obvious than ever that the center of interest in the protective controversy had shifted from the iron schedule to others, especially to Schedule K (wool and woollens). The progressive reduction of duties which had gone on since 1890 was carried a stage further. Not only iron ore was made free of duty, but also pig-iron, scrap-iron (already made free in 1909), iron in slabs and blooms, Bessemer steel ingots, and those forms of crude iron which are used for admixture in the steel-making processes, such as spiegel-eisen and ferro-manganese. Barbed wire and galvanized wire, such as is used for fencing, also became free: a concession to the farmers which under the actual conditions of supply was of little real consequence. Steel rails too went on the free list. Moderate *ad valorem* duties were imposed on other manufactures of iron, rising as the products became further advanced beyond the crude stage. Bar iron, for example, was dutiable at 5 per cent., steel bars at 8 per cent., structural shapes at 10 per cent. Tin plate, that old bone of contention, got 15 per cent.; tubes and pipes, 20 per cent. The drag-net clause, on manufactures of iron and steel "not otherwise provided for," imposed 20 per cent.,—no small reduction from the previous duty of 45 per cent.

A sweeping clause put all agricultural implements on the free list. "Plows, harrows, headers, harvesters," and so on in an extended enumeration; "cotton gins, machinery for use in the manufacture of sugar, wagons and carts, and all agricultural implements of any kind or description, whether specifically mentioned herein or not, including repair parts,"—all were admitted free. The effects to be expected from this clause were typical of those to be expected from the changes in the iron schedule, and indeed from the act at large. Most of the articles were not likely to be imported, nor were their prices likely to be lowered. As a rule, agricultural implements are made in the United States not only as cheaply as in foreign countries, but more cheaply. They are great articles of export. This is true especially of agricultural "machinery" in the narrower sense,—headers, harvesters, threshing machinery; it is true also of such implements, hardly to be classed under "machinery," as plows, harrows, horse-rakes, drills, wagons and carts. It is true even of most of those implements, of a still simpler sort, which have come down with comparatively little change from older days,— scythes, sickles, hoes, spades, and the like. Yet among the last mentioned, though as a rule the American tools are as cheap in price as the foreign, or superior in quality and effec- tiveness, there were at this time some which could perhaps be made more cheaply abroad and hence were likely to be imported. A few specialties, like sheep shears, hedge shears, pruning shears, seemed to belong in the class of importable implements; their free admission meant lower prices, and embarrassment, at the least, for domestic producers.

In the main, however, the changes in the iron and steel schedule signified little. There might be an increase in the importation of certain specialties; and some seaboard regions, more easily reached from abroad by water than from the centers of domestic production by land, might import sporadic supplies of crude iron. In the main, the course of production within the country, the sources of supply, the range of prices, would not be affected. The time had gone by when the protective system was of real consequence for the iron and steel industries. For good or ill, it had done its work.

Some minor items may be briefly noted. Hides, made free in the act of 1909 after so hot a debate, of course remained free; and now leather, and boots and shoes as well, were added to the free list. Wheat and flour, cattle and meats were also free. In the House an endeavor was made to retain duties on wheat and cattle, while abolishing those on flour and meats; an attempt to relieve the consumer and yet keep a show of protection for the farmer, which was obviously stultifying. Good sense prevailed in the end, and the duties on all these food products were swept away. The change was not likely to be of moment for the immediate future,—barring some border trade, and occasional importations in bad seasons. Eggs, milk, cream, went on the free list: again articles in which only a small border trade would be encouraged. Coal and lumber also went on the free list at last; the remnants of duties retained in 1909 were swept away.

A general anti-dumping section was maintained, substantially the same as that in the tariff act of 1909. The Secretary of the Treasury was authorized to impose additional duties equal to the amount of any grant or bounty on exportation given by any foreign country. The provisions for maximum and minimum duties, which played so large a part in the debates on the tariff of 1909, were dropped entirely.

The wide use of *ad valorem* duties called for a revision of the administrative sections commonly tacked on to revenue acts. This part of the tariff system had given occasion for constant patching, from 1789 to the present day. Even in the acts of 1890, 1897, and 1909, in which *ad valorem* duties were replaced by specific, wherever thought feasible, so many of the former remained that in each successive measure the provisions against fraud were made more stringent, or new administrative features devised. In 1890, the Board of General Appraisers had been established, having power to decide definitively on questions of facts which previously had gone to the courts and clogged them. In 1909, the Court of Customs Appeals was added, with exclusive jurisdiction over the strictly legal questions arising under the customs acts. It is surprising, in view of the strong desire of the then dominant party to strengthen the protective system, that the provisions concerning declaration, valuation, collectors' powers, and the like, should still have left so many loopholes for the dishonest importer. Yet this was the case; and modification of the sections covering such matters was still necessary in 1913. It is but just to note that the Taft Administration had given consideration to the same problems, and had appointed committees of Treasury officials to recommend improvements. The Democrats under Mr. Underwood's leadership also gave them earnest attention. The pertinent sections of the tariff accordingly were largely rewritten. That they were substantially improved was the judgment of specialists competent on this intricate subject.[1]

---

[1] See the analysis of these sections made in the *Quarterly Journal of Economics*, Nov., 1913, by Mr. James F. Curtis, who was an efficient Assistant

The penalties for fraud were made, not indeed heavier but more certain ; litigation on contingent fees (a great abuse) was prohibited ; the powers of collectors were strengthened. A clause that aroused strong opposition sought to give opportunity for the examination of the books of importers and foreign manufacturers suspected of dishonest practices. After much discussion, and vehement protest from persons interested, the clause was so framed as to give the Secretary of the Treasury discretionary authority to impose an additional duty of 15 per cent. in cases where there was refusal to submit books and records. On other matters also a discretionary power was given the Secretary of the Treasury : a mode of procedure much wiser than that of rigid prescription by law. Not of least interest to economists and others having occasion to study the course of foreign trade were provisions for the better collection and arrangement of the statistics of imports. There was ground for suspecting these of serious inaccuracies in the past.

On the whole, the administrative provisions were well drawn. How far they would succeed in making the new system work satisfactorily could not be said in advance. As has already been remarked, no great trouble is likely to arise with *ad valorem* rates when they do not exceed some such figure as 30 per cent. But when goods are subjected to *ad valorem* duties as high as 45, 50, 55, even 60

Secretary of the Treasury under the Taft Administration and had abundant experience with the government's difficulties.

per cent. (for example on silk piece goods, silk apparel, china ware) the temptation to evasion becomes so strong that all the penalties in the world will not entirely prevent it. When specific duties are abandoned because deemed suspicious or impracticable, the only safe administrative policy is to keep the *ad valorem* rates moderate.

CHAPTER X.

THE tariff act of 1913 remained in force nine years. A glance at the dates of the acts of the preceding forty years —1883, 1890, 1894, 1897, 1909, 1913—shows that one only, that of 1897, had a longer life. The application of moderate duties for nearly a decade, from 1913 to 1922, might have been expected to yield useful experience on some at least of the disputed points of the controversy.

True, it is only on a limited range of questions that helpful conclusions could reasonably be looked for. No trained observer would expect that experience could contribute much toward settling the fundamental question—the effect of such legislation on the general welfare through the greater or less output of material goods. We have here the familiar case of the intermingling of conflicting factors, of confused currents and cross currents. There is no way of disentangling the effects of a change in tariff legislation from those of the many other influences.

It might be otherwise, however, with one important phase of the controversy. What is the effect of a moderation of duties on the protected industries themselves? Would wool-growing, for example, quite disappear from the

447

United States under free wool? Would foreign competition practically sweep away the domestic woollen manufacture under a simple duty of 35 per cent on woollen goods? If sugar were free of duty would it continue to be made at all in Louisiana and the states producing beet sugar? In all these cases, and in many more, the protectionists predicted that disaster would ensue from such reductions as were made in the act of 1913. The revisionists on the other hand maintained that the rates of 1913, on manufactured goods at all events, were high enough to be "competitive"; that they were such as to enable these protected industries to hold their own, even though importations might be somewhat larger and competition from abroad somewhat sharper. For myself I have long been of the opinion that the extent to which most of the manufacturing industries depend on high protection is habitually exaggerated, and that the industrial readjustment consequent on legislation like that of 1913 would not be far reaching. Certainly the scientific observer would watch the outcome with no little curiosity; and a decade of experience under normal conditions would go far toward supplying an answer.

But, as everyone knows, the years during which the tariff act of 1913 was in force were as far from normal as could be imagined. The war of 1914–18 turned everything topsy-turvy. To American manufacturing industries it served as protection more effective than any tariff legislation could possibly be. Not only was foreign importation of competing products completely eliminated, but American goods such as previously had been made at home only under the shelter of high duties were exported to neutral markets. And the years immediately following the war were no less abnormal. We are not a whit wiser than before concerning the extent to which the manufacturing industries, great and small, depend for their existence on the unflinching maintenance of high protection. Consequently when the election of 1920 brought the Republicans into power again and made it certain that the tariff policy of 1913 would be reversed, the debates, so far as concerns this point, were carried on as much in the air as ever. The protectionists predicted ruin unless high duties were restored, but their predictions rested on no more secure basis than in 1913. Those who believed that a considerable reduction of duties could be made without causing an industrial overturn could only argue on the same lines of general reasoning as before. The experiment of 1913 was quite inconclusive.

There was not only this negative element in the tariff situation of 1921–22. Some positive factors were present which had not affected any of the previous revisions. Two had profound influence. The feeling for national self-sufficiency was intensified by the war; and the representatives of the agricultural West supported high protection with a vehemence never shown before.

The first of these is easy to understand. It showed itself in all countries after the war and everywhere served to strengthen and enlarge protection. Everywhere this nationalist feeling has intermingled confusedly with the cruder

29

and more familiar phases of protectionism.   The experiences of the struggle might easily lead a person who was without prejudice for or against free trade to accede to measures for securing, regardless of cost, a domestic supply of articles indispensable in war.   The ordinary protectionist ignores or denies that the stimulation of domestic supply involves any increase of cost at all or any economic drawback whatever. He simply finds in these experiences a further argument for bolstering up every branch of domestic industry.   The trend toward protection, strong enough before the war, became even more strong after its close.

The effect of the great war of 1914–18 and of the participation of the United States in that war was different from the effect of the civil war of 1861–65.   During the conflict of 1917–18 itself nothing whatever was done toward changing the tariff system.   This was due to several causes.   One was that no considerable revenue could be got from import duties.   Taxation, resorted to in any case only by way of supplementing the enormous loans, took the form of the income tax and the excess profits tax.   No less important was the circumstance that the political situation made a resort to customs duties impracticable.   The two parties, Republicans and Democrats, were almost evenly divided in the 65th Congress (1917–19), the Democrats having the slightest of majorities both in the House and in the Senate. There was a general feeling too, that all energies should be turned to prosecution of the war without distraction from party strife. Accordingly a truce was arranged on the tariff question. It was tacitly agreed that no increase in protective duties should be made; and it happened that hardly any duties were available for revenue purposes except such as would also involve protection. Hence it was that during the war itself no change whatever was made in the protective system.

It was after the election of 1920 and the complete rout of the Democrats that the tariff once more came to the fore. And then it was affected by war experience, partly because of a general feeling that there should be greater preparedness for any subsequent conflict, and partly because of the existence of the so-called "war babies." Sundry industries had sprung up with a mushroom growth during the period when the war gave protection even to the point of prohibition, and when the normal conditions of trade began to be restored they were confronted with the probability of serious competition from foreign producers.

The second factor that had a marked effect on the course of tariff legislation, the attitude of our western agricultural regions, was, like the first, an aftermath of the war. But in this case the influence at work was quite different from military fervor. The impelling force was the severe decline in prices from which the farmers suffered in 1920–21. They were hardest hit by the sharp industrial revulsion which began in the latter part of 1920. The prices of wheat, corn, meats, cotton, suddenly were cut to one-half, even to one-third of the war figures. The farmers were as helplessly ignorant concerning the cause of this decline as they had been concerning the previous rise. They clamored vociferously for a remedy. Their political representatives, hardly less at sea than the rank and file and eager to ferret out some sort of response to their constituents, turned to the tariff. All the popular debates of the last generation had inculcated the belief that the mere imposing of a duty served at once to benefit the domestic producer. In a time of distress this notion of the wonder-working effect of an import duty naturally led the leaders to propose, and the rank and file to welcome, immediate and drastic tariff changes. In the spring of 1921, an "Emergency" tariff act (May 27th) imposed high duties upon wheat, corn, meat, wool, sugar. Originally passed with a provision that the duties should be in force for six months only, it was reenacted step by step and remained in effect until the final passage of the act of 1922. As a means of meeting the emergency of the time it was hardly more than an amiable gesture. The prices of the several products continued to decline; hardly a better proof could be found of the failure of tariff duties to serve as a remedy of immediate efficacy.[1]

But this Emergency act, negligible though it was in its immediate effects, was of large consequence on the political situation and on the eventual character of the permanent tariff. By it the representatives of the agricultural states had committed themselves to a policy of high and even

[1] See a report of the Tariff Commission on Operation of Rates in the Emergency Tariff Act, Senate Document 224, 67 Congress, 2d Session.

ruthless protection. They had got from the other states, and especially from the manufacturing sections, all they wanted—*carte blanche* to fix as they pleased the duties on their products. When it came to the duties on manufactured articles, they could not easily oppose, as they had done in 1909, rates which seemed burdensome on the consumers. Thus no moderating influence was of avail in the 67th Congress. The Democrats were hopelessly outnumbered, and even in their slender minority not a few were committed by having previously bowed to the agricultural clamor. Among the Republicans a word of protest was heard now and then, but was hardly listened to.

The outcome was a tariff with rates higher than any in the long series of protective measures of the whole period. It went beyond the acts of 1890, 1897, 1909. The special conditions of 1921–22 led to an extreme of protection which few had thought possible.

The victory of the Republicans in the election of 1920 had been overwhelming, and their control of both houses of Congress was complete. Even though in this election, as in that of 1896, the tariff issue had played a minor part, a return to the traditional policy of their party was the certain consequence. Yet the act of 1922 had a legislative career unexampled for length. The Ways and Means Committee of the House began hearings on the tariff as early as January, 1921; that is, in the old Congress, in anticipation of the coming change of administration. Its bill, further elaborated by the same Committee of the new Congress, was

introduced in the House on June 29, and passed by that
body July 21. It was under discussion in the Senate for
more than a year. The Finance Committee of the Senate
did not submit it to that body until April, 1922; it was
passed by the Senate August 19. After the usual compromises in a Conference Committee of the two Houses, it
finally became law on September 19.

The Senate in most cases raised duties above the figures
proposed by the House. This more extreme policy was due
in part to the greater influence exercised by the states of the
Far West, whose representation, small in the House, was
large in the Senate. Hence it came to the fore most pro-
nouncedly in the case of the agricultural commodities. In
good part it was due also to the tradition of mutual concession and mutual support which senatorial courtesy has
engendered. The senators, always in the habit of acceding
to the wishes of their colleagues in what concerns the confirmation of presidential appointments, naturally yield to
one another on other matters also, and not least on this
one of tariff rates on the products of their several states.

The details of the bill were settled, as usual in cases of
disputed and complicated legislation, by a Conference
Committee of the two Houses. That committee of six
members worked with feverish haste for about a fortnight,
and submitted to the two bodies the bill in what was of
necessity its final form. At this last stage of the legislative
procedure no careful scrutiny is possible of the details of the
compromises and readjustments made by a Conference

Committee. Barring an occasional disagreement on some matter of outstanding moment, the measure as elaborated in the committee must be accepted; the only alternative is to forego action completely. A more vicious system for reaching a settlement could not well be imagined. The evil is an old one, rooted deep in our political system; nor is a remedy in sight.

On agricultural products there was a list of duties on any and every sort of item, of the kind familiar in our tariff history. Most of them were as devoid of economic significance in their permanent form as they were in the temporary form of the Emergency Tariff Act. Wheat became dutiable at 30 cents a bushel, as compared with a rate of 25 cents in the Tariff Act of 1909; rye 15 cents (10 cents in 1909). Corn remained at 15 cents a bushel. Beef bore a duty of 3 cents a pound, lamb of 4 cents a pound; the rates of 1909 were 1½ and 2 cents. There followed the usual list of petty or innocuous duties, from eggs to reindeer meat, peanuts to acorns. California, in which the protectionist sentiment had become curiously vehement and which it was perhaps thought desirous to placate on political grounds, was soothed by duties—either as high as in 1909 or higher—on lemons, nuts, prunes, and so on.

Still further concessions to the farmers appeared in the free list. Agricultural implements were admitted free, as they had been in 1913: such as plows, harrows, headers, reapers, cotton gins, and what not. Even wagons and carts were not dutiable. It was another empty gesture. As has already been said,[1] such articles are made in almost every case more cheaply in the United States than abroad; none except fragmentary imports come in and it makes no difference whether these odds and ends are free or dutiable. Binder twine too remained free: still another empty gesture. Potash also was left free at the last moment, the Conference Committee recommendation for a duty being overthrown in the House. Here the supply must come mainly by importation, and a duty would mean a real tax. But its largest use is for fertilizer; and though the industry was a war baby, it was not allowed to get sustenance at the expense of the farmers.

The aggregate effect of all the duties on agricultural products, both as regards their advantage to the agricultural producers and their burden on consumers, could not be considerable. It would be going too far to say that they must be without effect. The duty on wheat, for example, while of no influence upon the general trend of wheat prices, is likely to be of some significance in the spring wheat regions of the Northwest in seasons when the crop is scanty. In such seasons Canadian wheat, if free of duty, would sensibly mitigate a rise in the price of the hard grain which millers must have for certain grades of flour. Similarly, California lemons will sell for somewhat more, and the consumers will have to pay somewhat more, because of the obstacle which a duty places on the Sicilian article. But when all such items are added up, the total comes to little.

---

[1] See p. 441.

The significance of these duties, to repeat, was not so much economic as political.

With two important articles in the agricultural schedule the case is different. Sugar and wool are of large consequence.[1] Their general significance has been sufficiently considered in previous chapters. It will suffice here to note what action was taken in 1922.

On sugar the influence of the Far West again was potent; the beet sugar producers of that region dominated this part of the tariff field. The "full" duty was made 2.206 cents, as against $1\frac{1}{3}$ in the act of 1909 and $1\frac{1}{4}$ under the act of 1913. Cuban sugar, it will be remembered is entitled to a reduction of 20 per cent. under the reciprocity arrangement. The duty on Cuban sugar had been exactly one cent a pound under the act of 1913; it now became 1.7648 cents. This was practically the rate fixed by the Senate; the House rates had been a little lower.

In one important respect, the sugar situation in 1922 had become different from that of earlier years. The Cuban duty was now the effective duty. The imports were almost exclusively from that island, and were almost certain to be so confined in subsequent years. The predominance of Cuban imports and the virtual cessation of full-duty imports had begun before the great war; even then the Cuban reciprocity rate (1 cent under the act of 1913) had been the

---

[1] On sugar, see pp. 305, 397; on wool, 291, 328. I refer also to the discussion of these duties in *Some Aspects of the Tariff Question*, chapters iv–viii (sugar) and chapter xix (wool).

effective rate. The great increase of production in Cuba
during the war made it quite certain that the supply from
this quarter, when added to the domestic and non-dutiable
sugar, would meet all needs, and (barring an occasional
flurry) would prevent any full-duty sugar from coming in.
Accordingly the advance in the duty from 1 cent to
(roughly) 1¾ cents measures the effective increase of protection to the domestic producers and of burden on the domestic consumers.

On wool the changes were less simple. It was inevitable,
after the triumph of the Republicans at the election of 1920,
that a duty should be reimposed. The Emergency Tariff
Act of the spring of 1921 had already levied a duty of 15
cents per pound,—high beyond precedent, but avowedly
temporary. When the definitive rate was established in
the permanent tariff, this extreme figure was not maintained; yet the duty was still left in effect higher than in any
previous measure. The enhancement ensued mainly from a
change in the plan of assessment. The new plan, considered in its technical aspects, was an improvement; but
it was applied in such way as to bring to the wool growers
greater and more effective protection than ever before.

The change in assessment consisted in using the scoured
content—the clean fibre—as the basis of the duty. In all
previous acts the specific duty had been on the wool "in
the grease"; that is, on the wool as it comes from sheep's
back, with all the fatty matter which in the natural state is
mingled with the fiber. The percentage of fatty matter

varies greatly for different classes of wool, and a duty on wool "in the grease" is therefore of very varying effect. It is relatively high on the more greasy wools, relatively low on those less so. It has been not inaccurately characterized as a duty mainly on dirt. The practical exclusion from the United States, under this kind of levy, of wools of the more greasy sort had long been recognized. The Tariff Board of 1911 had accordingly recommended that the wool duty be assessed upon the basis of clean content, that is, on the wool after it has been scoured and has become ready for manufacturing use. The Tariff Commission in 1921 recommended the same plan; and it was finally adopted in the act of 1922.

The duty was made "31 cents per pound of clean content." The House had proposed a duty of 25 cents; the Senate had raised it to 33 cents; in the Conference Committee a compromise at 31 cents was arranged, and this figure was settled. It will be observed that the Senate, which in general acceded more liberally to the demands of the agricultural interests, here also pushed the duty a notch further up. The consequence, to repeat, was in almost all cases to make the effective duty higher. In the Act of 1909, the duty on clothing wool had been 11 cents a pound; practically the same as in all the high protective tariffs since 1867. If clothing wool were to shrink to one third of its weight in the process of scouring, a duty of 33 cents on the new plan would be equivalent to the 11 cents rate of the old. The duty of 1922 (31 cents) was very near to this figure.

Most grades of imported wool, however, shrink to less than one third of their weight; therefore on most grades the new duty operated as an advance. The appended table indicates how considerable are the divergencies between the different grades and how preponderant are the cases in which the duty was made higher. On wools from Australia and South America, the two most important sources of imports, the effective rate was increased 40 and 50 per cent.[1]

COMPARISON OF AD VALOREM EQUIVALENTS GIVEN BY
AN 11-CENT GREASE WOOL AND A 31-CENT CLEAN-WOOL DUTY

	Cost in grease	Shrinkage	Cost clean	Old system		New system		Duty less (−) or greater (+) under new system
				Duty per clean lb. at rate of 11 cents per *grease* lb.	Ad valorem equivalent on clean foreign cost	Duty 31 cents per *clean* lb.	Ad valorem equivalent on clean foreign cost	
	(cents)	Per cent.	(cents)	(cents)	Per cent.	(cents)	Per cent.	Per cent.
Merinos:								
Patagonian.........	12	75	48	44	91.7	31	64.6	− 2
Cape..............	26	66	76.5	32.4	42.3	31	40.5	− 4
Australian 64s......	50	50	100	22	22	31	31	+ 4
Crossbreds:								
So. Amer. 58/60s....	32	45	58.2	20	34.4	31	53.3	+ 5
New Zealand 58s....	40	40	66.7	18.3	27.5	31	46.5	+ 6
So. Amer. 50s	26	36	40.6	17.2	42.3	31	76.3	+ 8
New Zealand 50s....	31	30	44.3	15.7	35.5	31	69.9	+ 9
New Zealand 36/40s.	15	25	20	14.7	73.3	31	155	+11

Still other circumstances brought it about that protection to the wool growers was made in reality higher. Under the

---

[1] I take this table from a valuable article by Dr. A. H. Cole in *The Quarterly Journal of Economics* for November, 1922, to which the reader is referred for a fuller discussion of this item and of others in the provisions concerning textiles.

previous system there had been some alleviation because of the much discussed provision concerning skirted wool.[1] Chiefly because of this the old duty had been equivalent to somewhat less than the nominal rate of 11 cents a pound,— probably somewhat nearer 8 cents a pound. This alleviation disappeared under the new system, the stated rate being applied in all cases without mitigation.

Still another concession to the wool growers appeared in an entirely new arrangement for carpet wool. This grade of wool, as the reader will remember, is hardly produced in the United States at all. Almost the entire supply comes by importation; the duty is in the main a revenue duty. By far the greater part of this imported carpet wool is used for the purpose which its name indicates, namely in the manufacture of carpets. A small fraction, however, at most 5 per cent., had been used in the manufacture of the less expensive grades of woollen cloths, being mixed with finer wool and also with some cotton, and enabling a serviceable fabric to be turned out at lowered cost. This use of carpet wool for clothing purposes had always excited in special degree the ire of the wool growers. The wool being admitted at somewhat lower rates than clothing wool, its use as a substitute, for clothing wool, even to a small extent, seemed to them an almost criminal evasion of the benign intent of the protectionist system. To the disinterested observer the utilization of perfectly good fibre for cheapen-

---

[1] See *Some Aspects of the Tariff Question*, p. 306, and the references there given, for an account of this provision and its effects.

ing perfectly good clothing would seem to be one of the
obviously commendable ways in which expenses are cut
down in this world. But, to repeat, it had always caused
wrath among the wool growers, and had always been a bone
of contention between them and the carpet manufacturers,
who wanted to get their wool as cheaply as possible.

The outcome in 1922 was that carpet wool became free
when used in making carpets. Nominally it was subjected to
a duty higher than ever before, 12 cents a pound (on the wool
in the grease.)[1] But it was provided that if wool of this
grade was actually used in the manufacture of carpets or
other floor coverings, and if the fact should be established
to the satisfaction of the Treasury authorities, it might be
imported and used in bond, and the duty remitted. In
other words, the carpet manufacturers were placated by
getting their material free of duty. The wool growers were
satisfied by getting a duty on these coarser grades, if used
for making cloths, which was higher than any ever before
imposed even on clothing wool itself; so high as to be prohibitory, as indeed it was meant to be. And to make sure
that the remission to the carpet manufacturers was not
abused, a special penalty of 20 cents a pound was imposed
in case any remitted wool should by chance prove to be used
in making products other than carpets. Here as elsewhere
the wool growers had it quite their own way.

Among manufactured articles, first attention may be

---

[1] In 1897 and 1909 the duty had been 4 cents a pound upon the
cheaper grades of such wool, 7 cents a pound on the dearer grades.

given to woollen goods, on which the duties are necessarily affected by those levied on the raw material. Let it be recalled that a long series of previous acts had contained a double set of rates on woollens: a specific duty which served to compensate for, or offset, the duty on wool; and an *ad valorem* duty which was designed to constitute the net or effective protective rate. Now, as in 1897, with the restoration of the wool duty this compound system was reëstablished. But it was somewhat simplified, because of the new form of the duty on wool. That duty being now upon the clean wool content,—on fibre as actually used in the mill,—the compensating specific duty could be made at the same rate as that on raw wool. Raw wool was dutiable at 31 cents per pound of clean content; hence the compensating duty on cloths should be nearly the same. Nearly the same, but not quite. In the process of manufacture there is some waste or disappearance of wool fibre. A trifle more than a pound of clean wool is required to make a pound of cloth. Consequently the compensating duty should be somewhat higher than that on the wool itself,—somewhat higher than 31 cents a pound. In the act of 1922 it varied from 37 cents to 45 cents.

These specific rates were made too high; the compensation was too great. The allowance for loss in manufacture was excessive. Similarly, that for the use of cotton in cotton-warp goods left the specific rate too high.[1] Under earlier acts,

---

[1] On the cheaper goods in which cotton warp is used the compensating duty became 24 cents a pound. This assumed that three fourths

from 1867 to 1909, the effect of the compensating system had been to make the effective protection on wool manu-factures much greater than appeared on the surface[1]; it now became once more a device for concealed protection. But it is to be said that under the new arrangement this outcome was less flagrant than before. The concealed protection, though not done away with, at least was sensibly reduced.

The *ad valorem* rate on woollens remained for the great majority of goods at 50 per cent. In 1887 and 1909 it had been 55 per cent. on the more expensive classes of goods;—those most likely to be imported. The 50 per cent. rate, supplemented as it was by the concealed protection from the compensating rates, remained on most woollens prohibitive. As had been the case under previous acts, the only imports that could come in would still be the selected grades of finer goods. The situation as a whole remained much the same as under the previous high protectionist acts. Yet it is to be said here also that the system was not pushed higher than before; indeed, the bars were slightly let down.

So far as concerns carpets, the compensating system of course entirely disappeared, since carpet wool was virtually free. The duty upon carpets and rugs in general was made 40 per cent.—the same rate as in 1909. On Oriental and other more expensive grades of rugs the duty was raised to 55 per cent., a sharp advance.

_____

(roughly) of the weight of the goods was in the wool used; an assumption far above the facts for most goods of this kind.

[1] I have discussed this phase of the compensating system with some fullness in *Some Aspects of the Tariff Question*, ch. xx.

On silk goods a change in form was made even more marked than in the case of woollens. It will be remembered that in 1897 a highly elaborate system of specific duties had been imposed in this schedule, and that the same system had been retained in 1909. The silk manufacturers in 1921 proposed again an intricate scheme of specific duties, but with rates very sharply advanced. In the bill as passed by the House this scheme had been embodied. In the Senate, however, an abrupt change was made. The entire system of specific duties was swept away; in its place a simple *ad valorem* duty of 55 per cent. was imposed upon woven fabrics of silk,—the important and representative category of silk goods. This was a return to the plan which had prevailed from the Civil War until 1897. The rate of duty in 1864 had been 60 per cent., in 1890 50 per cent., and now was made 55 per cent. The return to the old system seems to have been due to apprehension of the political consequences of the extremely high duties proposed by the manufacturers. Apparently it was feared that the finger of scorn would be pointed at specific rates which were higher even than those of 1897 and 1909; and they were abandoned. As the manufacturers themselves had ample protection under the *ad valorem* duty of 55 per cent., the change was accepted with little opposition. Indeed, the silk schedule, notwithstanding the size of the industry and the quantitative importance of the duties, has never aroused as much debate as the other duties on textiles.

On cotton goods there was again a change in form, and

30

again rather an alleviation than an aggravation of the duties. The *ad valorem* duties which alone had been permitted in 1913 were replaced by specific duties; but these were arranged on a plan different from that of the preceding acts levying specific duties. The details of the newly adopted system are too complicated for detailed description. The basis of classification, both for yarns and cloths, was the yarn count,—directly so, as was natural, for the yarns themselves, and indirectly so for the cloths in that they were classified according to the yarns used in weaving them. The rates were made progressively higher as yarns and cloths were finer. In so far, the scheme was like that of 1913; then also the *ad valorem* rates had varied according to the yarn count; and it was different from the legislation of 1890 and 1897 in that the specific duties then had been arranged on a quite different basis. Yet notwithstanding the return to specific duties, these were still supplemented by provisos for minimum *ad valorem* rates, also arranged on a progressive scale. The *ad valorem* minima ranged from 5 per cent. on the coarsest yarns to 45 per cent. on the finest cloth; with a further proviso that the duties should in no case exceed 45 per cent. Miscellaneous cotton manufactures, not specially provided for in the enumeration of the various classes of goods (an important and representative category) became dutiable at 40 per cent.; in 1897 and 1909 this rate had been 45 per cent. The system was ingenious and consistent, and was among the improvements in the technique of tariff making which are to be credited to the Tariff Commission.[1] The substantive effect remained virtually the same as in 1897 and 1909, and indeed in 1913. On the cheaper and medium grades of cotton manufactures the duties remained such as to prohibit importation. A few finer grades and specialties might continue to be imported, on which duties would virtually be in the nature of revenue taxes.

On cotton hosiery, a much disputed article in previous acts, a change was made essentially the same as that in the duties on silks. A simple *ad valorem* duty of 50 per cent. was substituted for the cumbrous specific system which had been used in 1899 and 1909. Here too the fear of political consequences from imposing extreme duties demanded by the manufacturers led to a complete simplification and to some moderation. As in the case of silks, the duty remained prohibitive on the great bulk of the products.

On the whole, textiles showed no such marked accentuation of the protective policy as did the articles in which the agricultural West was interested. The difference was significant of the character of the act and of the forces which led to its enactment. True, as will appear presently, some extraordinary duties were imposed on various items among the manufactured goods. The policy of keeping the rates at a level about the same as in the previous highly protective acts, though followed in the textile schedules, was by no means consistently maintained. Yet as regards the bulk of the textiles themselves, protection was accepted in the main as it had stood in the Acts of 1897 and 1909. It was in

---

[1] *Cf.* what is said below, pp. 481.

other directions that the more extreme advances appeared.

On iron and steel there was a resumption of some duties which had been omitted in the Act of 1913. Pig iron paid 75 cents a ton; on steel rails, that old bone of contention, the rate was $\frac{1}{10}$ cent a pound, or $2.20 per ton. These are puny figures compared to those of a generation ago. Iron ore continued to be admitted free. The whole schedule had ceased to be of much consequence in the protective controversy, at least so far as concerns the heavier and half-manufactured forms of iron and steel. In earlier years these stood in the forefront of the protective controversy—a place taken after 1890 by sugar, wool, and the textiles. Some ferrous specialties, such as ferro-manganese, molybdenum, tungsten, caused debate, especially with reference to their use in war, and with the usual utilization of the war argument by the domestic producers and their legislative sponsors. The economic effects of these changes in duty cannot be great, though some particular interests will profit largely from them.

The general accentuation of protectionist feeling led to some advances of duty which cannot be said to have even a remote connection with preparedness for war and indicate the extremes to which the policy was carried. Chinaware went up to 60 per cent. when plain white; when painted or ornamented to the unprecedented figure of 70 per cent. "Jewelry commonly and commercially so known"—that is, cheap imitation jewelry—and a long list of like metal articles, such as buckles, buttons, powder-cases—and even vanity cases!—became dutiable at 80 per cent. Toys too, which the dreadful Germans had supplied largely under pre-war conditions, and which the enterprising Japanese had supplied in very poor quality during the war, were now taxed at inordinate rates in order to bolster up some domestic manufacturers who had begun operations under the abnormal conditions. This war baby got a rate of 70 per cent. It is somewhat amusing that dice, which are mentioned in close proximity to toys, remained dutiable at only 50 per cent. Cotton gloves were also subjected to very high duties. It will be remembered that the manufacturers of this article had maneuvered successfully for high duties in 1909; now they got duties even higher. It was provided that the duty, which is another of the combined type (*ad valorem* and specific) should not exceed 75 per cent. *ad valorem;* a legislative confession that this rate was likely to be reached and was not regarded as excessive. The English manufacturers, it may be noted, also had asked and obtained protection in their own country against the German makers of this article. No military or political ground can be imagined for refusing to accept a supply even from the Germans, if, as seems to be the case, they can make it cheaper and better. Lace window curtains also were given combined specific and *ad valorem* duties, which in no case were to be less than 60 per cent. Laces in general paid 90 per cent.[1] There is only one case in our entire tariff history in

---

[1] Some curious episodes leading up to this duty are explained in Dr. Cole's article.

which an *ad valorem* duty as high as this has been imposed—the 100 per cent. rate on brandies and spirits in the revenue tariff of 1846, which obviously was of quite a different character. Combined specific and *ad valorem* duties in later protective tariffs not infrequently brought an effective total as high or even higher; but it was veiled by the specific part of the combination, as was the case with similar provisions in the present tariff. A straight protective *ad valorem* tax of 90 per cent. was unexampled.

Hardly less overt were certain inordinate duties which, though in form of the combined *ad valorem* and specific type, in fact rested entirely on a value basis. Thus pocketknives, if valued at 40 cents a dozen or less, paid one cent *each* and in addition 50 per cent. *ad valorem;* if valued between 40 cents and 50 cents a dozen, 5 cents *each* plus 50 per cent. *ad valorem;* and so on. I put "each" in italics because a thin veil was thrown over the procedure—an indication of an uneasy conscience?—by fixing the valuation points according to the dozen but the duties according to the piece. Figuring both in the same way (by the dozen) we get the following results:

PENKNIVES, POCKETKNIVES, AND THE LIKE

	Duty	Duty reduced to *ad valorem* Terms	
		Max.	Min.
Value up to 40 cents doz.	12 cts. doz. + 50%	...	80%
" 40 @ 50 cents doz.	60 " " + 50%	200%	170
" $.50 @ $1.25 doz.	$1.32 " " + 55%	319	160
" $1.25 @ $3.00 doz.	$2.16 " " + 55%	228	127
" $3.00 @ $6.00 doz.	$3.00 " " + 55%	150	100
Over $6.00 doz.	$4.20 " " + 55%	125	...

The same method was applied to clippers, razors, guns and rifles; and in all these cases the duties, when reduced to a single *ad valorem* rate, were extremely high, ranging from 75 per cent. to over 400 per cent.

No marked changes were made in the free list, notwith-standing endeavors in that direction in one or the other of the two Houses. Cotton of all kinds finally remained free, although the Senate had put a duty on long staple cotton, of which some slight production is now undertaken in the irrigated region of Arizona. Hides also remained free, after long and acrimonious debate. The agricultural representatives were finally forced to accede to this, as an offset to their insistence for keeping boots and shoes on the free list, and leather as well. Coal remained free, with a provision (aimed at Canada) by which, if any country imposed a duty upon United States coal, the same duty was to be levied upon coal when coming from that country. Books in foreign languages had been made dutiable by the House, but were left free, as were all books in any language if imported by colleges and educational institutions for their own use. The friendliness to education did not avail, however, to retain on the free list scientific and laboratory apparatus imported by colleges and like institutions; in all cases this was hereafter to pay a duty of 40 per cent. Similarly, glass instruments for chemical, pathological and pharmaceutical use were no longer free for hospitals and educational institutions, as they had been before; they were to pay 65 per cent. Bread was put on the free list a quite innocuous provision so far

as the economic effect was concerned, and a characteristic
sop to sentimentality.

Among the most hotly debated paragraphs were those
fixing the duties on coal tar products and dyestuffs. They
were closely connected with the administrative provisions
of the act, to which further reference will presently be made.
The history of this set of duties makes a long story, and the
economic situation was highly complicated. Only a brief
sketch is possible here.

The war argument was used to the limit. Before 1914 the
supply of dyestuffs, the most important of the coal tar
products, came almost exclusively from Germany. During
the war there had been great shortage, speculation, advances in prices, a hothouse domestic industry. At its close
the domestic producers were dismayed, and urged their
case before Congress and the public with great insistence.
On the other hand the circumstance that there were large-
scale combinations in the industry and that the unpopular
Dupont concern was among the most important producers,
roused suspicion and some hostility.

Regarded from the strictly economic point of view the
industry does not seem to be adapted to American ways.
In the technical parlance of economics, it lacks a comparative advantage. Its processes are painfully detailed and
elaborate, highly trained and highly paid labor being applied
slowly and carefully to a variety of products. Each one of
these products is turned out in small amounts; a possible

exception is synthetic indigo, of which there is something like mass production. In the main it is adapted to the German industrial ways and traditions: exact applied science; patient experimenting; a technical staff and its trained technical assistants, to be had at comparatively low salaries and wages; large-scale operations but not mass production. Some bad things were said of the tricks of the German dyestuffs producers and merchants, and of the unscrupulousness of their competition. Apparently much of this was true, but hardly more true than of the same industry elsewhere; the business seems to lend itself to the worst features of the competitive system. The United States had not failed before the war to develop some chemical industries without high protection, but these were of a different type from the higher grades of coal tar products. Here as in other directions the successful American industries are those turning out great quantities of a single product by large-scale methods.[1] My impression is that not lack of aptitude for chemical industries as such, not great scarcity of trained chemists or lack of ability on their part, but the character of the dyestuffs part of the industry mainly explains the pre-war situation. As a matter of the international division of labor, the people of the United States probably would do well to turn

---

[1] See an instructive article by Mr. L. H. Baekeland, a chemist distinguished in the industrial application of his subject, in *Harper's Magazine*, April, 1917.

I refer also to what I have said in general of the principle of comparative costs and of its application, in my book *Some Aspects of the Tariff Question*, ch. iii.

to other things in which they work to better advantage, and get their dyestuffs from Germany. And—to go on with the purely economic aspects of the case—the war stoppage of supply raised the old question whether it is worth while to restrict the advantages of the international division of labor because of a possibility of its sudden disruption.

But quite a different phase of the war argument was urged in this case. The cool economic considerations, not of a sort to receive attention under any circumstances from the dominant party, were quite disregarded because of the stress laid on the chemical industries, and especially on the manufacture of coal tar products, for the direct service of war. The same plant can be used for making dyestuffs and the like in time of peace, for explosives and for poison gas when war comes. The line of reasoning is similar to that applied in favor of subsidizing a merchant marine: the ships can be used for the ordinary purposes of transportation during peace, and can serve as an auxiliary navy or transport system in time of war. The plea is more dramatically effective as regards the coal tar products: be prepared to make your own explosives and poison gas! It was pushed to the hilt; and in this case once more the general protectionist atmosphere caused it to be welcomed, with little endeavor to ascertain just how far the military needs went, or whether each and every kind of coal tar product had to be bolstered up at home in order to meet these needs.

On the other hand domestic producers were so uncertain of their own position—so impossible was it to say just how much they had to fear from their dreaded German competitors—that they urged at first a complete prohibition, at least for a couple of years. In fact a virtual prohibition had existed since the close of the war through certain administrative regulations, and had been sanctioned by a temporary act of Congress. The proposal for the so-called embargo, however, proved unpopular, and though put in the bill as presented by the Ways and Means Committee to the House, was struck out by the House itself. After long debates in the Senate, and with no little vacillation, it finally was dropped from the act itself. In its place came some extremely high duties, and some general administrative provisions which had no logical connection with the coal tar products themselves but which nevertheless were expected or hoped to be applied to them.

The new rates of duty were extremely high. In 1916, when the war shortage of dyestuffs roused attention duties had been imposed upon dyestuffs of 30 per cent. *ad valorem* plus 5 cents per pound. In the act of 1922 these rates became 40 per cent. *ad valorem* (55 per cent. until 1924) plus 7 cents per pound on the intermediate products; and 45 per cent. *ad valorem* (60 per cent. until 1924) plus 7 cents per pound on the finished coal tar dyes. The combination of specific and *ad valorem* duties was used, as it has been so often in the protective acts, to make sure that both the cheaper and the dearer forms should be saddled with an effective high duty.[1]   Much more important was the pro-

---

[1] On intermediates the specific duty of 7 cents a pound, reduced to an *ad valorem* equivalent on the basis of 1921 prices, ranged from 2½ per

vision that these *ad valorem* rates should be assessed, not under the ordinary procedure, but with "American valuation"; not on the basis of foreign market value, but on that of the selling price in the United States of a similar article of domestic production. Of the controversy that centered about American valuation in general more will be said presently. The effective duty was made very much higher by its application, and this special treatment was made obligatory for the coal tar products, and for them only. Alone in the act they were thus singled out. There were further provisions for the proper labeling and description of these articles, and (elsewhere in the act) for the application of special restrictions for the prevention of the "unfair competition"; provisions entirely proper and likely to meet a real need of combating unscrupulous competition. The rates themselves, to repeat, were extremely high. Both the

---

cent. on the most expensive of the intermediates (m-Nitro-p-tolindine) to 117 per cent. on Naptholine, a cheap substance; making the total rate vary—after adding 55 per cent. *ad valorem* duty—from 57½ per cent. to 172 per cent. On finished dyes the total rate ranged similarly from 61 per cent. on a very expensive dye, Erythrosine, to 90 per cent. on Sulphur Black, a cheap dye very largely used. On the last named, as on other dyes of large consumption, the duties were quite prohibitory. Figures on prices and production, and a mass of information on the entire industry, are to be found in the successive Censuses of this industry published by the Tariff Commission.

In computing these figures of *ad valorem* equivalents I have used the *ad valorem* duties of 1922–24, since these are applicable for comparison with the prices of 1921, the nearest available date. It must be remembered, too, that the *ad valorem* duties themselves are on the American valuation; this procedure bringing about a marked advance in the effective duty.

industrial and the military conditions are so extraordinarily complex as to render the problem quite the most difficult I have encountered in the whole history of tariff legislation. But it is certain that the military excitement caused the protective policy to be applied more rigorously than would have been the case if these two factors had not combined, and more so than was justified by either if taken by itself.

I turn now to the administrative provisions, and especially those bearing on the assessment of *ad valorem* duties, such as these high rates on coal tar products. Early in the session and without reference to the dyestuffs, it had been proposed there should be a radical change in the assessment of *ad valorem* duties: they should be levied hereafter on the basis of what was called "American" valuation, that is, on the value in the United States of a "comparable and competitive" article of domestic production. Not a little of pseudo-patriotic bombast was heard in favor of this "American" valuation. Strictly, the problem is one of administrative procedure. It ought to have been divorced entirely from the protective controversy. Unfortunately it is extremely difficult to secure this sort of divorce; any and every matter relating to import duties gets a tinge from the all-pervasive partisan atmosphere. In the act as finally passed there was a curious set of provisions. In the main, American valuation was discarded. *Ad valorem* duties were to be assessed in the first instance either on the foreign value of the goods at the time and place of purchase, or on the export value (at that time and place), whichever of these two being the higher. Some further provisions, however, brought modifications. If neither the foreign nor the export value could be ascertained, the duty was to be assessed upon what is called the "United States value"—the value of the *imported* commodity in the United States, less duty, cost of transportation and other expenses. This is a plan for applying *ad valorem* duties which has much to say for itself and might indeed have been made of wider application. If none of the preceding values could be ascertained the duty was to be assessed upon the "cost of production" abroad. This could hardly be more than an empty provision, since the three preceding can be ascertained in almost every case more readily than cost of production. Finally, if all the others fail, the duty was to be assessed upon the "American selling price,"—the American valuation which the pseudo-patriots had tried to apply universally. Its application would cause the same *ad valorem* figure to bring a very much heavier effective duty than any of the other alternatives. But it was to be used (barring the one case of coal tar products, just mentioned) only in the last resort, and only if the President exercised certain discretionary powers given him elsewhere in the act.

The discretionary powers given the President had no logical connection with the administrative provisions themselves, and the collocation of the two can only be explained by the vacillations and compromises under which the act finally got its shape. They were connected with still another

feature unique in the tariff of 1922. This was the explicit
legislative statement, appearing for the first time on the
statute book, that the principle underlying the legislation
was that of equalizing costs of production. "In order . . .
to put into force and effect the policy of the Congress by
this Act intended, whenever the President . . . shall find
it shown that the duties fixed in this Act do not equalize
the differences in costs of production in the United States
and the competing foreign countries," he was authorized
to raise or lower the duties for the purpose of equalizing
these costs; with the limitation, however, that the total
increase or decrease of duties should not exceed 50 per cent.
Before applying this power, however, investigations of
costs of production were to be made by the Tariff Commission, and the President's action was to be based upon the
recommendation of the Commission. And then followed,
curiously enough, the power to apply "American selling
price" in the assessment of *ad valorem* duties. The President, on "finding" that the differences in cost of production
in the United States and the principal competing country
could not be equalized by raising or lowering duties, was to
issue a proclamation to that effect, and thereupon the
"American selling price" was to be the basis of an *ad valorem*
duty on the article in question; with the proviso, however,
that the *ad valorem* rate itself, while it might be decreased
50 per cent., should not be increased. The basis of valuation become different; thereby the effective duty, at the
same nominal rate, would be higher. This tortuous arrange-

ment is not easy to understand and still less easy to justify. It was doubtless adopted as a device for saving the face of those who vowed they would never give up American valuation.

The notion of equalizing costs of production had become a sort of fetish among the protectionists. I say nothing here of its weakness from the point of view of economic principle, having indicated elsewhere[1] that it seems to me fatally unsound as a matter of tenable or consistent theory. It is the question of practicability in administration that was now raised by its being set up in the tariff law. The rule was proclaimed, and an endeavor was made to apply it, quite without regard to the most obvious realities. It is difficult enough to ascertain costs of production in the United States. True, with compulsory adoption of uniform methods of cost accounting by American establishments; with a large staff of accountants to examine books and check returns from a considerable number in each branch of industry; with some careful procedure for arriving at a mean between the high cost and the low cost producers —representative figures can be secured for American articles of a standardized sort. But can it be imagined that any officials in the United States could do this sort of thing for foreign products? that foreign producers would permit such a control of their accounts and figures as alone would make it possible to ascertain trustworthy comparable figures for the competitive articles in foreign countries? These diffi-

[1] See *Free Trade, the Tariff and Reciprocity*, ch. vii.

culties, great enough in case of standardized articles, obviously become immensely greater with specialties, and perhaps most difficult of all with goods produced at joint cost ("by-products"). These classes include many of the contested items for which resort to the flexible powers was likely to be sought. A biased or subservient Tariff Commission might make a pretense of having found accurate figures. A basis of well-ascertained fact is almost impossible to find, or if found, to keep up to date. Those who advocated this as a "scientific" solution of the tariff question were obsessed by formula and surprisingly unable to face the realities.

A distinctive feature in the history of the Act of 1922 is that for the first time a Tariff Commission was lending its aid to Congress. How serviceable did the Commission prove?

The Tariff Commission was established by an act of 1916,—an act combining some revenue provisions (including increases of duty upon dyestuffs) with those for the establishment of a Tariff Commission. The Commission was the result of a demand from many quarters for some more intelligent or discriminating procedure than that which had characterized the legislative history of tariff measures during the preceding generation. Neither political party was greatly in favor of the step. But it was strongly urged by the Wilson administration, and with some reluctance Congress gave it a trial. Unlike the Tariff Board of 1911, which was set up by President Taft under very vague statutory

31

powers,[1] it was deliberately and specifically established by Congress; with six Commissioners (not more than three of any one party) large powers of investigation, a considerable appropriation. Many of its sponsors had a vague hope that in some way the Commission would be an agency for fixing rates once for all and for removing the tariff question from the legislative sphere,—for "taking the tariff out of politics." A more rational and discriminating expectation was that it might be of service to Congress in arranging rates with more care, more consistency, better methods. How serviceable did the Commission prove?

Needless to say, it could not fulfill the Utopian expectations entertained in some quarters. No sensible person conversant with our political ways could suppose that Congress would put into the hands of any such body the settlement of questions of policy. As just stated, its powers as regards rates of duty were specifically restricted. The changes which it might recommend to the President, on the basis of differences in cost of production, were not to go beyond 50 per cent of the duties set by Congress; and no articles on the dutiable list were to be free, nor any on the free list dutiable. But there was wide scope for usefulness in other directions. The Commission might readily be helpful on such matters as more careful arrangement of the schedules, more accurate enumeration of the articles, greater consistency between the duties on raw materials and manufactures. Much of the phraseology of the tariff acts has been mechanically

[1] See p. 405, above.

copied from one measure into the next, regardless of changes in industrial methods and in commercial terminology. There has been abundant room for improvement in these technical matters. As regards rates of duty and substantive effects, even though questions of policy must be left to Congress, that body might at least be provided with more complete and more exact information than had been available in the past. What use should then be made of the data of course must depend, as with all legislation, on the character and intelligence of the legislators. Something at all events is gained if those who are intelligently solicitous for the public interest can secure trustworthy information.

These modest but feasible objects may be fairly said to have been in good measure attained in 1922. The textile schedules, as has already been noted, were better constructed than ever before; especially that on cottons and the marked simplification of the silk schedule was mainly due to the information supplied from the Tariff Commission concerning the duties proposed by the domestic producers and finally discarded. The agricultural schedule itself, much affected and indeed distorted though it was by the unusual political conditions, was better arranged than ever before. Most striking of all was the draftsmanship of the paragraphs relating to coal tar products and dyestuffs. It has just been pointed out that these were the occasion of bitter contention. Yet in the listing of the articles, and in their arrangement under the several heads of crude products (in the main left free of duty), intermediates, and finished products such as dyestuffs, the Tariff Commission's proposals were left unchanged throughout the legislative history of the measure. The paragraphs relating to them were drafted in the office of the Commission; the language so drafted was incorporated in the act in every detail. When it came to the rates of duty, the question of embargo or no embargo, American valuation, there was uncertainty, compromise, shift back and forth, in the various stages of the prolonged session. The height to which the protective policy should be carried was settled by Congress. But the technical form was accepted as it came from the experts of the Commission. This was the case not only with the paragraphs relating to the coal tar products, but with the entire chemical schedule. That schedule as it stood in previous acts, never well constructed and copied mechanically from one tariff to another through many revisions, had become in many respects not only ill-arranged but quite obsolete. It was now in better form than ever before.

Still another good result achieved from the labor of the Tariff Commission was a great improvement in the general administrative features of the customs system. A glance at the law as enacted will show that a very large part of it, roughly one third of the printed matter, is contained in Title IV, "Administrative Provisions." This title had a curious history.

Several years before, long before a general revision of rates of duty was under consideration, the Tariff Commission had undertaken an examination of the laws regulating

administrative procedure. They were found to be in hope-
less confusion. Some improvements had been made in
1913,[1] but the general frame work had been left unchanged.
The provisions concerning the collection of duties, the
functions of the various officers, the organization of the
custom houses, and the like, ranged in date from the end of
the eighteenth century to the end of the nineteenth. Many
of them, though still on the statute book, were quite obsolete.
Often they were inconsistent with each other. Some had
been drafted with reference to the conditions of a century
ago, when ocean transportation took place in sailing vessels,
and were quite impossible of application to the modern
steamship. The Commission prepared an entirely new
draft designed to bring order into the confused mass. In
the main it proposed nothing new, but simply codified the
existing laws, rejecting what was superfluous and obsolete,
simplifying what was to be retained. A few substantive
changes were made, and to these attention was called in the
report to Congress which accompanied the bill, attention
being also called to possible alternatives. Hardly a contentious question was involved. It was merely a matter of
bringing about a reform, obviously called for, in an important administrative procedure.

To this draft, at the time it was submitted to Congress,
no individual and no committee was willing to give a
moment's attention. The very circumstance that it was a
humdrum, uninteresting, undramatic piece of work doubt-

---

[1] *Cf.*, p. 444, above.

less acounts for the fact that no one was willing to give it the slightest heed. But in the course of the discussions of 1921–22 the proposal for assessing *ad valorem* duties on the "American valuation" led the House Committee to look into the paragraphs upon this subject in the Commission's draft; paragraphs which were in the main a codification of the longstanding system of assessing duties upon the foreign value at the time or place of exportation. They did not fit at all into the then favored scheme of American valuation. But the discovery of this convenient formulation of the existing practise led to the discovery that there was a great deal more in the Commission's draft. With very little discussion, the Committee came to the conclusion that the project was good and incorporated in the House bill virtually the whole of the draft. Changes were made, of course, in the paragraphs relating to the disputed matter of valuation; and on some other contentious matters also amendments were inserted. In the main, however, the elaborate proposals of the Commission were accepted without change. Much the same happened in the Senate. There too the valuation paragraphs were changed and rechanged, and finally emerged in the shape which has already been explained. Some modifications in phraseology were also made elsewhere, largely at the suggestion of customs officials; and a few provisions of substantive importance were added, the consideration of which would carry us too far afield, and which did not affect the main body of the draft. Upon the whole the work of the commission was accepted, and a great improvement thus brought about in the clearness and workableness of this part of the tariff system.

Something may be said in conclusion of the character of the debates on the measure and of the character of the measure itself. Perhaps most noteworthy in the debates was the constant insistence by the sponsors of the act on the principle of equalizing costs of production. As I have already remarked, it was embodied for the first time in statutory language,—declared by Congress to be the principle on which the tariff system is founded. Talk of this sort was more to the fore than at any previous time. And not only this; it was pushed to further extremes than ever before, both in the rates themselves and in their advocacy or justification. There were not wanting senators who expressed their willingness to impose a duty of 500 per cent. or 1000 per cent. if such rates were necessary for the sacred purpose of equalizing costs of production.[1]

---

[1] The following colloquy in the Senate may be quoted (Congressional Record, 67th Cong., 2d Session, p. 12514).

"MR. STANFIELD. Mr. President, does the Senator from Wisconsin want to see American labor put out of employment and American industries closed because he objects to imposing a rate which he thinks would startle the American people and prejudice them against the principles of the Republican Party?

"MR. LENROOT. Does not the Senator think that a rate can be fixed so high that it is better for America to have the labor doing something else?

"MR. STANFIELD. Not if that rate is necessary to equalize the difference in the cost of production of the foreign article which comes in competition in the American market with the American produce.

So far as concerns the range of rates, the protective system was carried further than ever before. The session began with hot enthusiasm for a new tariff. Between the feeling of exultation in the dominant party from their overwhelming victory at the polls and their eager search for a remedy to meet the industrial depression of 1921, the protectionist feeling was more fervid than ever before. There was an unmistakable cooling as the months went on. Depression had largely run its course; some revival of industrial activity set in. Elections to fill congressional vacancies and primary elections went against the stand-pat Republicans. Yet the path once entered upon could not well be left. The extreme policy was put through to the bitter end.

"Mr. LENROOT. Then I do not know where the Senator would stop. The Senator from Idaho (Mr. Gooding) says he would stop at tea, but, if it required 1000 per cent. to equalize the difference in the cost of production, I take it the Senator from Oregon agrees with the Senator from Idaho, and that they are both willing to tax the American people 1000 per cent. for the privilege of having an article manufactured in the United States. I am not; that is all.

"Mr. STANFIELD. May I answer the Senator's question as to where I would stop?

"Mr. LENROOT. Yes.

"Mr. STANFIELD. I would stop when the rate is so high that it is not necessary to equalize the difference in the cost of production in this country and abroad, including labor and the other elements of cost.

"Mr. LENROOT. So if it required 5000 per cent. the Senator would vote for it.

"Mr. STANFIELD. It would make no difference, because it would pay the American people to be kept employed. If American labor is out of employment the price makes no difference, because they have no purchasing power."

With this may be compared the discussion in the Senate in 1909, referred to at p. 364, above.

CHAPTER XI

THE TARIFF ACT OF 1930

THE Tariff Act of 1930 was passed under conditions quite different from those that obtained for the long series of preceding measures. The successive acts from 1883 to 1922 are all explicable on the ground of some special occasion for a general revision: either an admitted need of overhauling, or a party overturn, or some financial or economic stress. For several years before the act of 1883, it had been agreed on all hands that the rates established during and after the Civil War needed to be readjusted. The three acts of 1890, 1894, 1897 were the results of federal elections and political upsets. President Cleveland, largely influenced by fiscal difficulties, had thrown down the gauntlet on the tariff question in his famous message of 1887; that was the issue in the election of 1888; the Republicans, having elected President Harrison and a Congressional majority, passed the McKinley act of 1890. Their defeat in 1892 led to the Wilson "free trade" act passed by the Democrats in 1894. The return of the Republicans to power in 1896 was naturally followed by the Act of 1897 with its accentuated protective duties. Among all in the list the tariff of 1909 was least occasioned by a specific exigency; yet the financial crisis of 1907 and the contested election of 1908 were factors. That of 1913, with its lowered rates, was the result of the Democratic victory in the election of 1912. Finally, the act of 1922 is explicable from the nationalistic feeling fostered by the war and the disastrous economic collapse of 1920–21.

Nothing of this sort can be said in explanation of the tariff of 1930. There had been no political overturn. The tariff question had played no part in the presidential election of 1928. Neither party had made a demand for general revision, upward or downward. There was no economic pressure. Not only during the campaign, but during most of the time when the measure was under consideration, the country was at the top of a boom. Although the familiar bogie of impending breadlines under free trade was trotted out here and there in the course of the campaign, there was no whisper of existing distress from that sinister cause. The crisis of the autumn of 1929 did not occur until the character of the measure was settled. The most that was alleged on the score of industrial distress was the plea, made during the last month or two of debate, that some settlement of the tariff uncertainty would help toward starting the wheels of business again.

The explanation of the act of 1930, then, must be sought in other directions. It turns on some peculiarities in the economic conditions of the decade 1920–30, and especially on those of the agricultural situation. What part these played will appear in the narrative of the proceedings of Congress.

A special session was called by President Hoover for June of 1929; it was to deal primarily with the agricultural situation. All that was suggested by him on the tariff was that duties on agricultural products should be raised by way of helping the farmers, and that any manufacturing industries 'that were seriously depressed should be helped in the same way and on similar grounds. There was to be limited revision, to cure specific ills. This, it was hoped and expected, could be accomplished in comparatively short order. But the program came to nothing in the Committees that initiate and guide legislation and in the maneuvers of the leaders and steersmen of the dominant party. The special session dragged on, merged into the regular session in December, and the tariff law was not enacted until June, 1930.

The difficulty, as already intimated, was mainly in our political system. The accepted procedure, not new in 1930 but then more firmly established than in previous years, deserves description. In each of the two committees which deal with the tariff—that on Ways and Means in the House and that on Finance in the Senate—the traditions and methods are ideal for log-rolling. The House Committee consists of 25 members, of whom 15 are Republicans. The framing of a tariff bill is in the hands of the majority members; they simply present the

bill, once they have constructed it, to the minority for inspection. Each of the 15 Republicans is chairman of a
subcommittee of three which considers a particular
schedule—textiles, metals, chemicals. There is naturally
a tendency that each chairman shall be assigned to a
schedule because he represents constituencies interested
in that schedule. The Massachusetts member is likely to
be chairman of the subcommittee on textiles, the Penn-
sylvanian of that on iron and steel, and so on. Each subcommittee chairman has with him two other members,
and these in turn are chairmen of other subcommittees.
The chairman is naturally deferred to by the other two,
and in turn there is deference to these when they become
chairmen of the subcommittees on their articles. At a
meeting of party members as a body (that is, the 15 Republicans) each subcommittee has its program, reached
by the process of give and take; and each member lets
the others have their way, provided his own proposals
are not interfered with. There are public hearings before the Committee as a whole; but the inside party committees have none such,—they act in seclusion. There
could scarcely be a more effective device for trading.

In the Senate, while the procedure in important respects
is different, the outcome is much the same. The rules
and ways of the upper house are different from those of
the lower. More particularly, the Senate Committee on
Finance is unable to control the course of legislation as
firmly as the Ways and Means Committee in the House.

The Senate Committee has nineteen members, of whom eleven are Republicans, and eight are Democrats. It divides its work on the tariff between subcommittees as is the case in the House, and the presiding officer for each subcommittee is a member of the majority (Republican) party. But each also has members from the minority party, and the hearings are formal and open. After these hearings, the eleven Republicans get together "informally" and prepare the tariff bill. What discussions take place in these private meetings, what influence the chairman of a subcommittee has on his schedule, what is the amount of give and take between them all, can only be guessed. Most important, as just intimated, is the circumstance that there are no Senate rules for closure, that debate on the floor can be indefinitely prolonged, and that amendments can be proposed and pushed by individual Senators. There is thus give and take within the Committee; but when the Senate finally acts, it is with confusion and often with inconsistency.

In either body the only possibility of critical control or adherence to any guiding principle is in an able, firm, far-seeing chairman—some one with the qualities of a leader and statesman. But here again the system and the traditions are not propitious. Chairmen in both houses are appointed by seniority. While this is merely a matter of precedent and tradition, it yet is so firmly settled as to have become unwritten law. The member longest in service automatically becomes the committee head. Let a man get a start on a committee, and let him be steadily reelected by his district or state, and he is sure to become in time its chairman. The system is not without its advantages. It does prevent bargaining between factions and individuals about the chairmanships, and does prevent favoritism and intrigue in the selection. And on rare occasions, in times of stress and of unmistakable need for strong leadership in a given committee, there is departure from the system. But under the usual conditions it gives no guarantee or even promise of competent leadership or consistent policy. On the tariff the log-rolling process goes on without mitigation.

The result in 1929 was a curious and unexpected one. The House Committee did make a half-hearted attempt at "limited revision." It was an open secret that in doing so it acted in conformity to the well-understood wishes of the President. But the attempt was no more than half-hearted. The tariff bill as reported by the Committee to the House contained concessions to the farmer element in the form of higher duties on agricultural products, but contained also a large number of increases in the rates on other goods—changes sometimes great and sometimes small, sometimes on important articles and again on petty ones. The House itself went even further. This and that Representative and district felt that fair treatment had not been accorded, and wanted a share in the largesse; and indeed the bill evidently represented no consistent policy, but merely the compromises and concessions within the Committee itself. The House revolted. Amendments were liberally accepted by the Committee, such as to bring about a distribution of favors all around. Everybody got pretty much what he wanted. Constructed in this fashion, the bill passed the House and made its way to the Senate. [1]

The Senate Committee on Finance dealt with the measure in much the same way. It is true there were premonitory symptoms of protest, and there was uneasiness about the policy of forcing the rates up all along the line. But the Senate Committee was no better fitted than that of the House for a firm handling of the matter. There too the traditional ways could not but lead to log-rolling and trading. True, the Committee had in Senator Smoot a

---

[1] The House bill went through three stages. (1) A first draft, made by the 15 Republican members contained not only the increase in agricultural rates, but a good number of others also; yet conformed fairly well to the President's proposal for limited revision. (2) A second draft was made, after much pressure from a caucus of the Republican members, containing a large number of other advances; this was submitted to the House. (3) A third draft then emerged, designed to conciliate opposition; there being amendments on the floor of the House offered *by the Committee*. These amendments advanced rates still further. No other amendments were considered, and indeed none could be considered. The Committee amendment had priority, and by the time these had been acted on, the hour fixed for the close of debate and for the final vote had come.

For an instructive account of the general legislative procedure during the session, see an article by A. W. Macmahon, in the *American Political Science Review* for Feb. 1930, pp. 38–59. In this article attention is more particularly given to the tactics followed with regard to the export debentures.

chairman who was experienced, and was respected for ability. But he was not only an out-and-out protectionist of the most intolerant stamp, but was strongly interested in his own region and its own product, beet sugar; not regarded as an impartial or disinterested person, and not entitled to be so regarded. To secure what he wanted for his people, he had to allow his colleagues what they wanted for theirs. The bill as reported by the Senate Committee was proclaimed to have more decreases from the House rate than increases. But here again there was no consistency. The changes were haphazard, a bit more here, a bit less there. They represented the familiar process of mutual concessions within the Committee. All pretense of limited revision disappeared.

Then came a veritable collapse. The representatives of the farmers, and especially those from the Northwestern and Mountain States, revolted. The insurgents had long complained that the manufacturing states, especially those of the East, had been getting the lion's share of the tariff favors. Now, even though the farmers were granted something in the way of higher duties on the agricultural products, the manufacturers, already overfavored, were getting more and still more. A smouldering resentment broke into open flame.

This outburst was not due solely, probably not in major part, to the way in which the tariff question was handled. It came chiefly because of a feeling that the farmers were not getting their fair share of legislative aid at large. The Republican leaders had not acceded to the demands for direct aid to agriculture through export bounties (disguised as export debentures). The Coolidge administration had been opposed to any and all schemes of this kind; and it was known that Mr. Hoover, as a member of the Coolidge cabinet, had been heartily in accord with this opposition. As President his stand in 1929 was overt and uncompromising. Under strong pressure from the White House the act for agricultural relief, passed by Congress earlier in the session, had been stripped of the export debenture provisions. The insurgents succeeded in again inserting these provisions in the tariff bill as an amendment in the Senate; eventually in the Conference between House and Senate they were cut out.

This ultimate outcome was not unforeseen, and the farmers felt that they were abandoned. During the presidential campaign the Republicans—and the Democrats not less—had made vague but vociferous promises to do something real for them. Higher duties on agricultural products were entirely welcome to them, and the Republican leaders were more than willing to give them all they wanted. But it was clear that this could not be of any large benefit to the farming constituencies; and the insurgents were in no mood to sanction the duties that were alleged to bring real and supposedly great benefit to the Eastern constituencies. A curious spectacle was presented. All hands agreed to pile on the agricultural duties; but on other commodities many proposed increases were summarily voted down by a Senate coalition of insurgents and Democrats. The Democrats were as little consistent as the members of the dominant party. While they joined in votes to make the agricultural duties higher, each member was quite frank, as regards other duties, in getting for his own constituents whatever could be got. In the main they were glad to make political capital by helping the insurgents in breaking up the plans of the Republican leaders.

Even more unexpected than the revolt of the insurgents was another overturn, which soon followed it and partly nullified it. Senator Grundy of Pennsylvania, a protectionist of the most rigorous stamp, newly appointed to a vacant seat by his Governor, took a hand. By turning to the approved and reliable method of mutual concessions, he engineered an arrangement with the insurgents by which rates on agricultural products were to be advanced, while in return those on industrial articles were to be similarly favored. The bargain was kept, to be sure, only in a half-hearted way. As the individual items were taken up in the Senate and became subject to amendment from the floor, the changes were sometimes in one direction, sometimes in another. There was no rhyme or reason in it all; a deviation from the agreement here, a return to it there; duties shoved up on one motion, then shoved down on the next. The situation toward the close of the Senate's proceedings was nothing less than chaotic. [1]

Finally, after a year of long and wearisome sessions in which all pretense of leadership oozed away, the bill passed the Senate, and went as usual to the Conference Committee of the two houses. And it was there, as usual, that the details were settled. The amendments made in the Senate had been numerous as well as haphazard. The House provisions, though they had been guided more firmly, were hardly based any more on a consistent policy. The Conference Committee necessarily proceeded with speed—such has always been the case under the pressure of the closing days of the session— and patched up a compromise in sessions that were doubtless the most wearisome of all. Inevitably there was again concession, give and take, exchange of favors. The details, some of them highly important, were settled by a few individuals; by what processes and under what exchanges and compromises, was as much shrouded in secrecy as in previous tariff settlements.

So shaped, or rather shapeless, the bill at last went to President Hoover. He was besieged—so it was reported and was indeed most probable—by innumerable letters and telegrams asking him to veto it. That the measure was not at all in accord with his recommendations and

[1] A compact statement of the Senate's action, with details concerning the votes, is in an article by A. W. Macmahon, in the *American Political Science Review,* Nov. 1930, pp. 920–926.

wishes was clear enough. Probably it might have been much more in accord with them if he had said at an early stage in the session that he would veto anything that went beyond "limited revision." But no such firm stand had been taken. When the bill finally came to him, he could hardly do otherwise than approve. His party could not go before the country stultified by having nothing whatever to show for a year's prolonged and conspicuous labor. Some faint pretense there was by him and the other party leaders that this was a good measure, or good enough, or not so bad. But the judgment of sober men of all parties, and even of the staunch protectionists, was that there had been a sad exhibition of political ineptitude.

One saving element was supposed to be in the modification and strengthening of the flexible provisions initiated in 1922. Here, it was said by the defenders, the means were provided for straightening out all kinks and for making the tariff system defensible. Before proceeding to this phase of the legislation, it may be well to look at some of the rates in detail.

First, the agricultural commodities. Among these sugar was the most significant. It has already been pointed out that the sugar tax, which in 1890 had been mainly one for revenue, had come to be the most important part of the protective system, surpassing in economic and political consequence the duties formerly dominant,—those on iron and steel, textiles, wool. It illustrated also better than any other the tortuous course of the legislative proceedings of 1929–30, and the absence in them of any controlling principle.

The duty on Cuban raw sugar—the rate which alone signifies—had been fixed at 1.76 cents per pound in 1922. It was put at 2.40 in the bill as passed by the House. The report of the Senate Finance Committee put it at 2.2 cents; the Senate Committee of the whole lowered it to 1.76 cents (the figure of 1922,—this was during the brief interval when the insurgents were in command and were "slashing" rates); the Senate, when at last it passed the bill, made the figure 2.0 cents; and in the law as finally enacted it became 2.0 cents.

The economic effects of the sugar duty have been dealt with in the preceding pages. During the decade 1920–30, as in the pre-war years, about one-half of the supply came from Cuba, the other half from the domestic and quasi-domestic (duty free) sources,—Louisiana, the beet-sugar states of the west, Hawaii, Porto Rico, the Philippines. The economic situation was by no means simple, yet in the main clear enough: an industry of great quantitative importance, in a state of depression which was in the main a long-continued aftermath of the war; clamoring for protection on which it was in part dependent and in part not; posing as a representative of the farmers, when in fact the great bulk of the farmers were affected only as consumers.

In the handling of the sugar duty during the session of 1929–30 one thing was even more clear. The supposed underlying principle of protection—the equalization of competitive conditions, through duties based on differences of cost—was in this case quite ignored. The sugar producers, especially the beet-sugar people, asked all they thought it possible to get; the Republicans in House and Senate gave them, more or less grudgingly, what seemed necessary to fulfill campaign pledges and to hold their party associates in line. The final rate was merely the result of give and take, maneuvering and compromise.

It is to be admitted that the difference in cost was by no means easy to measure. The case of sugar presented in extreme form the difficulties in the way of applying the principle. The notion that there is one uniform cost abroad and another uniform cost at home, and that comparison between them is a simple matter, probably holds good in no case whatever. There are varying costs for every article, both within the country and without. The range and the nature of the differences are hard to make out. Even when accurate accounting data are to be had, and are carefully analyzed and compared, the best that can be done is to settle on some approximate and fairly representative figure. Sugar presented an extreme case of the kind, the cost figures showing a perplexing variety on both sides of the customs line. There was the added complication that the strictly domestic production of sugar, in Louisiana and the beet-sugar regions, was comparatively small, and that the quasi-domestic output in Hawaii, Porto Rico, and the Philippines, was very large. The sugar from these regions was affected by the duty quite as much as that of strictly United States production; but the domestic producers regarded the dependencies as outsiders, as rivals and competitors, having no claim to aid such as the farmers deserve. And even for the Louisiana and the beet-sugar producers the final figures of cost showed very large disparities. The Tariff Commission's inquiry in 1922–23 brought into sharp relief still another difficulty, namely, that the bias of the inquirer affects the conclusions. According as he is an unrelenting protectionist or a moderate one or an anti-protectionist, his figure is different. A majority of the Commission (at this time made up of five members only, there being one vacancy) put the difference in cost at 1.23 cents; a minority of two, more uncompromisingly protectionist, found it to be at least as high as the rate then in effect, 1.76 cents. A fair-minded, well-equipped and well-trained observer, Mr. P. G. Wright, concluded that a figure somewhere between 1.25 and 1.50 would conform to the existing differences of cost between American and Cuban producers. [1]

The thing important for the present discussion is that such figuring played no part in the doings of 1929–30. The plea was that the price of sugar was low, and that something must be done for the farmers (chiefly in the Mountain States) who grew sugar beets. No one pre-

---

[1] P. G. Wright, *Sugar in Relation to the Tariff,* 1924, p. 246.

tended that the difference in cost was greater than it had
been ten years before or five years before. There was
depression, felt not only by the growers but by the manufacturers who buy the beets and sell the manufactured
sugar. Recovery from the post-war collapse had been
slow; foreign and domestic producers alike had to face
low prices. But there was no suggestion that the *difference* between the two in cost and price had changed—that
there was anything in the relative figures to give occasion
for a higher duty.

The same policy—concession to the farmers, little
bother about the cost principle—appeared in the rates on
other agricultural articles. Among these, some were important and some trivial; but there was a similarity of
spirit in the handling of all.

Among the important articles was wheat; though it is
to be noted that, while the article was important, the
duty was much less so. The duty had been 30 cents a
bushel in 1922. That was thought a high rate; it was
explicable not only by the then depressed state of farming, but by the post-war burst of nationalism and protection. The Tariff Commission subsequently made an investigation of costs—the difference of costs between the
United States and Canada for hard winter wheat—and
had recommended a rate of 42 cents a bushel, which was
put into effect in 1924. That figure was retained in the
act of 1930,—42 cents a bushel.

The cost investigation in this case illustrated another

difficulty in the application of the principle, arising from the influence of climatic conditions and in crop fluctuations from season to season. The Tariff Commission's calculations of cost had been made for a period of three years. During these, as it happened, the rain-fall (the dominant factor) had been favorable for Canada, unfavorable for the United States. This divergence led to an appearance of great difference in costs. Almost immediately afterwards, the climatic conditions had turned the other way. If the difference in cost had been investigated in the same way for a longer period—five years or ten—there would have been quite another showing. The figuring of costs is a particularly difficult and dubious matter in the case of agricultural commodities; most of all in the United States, where the farmers' spokesmen have thought it necessary to curry favor with the farmers by exaggerating their ill fortune. The necessity for eliminating climatic variations, obvious in all cases, is particularly important for the wheat growing North West, where all depends on an irregular and somewhat precarious precipitation. No one could reasonably suppose that there was really a continuing difference in cost such as happened to appear for the three year period covered by the Tariff Commission and used as the basis of the duty of 42 cents. None the less the opportunity to do something for the farmers by raising the duty on wheat was welcomed by the Tariff Commission in 1924–25 and by Congress in 1930, and the duty, to repeat was left at that figure.

Another important commodity was cotton; and here not only was the commodity important, but the full weight of the duty was certain to be felt. Raw cotton of the grade grown in the South had been free of duty from time immemorial—it was obvious that no duty could signify. But now cotton of long staple (that only) was subjected to a duty of seven cents a pound.[1] This grade, used chiefly for cotton knit goods, had long been supplied solely by importation, almost all from Egypt. The Imperial Valley—that remarkable low lying region, transformed from a desert to a garden by irrigation from the Colorado river—had been found advantageous for raising it. The cotton growers there, like the fruit growers in California, who had long been almost ferociously insistent on duties for their products, were clamorous to have a share of the legislative favors. The planters of the South at large were naturally lukewarm, but quite as naturally were unready to object.

The item had a curious and not uninstructive course in the legislative history of the act. Cotton had been left free in the bill as passed by the House, still free in the bill as presented to the Senate by the Finance Committee of that body. But in the Senate Committee of the Whole, at the stage when the insurgents were in command and were determined as well as incensed, the Senate inserted a duty of seven cents. To the Westerners it

---

[1] The same duty had been in force during the short period of the Emergency Act of 1921.

seemed that the Eastern cotton manufacturers were opposed to a duty which the growers wanted,—another in the long standing list of grievances. This amendment was not eliminated from the bill as passed by the Senate or as it ran the gauntlet of the Conference Committee. It is not easy to guess how it came to be retained in the sessions of that potent and secretive body, but finally incorporated in the act it was.

Another much discussed set of agricultural articles were the meat and dairy products. Here, too, the farmers got what they wanted. The duty on cattle went up from figures running ½ to 2 cents a pound to higher ones of 2½ to 3 cents; that on beef from 3 cents to 6 cents. On sheep the advance was from 2½ to 5 cents, on mutton and lamb from 4 to 7 cents. On swine it was from ½ to 2 cents, on ham and bacon from 3 cents to 3¼ cents; with which may be noted that on corn from 15 to 25 cents a bushel. On milk and cream the duties were nearly tripled; on butter and eggs were raised less. Live poultry also felt a heavy hand,—8 cents a pound instead of 3 cents.

Related to the duty on meat, yet presenting economic problems quite different, was that on hides. Here, as has been already pointed out, [1] there were large and continuing imports, as well as great domestic production. And here, as in previous years, there was divergence of interest between the producers of raw material and the

---

[1] See above p. 378.

manufacturers. The shoe manufacturers in general
wanted hides and leather to remain free, as they had been
in 1922, and were willing that shoes should remain free
if hides also remained free. But some manufacturers of
particular grades wanted duties on shoes. The situation
in the manufacturing industry was of the sort familiar in
tariff history; an enormous domestic production, imports small but special qualities continuing to come in
(vagaries of fashion); a spurt for the time being of larger
imports of the special sort. The final outcome was a duty
of 10 per cent on hides, 15 per cent on leather, 20 per
cent on shoes.[1]

Some of the other changes in agricultural duties were
mere pretense; others meant something but not much;
still others might raise questions of larger significance.
Futile were the higher duties on swine and their meat, and
on corn. These things were articles of export, not of
import. To give the farmers higher duties on them was
a continuation of the old process of trying to throw dust

---

[1] The vagaries of the session are again illustrated by the ups and
downs of the hide duty. Briefly the history was:

Duty on hides

In the bill as passed by the House....................15%
"   "   "   " presented to the Senate by the Finance
              Committee.............................17½
"   "   "   " fixed by the Senate in Committee of
              the Whole............................free
"   "   "   " passed by the Senate..................free
"   "   "   " enacted 10%

in their eyes.[1] Dairy products were in the main a matter of domestic trade only. The duties on them were of significance chiefly for the border trade with Canada,—the most obviously advantageous case of a trade labelled "foreign," but clearly akin to the domestic trade between our States. The duties had local effect here and there, and so were not entirely negligible, yet in their bearing on the nation as a whole and on the farmers as a body were again hardly more than a gesture. Their important and lamentable effect was to irritate and even incense our neighbor across the border and seriously jeopardize friendly relations with them.

Of greater significance were the meat duties (other than on swine). They were of real importance, how-

---

[1] The Tariff Commission in 1928 went through the motions of making an investigation on the differences in cost of production for corn in Argentina and the United States. A few shiploads of corn—enough for a little chicken-feed—had happened to be sent to New York and San Francisco. Transportation as a cost played a great part in the Commission report. Half of the commissioners, strongly protectionist in spirit, reckoned as part of the "cost" of American corn the transportation charges by rail from the corn belt to San Francisco, which was supposed by them to be the "principal competing market"; and by thus loading the American cost, reached a figure of 35 cents as representing the excess of American over Argentine cost. The other half, less protectionist, treated New York as the principal market, and made the difference 12 cents a bushel. All the figuring was of a dubious sort; and the President, naturally and wisely, did nothing. The duty had been 15 cents a bushel in 1922; it is made 25 cents in 1930. The report of the Commission in this case is an example, unfortunately not the only one in its history, of ill-directed effort.

ever, not so much in relation to the tariff but because symptomatic of larger matters: the consumption within the country of all that was produced of these things, and the cessation of the exports. It became possible, even though not likely to be on a considerable scale for the time being, that some part of the consumption of the seaboard regions of the East would come to be supplied from Argentina. A new stage in economic development was setting in: the growing-up of the country to its agricultural capacities. Only the very first steps in this transition were now entered on, and years were likely to elapse before it went far. But the question began to loom up whether the United States was to adopt a policy not merely of fostering manufactures and a varied industrial structure, but one of complete self-sufficiency; a question of wider concern, economic, social, and international, than anything directly suggested or even considered in the debates. The chief thing then considered was the importation of "feeder cattle" from western Canada, whose competition with similar cattle from our own western ranges was thought dire. It was another case of border trade.

There was a long list of changes that were petty, such as must have made it difficult for the spokesmen of the farmers themselves to keep a sober face. Cabbages, celery, eggplant, lettuce, turnips, green peas and beans, tomatoes, clover seed, blue-berries,—all felt the heavy hand. So did hay and potatoes; obviously affected by the tariff merely at spots along the border, according to the transportation expenses of these bulky things. The Californians were appeased by higher duties on lemons, limes, grapefruit, plums, and prunes. The duty on tulip and narcissus bulbs was tripled; somehow these were dealt with as if the farmers were concerned. Onions and tomatoes, too, were hit hard; here, while some truck-farmers might be affected by early supplies from our Southern neighbors, the imports could not be more than a small fraction in the total consumption.

As I have already remarked, the representatives of the farmers were ready enough to accept and even demand higher duties on each and every agricultural product. Yet they could not but feel that few of them meant anything. Onions, tomatoes, cabbages, turnips, blueberries, peanuts —what of it all? No; if there was to be legislation for helping the farmers, it must be in other ways. The accepted line of action being that of direct relief for people who were in difficulties, the inevitable demand was that, so far as the tariff *not* be of such help, something else should be done. Hence the insistent pressure for aid to the farmers on similar lines, but really effective aid. The farmers were to get the essential benefit of the tariff— higher prices for their products than could be got under free trade—by some sort of bounty. Since they must of necessity sell abroad at the free trade price, let the equivalent of a tariff rate be secured to them at home. The devices proposed for securing this end were various, and their details do not concern us. It was the export deben-

ture plan that was fought for in 1930, and finally was
rejected by Congress. What is significant is the contention of the farmers that they must have, not mere sops,
but a real share in the favors that were being distributed.[1]

The contention was unanswerable. As the farmers and
the political insurgents saw it, the protective system being
with us once for all, its benefits and burdens should
be distributed impartially. Inevitably they were angered
when higher and higher duties were proposed on the
manufactured articles, and their own scheme for substantial aid to agriculture was swept aside. Thus the
duties on their products, inevitably futile as regards any
relief or even mitigation of the farmers' distresses, proved
no less futile politically.

On manufactured products, there was no such guiding
line of action as on the agricultural. For the latter,
higher duties all around had been promised, and they were
freely granted. On the manufactures nothing had been
promised except "limited revision," i.e. for industries that
could show they were in distress. The unexpected
vagaries of the session, the ups and downs of political

---

[1] On the duties on agricultural products, see J. D. Black, *Agricultu-
ral Reform in the United States,* ch. vii; a pamphlet on *Agricultural
Tariffs* by B. H. Hibbard and others, published in 1929 by the Raw-
leigh Bureau, Freeport, Ill.; and an article by P. G. Wright in the
Tariff Review, Nov. 1929. On the export debenture plan see J. S.
Davis, *The Farm Export Debenture Plan,* 1929; and for a general
discussion of the agricultural situation and the plan for relief, J. D.
Black, *op. cit.* Both are important.

alignment and legislative trading, led to much more. But it was often a matter of accident whether the proponents of a higher duty got what they wanted. Except for the one generalization that no duty was reduced in a way to matter to any domestic producer,[1] all that can be said is that the outcome will be chaotic.

Among the textile industries, the cotton manufacture more particularly presented claims on the ground of depression. Yet so much had been done for it in previous acts, and the structure of high protection had been so systematically built up, that little could be added. The complicated arrangement of duties set up in 1922 was retained, the figures being set somewhat higher. Indicative of the general trend are the ad valorem rates on the finer goods; they had been in general 45 per cent in 1922, and were now run up as high as 62½ per cent, and on some goods (e.g. the finer handkerchiefs) even as high as 67½ per cent. The real cause of trouble for the manufacture of most grades of cotton—indeed of all grades that weigh heavily in the domestic industry—was the extraordinary growth in the South; a semi-artificial and almost insensate growth, much promoted by a use of night-

---

[1] An exception to this generalization, but one instructive in another way as regards the tenor of the act, is the relegation to the free list of ammonium sulphate, an important ingredient in fertilizers. The act of 1922 had imposed a duty of ¼ cent a pound (about 12 per cent). The making of synthetic ammonia is a new and rapidly growing industry, such as would ordinarily be fostered under a highly protectionist policy; but here was another chance to show favor to the farmers, and the article was admitted free.

work so widespread as to shame our civilization. For the finer grades, the competition of rayon goods and the fashion of scant clothes for women were the main factors in the depression; and no advance of duties could be a remedy.

For woolens there was less claim on the ground of special depression; though the worsted branch was much affected, as indeed was the industry the world over, by the changes in fashion. As with cottons, so with woolens, the existing schematic arrangement of the duties was left untouched, but the rates were advanced on the finer goods. On these the ad valorem duty (i.e. protective part), which had been 50 per cent in 1922, was now made 60 per cent. It was these finer goods—the expensive qualities of cloths and dress goods—that alone were imported in any considerable degree, though the imports were still negligible compared to the total domestic production. The trend was the same as had appeared in the long series of tariff acts since 1867: persistent screwing up of the duties on the goods which cannot be made to advantage in this country, and yet failure to achieve the end apparently in view—that of shutting out the very last scrap of imported goods.

On silks the same sort of thing was done, but in this case without its being possible to allege any depression at all; the industry had prospered and grown mightily through the decade. Most silk goods were left as before, but here again the rates were made higher on the few fabrics that continued to come in. Among them the one bulking largest among the imports (and at that only a few millions' worth) was velvets; the rate was advanced from 60 to 65 per cent. The same increase appeared on silk apparel, and in the dragnet clause on silk manufactures not otherwise provided for.

There were sporadic changes on various other manufactures. On chinaware they were analogous to those in the textile list. Some grades here also continued to be imported, and in larger proportions than for the textiles. The duty on decorated china, already raised to 70 per cent in 1922, was again increased, by adding to this ad valorem rate a specific duty of 10 cents a dozen. Surgical instruments, put at 45 per cent in 1922, now were 55 per cent (the House bill had even proposed 70 per cent). Scientific glass instruments, on which the duty had been made 65 per cent in 1922, were now set at 85 per cent. On pocket-knives there was a petty advance, which is worth noting because indicative of the general petty procedure. Very high and complicated duties had been imposed in 1922. [1] In 1930 they were left untouched except for one item. On the very cheapest knives, worth 40 cents a dozen or less, the specific duty (additional to an ad valorem duty of 50 per cent) had been made 1 cent apiece in 1922. It now was just a bit higher—1¼ cents. On this lowest grade the compound duty of 1922

---

[1] On these rates in 1922, see pp. 470, 471, above.

(ad valorem and specific combined) had already been equivalent to 85 per cent; while on the other grades the range had been from 95 to 170 per cent. The very high rates on all the better grades had proved prohibitive of importation; but small imports of the cheapest grade still came in (a beggarly $100,000 a year). So here an attempt was made to get a higher duty, but in the end with only the slight advance just noted.[1]

An amusing list can be made of a series of duties that pursued the family from top to bottom. For the men, straw hats were subjected to much higher duties,—even higher than the Tariff Commission had recommended under the flexible provisions. The duty of 1922 had been equivalent to 60%, partly specific and partly ad valorem; the new one was about 150%. Women came in for attention of a similar sort; their leather gloves "embroidered or embellished" went from 70% to a compound rate equivalent to 140%. The children were not forgotten. The toy duties of 1922, one of the absurdities of that measure, were in general retained,—toys at 70%, dolls at 90%; but

---

[1] The history of the act shows that some individual producer and his (or their?) legislative representative pressed hard for getting a great increase on this small item. In the bill as passed by the House the specific duty had been 2 cents apiece; as reported by the Senate Finance Committee, 4 cents; as amended in the Committee of the Whole (insurgents!), 1 cent—i. e. the duty of 1922 unchanged; this refusal to advance the rate remained in the bill as passed by the Senate; finally it emerged from the Conference Committee with 1¼ cents.

some very cheap celluloid dollies were now subjected to still higher duties, again compound, equivalent to 160%. The boys naturally could not be let off more easily than the girls; and fire-crackers of the cheapest grades, which had been 8 cents a pound in 1922, now were put at 25 cents (about 135% on the value). Young and old were treated alike!

More important in industrial effect was a large increase in the duties on watch and clock movements—a complicated schedule, administratively bad, with compound duties (partly specific, partly ad valorem) graded according to the value of the articles. A curious case of duties lowered, and one illustrating again the tortuous history of the measure, is that of aluminum utensils; something in which householders were supposed to be interested, and in which the Secretary of the Treasury, dominant in the aluminum monopoly, was supposed also to be interested. The rate in 1922 had been 11 cents per pound plus 55 per cent. The House bill reduced it a trifle, to 11 cents plus 50 per cent; the Finance Committee left it there; the insurgents in the Senate cut it drastically, to 25 per cent flat, and so the bill as passed by the Senate left it; finally it emerged from the Conference Committee, and was fixed in the act, at 8½ cents plus 40 per cent—a lower rate than that of 1922, but still amply high enough to keep the imports down to a negligible figure. The metal itself (aluminum) on the other hand, came out with an increased duty. The figure had been 2 cents a pound in

1922. The House bill made it 5 cents, the Senate Committee left it at 5 cents, the insurgents cut it to 2 cents on the floor of the Senate; the Conference Committee settled it at 4 cents.

Some indication of the general trend in the act is given by a comparison of the average ad valorem rates, computed for each schedule. The averages stated below are reached by taking the imports for 1928, computing the duties then actually collected under the act of 1922 and their per cent on the imports, and then computing what would have been the per cent on the same imports if the duties of 1930 had been in force. Figures of this sort must be used with care; but they do indicate the direction in which the rates moved. They are taken from a compilation made by the Tariff Commission immediately after the passage of the act. It will be seen that there is some advance in each and every schedule, and that the greatest change is in the agricultural schedule.

AVERAGE RATES, BY SCHEDULES, IN THE TARIFF ACTS OF
1922 AND OF 1930

	Act of 1922 per cent	Act of 1930 per cent
1. Chemicals, oils, and paints	29.22	31.40
2. Earths, earthenwares, and glassware	45.62	53.62
3. Metals and manufactures of	33.71	35.01
4. Wood and manufactures of	7.97	10.49
5. Sugar, molasses, and manufactures of	67.85	77.21
6. Tobacco and manufactures of	63.09	64.78
7. Agricultural products and provisions	19.86	33.62
8. Spirits, wines, and other beverages	36.48	47.44
9. Manufactures of cotton	40.27	46.42

10. Flax, hemp, jute, and manufactures of....18.16   19.14
11. Wool and manufactures of.............49.54   59.83
12. Manufactures of silk....................56.56   59.13
13. Manufactures of rayon..................52.68   53.62
14. Paper and books.......................24.72   26.06
15. Sundries 21.97   27.39

Regarded as a whole, the act of 1930 must be characterized as futile. The new duties on manufactured goods were mostly of a petty sort; most noticeably so in such schedules as the cotton, silk, chinaware schedules. This or that article was more heavily taxed, and doubtless some domestic producers got an advantage. On the important branches of these industries the protective system had already been carried so far that no considerable further displacement of imports could be expected. As regards the odds and ends, the general economic conditions were such that imports were likely to flow in still.

Something more may be said here, even at the risk of repeating what has been said in earlier chapters, on the persistence of imports such as these, even in the face of duties raised again and again. The goods which continue to come in are in the main those to which much hand labor has been applied; things not made on a large scale with power and machinery. Among them some are particularly cheap, some are particularly dear; the poorest instruments and tools, and again the most exquisitely delicate. Often they present curious economic problems, being the results of eddies and cross currents that are outside the usual channels of trade. The domestic producer who wants to make one of them may succeed in working the Congressional procedure—his Congressman, the House and Senate Committees, the Conference Committee—so as to put through the precise kind and size of duty that will enable him to displace the foreigner. But often he will find that the imported article is not of the sort easily made with profit in a country where the great-scale industries are bidding high for good labor and keeping up the wages of good men. Quite probably, also, he will find that by the time he has set up his plant, laboriously learned it all, and got ready to supply the markets satisfactorily and in quantity, tastes and fashions have changed. "Something different" is wanted. Rapid adjustment to shifts in demand is not among the characteristics of a country with large plants and standardized ways. What with the continuance of demand for some of the old approved articles on the import list, the emergence of new specialties with changes in fashion and taste, the real and continuing advantages which other countries possess for one article and another—all these factors considered, the imports persist, and a certain minimum will always come in.

For the agricultural commodities, the same general characterization applies,—futility. The preceding account has indicated how the new duties were likely to be futile in their economic effects. They were even more so as moves in the game of politics. The farmers were not placated. The Republicans were in a dilemma from which they could not extricate themselves. They had proclaimed year after year that theirs was the party of prosperity, and that the high tariff was the grand instrument of prosperity. They had vociferously alleged that high duties were the cure for agricultural ills, and they could not do otherwise than apply their remedy. But, as must have been clear to the wiser heads amongst them, this was no panacea. When it came to sweeping government aid to the farmers, those same wiser heads had to face the hard fact that in reality there was no panacea, and the more drastic nostrums were rejected. The only hope was that the period of distress and distraction would run its course, and that some fortunate turn of crop variation and industrial recuperation would enable the party to say once more that it had saved the day. But for the time being there was nothing even in this part of the tariff act to save it from indifference, even disdain.

A measure passed under such conditions could satisfy no one. Hence more and more attention was given to the possibility of a change in system, through the delegation of power to the Tariff Commission.

The Tariff Commission, it will be recalled, had been designed at the start to be merely an investigating body, one to ascertain the facts and clear the air. While a long step was taken in 1922 toward making it something more, —a quasi-legislative board with powers to modify rates under the cost-difference principle,—its original functions were not disturbed. Even though the new powers and duties absorbed most of its energies and funds, it continued to make investigations and to maintain a portfolio of informational data. Much had been hoped from work of this kind. The ten year experience after the war, the period during which the Tariff Commission had a chance to function, did something toward justifying these hopes. Administrative features were clarified and improved. The lines of classification in adjusting complicated duties (for instance, on chemicals, cotton textiles, wool) were more carefully laid down. Few of these changes, however, were of large consequence. During the session of 1929–30, as during that of 1922–23, Congress in the main went the same old way. Congressional Committees indeed utilized the material of the Tariff Commission, and borrowed copiously from its documents and from its experts. But it was done chiefly for making points in debates or in Committee hearings, or for enabling a Congressman to see just what the figures meant for his party or his constituents. There was nothing in the experience of the decade to show that the essential problems were handled in Congress with a different result or in a different spirit.

Nor can it be said that the new and stronger powers given the Commission in 1922—the flexible provisions—improved the general situation. The Commission made a number of investigations and recommended a number of changes, and sundry duties were readjusted. These matters absorbed most of its attention and most of its funds. But there were great drawbacks and sad defects. Among the drawbacks, the most obvious was the time taken for investigations and findings. As I have already said, the ascertainment of costs in the United States and abroad is at best a difficult matter, and some time must be taken for it. But the Commission followed a pedantic procedure. It pretended to achieve the impossible—figures exact to a fraction of a cent. It should have taken short cuts, reached results approximate and sufficiently accurate, and on this basis made prompt reports. There was more than this to criticize; not only errors of judgment, but dissension and bad spirit. There were quarrels within the Commission which made conspicuous the main defect. The Tariff Commission was supposed to be a judicial body, standing aloof from any controversial questions, not biased by any beliefs which its members might entertain on general economic policies. It was sadly lacking in any such spirit. Too obviously its leading members were actuated in their conclusions by a wish to make protection higher, and to shape and interpret the cost figures so as to bring about higher duties. The protectionists themselves, while quite willing and even glad to accept the results, could not feel respect for a body which obviously was not holding to a high standard.

This record of ill performance was chiefly the result

of bad traditions and practices which infect the whole of the government's machinery. The spirit of the dominant party was all against any real change from the traditional ways. The Tariff Commission was accepted not as a step toward reform but as a sop to the business critics and the reformers. After the Republicans came into power in 1921, there was inevitably pressure for the appointment of men who would represent this or that section of the country, and "look out" for its interests. And the political conditions of the decade were unfavorable to a high standard. President Harding had been active in securing the adoption of the flexible provisions, but in the appointments to the Commission which was to administer them he followed the good old ways of accommodating friends and associates. President Coolidge cannot be said to have attained, at least in this part of the government's work, to a higher level. The make-up of the Commission was not such as to command respect either for intellectual capacity or for judicial spirit.

All this experience, however, discouraging though it might be, was not to be set down as conclusive. Moves for improvement in our political system proceed by slow steps. There is no immediate attainment of the goal, but trial and error, sobered sense, gradual advance. The various Commissions established of late by the Federal Government—the Interstate Commerce Commission, the Federal Trade Commission, even the Federal Reserve Board—all had this sort of history. The politicians tried to feather their nests; the "interests" tried to shape the new political instruments to their ends. As time went on, standards became higher. There was still much to be said in favor of the permanent Tariff Commission, on the supposition that it could be made up of high-minded and able men, ready to carry out loyally the policy laid down by the legislature, desirous of doing so in the right spirit and in the best way.

It was this sort of feeling that affected the provisions in the Act of 1930. As regards the powers and duties of the Commission no changes of moment were made. There had been proposals for modification, but in the end nothing came of them. The machinery remained the same: investigation of differences in cost of production, report to the President and "determination" of a new duty by him. The powers of the Commission were restricted, as before: it could not make (i.e. recommend) increases or decreases which would change rates by more than 50 per cent; and it could not remove articles from the dutiable list to the free list, or vice versa. It was perhaps of moment that the Commission was required to make investigations, not only of its own motion, but on request of the President, and on resolution by either House of Congress.

The outstanding change was in regard to personnel. The terms of office of the existing Commissioners were abruptly cut off, and the President was empowered to set up an entirely new body, re-appointing incumbents or not as he saw fit. The salary was raised (from $7,500 to $11,000) by way of making it easier to secure men of the desired quality. The hope was that a Commission completely remade would not only command greater respect and improve the details of the schedules, but would modify "inequitable" or "unjust" or "unwarranted" rates, and make the tariff "right." What could be accomplished in this direction, lies at this writing (1930) in the lap of the gods.

APPENDIX.

Imports, Duties, and Ratio of Duties to Imports, 1860–1907.

(*From the* " Statistical Abstract.")

(00,000 omitted.)

Fiscal Year Ending June 30.	Imports.			Duties Collected.	Per cent. of Duties to Dutiable Imports.	Per cent. of Duties to Total Imports.
	Free.	Dutiable.	Total.			
1860	68.4	267.9	336.3	52.7	19.67	15.67
1	67.4	207.2	274.6	39.0	18.84	14.21
2	49.8	128.5	178.3	46.5	36.19	26.09
3	30.0	195.3	225.4	63.7	32.62	28.28
4	38.2	262.9	301.1	96.5	36.69	32.03
5	40.1	169.6	209.6	80.6	47.56	38.46
6	57.1	366.3	423.5	177.0	48.93	41.81
7	17.0	361.1	378.2	168.5	46.67	44.56
8	15.1	329.7	344.8	160.5	48.63	46.49
9	21.7	372.7	394.4	176.5	47.22	44.65
1870	20.2	406.1	426.3	191.5	47.08	42.23
1	40.6	459.6	500.2	202.4	43.95	38.94
2	47.7	512.7	560.4	212.6	41.35	37.00
3	178.4	484.7	663.1	184.9	38.07	26.95
4	151.7	415.7	567.4	160.5	38.53	26.88
5	146.5	379.8	526.3	154.5	40.62	28.20
6	140.6	324.0	464.6	145.2	44.74	30.19
7	140.8	299.0	439.8	128.4	42.89	26.68
8	141.3	297.1	438.4	127.2	42.75	27.13
9	142.5	296.7	439.3	133.4	44.87	28.97
1880	208.0	419.5	627.5	182.7	43.48	29.07
1	202.5	448.1	650.6	193.8	43.20	29.75
2	210.7	505.5	716.2	216.1	42.66	30.11
3	206.9	493.9	700.8	210.6	42.45	29.92
4	211.3	456.3	667.6	190.3	41.61	28.44
5	192.9	386.7	579.6	178.1	45.86	30.59
6	211.5	413.8	625.3	189.4	45.55	30.13
7	233.1	450.3	683.4	214.2	47.10	31.02
8	244.1	468.1	712.2	216.0	45.63	29.99
9	256.6	484.8	741.4	220.6	45.13	29.50
1890	266.1	507.6	773.7	226.5	44.41	29.12
1	388.1	466.4	854.5	216.9	46.28	25.25
2	458.1	355.5	813.6	174.1	48.71	21.26
3	444.2	400.3	844.4	199.1	49.58	23.49
4	379.0	257.6	636.6	129.6	50.06	20.25
5	376.9	354.3	731.2	149.4	41.75	20.23
6	368.9	390.8	759.7	157.0	40.18	20.67
7	381.9	407.3	789.2	172.7	42.41	21.89

Imports.

Fiscal Year Ending June 30.	Free.	Dutiable.	Total.	Duties Collected.	Per cent. of Duties to Dutiable Imports.	Per cent. of Duties to Total Imports.
1898	291.5	295.6	587.1	145.4	48.80	24.77
9	299.7	385.8	685.4	202.0	52.07	29.48
1900	366.8	463.8	830.5	229.4	49.24	27.62
1	339.1	468.7	807.8	233.6	49.64	28.91
2	396.5	503.2	899.8	251.5	49.78	27.95
3	437.3	570.7	1,008.0	280.7	49.03	27.85
4	454.1	527.7	981.8	258.2	48.78	26.30
5	517.1	570.0	1,087.1	258.4	45.24	23.77
6	548.7	664.7	1,213.4	293.9	44.16	24.22
7	641.9	773.4	1,415.4	329.5	42.55	23.28
8	525.7	657.4	1,183.1	282.3	42.94	23.88
9	599.4	682.3	1,281.6	294.4	43.15	22.99
1910	761.4	785.8	1,547.1	326.3	41.52	21.11
11	777.0	751.0	1,527.9	309.6	41.22	20.29
12	881.5	759.2	1,640.7	304.6	40.12	18.56
13	987.0	780.0	1,767.0	312.3	40.05	17.69
14	1,152.4	754.1	1,907.0	284.0	37.60	14.88
15	1,033.0	616.0	1,648.4	206.0	33.43	12.49
16	1,496.0	683.2	2,179.1	210.0	30.67	9.62
17	1,853.0	815.0	2,667.3	221.5	27.18	8.31
18	2,118.0	747.4	2,865.0	180.2	24.11	6.30
Year Ending Dec. 31.						
1919	2,711.5	1,116.3	3,828.0	237.5	21.27	6.20
20	3,116.0	1,986.0	5,102.0	326.0	16.40	6.38
21	1,564.3	993.0	2,557.0	292.4	29.45	11.44
22	1,888.2	1,185.5	3,073.8	451.4	38.07	14.68
23	2,165.1	1,566.6	3,731.8	566.7	36.17	15.18
24	2,118.1	1,456.9	3,575.1	532.3	36.53	14.89
25	2,708.8	1,467.4	4,176.2	551.8	37.61	13.21
26	2,908.1	1,500.0	4,408.0	590.0	39.34	13.39
27	2,680.0	1,483.0	4,163.1	574.8	38.76	13.81
28	2,678.6	1,399.3	4,077.9	542.3	38.76	13.30
29	2,880.1	1,458.4	4,338.6	584.8	40.11	13.55

This table is taken from the "Statistical Abstract of the United States." The figures given in different editions of the "Statistical Abstract" have not always been

consistent. Those given in the table are from the edition
of 1891 for the earlier years (1860–68), and from the editions of 1895 and 1912 for the later years. They indicate
"net imports," *i.e.*, imports less re-exports, for 1860–66;
from 1867 on, they indicate "imports for consumption."
Substantially, these two forms of statement come to
nearly the same thing. The significant changes will
be easily noted. The sharp rise in the average rate (per
cent. of duties to imports) between 1861 and 1865 shows
the extent to which the legislation of the war affected the
general character of the tariff system. The average rate
on dutiable articles, after reaching its war maximum in
1866, declines somewhat for a few years thereafter. From
1872 to 1875, there is a further fall, in consequence of the
ten per cent. reduction of 1872 ; after 1875 the rate goes
up again, and then remains fairly steady until 1883. The
act of 1883 brings a distinct rise in the average rate on
dutiable articles ; the act of 1890 a still further rise, bringing in 1894 the maximum for the whole period (50.06 per
cent.). The abrupt increase in the free imports in 1873 is
the result of the abolition of the tea and coffee duties in
1872, which causes also the fall in the average per cent. of
the duties collected as compared with the total imports.
The abolition of the sugar duty in 1890 brings a similar
abrupt increase of the free imports in 1891 and 1892, and a
similar fall in the ratio of duties collected to total imports.
The act of 1894 brings a distinct lowering of the average
rate of duty ; that of 1897 raises the average to the figures

that had prevailed under the acts of 1883 and 1890. From 1897 to 1912 there is a slow decline in the average rate of duty, due to the circumstance that the free imports form a larger proportion of the total, which again is due to a tariff so high as often to prohibit the importation of dutiable articles. After 1913–14 there is a marked decline, due partly to the reductions in duty under the Act of 1913, but in good part to the fact that imports free of duty from non-European countries rose rapidly, in terms of money value, during the great war and immediately after its close.

INDEX

A

Adam Smith quoted, 364

Ad-valorem duties, 159, 303, 434, 518

Ad-valorem duty on woollens, 207, 293, 333, 340, 393, 428, 464, 514

Administrative sections of tariff of 1913, 443; of 1922, 477, 485; of 1930, 522

Agricultural products, duties of 1883, 248; of 1890, 274; in 1909, 367; free in 1913, 443; duties of 1922, 445; duties of 1930, 500, 520

Agricultural implements free in 1913, 441; in 1922, 455

Aldrich on tariff of 1909, 375

"American valuation" in 1922, 476, 477

Average rates of duty, 1860–1929, 528

B

Bar-iron, duty of 1883, 244

Beet-sugar and protection, 396, 426, 502

Blankets, duty of 1867, 205, 214; of 1883, 242

Books, duty of 1922, 471

C

Canada's tariff relation to U. S. in 1909, 402

Canada, reciprocity treaty with, defeated in 1910, 414

Carpets, duty of 1867, 214; of 1890, 266

Carpet wool, duty of 1867, 201; of 1883, 239; of 1890, 257; of 1897, 331; free in 1913, 427; duty of 1922, 461

Charcoal iron, 54, 131

Clay and the tariff, 74, 85, 96

Cleveland, on the tariff, 253, 256; does not sign act of 1894, 290, 320

Coal, duty in 1872, 185; in 1894, 298; in 1897, 342; in 1909, 380; free in 1913, 443, and in 1922, 471

Coal-tar products, duty of 1922, 472

Coffee, free in 1846, 114; duty reduced in 1870, 179; repealed in 1872, 184; expediency of, 186

Colonies, industrial state of, 8

Compensating system on wool and woollens, 196; abolished 1894, 292; re-established 1897, 333; abolished 1913, 429; re-established 1922, 463

"Competitive tariff" in 1913, 418, 431

Compromise tariff of 1833, 110

Conference committee on tariff in 1883, 233; in 1890, 289; in 1897, 328; in 1909, 376; in 1913, 417; in 1922, 454; in 1930, 499

Congressional procedure in dealing with the tariff, 491

Copper, duty of 1869, 219; of 1883, 245; of 1890–97, 272, 343; statistics, 455

CAPRICORN TITLES

36

201. *Hauser*, DIET DOES IT. $1.35.
202. *Moscati*, ANCIENT SEMITIC CIVILIZATIONS. $1.65.
203. CHIN P'ING MEI. $2.45.
204. *Brockelman*, HISTORY OF ISLAMIC PEOPLES. $2.45.
205. *Salter*, CONDITIONED REFLEX THERAPY. $1.85.
206. *Lissner*, LIVING PAST. $1.95.
207. *Davis*, CORPORATIONS. $2.45.
208. *Rodman*, CONVERSATIONS WITH ARTISTS. $1.45.
209. *Falls*, GREAT WAR. $1.95.
210. MEMOIRS OF A RENAISSANCE POPE. $1.95.
211. *Schachner*, FOUNDING FATHERS. $2.45.
212. *Viereck*, UNADJUSTED MAN. $1.85.
213. *Cournos*, TREASURY OF CLASSIC RUSSIAN LITERATURE. $2.45.
215. *Guerdan*, BYZANTIUM. $1.45.
216. *Mandeville*, FABLE OF THE BEES. $1.65.
217. *Bradford*, OF PLYMOUTH PLANTATION. $1.65.
218. *Taylor*, COURSE OF GERMAN HISTORY. $1.45.
219. *Frankfurter*, LAW & POLITICS. $1.75.
220. *Shelby Little*, GEORGE WASHINGTON. $1.95.
221. *Peterson*, ANCIENT MEXICO, $1.65.
223. *Isaacs*, IMAGES OF ASIA. $1.85.
224. *Krafft Ebing*, ABERRATIONS OF SEXUAL LIFE. $1.95.
226. *Grekov*, SOVIET CHESS. $1.65.
227. *Ernst-Loth*, REPORT ON THE AMERICAN COMMUNIST. $1.45.
228. *Adler*, THE PROBLEM CHILD. $1.85.
231. *Fine*, FIFTY CHESS LESSONS. $1.45.
233. *Barraclough*, ORIGINS OF MODERN GERMANY. $2.45.
235. *Skeat*, ETYMOLOGICAL DICTIONARY. $2.45.
236. *Hauser*, GAYLORD HAUSER COOK BOOK. $1.65.
237. *Fulop Miller*, THE JESUITS. $2.45.
238. *Shenton*, RECONSTRUCTION. $1.75.
239. *Blitzer*, COMMONWEALTH OF ENGLAND. $1.65.
240. *Wright*, GREAT AMERICAN GENTLEMAN. $1.65.
241. *Braeman*, ROAD TO INDEPENDENCE. $1.65.
242. *Bridgebaugh*, CITIES IN THE WILDERNESS. $2.65.
243. *Bridenbaugh*, CITIES IN REVOLT. $2.65.
244. *de Riencourt*, COMING CAESARS. $1.95.
246. *Weinberg*, THE MUCKRAKERS. $2.45.
247. *Hays*, FROM APE TO ANGEL. $2.65.
248. *James*, ANCIENT GODS. $2.25.